The Treatment of Drinking Problems

A Guide for the Helping Professions

Fifth Edition

The Treatment of Drinking Problems

A Guide for the Helping Professions

Fifth Edition

E. Jane Marshall
Institute of Psychiatry, King's College London

Keith Humphreys
Veterans Affairs and Stanford University Medical Centers

David M. Ball
Institute of Psychiatry, King's College London

With contributions from

Griffith Edwards
Former director of the Addiction Research Unit
Sole author of the first and second editions
Lead author of the third and fourth editions

and

Christopher Cook
Durham University
Co-author of the third and fourth editions
Author of Chapter 16 in this edition

CAMBRIDGE
UNIVERSITY PRESS

CAMBRIDGE UNIVERSITY PRESS
Cambridge, New York, Melbourne, Madrid, Cape Town, Singapore, São Paulo,
Delhi, Mexico City

Cambridge University Press
The Edinburgh Building, Cambridge CB2 8RU, UK

Published in the United States of America
by Cambridge University Press, New York

www.cambridge.org
Information on this title: www.cambridge.org/9780521132374

First edition published in 1982 by Wiley Blackwell
Second edition published in 1985 by McGraw Hill Higher Education
Third edition published in 1997 by Cambridge University Press
Fourth edition published in 2003 by Cambridge University Press

First published 2010
4th printing 2012

Printed in the United Kingdom at the University Press, Cambridge

*A catalogue record for this publication is available from the
British Library*

Library of Congress Cataloguing in Publication data

Marshall, E. Jane.
The treatment of drinking problems : a guide for the helping
professions. – 5th ed. / E. Jane Marshall, Keith Humphreys, David M. Ball ;
with contributions from Griffith Edwards and Christopher Cook
    p. cm.
Rev. ed. of: The treatment of drinking problems / Griffith Edwards, E. Jane
Marshall, Christopher C.H. Cook. 4th ed. 2003.
Includes bibliographical references and index.
ISBN 978-0-521-13237-4 (pbk.)
1. Alcoholism–Treatment. I. Humphreys, Keith. II. Ball, David M. III.
Edwards, Griffith. Treatment of drinking problems. IV. Title.

RC565.E38 2010
616.86′106–dc22   2010020796

ISBN 978-0-521-13237-4 Paperback

This book is dedicated to anyone struggling with a drink problem

Contents

Foreword
Welcoming the fifth edition

The publishing history of this book since its first appearance in 1982, is outlined in the editorial note that immediately follows this Foreword. It is exciting to see a previously British text now become an Anglo-American production. I want to commend this most recent contribution, and congratulate the current writing team on a job eminently well done. But I want also to try to identify what I see as a key intention which has guided the development of this book throughout its history and up to the present point.

This manifestly is a book committed to enhancing the motivation and commitment of the professionals who will make the treatment happen. I believe that the present volume like its predecessors has, as a core intention, the purpose of persuading all manner of professionals practising in this arena, whether they are dedicated to a specialist career or are for the first time encountering a drinking problem in some generalist setting, that they must learn how best to use themselves as agents of change. Treating drinking problems is portrayed in this volume as embedded in human interactions rather than a tick-box enterprise. The reward that can come from the varied and challenging engagement with this type of experience, potentially offers to the practitioner considerable reinforcement in terms of heightened understanding of the human condition and of one's own human potential as therapist. There are few other areas of practice where skilled intervention can so greatly help an individual to turn their life around. In some ways the deeper intention of this book is itself to act as change agent, with the relevant professions the target for change.

There are, no doubt, several other intentions woven into this fifth edition which the authors themselves would identify if asked so to do: the staying close to reality; optimism coupled with the admitting of difficulties and frustrations; the definition and interpretation of the science base and repeated consideration of how science and the wisdom of clinical experience are to be brought together; the rejection of stereotype; acknowledgement of the diversity of settings where the problems will be encountered; the reality of dependence as dimension rather than category and with non-dependent drinking also within the remit. Those threads and more are embedded within a book which in masterly fashion speaks to the reward to be found in the treatment of drinking problems. The quality of the writing serves to support the ambitions of this book.

Griffith Edwards
National Addiction Centre

A note on the fifth edition

The Treatment of Drinking Problems: A Guide for the Helping Professions was first published in 1982 as a single author text. That author, Griffith Edwards, wrote that he had drawn freely from the 'two major resources which must be the foundations of any treatment text – the worlds of clinical experience and of scientific research'. He acknowledged the many clinical colleagues with whom he had worked for over 20 years at the Maudsley and Bethlem Royal Hospitals. This edition appeared in 1982 and was translated into German, Spanish, Portuguese, Japanese and Swedish. The second edition appeared in 1987, again as a single author work.

The third edition was published in 1997 with Griffith Edwards as senior author and Jane Marshall and Christopher Cook as 'equal partners in the writing team'. The book was substantially revised and four new chapters added. The same writing team contributed to the fourth edition (2003).

The fifth edition has been entrusted to a new writing team, Jane Marshall, Keith Humphreys and David Ball. Jane Marshall contributed to the third and fourth editions and so offers continuity. Keith Humphreys brings a North American freshness to the text and David Ball a clinician–scientist perspective. Christopher Cook, addiction psychiatrist and priest/theologian, now a Professorial Research Fellow at Durham University, has maintained links with the team, and contributes a new chapter on spiritual and religious issues in treatment. To have been entrusted with a book of this nature is an honour, but brings with it a very great challenge. How does one develop the subject, while at the same time staying faithful to the essence of the original text? The current authors owe an enormous debt of gratitude to Griffith Edwards for his generosity in passing on and supporting the project and 'keeping faith' with it. They have endeavoured to ensure that the book is as fresh and relevant to the clinician of today as it was almost 30 years ago. Some text originally contributed to earlier editions is reproduced verbatim or with editing and enlargement in the present edition.

Introduction

This book is intended for anyone, generalist or specialist, whose responsibilities bring them into contact with people who have drinking problems. We hope that generalists will find it a helpful introduction to the field, and that generalists and specialists from all backgrounds will use it to enhance their diagnostic and therapeutic skills.

Drinking problems occur across all social structures and cannot be neatly confined to the specialist addiction sector. The text considers the treatment of drinking problems across the range of approaches from informal, through non-specialist to specialist treatment. Most drinking problems are not encountered in specialist care, so we are keen to highlight the benefits of early interventions in reversing, preventing or delaying the progression of alcohol problems. The broadening of the base of treatment means that generalists from a variety of fields including primary care, the general hospital, Social Services and the criminal justice system are involved in the identification of alcohol problems, the provision of brief interventions and referral onwards for specialist treatment. Specialist treatment begins with a comprehensive assessment of the individual and usually involves a 'package' of treatments, ideally evidence-based. Because many professional groups are employed in the specialist field, we have employed the generic word 'therapist' to describe the person doing the helping and hope that the text is equally relevant to the needs of psychiatrists and other medical practitioners, nurses, psychologists, social workers, occupational therapists and counsellors. Different professional groups inevitably bring their own skills to the treatment of drinking problems, but there is much in common and we have much to learn from each other. The fifth edition of the book describes screening and brief interventions for hazardous and harmful drinking as well as the specialist treatment of alcohol dependence and the different settings in which alcohol problems are encountered.

The authors have sought to retain the spirit of previous editions and, in particular, to maintain the style, accessibility and readability of the book.

The chapters are grouped into two parts. Section 1, 'Background to understanding' comprises Chapters 1–8, while Section 2, 'Treatment: context and content' (Chapters 9–18) considers non-specialist and specialist interventions and includes chapters on Alcoholics Anonymous and spirituality.

As women are now drinking more in the UK and the USA, we have not included a separate chapter on women's issues but have chosen to weave material about women drinkers throughout the book.

Section 1: Background to understanding

Definitions of drinking problems (Chapter 1)

This chapter opens with a number of vignettes describing the many faces of drinking problems and this is followed by an account of 'sensible' drinking guidelines. Three categories of alcohol misuse are defined: hazardous drinking, harmful drinking and alcohol dependence. The clinical genesis of the concept of the alcohol dependence syndrome is outlined, the individual elements of the syndrome are discussed and the relevance of an understanding of dependence to the specifics of treatment is considered.

Alcohol as a drug (Chapter 2)

Alcohol is a drug which has important pharmacological and toxic properties upon most systems in the human body. Knowledge of these pharmacological effects is basic to understanding the problems that arise from its use as well as the treatment adopted. The language in this chapter is necessarily technical but we have tried to write it in a way that is accessible to the non-medical reader.

Causes of drinking problems (Chapter 3)

This chapter endeavours to explain why some people and not others develop drinking problems. Environmental factors, such as the availability of alcohol and cultural norms, are addressed as well as economic factors, genetic predisposition and psychological mechanisms. The relevance of these factors to the practical business of treatment is discussed.

Alcohol-related problems (Chapters 4–7)

These four chapters deal with the complications of alcohol problems which encompass a number of domains: social (Chapter 4); physical (Chapter 5); psychiatric illness and co-morbidity (Chapter 6); alcohol and other drug problems (Chapter 7).

Various presentations (Chapter 8)

This chapter describes a number of clinical presentations spanning the life course, presentations encountered by clinicians on a daily basis: the 'young' drinker, the patient on a general hospital ward, the patient from a different cultural background, the older patient.

Section 2: Treatment: context and content

Introduction, settings and roles (Chapter 9)

Only a small minority of people with drinking problems actually make contact with specialist services. We take a broader view of where problem drinkers may find help, and in this chapter we explore help-seeking trajectories which include informal, non-specialist and specialist treatment paths. We recognize that treatment is often 'messy' and complex, and that support can be derived from a number of sources and vary over time.

Non-specialist settings (Chapter 10)

Non-specialist settings offer the opportunity to intervene earlier in the life course/drinking career before problems become severe. Even a small intervention made early enough can have significant long-term impact. A number of non-specialist settings are described, ranging from primary care to the workplace. We include general psychiatry services where drinking problems are all too often overlooked, despite the capacity to treat them. Case finding and detection are considered, and this is followed by a review of biological markers and screening questionnaires. Intervention within the non-specialist setting is described, and a more detailed account of brief motivational interviewing and medical management given.

Assessment as the beginning of therapy (Chapter 11)

This chapter covers practical issues related to the art and technique of history-taking. Separate sections describe the assessment interview with the patient and spouse, and outline an approach to case formulation.

Withdrawal states and treatment of withdrawal (Chapter 12)

Detoxification is an important prelude to the further treatment of the dependent drinker. This chapter covers the medical and clinical basics of alcohol withdrawal, but also guides the non-medical reader as to the underlying principles. The diversity of withdrawal states, the choice between community and in-patient settings and the correct use of medication are all addressed.

The basic work of treatment (Chapter 13)

Here we emphasize that the relationship between the therapist and patient or client is as important as the treatment techniques or therapeutic tactics used. Likewise, changing behaviour is impossible without significant motivation on the part of the patient, and the nurturing of this motivation is core work for the therapist. Some guiding principles for working with the patient are given, together with a discussion of the framework and content of sessions. We consider the thorny question of how to deal positively with relapse and basic work with the family of the drinker. 'House keeping' issues, such as the spacing of appointments and the duration and termination of treatment, are also considered.

Specialist treatment (Chapter 14)

Chapter 14 reviews the evidence base for specialist treatments, with a particular focus on motivational interviewing and motivational enhancement therapy, cognitive behavioural therapy and pharmacotherapy. We lay particular emphasis on the view that treatment should be research based.

Alcoholics Anonymous and other mutual-help organizations (Chapter 15)

Alcoholics Anonymous (AA) is an international self-help organization that has helped countless millions of people with drinking problems since it was founded in 1935. This chapter provides an introduction to how AA operates and to its beliefs and practices. The importance of effective co-operation between treatment professionals and AA is emphasized.

Spiritual and religious issues in treatment (Chapter 16)

Spiritual and religious issues are important in all areas of healthcare because of their influence on outcomes and in helping to understand the whole person and their meaning and purpose in life. They have particular resonance in the addiction field because addiction can be viewed as a fundamentally spiritual problem which affects the common humanity of the drinker. This chapter explores the meaning of spirituality and religious belief, considers the spiritual 'fallout', which occurs as a result of addiction, and tries to make sense of what all of this means when working with someone who has an alcohol problem.

Working towards normal drinking (Chapter 17)

For patients who are not significantly alcohol dependent, normal or 'controlled' drinking may be a feasible and preferred goal. The criteria for supporting this choice are outlined and treatment approaches discussed.

When things go wrong and putting them right (Chapter 18)

This is a practical chapter that deals with common clinical situations where treatment comes up against difficulties: the therapeutic impasse. It considers how to unblock or reconfigure the therapeutic strategy in such situations in order to get on course again

Section 1

Background to understanding

Background to understanding

Definitions of drinking problems

What is a 'drinking problem'?

The treatment of 'drinking problems', at first blush, may seem to be a frustratingly vague topic for a book. It doesn't define the problem in terms of a particular treatment setting or by a particular amount or pattern of alcohol consumption; nor does it equate the problem with the criteria of any particular diagnostic system. Rather it is a common-sense, broad-brush description grounding the issue in actual drinking behaviour that causes problems. Such drinking problems may be perceived differently by the individual, their social network, family and society at large, even to the point that what some consider a problem others consider to be of no concern at all. However, within this melting pot of behaviours there is a semblance of structure, related to the multiple domains that map onto the specific classifications of alcohol problems, which provides a means of communication, signposts treatment, indicates prognosis and forms the basis for research.

The many faces of drinking problems

To many workers in the field, including readers of prior editions of this volume, the phrase 'drinking problem' conjures up thoughts of cases like this one.

> Robert is a 45-year-old unemployed white male who was admitted to the in-patient alcohol unit for medically assisted withdrawal from alcohol for the second time in 1 year. He began drinking heavily in his teens, with only a few months of abstinence since, all of them stimulated by short-term contacts with treatment professionals and Alcoholics Anonymous, none of which resulted in lasting change. His wife became fed up with his drinking 5 years ago and kicked him out of the house, and he has lived in shelters, halfway houses, single-room occupancy hotels and other marginal housing arrangements since, including periods when he slept under a bridge with his 'bottle gang'. In morning group on the ward, his hands shake as he holds his cup of tea and tells his doctor and fellow patients in a trembling voice that 'this time, I'm really going to make a go of it'.

Individuals with severe alcohol dependence seen in specialist care settings, such as Robert, are familiar to anyone who works in the alcohol field, and remain a major focus of this edition of this book. Yet drinking problems occur and present across all social structures and health resources, and are not neatly confined within the specialist addiction sector. This text, professing to address the treatment of drinking problems, considers the whole range of approaches: from informal through non-specialist to specialist services. As such it does not merely comment on the treatment of established alcohol dependence but also examines interventions that may reverse, prevent or delay the progression of alcohol problems. This brings cases like the following into the ambit of this volume.

Michael is a 50-year-old successful salesman of Indian descent. He is slightly overweight and is being monitored regularly by his primary care physician for elevated blood pressure. His doctor is mystified by the difficulty they experience in bringing Michael's blood pressure under control; the medications and diet recommendations do not seem to be working. During an early afternoon appointment, the doctor notices that Michael seems slightly tipsy and asks if he has been drinking. Michael smiles and says: 'Of course, a three martini lunch with clients is standard practice in the sales game. But it's not like I'm an alcoholic or anything: I've got a job, a house, a great family and I'm a star performer at my firm. So, on the blood pressure, are you going to switch my medication or what?'

Emily is a 22-year-old honours college student whose roommate brings her to the Accident and Emergency Department (Emergency Room) at midnight on a Saturday for treatment of facial bruising and a cracked tooth. Emily had been assaulted by her boyfriend, who was convinced that she had been flirting with the barman. Emily's boyfriend goes on pub crawls many times during the week; she accompanies him only on weekends. Her boyfriend is under arrest and Emily is sobbing hysterically that she doesn't want him in jail. With slurred words, she protests: 'He's not really like that – it's the drink that makes him act that way. I've been after him to cut back'. Emily attempts to leave as soon as her injuries are treated, but the doctor asks her to wait a moment so that the alcohol liaison nurse can have a word with her. 'About my boyfriend's drinking?' Emily asks. 'No', says the doctor kindly, 'about yours'.

George was a hard-working, well-respected judge before he retired at 65 years of age; in fact his wife described him as having a tendency to be a bit of a 'workaholic'. On retirement he had experienced long periods of boredom, something he had rarely felt before, and consequently he spent more time practising his hobby of wine tasting. One Monday, after a particularly indulgent weekend, shortly after entering a wine bar with his wife, he experienced an episode of loss of consciousness, bit his tongue and was incontinent of urine. Believing that George had suffered a stroke, his wife telephoned an ambulance which took George to hospital, where he was admitted to the clinical decision unit overnight and next day transferred to a neurology ward for further investigation. Two days later, he started to become confused and suspicious, and during an MRI scan leapt off the trolley, pulling out his intravenous line. 'That machine is trying to read my mind!' he yelled, maintaining that the stolen personal information would be used by the criminal fraternity to destroy his family in a final act of revenge. He was restrained by the hospital security team and following a short period of sedation with benzodiazepines he recovered, but still finds it difficult to understand this frightening period in his life.

A population perspective on drinking

Drinking within a population can be envisaged as a continuous spectrum ranging from non-drinkers, through 'sensible drinkers', to those described in the examples above: 'hazardous drinkers', 'harmful drinkers' and 'dependent drinkers'. The proportion of any given population in these categories varies, with both alcohol availability and acceptability being important determinants.

Sensible drinking or 'normal drinking'

Quantity/frequency definitions

In the UK the drinking guidelines formulated by the Royal Colleges of Physicians, Psychiatrists and General Practitioners converged in the mid-1980s to define low-risk drinking as being less than 21 units of alcohol per week for men and less than 14 units per week for women (1 unit = 8 g alcohol) (British Medical Association, 1995). Consumption of 22–50 units per week for men and 15–35 units per week for women was considered as hazardous, and consumption of over 50 units per week for men and 35 units per week for women as harmful. In 1995, the Department of Health moved from weekly to daily limits, and advised that 'regular consumption of between 3 and 4 units a day by men of all ages will not accrue significant health risk' (Department of Health, 1995, p. 32). Likewise women were advised that 'regular consumption of between 2 and 3 units a day by women of all ages will not accrue any significant health risk' (Department of Health, 1995, p. 32). These guidelines, based on epidemiological data of alcohol-related morbidity and mortality, are similar to those available in other countries (Tables 1.1 & 1.2).

For instance, US guidelines advise that 'those who choose to drink alcoholic beverages should do so sensibly and in moderation – defined as the consumption of up to one drink per day for women and up to two drinks per day for men' [an American standard drink contains 14 g of ethanol] (US Department of Health and Human Services and US Department of Agriculture, 2005, p. 44). Recently the Australian National Health and Research Council recommended that neither men nor women should exceed 2 standard drinks per day (1 standard drink = 10 g) (National Health and Medical Research Council, 2007).

'At risk' drinking is commonplace and young drinkers are particularly prone to drinking in this fashion. Using data from the National Longitudinal Alcohol Epidemiologic Survey, Dawson and colleagues calculated that a third of drinkers never exceed moderate alcohol consumption, a third do so occasionally and for the rest it was their usual behaviour (Dawson, Archer & Grant, 1996). Furthermore, 88% of the alcohol was consumed in a risky fashion. Similarly, in the UK, the General Household Survey for 2006 reported that 40% of men and 33% of women had exceeded daily sensible limits in the preceding week (Goddard, 2008). In Australia, data from the 2007 National Drug Strategy Household Survey revealed that some 24% of males and 17% of females reported drinking more than the recommended guidelines for acute harm on at least one occasion a month (more than 6 standard drinks for men and 4 for women), and 10% drank in excess of guidelines for chronic alcohol-caused problems (more than 4 standard drinks for men and 2 for women on an average day) (Australian Institute of Health and Welfare, 2008). Previous analysis from these surveys indicate that 62% of the alcohol consumed was at

Table 1.1. Example of standard drink sizes in different countries.

Country	Standard drink (grams of ethanol)
UK	8
Ireland	10
The Netherlands	9.9
Australia	10
New Zealand	10
France	10
Italy	12
South Africa	12
Canada	13.6
USA	14
Japan	19.75

Source: http://www.icap.org/table/InternationalDrinkingGuidelines.

Table 1.2. Examples of recommended drinking limits for drinking in different countries (grams of ethanol).

Country	Men	Women
Australia	20 g/day	20 g/day
New Zealand	30 g/day or 210 g/week	20 g/day or 140 g/week
UK	24–32 g/day or 168 g/week	16–24 g/day or 112 g/week
France	30 g/day	30 g
The Netherlands	39.6 g/day	19.8 g/day
USA	14–28 g/day; 196 g/week	14 g/day; 98 g/week
Canada	27.2 g/day; 190 g/week	27.2 g/day; 122 g/week

Source: http://www.icap.org/table/InternationalDrinkingGuidelines.

a risky/high-risk level for acute harm, and this was particularly pronounced in the 14–17 and 18–24-year age groups in which this accounted for more than 80% of the alcohol consumed (Chikritzhs et al., 2003). Similarly, in the UK between 63% and 75% of alcohol is consumed in a non-sensible manner, particularly by younger adults (Williamson, 2007).

Categories of alcohol misuse: alcohol use disorders

Three categories of alcohol misuse make up the top three tiers of the pyramid in Figure 1.1, namely hazardous drinking, harmful drinking and alcohol dependence (Edwards, Arif & Hodgson, 1981). Hazardous drinking refers to drinking that has not yet accrued any harm, but exceeds sensible and safe limits. Harmful drinking describes drinking behaviour that incurs harm. The division between these two is somewhat arbitrary and dependent on the ability to detect harm. For example, the use of markers sensitive to alcohol-related liver damage could shift those previously oblivious of this harm into the harmful category. Finally the development of symptoms suggestive of dependence indicates the diagnosis of alcohol dependence.

Hazardous drinking

Hazardous drinking refers to drinking above a certain limit that places the individual at risk of incurring harm. It was described by Edwards and colleagues in a World Health Organization (WHO) report as:

> Use of a drug that will probably lead to harmful consequences for the user – either to dysfunction or to harm. This concept is similar to the idea of risky behaviour. For instance, smoking 20 cigarettes each day may not be accompanied by any present or actual harm but we know it to be hazardous (Edwards, Arif & Hodgson, 1981, p. 228).

The WHO *Lexicon of Alcohol and Drug Terms* described hazardous use of a substance as:

> A pattern of substance use that increases the risk of harmful consequences for the user. Some would limit the consequences to physical and mental health (as in harmful use); some would also include social consequences. In contrast to harmful use, hazardous use refers to patterns of use that are of public health significance despite the absence of any current disorder in the individual user. The term is used currently by WHO but is not a diagnostic term in ICD-10 (World Health Organization, 2010).

Hazardous drinking usually applies to anyone drinking over the recommended levels. One common pattern of hazardous use is 'binge drinking'; for example, defined as drinking in

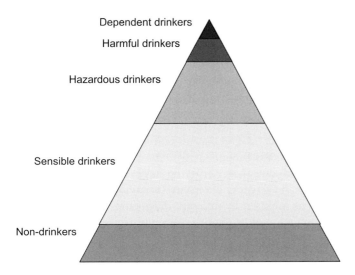

Dependent drinkers

Harmful drinkers

Hazardous drinkers

Sensible drinkers

Non-drinkers

Figure 1.1. Drinking within the population. The areas are not accurate representations of the relative proportions of those exhibiting differing drinking behaviours as this varies between populations.

excess of 8 units per day for men and 6 units per day (or in one episode) for women. Binge drinkers are at risk of harm, even though they may not exceed the 'safe' weekly limits. Binge drinking is not represented in Figure 1.1 or in the diagnostic criteria, because it is not specific to any level of consumption: hazardous, harmful and dependent drinkers may all have drinking binges. The term and its synonyms (e.g. bouts, benders) have no firm definition in everyday speech or in clinical practice.

Hazardous drinkers do not usually seek help for an alcohol problem. They are typically picked up opportunistically in the primary care or general hospital setting.

Harmful drinking

Harmful psychoactive substance use was described by Edwards and colleagues in their 1981 WHO report as 'use of a drug that is known to have caused tissue damage or mental illness in the particular person' (Edwards, Arif & Hodgson 1981, p. 228). Unlike hazardous drinking, harmful use is a diagnostic term within the International Classification of Diseases (ICD-10) where it is defined as:

> A pattern of psychoactive substance use [in this case alcohol] that is causing damage to health. The damage may be physical (as in cases of hepatitis from the self-administration of injected drugs) or mental (e.g. depressive episodes secondary to heavy consumption of alcohol) (World Health Organization, 1992, pp. 74–75).

Harmful use commonly, but not invariably, has adverse social consequences; social consequences in themselves, however, are not sufficient to justify a diagnosis of harmful use. The equivalent diagnosis in the *Diagnostic and Statistical Manual of Mental Disorders* (DSM-IV-TR) is that of alcohol abuse (American Psychiatric Association, 2000). This is defined as a 'maladaptive pattern of substance use [in this case alcohol] leading to clinically significant impairment or distress' (American Psychiatric Association, 2000, p. 199). In the absence of a diagnosis of alcohol dependence, the criteria include at least one of the following alcohol-related recurrent behaviours: failure to fulfil major obligations; use in situations in which it is physically hazardous; legal problems; continued use despite persistent or recurrent social or interpersonal problems caused or exacerbated by the effects of alcohol.

Harmful drinkers usually present to primary care, the general hospital, the criminal justice system and to Social Services.

Alcohol dependence (syndrome)

The tip of the pyramid in Figure 1.1 represents the dependent drinker. These individuals typically have a history of alcohol-related problems, and may present directly to alcohol services but often present to other services. Moderately dependent drinkers will show evidence of tolerance, alcohol withdrawal and impaired control over drinking. Severely dependent drinkers typically have long-standing problems and a history of repeated treatment episodes.

Based somewhat on the traditions imposed by different diagnostic systems, some scientific and clinical work on this population of drinkers has been organized under the concept of 'alcohol dependence' (e.g. studies using the DSM-IV-TR), whereas other work has been informed by the concept of the 'alcohol dependence syndrome' (e.g. studies using the ICD-10). Etymologically, the English word 'syndrome' derives from the Greek 'syn' meaning together and 'dromos' meaning running. Thus the 'alcohol dependence syndrome', as operationally defined by the ICD-10, is a collection of symptoms that 'run together' including a compulsion to take alcohol, difficulty with control, withdrawal symptoms and relief drinking, tolerance, predominance and persisting use despite evidence of harm. Nonetheless, the ICD-10, like the DSM-IV-TR, requires only three of the criteria to be present, and so perhaps the strict definition of syndrome, as 'consistently occurring together', should not apply to the ICD-10. The DSM-IV-TR criteria are similar and include tolerance, withdrawal symptoms, taking of alcohol in greater amounts than intended, desire or unsuccessful attempts to cut down, spending extensive time in activities to obtain alcohol or recover, giving up of activities and persistent use despite associated problems (Tables 1.3 & 1.4).

A mechanistic approach to the diagnosis of dependence is insufficient. Dependence cannot be conceived as 'not present' or 'present', with the diagnostic task then completed. The skill lies in being able to recognize the subtleties of symptomatology, which will reveal not only whether this condition is there at all but, if it exists, the degree of its development. What has also to be learnt is how the syndrome's manifestations are moulded by personality, by environmental influence or by cultural forces. It is the ability to comprehend the variations on the theme that constitute the real art. However, for those who wish to revisit diagnostic criteria these are presented in Tables 1.3 and 1.4. If the therapist cannot recognize *degrees* of dependence, they will not be able to fit their approach to the particular individual, and they may retreat into seeing 'addiction to alcohol' as a fixed entity from which all individuals with drinking problems are presumed to suffer, for whom the universal goal must be total abstinence and with the treatment which is offered universally intensive. The needed skill is the development of a discriminating judgement, which is able in each case to sense out the degree of dependence, identify a rational treatment goal with that person and propose a treatment plan fitted to their goal.

Clinical genesis of the concept

A syndrome is a descriptive clinical formulation which is, at least initially, likely to be agnostic as to causation or pathology. The existence of alcohol dependence has been evident to acute observers for many years (e.g. Thomas Trotter's essay of 1804), but in the 1970s a detailed clinical description was enunciated within a syndrome model (Edwards & Gross, 1976). It was suggested

Table 1.3. The DSM-IV-TR criteria for alcohol dependence.

A maladaptive pattern of alcohol use leading to clinically significant impairment or distress, as manifested by three (or more) of the following, occurring within a 12-month period.

1 Tolerance, as defined by either of the following:

   (a) a need for markedly increased amounts of alcohol to achieve intoxication or desired effect;

   (b) markedly diminished effect with continued use of the same amount of alcohol.

2 Withdrawal, as manifested by either of the following:

   (a) the characteristic withdrawal syndrome for alcohol;

   (b) the same (or a closely related) substance is taken to relieve or avoid alcohol withdrawal symptoms.

3 Alcohol is often taken in larger amounts over a longer period of time than was intended.

4 There is a persistent desire or unsuccessful efforts to cut down or control alcohol use.

5 A great deal of time is spent in activities necessary to obtain alcohol, use alcohol, or recover from its effects.

6 Important social, occupational or recreational activities are given up or reduced because of alcohol use.

7 Alcohol use is continued despite knowledge of having a persistent or recurring problem that is likely to have been caused or exacerbated by alcohol (e.g. continued drinking despite recognition that an ulcer was made worse by alcohol consumption).

Source: American Psychiatric Association (2000).

Table 1.4. The ICD-10 criteria for alcohol dependence syndrome.

A cluster of physiological, behavioural and cognitive phenomena in which the use of alcohol takes a much higher priority for a given individual than other behaviours that once had greater value. A central descriptive characteristic of the dependence syndrome is the desire (often strong, sometimes overpowering) to take alcohol. There may be evidence that the return to alcohol use after a period of abstinence leads to a more rapid reappearance of other features of the syndrome than occurs with non-dependent individuals.

Three or more of the following have been experienced or exhibited at some time in the previous year.

(a) Strong desire or sense of compulsion to take alcohol.

(b) Difficulties in controlling alcohol-taking behaviour in terms of its onset, termination or level of use.

(c) A physiological withdrawal state when alcohol use has ceased or has been reduced, as evidenced by: the characteristic withdrawal syndrome for alcohol; or use of the same (or a closely related substance) with the intention of relieving or avoiding withdrawal symptoms.

(d) Evidence of tolerance, such that increased dosages are required in order to achieve effects originally produced by lower dosages.

(e) Progressive neglect of alternative pleasures or interests because of alcohol use, increased amount of time necessary to obtain or take alcohol or recover from its effects.

(f) Persisting with alcohol use despite clear evidence of overtly harmful consequences, such as harm to the liver through excessive drinking, depressive mood states consequent to heavy substance misuse or alcohol-related impairment of cognitive functioning. Efforts should be made to determine if the user was actually, or could be expected to be, aware of the nature and extent of the harm.

Source: World Health Organization (1992).

by Edwards and Gross that clinical observation revealed a repeated clustering of signs and symptoms in certain heavy drinkers. Further, it was postulated that the syndrome existed in degrees of severity rather than as a categorical absolute, that its presentation could be shaped by pathoplastic influences rather than its being concrete and invariable and that alcohol dependence should be conceptually distinguished from alcohol-related problems. This clinically derived formulation was at that stage designated as only provisional, and within the general research tradition of psychiatric taxonomy the *validity* of the syndrome had then to be determined.

Alcohol dependence: establishing syndrome validity

Following the original description, research has tested multiple aspects of validity. The overall conclusion to be drawn from this, by now extensive body of research, is that the syndrome is a reality rather than a chimera of the clinical eye. That is not to say that all elements are in psychometric terms equally well tied into the syndrome. Within a psychometric perspective, some elements may be redundant, and difficulties have been encountered in operationalizing elements, such as narrowing of repertoire, subjective change and reinstatement.

Elements of the alcohol dependence syndrome

The elements of the syndrome as originally formulated by Edwards and Gross will now be discussed sequentially below rather than the more restrictive formulations described in ICD-10 or DSM-IV-TR (Edwards & Gross, 1976). The alcohol dependence syndrome is a hypothetical construct which formal diagnostic criteria index to some extent. However, it is important to appreciate that the symptoms of this hypothetical construct are not, strictly speaking, equivalent to a diagnostic symptom list.

Narrowing of repertoire

The ordinary drinker's consumption and choice of drink will vary from day to day and from week to week; they may have a beer at lunch on one day, nothing to drink on another, share a bottle of wine at dinner one night and then go to a party on a Saturday and have several drinks. Their drinking is patterned by varying internal cues and external circumstances.

At first, a person becoming caught up in heavy drinking may widen their repertoire and the range of cues that signal drinking. As dependence advances, the cues are increasingly related to relief or avoidance of alcohol withdrawal, and their personal drinking repertoire becomes increasingly narrowed. The dependent person begins to drink the same whether it is a workday, weekend or holiday; the nature of the company or their own mood makes less and less difference. Questioning may distinguish earlier and later stages of dependence by the degree to which the repertoire is narrowed. With advanced dependence, the drinking may become scheduled to a strict daily timetable to maintain a high blood alcohol. More careful questioning will, however, show that even when dependence is well established, some capacity for variation remains. The syndrome must be pictured as subtle and plastic rather than as something set hard, but as dependence advances the patterns tend to become increasingly fixed.

Salience of drinking

The stereotyping of the drinking pattern as dependence advances leads to the individual giving priority to maintaining their alcohol intake. The spouse's distressed scolding – once effective – is later neutralized by the drinker as evidence of a lack of understanding. Income, which previously had to serve many needs, now supports the drinking habit as the first demand. Gratification of the need for drink may become more important for the individual with liver damage than considerations of survival. Diagnostically, the progressive change in the salience given to alcohol is important, rather than the behaviour at any one time. The individual may relate that they used to be proud of their house but now the paint is peeling, used always to take the children to football matches but now spend no time with the family, used to have rather conventional moral standards but will now beg, borrow or steal to obtain money for alcohol.

Increased tolerance to alcohol

Alcohol is a drug to which the central nervous system (CNS) develops tolerance (see Chapter 2). Individuals themselves report on tolerance in terms of 'having a good head for liquor'. Clinically, tolerance is shown by the dependent person being able to sustain an alcohol intake and go about their business at blood alcohol levels that would incapacitate the non-tolerant drinker. This does not mean that their functioning is unimpaired – they will be a dangerous driver, but because of their tolerance they will (unfortunately) still be able to drive. Furthermore, an individual may present with very high blood alcohol concentrations that would be fatal for the non-tolerant, yet not appear intoxicated, engage in a constructive interview and even remember it afterwards! Acute tolerance, which any normal subject will experience in response to even a single dose of alcohol, needs to be distinguished from the chronic tolerance, which is a feature of the dependence syndrome.

Cross-tolerance will extend to certain other drugs, notably the sedative-hypnotics such as benzodiazepines, which means that the person who has become tolerant to alcohol will also have a tolerance to these drugs and vice versa. Indeed, this cross-tolerance can be exploited by using benzodiazepines to prevent and manage alcohol withdrawal symptoms during detoxification. The rate of development of tolerance is variable, but the heavy drinker who is not dependent can manifest tolerance. In later stages of dependence, for reasons that are unclear, the individual begins to lose their previously acquired tolerance and becomes incapacitated by quantities of alcohol which they could previously handle. They may begin to fall down drunk in the street.

Withdrawal symptoms

At first these symptoms are intermittent and mild; they cause little incapacity, and one symptom may be experienced without others. As dependence increases so does the frequency and severity of the withdrawal symptoms. When the picture is fully developed, the individual typically experiences severe multiple symptoms every morning on waking and perhaps even in the middle of the night. Questioning often reveals that the severely dependent individual experiences mild withdrawal symptoms (which they recognize as such) at any time during the day when their alcohol level falls. Complete withdrawal is therefore not necessary to precipitate disturbance.

The individual often remembers rather exactly the dating of the period when they first began to experience withdrawal, and there is no necessary association with a sudden increase in alcohol intake.

The spectrum of symptoms is wide and includes tremor, nausea, sweating, sensitivity to sound (hyperacusis), ringing in the ears (tinnitus), itching, muscle cramps, mood disturbance, sleep disturbance, hallucinations, generalized (*grand mal*) seizures and the fully developed picture of delirium tremens. There are four key symptoms, outlined below.

Tremor

This nicely illustrates that it is *degree* of symptom experience that is essential to the clinical observation, rather than a recording in the case notes simply that the individual does or does not experience withdrawal tremor. Shakiness may have been experienced only once or twice, or intermittently and mildly, for example, after a heavy binge, or it may be experienced every morning and to a degree which is incapacitating, or with many intervening intensities and frequencies. As well as the hands shaking, there may be facial tremor or the whole body shaking. The therapist has to cultivate an awareness of something equivalent to the Richter scale used to categorize the strength of earthquakes, and look out for the individual saying that they rattle their morning teacup against the saucer. In the extreme case, a drinker may rely on the kindness of the barmaid to lift the day's first pint to their lips.

Nausea

The individual who is asked only whether they vomit may well deny it. Their experience, however, may be that if they attempt to clean their teeth in the morning, they will retch; or they may never eat breakfast because they know it would be too risky. A common story is that most of the first drink of the day is vomited back.

Sweating

This may be dramatic; the individual wakes regularly in the early hours of the morning with soaking sweats. At the earlier stages of dependence, they may report no more than feeling clammy.

Mood disturbance

In the earlier stages, individuals may phrase the experience in terms of 'I'm a bit on edge' or 'my nerves are not too good', but when dependence is fully developed they may use vivid descriptions to indicate a state of appalling agitation and depression. Often the anxiety seems to be characterized by a frightened reaction to loud noises or traffic (sometimes with a phobia of crossing the road), fear of someone approaching from behind and fright at 'the twigs on the trees rubbing together'. A co-occurring mood disorder may at times exacerbate withdrawal symptoms.

Relief or avoidance of withdrawal symptoms by further drinking

In the earliest stages, the individual may be aware that a drink at lunchtime 'helps to straighten me up a bit'. At the other extreme, an individual may require a drink every morning before they get out of bed, as a matter of desperate need. As with withdrawal symptoms, relief drinking must not be conceived as only a morning event; the individual may wake in the middle of the night for the drink, which will abort incipient withdrawal. They may be aware that if they go 3 or 4 hours without a drink during the day, the next drink is valued especially for its relief effect. Relief drinking is cued not only by frank withdrawal but also by minimal symptoms of subacute withdrawal, which signal worse distress if drink is not taken. The dependent individual may try to maintain a steady alcohol level which they have learnt to recognize as comfortably above the danger level for withdrawal, and to this extent their drinking is cued by withdrawal avoidance as well as withdrawal relief.

Clues to the severity of an individual's dependence are often given by the small details they provide of the circumstances and timing of the first drink of the day, and their attitude towards it. If they get up, have a bath, dress and read the paper before that drink, then dependence is not very advanced. A housewife who finishes her morning chores before having her first drink is at a different stage of dependence from the woman who is pouring whisky into her first cup of tea. Someone engaged in relief drinking may have ritualized the procedure. A man may go to the early-morning pub at 7 am and go straight up to the bar, where the barman will know immediately to give him a pint of lager, which the man will grab at clumsily with both hands and drink down fast. He may go to the lavatory and vomit some of this pint back, but he can then drink the next pint at greater leisure, and he will know that within 20 or 30 minutes of walking into that pub 'the drink will have cured me'. A drinker may relate that they know the exact quantity of alcohol required for this 'cure' and the exact time interval for the alcohol to take effect, and they report also that the 'cure' is repeatedly so complete as to be almost miraculous. Sometimes they describe what is, presumably, a conditioned response; the mere fact of having a glass in their hand gives relief.

That the dependence syndrome is a plastic condition rather than something immutable is brought out again by the way this particular element is shaped by social and personal factors. For some the idea of keeping drink in the house may be so against subcultural expectations that they will always wait for the pubs to open rather than 'keep a drink indoors'. The person of rigid personality may endure considerable withdrawal for some hours rather than take a drink before lunch. To understand fully what the individual reports always requires that these shaping factors are taken into account.

Subjective awareness of compulsion to drink

The conventional phrases used to describe the dependent person's subjective experience are not altogether satisfactory. For instance, awareness of 'loss of control' is said to be crucial to understanding abnormal drinking and sometimes they say, 'If I have one or two, I'll go on', or 'If I go into the pub, promises don't mean anything', or 'Good resolutions dissolve in alcohol', or 'Once I've really got the taste of it, I'm away'. Control is probably best seen as variably or inter-mittently impaired rather than 'lost'. Although 'loss of control' has in some of the classic texts been pictured as the touchstone for diagnosis of addiction to alcohol, it is obvious that many so-called 'social drinkers' at times drink too much and are sorry and embarrassed afterwards.

The experience of 'craving' is often wrapped up in conventional phrasing. The patient may describe it in unambiguous terms – they are 'gasping for a drink' or report that 'a drink will hit the spot'. The subjective interpretation of the withdrawal may, however, be much influenced by environment, and the person who is withdrawing on a hospital ward may not experience any craving. Cues for craving may include the feeling of intoxication as well as incipient or developed withdrawal, mood (anger, depression or elation) or situational cues (being in a pub or with a drinking friend).

The individual who is in a withdrawal state (or partial withdrawal) may report that they are compulsively ruminating on alcohol and that they have hit on the strategy of blocking these ruminations by bringing in other lines of thought.

Reinstatement after abstinence

When alcohol dependent patients begin to drink again following a period of abstinence they relapse, sooner or later, into the previous stage of the dependence syndrome. The time course is extremely variable. Typically, the person who had only a moderate degree of dependence may take weeks or months to reinstate dependence, perhaps pulling back once or twice on the way. A severely dependent individual typically reports that they are again 'hooked' within a few days of starting to drink, although even here there are exceptions: on the first day they may become abnormally drunk and be surprised to find that they have lost their tolerance. Within a few days they are, however, experiencing severe withdrawal symptoms and drinking for relief, the subjective experience of compulsion is reinstated, and their drinking is back in the old stereotyped pattern. A syndrome that had taken years to develop can be fully reinstated within 72 hours of drinking or sooner, and this is one of the most puzzling features of the condition.

Should dependence be diagnosed in the absence of withdrawal symptoms?

As noted above, the term syndrome suggests that certain symptoms and signs 'consistently run together'. In contrast, the 'pick and mix' nature of both the ICD and DSM diagnostic criteria permit the diagnosis of alcohol dependence in the absence of withdrawal symptoms. As such, this approach will probably catch in the net many people who are drinking heavily but who are not experiencing any features of physical dependence upon alcohol. The question is important and not merely semantic. In a large US household survey, Schuckit and colleagues found that subjects who were positive for DSM-III-R alcohol dependence differed markedly according to whether physiological symptoms (withdrawal or tolerance) were or were not present. Those with physiological symptoms drank more heavily than the others and experienced more adverse consequences from their drinking (Schuckit et al., 1998). In another population study, the experience of tremors was predictive of poorer 1-year outcome and chronicity (Hasin et al., 2000). A syndrome by its nature is a state difficult to differentiate absolutely from non-syndrome, and whilst some may understand the presence of withdrawal symptoms as merely a measure of severity, others recommend that the diagnosis of alcohol dependence be reserved for those who have experienced withdrawal symptoms to at least some degree. Our own view is that clinicians should weigh withdrawal symptoms more highly than the other diagnostic criteria when judging how severe a case may be, and we hope that those currently developing the DSM-V will consider adopting a similar approach.

The time element

To discuss the severity of dependence inevitably introduces consideration of the time element. The longer someone has been putting themselves through repeated cycles of withdrawal and relief, the more severe the dependence they will have contracted. However, note also has to be taken of the rapidity or gradualness of the transition between heavy drinking and dependence, and of the age at which dependence developed. Why dependence should have become manifest at a certain phase in the life of a drinker is unexplained. Whatever the underlying causes, it is rather typical for the man with a long-standing heavy alcohol intake to be able to identify a transition period of about 12 months during which the dependence symptoms had their onset and a quickly mounting severity. Women typically experience a more 'telescoped' onset of dependence symptoms. With other cultures, personalities and patterns of drinking, dependence may arise earlier or later in life, after longer or shorter alcohol exposure, and may advance with greater or lesser rapidity.

In summary, to understand fully the individual's dependence, the present picture has to be related to its evolution over time, and the determinants of that evolution identified.

Why an understanding of dependence matters

Having outlined the diagnosis of dependence, the manner in which degrees of the syndrome's development are to be identified and the way in which personality and environment may shape the presentations, the question then arises: 'What is the practical purpose of such diagnostic work, the gain from developing this kind of diagnostic skill?' The answers are both general and specific.

The dependence concept and the brokerage of understanding

The realization that such a condition as alcohol dependence exists, and an understanding of the personal implications of this diagnosis, may often assist in the relief of the person's sense of muddle and bafflement. It can contribute to a helpful framework for personal understanding, and enable them to come to terms with a condition that they had previously only reacted to with confusion. The fact that alcohol is a drug which can produce dependence – 'a drug of addiction' – often comes as a surprise to a person's family as much as to the individual themselves. The diagnosis, if sensitively explained, can for the family too, mean a way of restructuring a reaction to a situation which previously engendered confusion, fear or anger. The spouse begins to realize that there is more than 'weakness of the will' that has to be understood; that expecting their partner 'to drink like other people' is not possible.

For the therapist, what flows from understanding the nature of dependence lies partly in accurate empathy for that person's experience. Baldly to impart no more than the diagnostic label – a sort of magisterial sentencing – is not what is meant by building up understanding.

Furthermore, it would be useful health education if the public in general were aware that alcohol has dependence potential. The public need to know more of the dangers and the danger signals, what dependence can mean for themselves, for someone in their family, for someone at work or for someone they meet in the pub. An understanding of alcohol dependence should become part of ordinary social awareness, but it is equally important that society understands that alcohol problems also commonly occur without dependence.

The relevance of an understanding of dependence to the specifics of treatment

The ability to diagnose dependence and recognize its degrees is vital to setting the treatment goal (see Chapters 10, 11 and 13). A severely dependent drinker is unlikely to be able to return to normal drinking, and the clinician's ability accurately to recognize the degree of dependence is vital to this important aspect of care (Edwards, 1986). Assessment of the person's degree of dependence is also relevant to the choice of withdrawal regime and a forewarning as to risk of delirium tremens or withdrawal fits (see Chapter 12). Understanding of the severity of relapse requires an ability to recognize whether dependence has been reinstated. Monitoring the progress of regression of dependence intensity over time is relevant to understanding the drinking career and drinking within the life course.

There is also the question of whether intensity of dependence should be seen as indicating the intensity of the required treatment – a variant of the matching hypothesis. There is common-sense appeal in the postulate that more heavily dependent drinkers should, say, be given more therapeutic time, be more readily admitted to in-patient care and be provided with more intensive follow-up. Some research does not, however, support that proposition (Edwards & Taylor, 1994) .

The range of drinking problems

It is essential to appreciate the full range of drinking problems that occur, and manifest themselves, in a rich variety of situations and settings. Even that cluster of symptoms which constitute the alcohol dependence syndrome, from the very outset were envisaged to vary in terms of severity and to be the subject of moulding factors including personal, environmental or cultural forces. The failure to develop a discriminating judgement, which permits an accurate assessment of the degree of severity of the problem, forces the individual to perceive drinking problems as a fixed entity for which the universal treatment goal of abstinence must be adopted. However, possessing this skill permits the therapist, in conjunction with the client, to identify a specific rational treatment plan from the whole range available.

References

American Psychiatric Association (2000) *Diagnostic and Statistical Manual of Mental Disorders*, Fourth edition, Text revision. Washington DC: American Psychiatric Association.

Australian Institute of Health and Welfare (2008) *2007 National Drug Strategy Household Survey*. Drug statistics series no. 20. Cat. no. PHE 98. Canberra, Australia: Australian Institute of Health and Welfare.

British Medical Association (1995) *Alcohol: Guidelines on Sensible Drinking*. London: British Medical Association.

Chikritzhs T, Catalano P, Stockwell T, et al. (2003) *Australian Alcohol Indicators 1990–2001: Patterns of Alcohol Use and Related Harms for Australian States and Territories*. Perth, Australia: National Drug Research Institute.

Dawson D A, Archer L D, Grant B F (1996) Reducing alcohol-use disorders via decreased consumption: a comparison of population and high-risk strategies. *Drug and Alcohol Dependence* 42(1), 39–47.

Department of Health (1995) *Sensible Drinking: The Report of an Inter-departmental Working Group*. London: Department of Health.

Edwards G (1986) The alcohol dependence syndrome: a concept as stimulus to enquiry. *British Journal of Addiction* 81(2), 171–183.

Edwards G, Gross M M (1976) Alcohol dependence: provisional description of a clinical syndrome. *British Medical Journal* 1(6017), 1058–1061.

Edwards G, Taylor C (1994) A test of the matching hypothesis: alcohol dependence, intensity of treatment, and 12-month outcome. *Addiction* 89(5), 553–561.

Edwards G, Arif A, Hodgson R (1981) Nomenclature and classification of drug- and alcohol-related problems: a WHO memorandum. *Bulletin of the World Health Organization* 59(2), 225–242.

Goddard E (2008) *General Household Survey, 2006: Smoking and Drinking among Adults 2006*. Newport, UK: Office for National Statistics.

Hasin D, Paykin A, Meydan J, Grant B (2000) Withdrawal and tolerance: prognostic significance in DSM-IV alcohol dependence. *Journal of Studies on Alcohol* 61(3), 431–438.

National Health and Medical Research Council (2007) *Australian Alcohol Guidelines for Low-risk Drinking: Draft for Public Consultation*. http://www.diabeteslife.org.au/portals/0/alcohol_guidelines_for_low_risk_drinking.pdf.

Schuckit M A, Smith T L, Daeppen J B, et al. (1998) Clinical relevance of the distinction between alcohol dependence with and without a physiological component. *American Journal of Psychiatry* 155(6), 733–740.

Trotter T (1804) *An Essay, Medical, Philosophical, and Chemical, on Drunkenness, and its Effects on the Human Body*. London: T N Longman and O Rees.

US Department of Health and Human Services and US Department of Agriculture (2005) *Dietary Guidelines for Americans 2005*. Washington DC: US Government Printing Office.

Williamson R (2007) Alcohol consumption and mental health. PhD thesis, London: University of London.

World Health Organization (1992) *The ICD-10 Classification of Mental and Behavioural Disorders Clinical Descriptions and Diagnostic Guidelines*. Geneva: World Health Organization.

World Health Organization (2010) *Lexicon of Alcohol and Drug Terms*. http://www.who.int/substance_abuse/terminology/who_lexicon/en/index.html.

**Section 1
Chapter**

2

Background to understanding

Alcohol as a drug

The purpose of this chapter

Humankind has 'enjoyed' a relationship with alcohol for many thousands of years. Indeed such drinks are imbued with symbolic significance when used within social, cultural and religious custom and ritual. Its properties have been familiar to countless peoples around the world for thousands of years. However, it is also a drug that has important pharmacological and toxic effects upon most systems in the human body. Knowledge of these pharmacological effects is basic to understanding both the problems that arise from its use as well as the treatment approaches adopted.

What's in an alcoholic drink?

The term alcohol is derived from an Arabic word for the black powder of purified antimony (*al-koh'l*) that was used as an early form of eyeliner. The word was subsequently generalized to mean purification and later adopted into the English language to describe the distillate of wine as 'alcohol of wine'. Pharmacologically, alcohol describes organic compounds characterized by a hydroxyl group attached to a saturated carbon molecule.

There are many alcohols including methyl alcohol (methanol, which is highly toxic and ingestion of 30 ml is potentially fatal), isopropyl alcohol (isopropranol – also highly toxic with symptoms being reported at doses as low as 20 ml) and ethyl alcohol (ethanol - the primary active ingredient in alcoholic drinks, (Figure 2.1). Alcohol-containing drinks consist mostly of water (H_2O), ethanol (CH_3CH_2OH) and flavours/colour. Ethanol has been called a 'stupid molecule' due to its simple structure, whilst the flavour, colours and congeners (related chemicals produced during fermentation) are sometimes called the 'dirt in the drink'. Ethanol is the subject of this chapter; however, the inaccurate term 'alcohol' is used in its place in deference to the common usage of this term whilst recognizing this inherent inaccuracy.

Pharmacology

Alcohol (ethanol) is a colourless liquid at room temperature, and freezes and boils at a lower temperature than water. In addition it is lighter than water and therefore has a lower density (Table 2.1).

The complexity of scientific notation

Various ways of expressing alcohol concentrations are employed in different texts. Usually concentration is expressed as a weight in a given volume of blood, breath or urine. In this chapter, blood alcohol concentrations are expressed as milligrams per 100 millilitres of blood

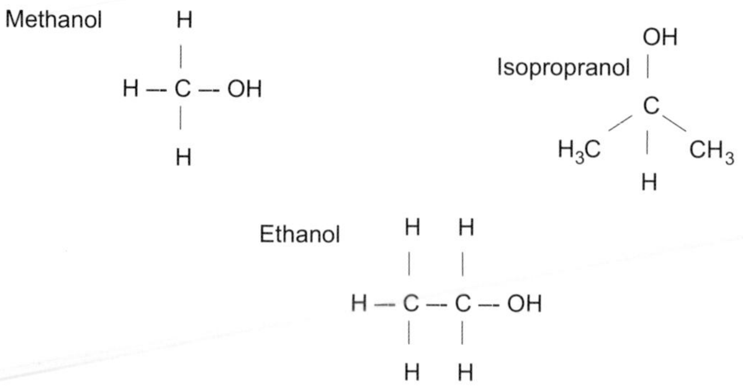

Methanol

H — C — OH

with H above and H below the central C

Isopropranol

H_3C — C — CH_3 with OH above and H below

Ethanol

H — C — C — OH

with H, H above and H, H below the carbons

Figure 2.1. Chemical structure of some alcohols.

Table 2.1. Properties of alcohol compared with water.

	Alcohol (ethanol)	Water
Formula	CH_3CH_2OH	H_2O
Appearance	Colourless clear liquid	Colourless clear liquid with a hint of blue
Molecular weight	46 g/mol	18 g/mol
Density	0.79 g/cm³ (liquid)	1 g/cm³ (liquid)
Melting point	−114°C	0°C
Boiling point	78.4°C	100°C

(mg/100 ml). It should, however, be noted that the following reported blood alcohol concentrations are all the same (see also Brick, 2004):

100 mg/100 ml
100 mg/decilitre (100 mg/dL)
100 mg/100 cc
100 mg per cent (100 mg%)
0.1 g/100 ml
0.1 g/decilitre
0.1 grams per cent (0.1 g%)
0.1 per cent (0.1%)

Laboratory studies may report a millimolar concentration and this can be converted to mg/100 ml by using the molecular weight. Thus the millimolar concentration (mmol) of alcohol is multiplied by the molecular weight 46 g/mol and divided by 10 to achieve the same concentration in mg/100 ml. In addition, clinical laboratories usually measure alcohol concentrations in serum rather than in blood. An approximate conversion between serum and blood concentration can be obtained by multiplying the value in serum by 0.85.

More confusing is the term 'proof', which has different meanings in the UK and the USA. Proof was used as measure of the concentration of alcohol, and 100% proof represents the lowest dilution able to sustain combustion, of equal amounts of gunpowder and the spirit under test, producing a clear blue flame. This represents a concentration of approximately 57% alcohol by volume (ABV) under the UK system with pure alcohol being 175% proof. In the USA, proof is double the concentration expressed by volume and therefore 100% proof is equivalent to 50% ABV. Thus, in the old UK system 70% proof spirit is 40% ABV or 80% proof in the USA!

Standard drinks worldwide

Standard drinks vary across different countries and this must be taken into account when reading the literature or using instruments that quantify drinking behaviour (e.g. the AUDIT questionnaire). In the USA drinks are often sold in ounces with 1 ounce ≈ 30 ml. Thus, 1 standard drink is approximately 1.5 ounces of 80% proof alcohol (see Table 1.1 for standard unit drink definitions from different countries).

The Great British unit

The UK has adopted the term 'unit of alcohol' to cope with the enduring consumption in public houses of beer in the Imperial Measure of pints (568 ml). Thus 1 pint of 'normal' strength beer (i.e. ~3.7% ABV) would represent 2 units. At first sight the choice of 8 g, as a definition of a unit, might seem to be an awkward figure; firstly, because it is a weight and drink is generally consumed as a volume; and, secondly, the number 8 complicates any mental arithmetic. However, the density of alcohol is less than water and 8 g expressed as a volume is 8/density = 8/0.79 ≈ 10 ml. As the strength of alcohol sold in the UK is expressed in terms of percentage alcohol by volume (ABV) this makes the calculation of the number of units very straightforward. Thus, the strength (ABV) is multiplied by the volume and divided by 100 to get the volume of pure alcohol in the drink. This is then divided by 10 to get the number of units.

Thus, for a 750 ml bottle of wine at 12% ABV the volume of pure alcohol in the bottle is 750 ml × 12/100 = 90 ml. This expressed as units is therefore 90 ml/10 ml, i.e. 9 units.

Absorption and distribution

Absorption of alcohol is relatively slow from the stomach but occurs rapidly in the small intestine, and the time to maximum concentration in the blood ranges from 30 to 90 minutes (Brick, 2004). The presence of food in the stomach slows absorption by delaying gastric emptying into the small intestine, thus slowing its entry to this part of the gut that is highly efficient at absorbing such substances due to the presence of villae, little projections into the gut, which dramatically increase the surface area available for absorption. Furthermore, the prandial state can differentially alter the efficiency with which drinks of differing alcohol concentrations are absorbed. The presence of carbon dioxide bubbles in fizzy drinks (e.g. champagne) increases absorption, whilst physical exercise reduces absorption. In addition, sugar-free mixers increase gastric emptying and absorption when compared with sugar-containing regular versions. Furthermore, peak blood levels are higher if the same quantity of alcohol is ingested in a single dose rather than in several small doses (Agarwal & Goedde, 1990).

Following absorption alcohol is distributed throughout the body. It is hydrophilic (water-loving) and therefore is distributed with water and can cross the placenta into the fetal circulation, and is also found in breast milk in lactating mothers.

Blood alcohol concentration (BAC) is very similar to tissue levels in most of the body except fat. The usually smaller stature and relatively higher proportion of body fat (or lower proportion of water) in women often leads to a higher BAC than would occur in men after an equivalent dose of alcohol. This may explain, in part, the increased vulnerability of women to certain types of tissue damage.

Excretion and metabolism

Between 90% and 98% of ingested alcohol is eliminated from the body by oxidation to carbon dioxide and water. Most of the alcohol that escapes oxidation is excreted unchanged in expired air, urine and sweat; elimination by these routes may increase after a heavy drinking bout or at elevated temperatures. Indeed presence of alcohol in expired air can be used to estimate the BAC using a breathalyser. The breath alcohol concentration (BrAC) can be used to calculate a presumed BAC level using a conversion factor, which varies between countries, and some breathalysers do this automatically as they are calibrated for blood. Breathalysers provide a more objective measure of alcohol levels than clinical examination alone, and are widely employed in motorists suspected of drink-driving offences. Countries set differing legal limits for driving; for example, this ranges widely across Europe from 0 to 80 mg/100 ml in blood.

Hepatic alcohol metabolism

The amount of alcohol oxidized per unit time depends on body weight. In the healthy adult the rate is limited to about 8 g, or 1 UK unit of alcohol per hour in a 70 kg adult, or 120 mg/kg per hour (Fleming, Mihic & Harris, 2006). The breakdown of alcohol in the liver is largely saturated, that is it takes place as quickly as possible, at low blood alcohol concentrations and, technically, this is called a pseudo-zero-order of metabolism in which the rate is constant and doesn't vary with alcohol concentration at the levels generally found during drinking. Breakdown can be faster in the heavier drinker (see below). Alcohol may undergo first pass metabolism (FPM) in the stomach, but 90–98% of ingested alcohol is metabolized in the liver. The major pathway is oxidation by alcohol dehydrogenase (ADH) to acetaldehyde (Figure 2.2). Acetaldehyde is highly toxic and is usually rapidly oxidized by aldehyde dehydrogenase 2 (ALDH2) to acetate. Acetate is then broken down to water and the gas, carbon dioxide.

The enzymes ADH and ALDH are under genetic control. Five classes of ADH have been described and the class I variety is largely responsible for the first step in alcohol metabolism in the liver (Figure 2.3). Class I consists of enzymes encoded by three different genes that demonstrate up to a 40-fold difference in the maximum speed of the reaction. At least four isozymes (different enzymes that catalyse the same reaction) of ALDH have been detected in humans. ALDH2, the isozyme largely responsible for the oxidation of acetaldehyde, exists in two forms, one of which is virtually inactive. Low-activity ALDH2, which is common in Oriental populations, leads to a flushing reaction when alcohol is taken – the so-called Oriental Flush Reaction. This reaction is unpleasant; therefore, individuals with low-activity ALDH2 are less inclined to drink and are thus less vulnerable to developing alcohol problems and dependence (Ball, Pembrey & Stevens, 2007). This is also the primary site of action for disulfiram (Antabuse®), a drug that acts by destroying the activity of ALDH2 and is used to help maintain abstinence in alcohol dependence (see Chapter 14). In essence, possessing this low-activity variant is similar to taking disulfiram constantly. The acetate formed from acetaldehyde is released into the circulation and is largely taken up by muscle and heart for oxidation via the tricarboxylic acid cycle (Fleming, Mihic & Harris, 2006) (Figure 2.4).

Although ADH is the major pathway for the oxidation of alcohol, it can also be oxidized by two other enzymes systems, the microsomal ethanol-oxidizing system (MEOS) located in the smooth endoplasmic reticulum (SER), and catalase, located in peroxisomes. The contribution of catalase is thought to be minimal. The MEOS is dependent on the cytochrome P450 system which is located on the SER. It usually plays a small role in the metabolism of alcohol, but this role increases with increased consumption. Chronic alcohol intake enhances MEOS activity by a process of inducing a form of P450 called CYP2E1 (cytochrome P450 2E1). The induction of CYP2E1 leads to an increase in the rate of alcohol metabolism and to an increased tolerance to alcohol and other drugs. Indeed CYP2E1 may be responsible for up to 10% of alcohol metabolism in chronic abusers.

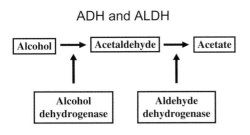

ADH and ALDH

Figure 2.2. Metabolism of alcohol.

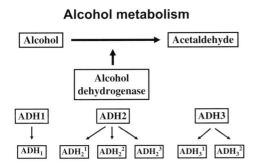

Alcohol metabolism

Figure 2.3. Genetic variation in alcohol dehydrogenase (ADH). There are three genetic variants in ADH2 and two in ADH3 that affect the speed of the enzyme.

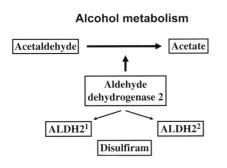

Alcohol metabolism

Figure 2.4. Genetic variation in ALDH2. There are two genetic variants in ALDH2, one of which is of low activity (ALDH2^2). Disulfiram, an aversive drug that is used to aid the maintenance of abstinence, destroys the activity of ALDH2 (effectively blocking the metabolism of acetaldehyde to acetate and causing an unpleasant and potentially dangerous reaction).

Extrahepatic alcohol metabolism

It is now accepted that alcohol is subjected to a FPM by the ADH isoenzymes, primarily ADH7, in the stomach, and that this represents some protection against the systemic effects of alcohol (Birley et al., 2008; Jelski et al., 2002).

Acute pharmacological effects

This section describes common acute effects of alcohol ingestion. The chronic effects are described in Chapter 5.

Cardiovascular system

Rarely will acute intoxication have serious consequences for the cardiovascular system. However, an alcohol binge, on top of a history of regular heavy drinking, has been associated with heart arrhythmias, commonly a supraventricular tachycardia (SVT), and this has been referred to as 'holiday heart syndrome'. (An SVT is an episode of a fast heartbeat, experienced as palpitations.) Spontaneous recovery typically occurs following abstinence.

Body temperature

Moderate amounts of alcohol can lead to peripheral vasodilatation, which can increase heat loss, but is associated with a misleading feeling of warmth. Furthermore, increased sweating can, in turn, lead to heat loss and a fall in body temperature. Large amounts of alcohol can depress the central temperature-regulating mechanism causing a more pronounced fall in body temperature.

Gastrointestinal tract

Alcohol can stimulate gastric acid secretion and release of gastrin, the hormone that causes the secretion of gastric acid, with lower alcohol concentration drinks being associated with a greater stimulation. Strong alcoholic drinks, however, cause inflammation of the stomach lining and produce an erosive gastritis.

Kidney

Alcohol itself produces a diuretic effect independent from the increased flow associated with the ingestion of large volumes of fluid. This diuretic effect is due to the suppression of vasopressin (antidiuretic hormone) release.

Respiration

Moderate amounts of alcohol may stimulate or depress respiration, whereas large amounts (e.g. 400 mg/100 ml or greater) produce depression of respiration.

Central nervous system

The effects of alcohol on the brain are dependent on dose, rate of rise in BAC and degree of tolerance. Typically, driving skill is affected at 30 mg/100 ml. Ataxia, inattention and slowed reaction times are evident at levels of about 50 mg/100 ml. Mood and behavioural changes occur at levels of approximately 50–100 mg/100 ml. At levels of 150–300 mg/100 ml there is loss of self-control, slurred speech and clumsiness. Individuals unused to heavy drinking are moderately intoxicated at BAC levels of 150–250 mg/100 ml and obvious intoxication is usually evident at 300 mg/100 ml. At BACs of 300–500 mg/100 ml individuals are usually severely intoxicated, and stupor and hypothermia may sometimes supervene. Hypoglycaemia and seizures are occasionally a feature of BACs in this range. Heavy drinkers become tolerant to the central nervous system (CNS) effects of alcohol and may on occasion have BAC levels of 500 mg/100 ml without obvious signs of intoxication. However, for non-tolerant drinkers, such levels are associated with depressed reflexes, respiratory depression, hypotension, hypothermia and death.

Sites of action

Alcohol is a relatively non-specific drug that interacts with multiple chemical messengers or neurotransmitter pathways. It does not have a specific interaction at a particular brain receptor, as is seen with opioid drugs, or via blocking a reuptake transporter, such as cocaine, but rather is thought to act at 'receptive elements', including neuronal proteins (e.g. receptors and proteins involved in neuronal signalling). Thus, the rewarding properties of alcohol are thought to be mediated in part by effects on the dopamine and opioid systems. However, the most profound effects, which are implicated in tolerance and dependence, are exerted on the gamma-aminobutyric acid (GABA) and glutamate systems (Nutt, 1999). GABA is the major inhibitory system in the brain and a balance is established with glutamate, the major excitatory system in the brain. Remarkably, the neurotransmitters for these two opposing systems are very closely related and can be produced from each other in one chemical step.

Alcohol and the GABA-receptor complex

As previously mentioned, GABA is the main inhibitory neurotransmitter in the brain. The $GABA_A$ receptor is like a ring doughnut that sits in the membrane of the neurons (Nutt, 1999). GABA facilitates the passage of chloride, a negatively charged ion, into the cell, through the channel, making the cell less excitable and thereby relieving anxiety. Alcohol enhances the GABA-mediated flow of chloride ions at some types of GABA receptors and this is determined by their subunit combination.

Alcohol and the glutamate receptor

Glutamate is the main excitatory neurotransmitter system in the brain. It acts on at least three different types of receptor and important for the effects of alcohol are the N-methyl-D-aspartate (NMDA) receptors (Nutt, 1999). Like $GABA_A$, the NMDA receptor is like a ring doughnut sitting in the cell membrane, in this case allowing the passage of positively charged calcium ions into the cell, thus making the cell more likely to 'fire'. Excessive influx of calcium is damaging to the neuron, and this has been termed excitotoxic damage; this mechanism is thought to be partly responsible for alcohol-related neuronal loss and cognitive impairment. Alcohol seems to act as a blocker of the NMDA channel, thus opposing the effects of glutamate.

GABA and glutamate in tolerance and dependence

On chronic exposure to alcohol the brain has to adapt to these GABA-enhancing and glutamate-blocking effects. Thus, for the brain to continue functioning in the constant presence of alcohol, there occurs a compensatory reduction in GABA function and an increase in glutamate function. When an individual who is physically dependent upon alcohol stops drinking, or cuts down suddenly, the alcohol is metabolized at a rate of approximately 1 unit per hour. Typically, the alcohol leaves the body within approximately 1 day, and this is too quick for the tolerant body to readjust and for the brain to rebalance these two systems. This relatively rapid metabolism of alcohol thus results in an imbalance between the GABA and glutamate systems that manifests itself by withdrawal symptoms including tremors, sweats, dry heaves and, for some, withdrawal seizures and delirium tremens.

Medically this can be prevented by replacing the alcohol with a benzodiazepine, which similarly enhances GABA-induced chloride flux, thereby restoring the balance between these two systems (Figure 2.5). By using a benzodiazepine with a long half-life and/or employing a reducing regime over several days, the brain is allowed the time needed to readjust to the absence of alcohol by restoring the balance between these two opposing systems.

Alcohol and the dopamine receptor

Dopamine plays a role in mediating the pleasurable consequences and salience of alcohol (Robbins et al., 2007). However, non-dopaminergic pathways are also involved. The mesolimbic dopamine system (ventral tegmental area → nucleus accumbens) plays a significant role in mediating the reinforcing properties of alcohol. In animal models, alcohol increases the firing of dopaminergic neurons and increases the release of dopamine from these neurons in the nucleus accumbens. It has been proposed that vulnerability to alcohol dependence is

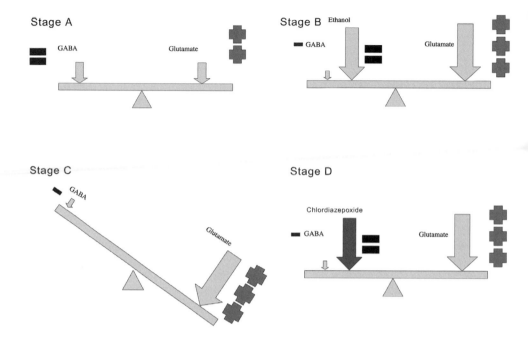

Figure 2.5. GABA and glutamate stages in tolerance and withdrawal. In the brain there is a balance between the inhibitory GABA system and the excitatory glutamate system (Stage A). Alcohol disrupts that balance and on chronic exposure the brain adjusts and adapts to the presence of alcohol (Stage B). When a physically dependent individual stops drinking, or cuts down rapidly, the brain cannot adjust sufficiently quickly and the individual develops symptoms and signs of physical withdrawal (Stage C). This balance can be restored and the withdrawal symptoms treated using benzodiazepines that are tailed off slowly allowing the brain to re-establish the balance between these two systems (Stage D).

associated with a hypofunctional mesolimbic dopaminergic system. Dopaminergic pathways are involved in mediating the pleasurable effects of alcohol (positive reinforcement). Reduced function in the mesolimbic dopaminergic system may be associated with a vulnerability to developing alcohol dependence.

Alcohol and the endogenous opioid system

The reinforcing and pleasurable effects of alcohol are mediated, at least in part, by activation of the endogenous opioid system (Figure 2.6). Alcohol consumption causes activation of the opioid system – in particular the β-endorphin pathways primarily originating in the nucleus arcuatus. This activity leads, in the β-endorphin pathways, to increased dopamine release in the nucleus accumbens by: (1) disinhibition of the tonic inhibition of GABA neurons on dopamine (DA) cells in the ventral tegmental area; and (2) direct stimulation of DA cells in the nucleus accumbens (Gianoulakis, 1998). Mu-opioid receptor antagonists such as naloxone and naltrexone block these central effects of β-endorphins and have been shown to reduce alcohol consumption in animal models and clinical settings (see Chapter 14) .

Reinstatement

One of the features that Edwards and Gross described as part of the alcohol dependence syndrome was that of rapid reinstatement (Edwards & Gross, 1976). How can we explain the

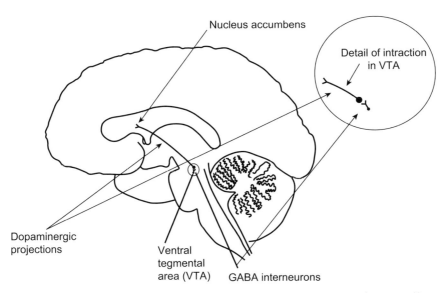

Figure 2.6. Diagram showing brain reward circuitry including dopaminergic projections from ventral legmental area (VTA) to nucleus accumbens with gamma-aminobutyric acid (GABA) interneurons.

process by which the individual with alcohol dependence, who has been abstinent for several years, develops severe alcohol withdrawal symptoms within days or weeks following relapse? In essence, this suggests that the brain does not 'reset' itself and that some form of tolerance persists long into abstinence. Indeed, there have been some reports that levels of the GABA-benzodiazepine receptor are lower in abstinent subjects in the absence of brain atrophy. Such changes could represent a vulnerability factor predisposing to the development of alcohol dependence, damage secondary to alcohol consumption and/or part of the biological under-pinning of reinstatement. Certainly it has been difficult to demonstrate a difference in GABA-benzodiazepine receptor function using challenge tests, and the biological mechanism of this clinical feature has yet to be elucidated (Taylor et al., 2008) .

Future directions

In recent years neuropharmacological research has helped to uncover the mechanisms underly-ing the actions of alcohol, the 'appetite' for alcohol and the biological basis of dependence. This has led to a renewed interest in pharmacotherapies for alcohol dependence with some promis-ing results. The challenge now is to integrate insights from the neuropharmacology, molecular genetics and clinical science with understanding from other and wider disciplines, particularly psychology. Drinking is a behaviour with multiple determinants, and the truly crucial questions will, in the long run, yield only to multidisciplinary (and interdisciplinary) research.

References

Agarwal D P, Goedde H W (1990) *Alcohol Metabolism, Alcohol Intolerance, and Alcoholism: Biochemical and Pharmacogenetic Approaches*. Berlin: Springer.

Ball D, Pembrey M, Stevens D N (2007) Genomics. In *Drugs and the Future*, D Nutt, T W Robbins, G V Stimson, M Ince, A Jackson (eds). London: Academic Press, pp. 89–131.

Birley A J, James M R, Dickson P A, et al. (2008) Association of the gastric alcohol dehydrogenase gene ADH7 with variation in alcohol metabolism. *Human Molecular Genetics* **17**(2), 179–189.

Brick J (2004) Characteristics of alcohol: chemistry, use, and abuse. In *Handbook of the Medical Consequences of Alcohol*, J Brick (ed.). New York: Haworth, pp. 1–6.

Edwards G, Gross M M (1976) Alcohol dependence: provisional description of a clinical syndrome. *British Medical Journal* 1(6017), 1058–1061.

Fleming M, Mihic S J, Harris R A (2006) Ethanol. In *Goodman and Gilman's: The Pharmacological Basis of Therapeutics*, 11th edn, L L Brunton, J Lazo, K L Parker (eds). New York: McGraw Hill, pp. 591–606.

Gianoulakis C (1998) Alcohol-seeking behavior: the roles of the hypothalamic-pituitary-adrenal axis and the endogenous opioid system. *Alcohol Health and Research World* 22(3), 202–210.

Jelski W, Chrostek L, Szmitkowski M, Laszewicz W (2002) Activity of class I, II, III, and IV alcohol dehydrogenase isoenzymes in human gastric mucosa. *Digestive Diseases and Sciences* 47(7), 1554–1557.

Nutt D (1999) Alcohol and the brain. Pharmacological insights for psychiatrists. *British Journal of Psychiatry* 175, 114–119.

Robbins T W, Cardinal R, DiCiano P, et al. (2007) Neuroscience of drugs and addiction. In *Drugs and the Future*, D Nutt, T W Robbins, G V Stimson, M Ince, A Jackson (eds). London: Academic Press, pp. 11–87.

Taylor C, Nash J, Rich A, Lingford-Hughes A, Nutt D, Potokar J (2008) Assessment of $GABA_A$ benzodiazepine receptor (GBzR) sensitivity in patients with alcohol dependence. *Alcohol and Alcoholism* 43(6), 614–618.

Background to understanding

Causes of drinking problems

3

The previous chapters have set out why alcohol is a drug, and described how some individuals use it to excess and to ill effect. This chapter turns to the crunch question: Why do some people and not others develop drinking problems?

Science points fairly consistently to five broad classes of factors that, on average across people, influence the likelihood of developing drinking problems (Table 3.1). Yet it has to be said that because individual lives frequently diverge from average effects, accounting for any individual case of drinking problems will always remain at least partly a matter of speculation not only by the healthcare provider, but by the individual and those around them.

Table 3.1 divides the factors that influence drinking problems into three levels, namely the societal, the family/community and individual. This framework is an oversimplification in a number of respects – most notably because the different factors interact across and within domains – but is useful as an analytic and descriptive convenience.

Availability of the drug

Drinking problems differ in an important respect from other problems of interest to psychiatry in that they can only occur in the presence of a particular environmental feature, namely alcohol. One can be depressed anywhere, or have schizophrenia anywhere, but one can only have a drinking problem where there is drink. And, broadly speaking, the more that drink is readily available, the more likely drinking problems are to occur, whether one is speaking of a society, a community or an individual.

The most fundamental ways societies determine alcohol availability are by laws regulating whether and under what conditions alcohol may be produced, sold and consumed. Alcohol is de jure or de facto illegal in some regions (e.g. in parts of the Middle East), all of which have an unusually low prevalence of drinking problems. The USA's experience of Prohibition has been represented in many movies and novels as actually having increased problem drinking, and this has become the posh view in many circles. However, in fact the opposite occurred, with cirrhosis and alcohol consumption dropping dramatically as the supply of alcohol was restricted (Blocker, 2006). Similar results were found during a strike in the national liquor industry in Finland (Mäkelä, 1980) where a dearth of supply led to reduced drinking problems.

Where alcohol is legal, it can be made less available through other policy actions; for example, laws restricting sale to particular licensees and times of day, as well as taxes which reduce access by artificially raising alcohol's price. Variations in supply can and do influence demand (Holder, 2000), just as demand can stimulate greater supply. Within individual countries over time, and in comparisons of different countries at any given time, reducing the real price of alcohol increases the overall consumption of alcohol by a population. Similarly, measures that make alcohol more readily available by reducing restrictions on its supply also tend to increase consumption. Manipulation of policy can therefore have enormous impact upon

Table 3.1. Five factors that often influence the development of drinking problems.

Factor	Level		
	Societal	Community/family	Individual
Availability of alcohol	Legal status of alcohol	Density of alcohol outlets	Alcohol available at home and at work
	Licensing, sale and tax laws	Family and social network alcohol availability	
Values and norms	Cultural drinking patterns	Drinking traditions	Religious beliefs
	Dominant religious traditions	Prominence of youth culture	Beliefs about alcohol
Economic situation	Presence of alcohol industry	Economic strain	Personal ability to afford alcohol
	National wealth/poverty	Class-related drinking patterns	
Genetics	Population risk/protective factors	Parental genes	Individual genes related to alcohol response
			Genes related to anxiety, depression and activity level
Disorder/chronic strain	Level of stability in society	Amount of disorder in community	Poor physical health/pain
		Marital conflict/family violence	Daily hassles

the alcohol consumption of a population. Conversely, failure to utilize such controls can allow alcohol consumption to escalate and related problems to reach epidemic proportions (Anderson & Baumberg, 2006; Babor et al., 2003, 2010; Edwards et al., 1994).

At a community level, factors such as the density and distribution of outlets may influence local incidence of alcohol-related road traffic accidents or violence (Gruenewald & Treno, 2000). Further, particular family and social networks are more or less 'wet', with some routinely providing alcohol at social, recreational and community events and others not doing so.

Individuals also vary in the amount of alcohol available in their daily life context. A well-stocked bar in the home makes heavy drinking easier; living in the country three miles from the nearest pub makes it harder. Certain occupations also offer unusually high access to alcohol, including working in a restaurant, bar or in the drinks industry itself. Selection, of course, plays a role in who takes such jobs, but this does not entirely explain the level of drinking observed. New employees in the drinks industry are likely to be relatively heavy drinkers, but they also further increase their alcohol consumption after working in that industry (Plant, 1979). This may reflect the ready availability of alcohol in that particular occupational environment.

Norms and values

Across countries with similar legal regimes, the prevalence and amount of drinking varies substantially. As drinking is often a social activity, and drinkers tend to make judgements about how much drinking is normal based on social comparisons, cultural norms of higher prevalence (i.e. few abstainers) and heavier volume drinking tend to reproduce themselves. This in turn leads to more drinking problems (Babor et al., 2003, 2010; Edwards et al., 1994).

The quantity of alcohol consumed is not the only characteristic of drinking that affects the occurrence of drinking problems. The pattern of alcohol consumption is also important. For example, different drinking problems are likely to arise in the woman who drinks 4 glasses of wine every day, as compared with the woman who drinks 3 bottles of wine in 2 days but who then drinks nothing for 2 or 3 weeks. Whilst the former is at greater risk of damage to the liver, brain and other organs, the latter is at greater risk of marital disharmony and other social problems.

Cultural norms can influence the pattern of drinking just as much as the amount. In France, habitual consumption of wine with meals is associated with a relatively high, but constant, per capita consumption, which predisposes towards chronic medical complications such as cirrhosis and certain cancers. In urban centres in the UK and North America, particularly amongst working class men, alcohol is more likely to be consumed away from the home and often in relatively large quantities at a sitting. This pattern of drinking to intoxication seems to be more likely to be accompanied by adverse social consequences such as marital disharmony, accidents, interpersonal violence and drunkenness offences.

Culture may also influence the ways in which people behave when intoxicated. Drunken behaviour is shaped not only by the biological effects of alcohol as a drug, but also by social and cultural expectations as to how people will behave whilst intoxicated (MacAndrew & Edgerton, 1970). This may influence, for example, the likelihood of drunken antisocial behaviour.

One important element of culture is religious practice. Virtually all of the factors described thus far had some bearing on this (e.g. the Protestant religious forces behind US Prohibition, the Islamic prohibition on alcohol affecting anti-alcohol values in the Middle East). People with alcohol problems are far less likely to engage in religious practices than the general population. In contrast, being raised in a mainstream religion is a potent protective factor against a young person developing an alcohol problem (Humphreys & Gifford, 2006) .

Values and norms also are potent forces on drinking problems at the community level. For example, some neighbourhoods (usually but not always due to the presence of universities), are part of youth culture, in which drinking, dating, mating and dancing are prevalent and intertwined. Communities also have drinking traditions, such as one can find in the Irish ethnic bars of Boston's Southie district, or, at the other extreme, the largely dry counties of parts of the US Deep South. Families too have their drinking traditions, which children observe and from which they learn. In some families, drinking heavily is a matter of pride and identity, e.g. 'He could hold his drink like a real McAllister'!

At an individual level, personal religious beliefs and values, as well as specific beliefs about alcohol, also may affect an individual's likelihood of developing drinking problems. In general, these effects are intuitive, i.e. more religious beliefs and more anti-alcohol beliefs lessen drinking problems. But, for a small portion of people, these same beliefs may make drinking more exotic, and hence unusually appealing.

Economic factors

The presence of a drinks industry, which can mass produce alcohol and then market it and sell it, causes a wide-scale increase in alcohol consumption and drinking problems. A number of undeveloped societies that had only locally made, low-strength, hard-to-create alcoholic beverages (e.g. the Haya Indians, who through an elaborate process made low-strength banana wine for ceremonial events [Carlson, 2006]), have seen a sharp rise of drinking problems with the arrival of stronger, attractively packaged, more easily acquired commercial alcoholic beverages such as the industry can provide.

Other economic influences on alcohol consumption are not deliberately manipulated, but follow in the wake of social change. In the 1990s, for example, rapid socio-economic changes in Eastern Europe led to increased availability of alcohol, increased consumption and increased drinking problems. This would suggest that, where possible, policy initiatives should be put in place as an intentional preventive measure, in advance of such changes. Equally, where controls on price and access already exist, they should not be removed solely for political, ideological or trade reasons, with their public health significance ignored.

The influence of supply upon demand for alcohol indicates that the alcohol-supply system (production, distribution, wholesale, import/export and retail sale) is an important consideration in any analysis of alcohol policy in relation to public health and safety. Many important questions are raised concerning the relationship between a multinational drinks industry and national governments, and the nature, strategy and determination of growth within this industry. In short, policymakers and researchers must ask: 'What drives the alcohol supply side?' (Edwards & Holder, 2000). It is important to remember that the supply system operates at a local as well as at the national and international level.

Economics also shape drinking because different forms of alcohol are linked in the public mind (often through advertising) with different economic classes. A well-off person may therefore drink wine rather than beer, not out of genuine liking but based on a sense that wine is what well-off people drink. These class distinctions are often socially reinforced: the factory worker who goes to the pub with his mates after work and orders a glass of sherry may endure substantial derision.

Personal finances may also shape the nature of drinking problems. Drink-driving arrests and boating accidents are more common among those who can afford such modes of transportation. Money may, to some extent, also allow a person to buy his or her way out of some drinking problems, at least in the short term; for example, by hiring a skilled barrister to have charges reduced or dismissed after an alcohol-involved mishap.

Economic strain in a community can also stimulate problem drinking. Multiple studies have shown that economic shocks (e.g. the closing of a factory and associated mass redundancy in the community) tend to be followed by increases in family problems, psychiatric care-seeking and disorder, all of which seem likely to have reciprocally positive relationships with problem drinking (Kiernan et al., 1989). At an individual level, some would argue that the stress of being unable to pay bills and otherwise make ends meet drives people to drink, others would disagree and assert instead that far from being victims of circumstance, problem drinkers bring such financial woes upon themselves. As usual, data have been unkind to such one-sided explanations: longitudinal research shows that while problem drinking does indeed generate economic strains for drinkers and their families, these strains in turn lead to a subsequent worsening of the drinking problem (Humphreys, Moos & Finney, 1996).

Genetics

Drinking problems tend to run in families (Ducci & Goldman, 2008). Family environment was often assumed to underlie this clustering, tending in some way to produce uniformity of behaviour. There is almost certainly some truth to this hypothesis. However, more recent research has attempted to disentangle the effects of family environment from those of heredity. By studying identical and non-identical twins, and children raised and apart from their biological parents, it is possible to separate the effects of 'nature' and 'nurture'. With only a few exceptions, such studies have tended to confirm that there is a genetic component to drinking behaviour and drinking problems, in addition to the undeniably important influence of the environment (Cook, 1994).

Two main approaches have been adopted to search for those genes that contribute to the vulnerability to drinking problems. The first, called linkage, tracks the behaviour, or problem of interest, through families and attempts to identify a coinheritance between a genetic variant and the condition. Finding this positive linkage implies that a gene around that variant may be involved. Such an approach is systematic, as the whole genome can now be studied with a relatively small number of genetic variants. However, this approach is not necessarily sensitive enough to identify the genes of small effect anticipated in addiction. The second method, termed allelic association, compares those demonstrating the problem with controls that do not. In essence, the distribution of genetic variants is compared between the cases and controls and a significant difference indicates that a gene very close to that genetic variant is involved. This approach is much more sensitive and can detect the genetic effects predicted to be involved in addiction. In addition, it is now possible to perform a 'whole genome scan' by studying a million genetic variants in a single reaction by using a 'DNA array' or 'DNA chip'. However, the field is littered with inconsistent findings, and the issue of false positives must be addressed statistically as the huge amount of data produced by these DNA arrays is evaluated. Any reported findings should therefore be viewed with a healthy degree of scepticism until robustly replicated.

What is inherited that in some way causes heavy drinking, alcohol-related problems or alcohol dependence? In most cases the answer to this question is not known. However, some clues are available and we may indulge in some informed speculation. For example, in Oriental populations a genetic variant of one of the enzymes involved in alcohol metabolism (aldehyde dehydrogenase 2: ALDH2) is responsible for a 'flushing' syndrome, which is manifested by an unpleasant physiological response to the ingestion of alcohol. Carriers of the mutant gene tend to drink little or no alcohol, since they feel unwell when they do so. This genetic effect, due to a single gene mutation, dramatically reduces the incidence of heavy drinking and thus the alcohol-related problems amongst those affected by it. Similar, but more subtle, effects in the way that the body 'handles' alcohol may influence the amount that Caucasian individuals drink.

There is also evidence of a genetic influence upon liability to alcohol dependence (Cook & Gurling, 2001). The exact brain reward mechanism by which this effect is conferred is not yet known, nor is it clear how much of any added risk is specific to alcohol dependence versus also posing a risk for a range of addictions. There is likely a shared genetic contribution during development to negative affect and behavioural under control, which can lead to psychological and behavioural problems in adulthood, including problem drinking (Hesselbrock & Hesselbrock, 2006).

Genetic effects also directly influence the incidence of adverse consequences given that someone is a drinker. For example, it would seem likely that particular organ systems (e.g. liver or brain) might be subject to genetic variation in vulnerability to alcohol-induced damage. This hypothesis is supported, for example, by one of the twin studies of drinking problems, which showed evidence for a genetic influence upon both alcohol-induced liver disease and alcoholic psychosis (Hrubec & Omenn, 1981).

How then can the evidence supporting the importance of both genetic and environmental causes for heavy drinking and drinking problems be brought together? The truth is, of course, that a behaviour such as alcohol consumption cannot be totally understood either on the basis of genes or environment alone, but only as a product of the interaction between a variety of genetic and environmental influences (Ducci & Goldman, 2008). Thus, one might see an individual as being more or less disposed to heavy drinking, or to particular alcohol-related problems, or to dependence upon alcohol. This level of predisposition determines the risk, or probability, of being a heavy drinker, or of suffering from a particular drink-related problem. If a combination of environmental and genetic risk factors exceeds a certain hypothetical threshold, then that individual will drink heavily or suffer a particular problem associated with their drinking.

We may now understand the enigma of the individual who drinks heavily, and escapes harm, or of the person who drinks moderately and suffers various complications. In the former case, the individual may be predisposed to heavy drinking by a combination of hereditary and environmental factors. However, at the same time, they may have a (genetic) constitutional resilience that protects them from liver damage, and they may learn (from their environment) social controls and patterns of behaviour that avoid public drunkenness, drink-driving or other alcohol-related problems. In the latter case, the reverse may be true. Thus, an individual may drink moderately as a result of minimal genetic and environmental predisposition towards heavy drinking and yet be subject to, say, liver disease owing to a genetic susceptibility of the liver to damage by alcohol.

Disorder and chronic stress

War, natural disaster and mass dislocation are commonly associated with increases in all types of substance use, unless the destruction is so great as to destroy the means of supply itself. Long-term political subjugation, as for example occurred with Native Americans, may also stimulate alcohol problems.

At the community/family level, disorder and stress may be experienced in a range of ways, but the most common is family conflict, be it ongoing squabbling between a couple married in misery, power struggles between adolescents and parents or outright physical violence within the family.

On an individual level, major negative life events and everyday hassles both appear to increase the amounts that people drink. A particularly common chronic stressor is poor health, particularly chronic pain (Brennan, Schutte & Moos, 2005). This may be explained on the basis that alcohol can temporarily relieve emotional anxiety and physical pain and is thus used as a means of coping (as invoked by the 'self-medication' and 'tension reduction' hypotheses). Psychological and physical strain factors would therefore appear to be an important risk factor for the development of drinking problems. However, the research evidence is not consistent and heavy drinking tends to cause further stress in the form of the problems that it generates (divorce, unemployment, ill health, and so on). There is also evidence that alcohol can exacerbate anxiety rather than relieve it. The association between heavy drinking and stress is therefore a complex one and it should not be seen as simple cause and effect.

Application to practical contexts

Some of the research described in this chapter remains academic in day-to-day practice. For example, efforts to help the problem drinker may be relatively uninfluenced by the knowledge that he or she has a strong family history of drinking problems. Nor will it be very important in practice to know whether that familiality is determined by genetic or cultural causes. However, neither should it be assumed that such matters are irrelevant to the practical contexts within which policies are made and clinical interventions offered.

Present or future applications of research and knowledge concerning the causes of drinking problems may be identified in the realms of prevention and treatment. Policy making, health and public education, individual and family counselling and drug treatments are all influenced in various ways.

Policy making is most obviously influenced by the wealth of research on the ways in which the availability and acceptability of alcohol within the community influence the epidemiology of alcohol-related problems (Babor et al., 2003, 2010; Edwards et al., 1994; Holder & Edwards, 1995). Taxation, legislation, service planning and workplace policies are all potentially effective tools of prevention. Such policies are known to be effective because of empirical research support. They are effective in practice because of the ways in which they influence the underlying causes of alcohol-related problems.

Knowledge of the causes of alcohol-related problems also influences face-to-face health education in clinical practice and public education in the wider community. For example, the question often arises as to what constitutes 'safe' or 'sensible' drinking. In truth, and as this chapter shows, the answer to this question will vary depending upon a range of individual and environmental vulnerability factors, many of which may be unknown. Because of this uncertainty, general guidelines for sensible drinking have been offered, which are estimated to be appropriate for most members of the population (British Medical Association, 1995; Royal Colleges of Physicians, Psychiatrists and General Practitioners, 1995; Royal College of Psychiatrists, 1986; and see Chapter 1). No drinking is, however, absolutely safe for all drinkers, on all occasions, and in all environments, and advice cannot properly be mechanistic. The child of the parent with a drinking problem, the person who is anxious or depressed or the drinks industry employee are examples of people at particular risk, who may find it difficult to adhere to simple advice in practice, because of either constitutional susceptibility or environmental pressures or both. Knowledge of the environmental and constitutional factors that make an individual vulnerable to drinking problems is therefore important, both to the professional asked to provide advice on such matters, and also to the individual wishing to make rational decisions about their own drinking.

In relation to the actual business of treatment, the matters discussed in this chapter are firstly relevant to the approach to case assessment which is outlined in Chapter 11. There it will be suggested that whenever assessing a patient, or planning their treatment, the requirement must be to look in detail both at the individual and their environment and to examine the multiple factors, both remote and current, which may bear on the genesis of that person's drinking problem. The research discussed in the present chapter gives that assessment-approach its scientific underpinning.

In addition to the population and individual contexts, knowledge of the causes of alcohol-related problems has application to the support and treatment offered to families. Although family therapy or family counselling are often not available as a component of treatment, our knowledge of the ways in which genetics and family environment contribute to the causation of alcohol-related problems would suggest that there is an important place at this level for both information-giving and psychological therapy. For example, knowledge of the way in which family rituals and routines are affected by alcohol misuse has been used as the basis of therapy for the alcoholic family (Steinglass et al., 1987; and see Chapter 4) .

Overall, it may be said that knowledge of the causes and predispositions to drinking problems is likely to offer a more informed, focused and effective approach to any area of engagement with alcohol-related problems. This is true regardless of whether the professional is working with individuals, groups, families or communities; whether in treatment or prevention; and whether their domain of interest is clinical, educational or political.

References

Anderson P, Baumberg B (2006) *Alcohol in Europe*. London: Institute of Alcohol Studies.

Babor T, Caetano R, Casswell S, et al. (2003) *Alcohol: No Ordinary Commodity: Research and Public Policy*. Oxford: Oxford University Press.

Blocker J S (2006) Did prohibition really work? Alcohol prohibition as a public health innovation. *American Journal of Public Health* 96, 233–243.

Brennan P L, Schutte K K, Moos R H (2005) Pain and use of alcohol to manage pain: prevalence and 3-year outcomes among older problem and non-problem drinkers. *Addiction* 100, 777–786.

British Medical Association (1995) *Alcohol: Guidelines on Sensible Drinking*. London: British Medical Association.

Carlson R G (2006) Ethnography and applied substance misuse research: anthropological and cross-cultural factors. In *Rethinking Substance Abuse: What the Science Shows and What We Should Do About It*, W R Miller, K Carroll (eds). New York: Guilford, pp. 97–114.

Cook C C H (1994) Aetiology of alcohol misuse. In *Seminars in Psychiatry: Alcohol and Drug Misuse*, J Chick, R Cantwell (eds). London: Royal College of Psychiatrists, pp. 94–125.

Cook C C H, Gurling H M D (2001) Genetic predisposition to alcohol dependence and problems. In *International Handbook of Alcohol Dependence and Problems*, N Heather, T J Peters, T Stockwell (eds). Chichester, UK: John Wiley & Sons, pp. 257–279.

Ducci F, Goldman D (2008) Genetic approaches to addiction: genes and alcohol. *Addiction* 103, 1414–1428.

Edwards G, Holder H D (2000) The alcohol supply: its importance to public health and safety, and essential research questions. The supply side initiative: international collaboration to study the alcohol supply, H D Holder (ed.). *Addiction* 95(Suppl 4), 621–627.

Edwards G, Anderson P, Babor T F, et al. (1994) *Alcohol Policy and the Public Good*. Oxford: Oxford University Press.

Gruenewald P J, Treno A J (2000) Local and global alcohol supply: economic and geographic models of community systems. The supply side initiative: international collaboration to study the alcohol supply, H D Holder (ed.). *Addiction* 95(Suppl 4), 537–549.

Hesselbrock V M, Hesselbrock M N (2006) Developmental perspectives on the risk for developing substance abuse problems. In *Rethinking Substance Abuse: What the Science Shows and What We Should Do About It*, W R Miller, K Carroll (eds). New York: Guilford, pp. 97–114.

Holder H D (2000) The supply side initiative as an international collaboration to study alcohol supply, drinking and consequences: current knowledge, policy issues, and research opportunities. The supply side initiative: international collaboration to study the alcohol supply, H D Holder (ed.). *Addiction* 95(Suppl 4), 461–463.

Holder H, Edwards G (1995) *Alcohol and Public Policy: Evidence and Issues*. Oxford: Oxford University Press.

Hrubec Z, Omenn G S (1981) Evidence of genetic predisposition to alcoholic psychosis and cirrhosis: twin concordances for alcoholism and its biological end points by zygosity among male veterans. *Alcoholism: Clinical and Experimental Research* 5, 207–215.

Humphreys K, Gifford E (2006) Religion, spirituality and the troublesome use of substances. In *Rethinking Substance Abuse: What the Science Shows and What We Should Do About It*, W R Miller, K Carroll (eds). New York: Guilford, pp. 257–274.

Humphreys K, Moos R H, Finney J W (1996) Life domains, Alcoholics Anonymous, and role incumbency in the 3-year course of problem drinking. *Journal of Nervous and Mental Disease* 184, 475–481.

Kiernan M, Toro P A, Rappaport J, Seidman E (1989) Economic predictors of mental health services utilization: a time-series analysis. *American Journal of Community Psychology* 17, 801–820.

MacAndrew C, Edgerton R B (1970) *Drunken Comportment*. London: Nelson.

Mäkelä K (1980) Differential effects of restricting the supply of alcohol: studies of a strike in Finnish liquor stores. *Journal of Drug Issues* **10**, 131–144.

Plant M A (1979) *Drinking Careers*. London: Tavistock.

Royal Colleges of Physicians, Psychiatrists and General Practitioners (1995) *Alcohol and the Heart in Perspective: Sensible Limits Reaffirmed*. London: Royal Colleges of Physicians, Psychiatrists and General Practitioners.

Royal College of Psychiatrists (1986) *Alcohol: Our Favourite Drug*. London: Tavistock.

Steinglass P, Bennett L A, Wolin S J, Reiss D (1987) *The Alcoholic Family*. London: Hutchinson.

4

Background to understanding

Social complications of drinking problems

When a problem drinker is standing before them, doctors can see the problems the person might 'carry with them': neurological impairment, medical complications, psychopathology and illegal drug dependence. These are all serious disorders worthy of clinical attention, and are accordingly addressed in other chapters of this book. But this chapter is about what cannot typically be directly observed in the consulting room, namely the web of family interactions, social networks and institutional responses that problem drinkers encounter in their daily lives. This surround can have a profound influence on the course of treatment and, indeed, on the drinker's entire life course. A drink-driving arrest can shock one patient into productive action but ruin the career of another. A network of drinking mates can undermine treatment, whereas a supportive but firm family can be a major aid to therapeutic progress. And a single alcohol-fuelled act of violence can have life long consequences, both for the perpetrator and the victim.

Before proceeding to specific social contexts in which drinking problems reverberate, we consider four important conceptual issues. Each shapes our understanding of how drinking problems unfold, and therefore has implications for clinical intervention.

Pinpointing the 'complications' of drinking problems in individual lives is rarely simple

Chapter 3 discussed the causes of drinking problems, which logically must precede them in time. This chapter addresses the complications, which logically must follow drinking problems in time. Yet a discerning reader will note that some problems (e.g. medical problems, difficult economic circumstances) are mentioned under both headings. Likewise, in the treatment of individual patients, clearly distinguishing putative causes from consequences can be quite challenging.

Marilyn is an attractive, 28-year-old woman who has been married to a successful business executive for 3 years. The couple planned a traditional family arrangement in which Marilyn would stay at home and focus entirely on rearing children. After a year of marriage, the relationship began to sour when the couple discovered that Marilyn was infertile. Marilyn reacted to this news by feeling like 'a failure as a woman', and suspected that her husband secretly held the same view. Until this point in her life, Marilyn had rarely consumed alcohol for fear that she would end up like her bullying, frequently drunk parents. Nonetheless, Marilyn began to drink regularly when she was home alone, despairing: 'What difference does it make?' She describes her husband as having steadily withdrawn attention and affection over the past 2 years. During this period her drinking increased, as did her depression and loneliness. She is typically severely intoxicated by 3 pm, and has severe headaches and vomiting most mornings. Her sexual relationship with her husband has all but ceased in the past year, starting when he called her 'repulsive' after finding her extremely intoxicated and naked on the bedroom floor. She has lately had the persistent anxiety that he is having an extramarital affair, and states that alcohol is the only thing that stops this fear from racing through her mind.

One could argue that the lesson of this sad situation is that Marilyn's drinking problems created complications for her marriage and her emotional well-being. Yet one could also argue that it was actually health problems and personal tragedy (e.g. infertility in someone who desperately wanted a child) that caused Marilyn's problem drinking, or that Marilyn's depression and anxiety had the adverse consequence of accelerating (or 'telescoping') the course of her incipient drinking problem. Or perhaps Marilyn acquired a genetic liability from her alcoholic parents and that is the true cause of her current misery. One could even argue that this married couple's perceptions of a woman's proper role (i.e. that she has no value other than as a mother) is causing drinking problems, marital unhappiness and depression. Even from this short case description, a number of other conjectures on the causes versus the complications of Marilyn's drinking could be made, much as one could stand in a river and speculate endlessly about which particular rivulet, eddy, rock and overturned tree stump is truly defining the water's course.

The question of whether causes and complications can be clearly made out in a complex life seems less academic when one recognizes how commonly patients want to know the answer to the 'big questions'; for example, 'Did something make me drink?' 'What share of this suffering is of my own creation?' 'What else will change if I get my drinking under control?' For the clinician to say 'there is no way to know if all of your problems would have befallen you even if you had never had a drink' is philosophically correct, but clinically inept, as it potentially destroys the patient's incentive to change. At the other extreme, for the clinician to hang every bad event in the patient's life on problem drinking could induce crushing guilt, inappropriate self-blame and false hope that life will be a bed of roses as soon as the cork is in the bottle.

There is no sense in a clinician pretending to have perfect understanding of what caused what in an individual's past, nor of shielding the patient from the fundamental uncertainties about such things, which are part and parcel of human existence. Speaking probabilistically is often the best course, i.e. 'Neither of us can know for sure if your marriage became unhappy because you started drinking heavily or the reverse, but I hope we can agree that it's more likely to get better in the future if you get your drinking under control'. As authors we adopt precisely the same probabilistic stance in this book. We highlight problems that we consider 'complications' because scientific evidence shows that they are prevalent in the drinking population and that they are usually made worse by drinking. These two facts make them worthy of the clinician's attention. Yet in using the term 'complication' we unhesitatingly acknowledge that, in any individual life, the complication may actually have been a cause of problem drinking, or for that matter both a complication and a cause.

One person's complication is another person's benison

Inexperienced clinicians frequently make the mistake of assuming that problem drinkers invariably define an adverse consequence of drinking as would those around them. A patient losing a job from problem drinking may distress the clinician, as well as the patient's spouse and children, but the drinker himself or herself may enjoy the new found free time and lack of responsibility. Another spouse, to the clinician's surprise, may be perfectly satisfied that her otherwise demanding and tiresome husband slowly passes out from heavy drinking each evening, granting her otherwise scarce peace, quiet and the run of the house. For these reasons, the experienced clinician will always assess the drinking surround neutrally, rather than subtly cuing the patient as to what should be considered a problem. After all, therapeutic leverage often comes more from what the drinker considers the complications of drinking than what others view as its downsides.

The social contexts of problem drinking are to some extent selected, and to some extent select

Problem drinkers do not choose the liver with which they were born, nor can their liver seek greener pastures when heavy alcohol consumption imposes added strain. In contrast, problem drinkers can often choose the social contexts in which they will and will not participate, and social environments, being composed of active, motivated people, can choose or not choose the problem drinker. For example, one of the interesting observations of social epidemiology is that people who tend to drink heavily have friends who drink heavily. This comes about in part through selection by the drinker, e.g. choosing to hang around in pubs or to drink at hours of the day that most people consider 'too early for a drink'. It also comes about by selection of other people; for example, the light-drinking relatives who slowly reduce contact so as to avoid exposure to a couple's drunken rows. This phenomenon helps explain why many heavy drinkers do not see themselves as above average in consumption: they drink about as much as those around them.

The clinical implication is that the clinician must conduct a 'higher-level' review of social complications that is not needed for medical or psychiatric consequences. Specifically, one must consider not only the consequences of problem drinking in the drinker's social environment, but how drinking got that person into that specific environment in the first place. One of the benefits of this awareness is that it can help the patient see new possibilities in life that are not apparent because they have drifted into their current range of social environments in order to support their drinking. So, for example, a problem drinker may be pleased to hear that rather than worry about how to get along with a demeaning boss and cope more effectively with menial pay as a warehouse worker (a job chosen because it allows drinking), bringing drinking under control can allow a new job where such concerns are irrelevant. The same principle often applies in romantic relationships, i.e. rather than attempt to divine which of a group of habitués at a dive bar is least likely to be physically aggressive on a date, a woman problem drinker can start seeking dates in locations not centred on heavy drinking.

In addition, this 'higher-level review' can guard against any tendency in the clinician to regard the patient as a passive victim of social environments, which is a 'story' that some patients like to tell and may even believe themselves. For example, the man who says he drinks heavily because he has no wife or friends, or because his children never visit, isn't acknowledging that his drinking may be causing others to drop him from their social networks in the first place.

A person's resources moderate the strength of the link between drinking problems and social complications

Consider two women with identical drinking problems. Each gets in her car and drives home from a late-night party while heavily intoxicated and is pulled over by a policeman who observes the car weaving out of the lane. In theory, the fates of these two women – their 'complications of drinking' – should also be identical, but in practice they may not be. If one of the women is a well-known author and the other is a short-order cook, or if one drives a Mercedes and the other a shambling jalopy, or if one is toothsome and charming and the other rudely stamped and verbally clumsy, the policeman may use his discretion differently. In the case of the more successful, or wealthier, or more appealing woman, a warning may suffice in his mind, 'Just this once', but for the less successful, poorer, less appealing woman no such mercy may be forthcoming.

The important lesson is that some people, whether through social standing, money, guile, good looks, charm or connections are unusually good at evading what would otherwise be the consequences of their drinking problems. The high-profile parade of spectacular drinking disasters among rich and famous people is often attributed to the media's obsession with celebrity. But an alternative explanation is equally plausible. Because such people are often insulated from the more minor complications of their drinking when their problem is less severe, they ironically enough may be more likely to progress to the point that they experience a complication that no amount of influence, money or fame can make disappear.

Clinicians, like anyone else, can have their judgement affected by a patient's wealth, charm and the like, and must guard against the tendency to buy into the patient's narrative that drinking cannot really be that serious because consequences have been largely eluded thus far. At the other end of the continuum, for a clinician to ignore the fact that social complications can come down unusually harshly on certain individuals could disrupt the therapeutic relationship, either by failing to appreciate the reality of the patient's life (e.g. the higher odds that a patient from a racial minority will be pulled over in 'random' traffic stops), or by overstating the seriousness of the drinking per se.

We now turn to domains in which social complications of drinking are commonly experienced: family, work/education, violence and other crime and financial stability/housing.

Family complications of problem drinking

Drinking problems can reverberate throughout a person's social network, including to friends and to distant in-laws who may be in contact only a few times year. But in almost all cases, the most profoundly affected people are the drinker's partner and children, upon whom we focus here.

The partner

We use 'partner' generically in this chapter to refer to the problem drinker's legally recognized spouse (of a different or the same sex) as well as to other significant romantic partnerships. Because clinical writings in prior eras often took as read that 'partners' were female and problem drinkers male, we emphasize here that we use 'partner' to refer to men as well as women, consistent with the rise of heavy drinking among women in recent decades (Grucza et al., 2008).

A history from the partner as an individual

The assumption is too often made that the purpose of taking a history from the partner is solely that of obtaining 'independent information'. What is frequently forgotten is the need to take a history from the partner as a person in his or her own right. The result is that, after months have gone by, it is suddenly realized that treatment is proceeding on the basis of much being known about the patient while the partner remains a cipher, and their interaction is hence inexplicable. Treatment of the patient is handicapped, and the fact that the partner may too need help is overlooked.

What has to be overcome is a subconscious social constraint – the feeling that it is embarrassing to interview someone about their own situation when their role is presumed to be that of someone coming to the clinic to talk about someone else's serious problem. How the initial history is to be taken from the partner in respectful, comfortable terms is fully discussed in Chapter 11.

How drinking problems affect the partner and the relationship

As mentioned, social networks to some extent select their members. In the case of couples in which one member has a drinking problem, this can result in social isolation as outsiders withdraw out of embarrassment, discomfort or fear. The non-drinking partner may encourage this isolation, either out of shame or from a desire to protect the drinking partner from criticism.

A frequent additional stressor is the unpredictability of what is going to happen. A woman may not know whether, when her partner gets back from the pub, he will be in a raging temper and attack her with his fists. A man might worry that this will be one of the nights that his partner gets drunk and humiliates them both in a social situation by being loud, crude or sexually inappropriate. The exhaustion that can be engendered by the experience of dealing with continuing distress and peaks of crisis over a period of years may be the partner's dominant complaint.

Historically, clinical writings have attributed much of the behaviour of wives of problem drinkers to psychopathology (e.g. a secret joy or sense of superiority that their husband was alcoholic). Yet a more direct explanation of the behaviour of many wives, and husbands as well, is that they continue to love the problem drinker despite it all. Orford and colleagues documented that cross-culturally, the allowing of second and third chances, the tolerance of abuse and disappointment, the efforts to control drinking are very commonly motivated by the fact that the partner worries about, cares for and wishes to help the problem drinker (Orford et al., 2005). This indeed is one of the stressors of such relationships, having to watch someone you love harm themselves or you, and constantly trying to judge where love ends and damaging over-indulgence begins.

In addition to emotional strain, partners of problem drinkers often face concrete realities that can be tangibly threatening; there is the risk of eviction if the rent is not paid, or violence may result in serious physical injury. Divorce, which often has significant adverse economic and psychological effects, is also a common result of problem drinking. More commonly, problem drinking creates a host of minor tangible problems that have to be coped with: no housekeeping money this week, electricity shut off for a day until the bill is belatedly paid, the neighbours complaining about the doors being slammed when the drinker got home last night, constant rowing, the drinker being unkempt or wetting the bed.

It would, however, be a mistake always to picture such relationships only in extreme terms. Extremes of suffering certainly occur with sad frequency, but there are all gradations. Sometimes the problem drinker's deportment when inebriated causes little distress. Perhaps the drinker becomes a bit silly and argumentative, or simply nods off and is difficult to drag up to bed.

Finally, there is every reason to have hope that the partner of a problem drinker can benefit substantially from the drinker's successful treatment. Moos and colleagues have found that spouses of remitted alcoholic patients score similar or somewhat better on mental health measures as community controls, and substantially better than spouses of actively drinking alcoholics (Moos, Finney & Cronkite, 1990). Much of what is sometimes put down to enduring psychopathology in partners of problem drinkers is therefore actually a reaction to a difficult situation that dissipates when the drinking problem is resolved.

The types of hardship that the partner may encounter are discussed in more detail in relation to taking the 'independent history' from the partner (see Chapter 11).

Relationships in which both partners have a drinking problem

This extraordinarily difficult situation is encountered more often than might be guessed from the prevalence rate of drinking problems. Heavy drinkers are unusually likely to marry other heavy drinkers, and drinking together can be a central activity in such relationships.

The story is usually that of a person with a drinking problem marrying someone else with an established and evident drinking problem. For one or both partners it may be a second marriage. They met perhaps in a bar or even in a hospital ward, and it is a marriage of convenience between drinkers. They have no knowledge of each other's sober beings, and are, sadly, likely to drag each other down further. Alcohol-related problems do sometimes develop in both partners in an already established marriage. Quite often the development is not simultaneous, but the wife seems to follow in the husband's footsteps, her drinking being in part perhaps a reaction to the stress of the husband's behaviour. Another type of marriage is where the partners have met at Alcoholics Anonymous, are both committed to 'recovery' and are able to give each other much support.

In general, where both husband and wife have a serious problem, it can be difficult to reach them with effective help. If they met in a pub and each purposefully married a drinking partner, the therapist may encounter a baffling pack of pathological motivations. In such instances, all that may be possible is to make the offer of help, try to maintain some sort of monitoring contact and wait for the happening which can provide the therapeutic opening; for example, one partner going into hospital with a physical illness. Where the heavy drinking has developed during the marriage, rather than being the foundation of the marriage, the possibilities for therapy are usually more hopeful. Both partners may simultaneously be able to seek help, or it may be necessary to start with the partner who is more motivated, or with any children who could benefit from the support of a treatment professional. If therapy can capture the potential for mutual understanding, which can exist between partners who have shared the same problem, an initially difficult situation can be turned to special advantage.

Coping styles of partners

Past perspectives on the alcoholic marriage (not to mention some which are still current) have often been rather negative in outlook (Orford et al., 2005). Recognition of this bias has given rise to a shift in emphasis, away from that of the presumed pathology of the partner and their status as victim, towards an attempt to understand their ability to cope with the stresses presented by an intimate relationship with an alcoholic.

Helping a partner change their *coping style* is a well-established part of alcohol treatment for couples (McCrady et al., 2002). A wide range of different styles have been identified, and different approaches to classification are suggested. However, research suggests that they may all eventually be reduced to three main options: engagement, tolerance or withdrawal (Hurcom, Copello & Orford, 2000; Orford et al., 1998). A few suggestions are made here as to the kind of behaviours that might be found under each of these headings.

Engagement involves strategies which involve assertiveness, taking control, emotional responses or offering of support. For example, a spouse may resort to *attack,* trying to control the drinker's behaviour by scolding, shouting, threatening to walk out or, on occasions, even by physical assault. The drinker is informed that a solicitor will be contacted 'first thing tomorrow morning'. Drink is poured down the sink, clothes thrown on the front lawn. *Manipulation* embraces a number of behaviours, such as seeking to shame the drinker, with the partner showing his or her own distress or emphasizing the children's suffering. *Constructive help-seeking* is a pattern characterized by behaviour such as asking the family doctor to speak to the problem drinker, visiting an Alcoholics Anonymous meeting, reaching out for support from friends and family or going to the public library and reading books on alcoholism and treatment.

Tolerance includes self-sacrifice, acceptance and inactivity. *Spoiling* may be a more active example of this approach: the partner nurses the drinker through hangovers, keeps dinner warm, shoulders the extra child care and so forth. Much is actively given to the problem drinker in such situations without much expectation of return. By contrast, *inaction* provides a more passive form of tolerance which simply accepts the status quo.

The third class of coping behaviour, withdrawal, is illustrated by the following example of *circumvention.*

> It's terrible really, but I suppose we've all got used to it. We'll all go to bed before he comes in at night and I'll pretend to be asleep when he comes into the room. I tell the kids to keep out of his way. Sometimes he gets back early, but if we're in the sitting room watching the television, more often than not he just goes out to the kitchen. I take the children on holiday, he doesn't come, and frankly we don't ask him.

Contact is so far as possible minimized, and there is emotional as well as physical avoidance. This might involve quite independent behaviours. For example, a partner/spouse might adopt an approach of *constructive management* in which self-worth is retained and the family looked after largely through the partner's efforts.

These various styles (summarized in Table 4.1) seldom exist in pure form, and there are other examples of coping behaviour which might be given. The choice of style may be influenced by the way in which the partner generally copes with life, by class expectations, by

Table 4.1. Examples of each of three main options for action open to partners of problem drinkers.

1 Engagement:
- attack
- manipulation
- spoiling (where used to attempt to induce change)
- constructive help-seeking

2 Tolerance:
- spoiling
- inaction

3 Withdrawal:
- circumvention
- constructive management

the type of behaviour which the problem drinker is manifesting and by the duration of the problem. The coping style employed at a particular time may be a response in a sequence of experiments in which the partner is searching around, trying first one tack and then another (Table 4.1).

Children

For the children of the problem drinker to be entirely forgotten by the therapeutic team is sadly all too easy. Their names and ages are noted in the initial history-taking, out of the corner of an eye there is the awareness of their continued existence, but the parents are the focus of attention and are taking up all the therapeutic time. There is the vague feeling that 'more ought to be done about the children', but the intention is all too seldom honoured.

Experiences to which children are exposed

The experiences of the child of a problem-drinking parent are varied, depending upon the degree of emotional support provided by either parent, the variety of other social and emotional supports which may be available, the age of the child when the parent developed the drinking problem and the child's level of ability to understand the problem drinker's behaviour and moods (Steinglass et al., 1987). Of great importance is the actual behaviour of the parent when intoxicated; if there is continued rowdiness, arguments or violence, the impact will be far more adverse than in those instances where drunkenness is not associated with verbal, physical or sexual aggression.

A drinking problem, of whatever degree or nature, which as its end-result produces what can be summarized as a bad home atmosphere is attacking the centre of what family life should be able to give to a child. This is the kind of family where the social worker will report that 'you know there is something wrong as soon as you walk in the door'. Whether it is more damaging for the mother rather than the father to be the person with the drinking problem is uncertain, and there may be a different impact on the boys and the girls in the family. If a parent when drunk continuously picks on a particular child, scolding them, finding fault, demeaning or hitting them, then that child is immensely at risk.

In some families, the drinking of a parent will lead to separation and divorce, hospitalization of a parent or even to death of a parent. Children may have to suffer criticism of their parents by family, neighbours or friends, and the behaviour of their parents may lead to embarrassment or shame. The behaviour of the drinking parent is likely to be unpredictable, and the behaviour of the sober parent may also be adversely affected in so far as the child is concerned – even to the point where the child views this parent less favourably than the problem drinker (Velleman & Orford, 1999).

Problems that children develop

At the psychological level, one common effect is a general rising of the anxiety level and depressive symptoms in the child (West & Prinz, 1987; Zeitlin, 1994). Further, the child may be very basically deprived of a satisfactory role model (Zeitlin, 1994).

The psychological damages, and the social disabilities which can result, will interact. In the school setting, anxiety may lead to social disability, poor academic performance and other problems. Boys are especially likely to display antisocial behaviour (West & Prinz, 1987). Children of both sexes may display temper tantrums or get involved in problems which come to the attention of the police (Zeitlin, 1994).

The absence of emotional regard within the home can mean that a child as an adolescent will develop particularly rejecting attitudes towards the parents, and enter precipitously into identification with an adolescent peer group. Such an extreme version of a normal process is not necessarily harmful, but the children from this disturbed home can be vulnerable to involvement with groups that are themselves disturbed and engaging in drug-taking or delinquency. These associations may in part represent a revenge on the parents, or substitute comfort or excitement to replace the good inner feelings that are so lacking. There can, however, be no fixed predictions as to how a child from a drinking home will meet adolescence. Another outcome may be that the child is clinging, desperately and anxiously involved in the home, tied to protecting the non-drinking parent and unable to make any identification with other young people (Table 4.2).

At any stage of childhood the possibility of actual physical damage must be considered. There is an association between drinking problems and non-accidental injury, and in childhood and adolescence the risk of physical assault may continue; the damage is often no more than bruising, but the risk of more serious injury is not to be discounted. Accidental injury may occur due to inadequate supervision. Sexual abuse of children is substantially more likely (Bear, Griffiths & Pearson, 2000; Velleman & Orford, 1999). An extended example of how to provide help for the child of parents who have drinking problems is discussed in Chapter 8.

Although the idea that 'adult children of alcoholics' suffer from a unique set of psychiatric problems enjoyed a lengthy vogue in clinical circles and the popular press, no psychiatric problems are unique to this population (Griffin et al., 2005). Recent, painstaking work suggests that, with the possible exception of an increased risk of drinking problems, the damaging effects of parental alcoholism on adults are mediated through stressors also found in other disturbed, non-alcoholic home environments: sexual abuse, physical violence, parental psychopathology and a conflictual family environment characterized by low cohesion, organization and expressiveness (Griffin et al., 2005). It also bears mentioning that many adult children of alcoholics are well adjusted, and even find ways to use their painful experiences to their advantage.

> Christmas celebrations were frequently spoiled during Kate's childhood, as a result of her father's invariable drunkenness. Even the normal routine of daily life had accommodated his unpredictable behaviour after 'a drink with colleagues' on the way home from work. When Kate married and started a family of her own, she and her husband therefore determined that they would never let drinking spoil their family life, and they translated this into agreed family expectations on what would constitute acceptable drinking and the occasions when drinking might be done.

Table 4.2. Problems experienced by children of problem drinkers.

- Anxiety
- Depression
- Low self-esteem
- Relationship difficulties
- Poor school performance
- Antisocial behavior
- Physical and sexual abuse
- Accidental injury
- Risk of alcohol-related problems in later life

Work and education

I wrote 30 job applications to various firms and told them I had been treated for a drink problem, was now sober and wanted to find my way back with everything in the open. I didn't get a single interview. So the next time I kept quiet about my drinking, spun a yarn about that year off work, handed in two out-of-date references, lied on the medical form, and got the job. And then? They checked things out, I was fired on Friday, and yes, it's stupid, but I've been drinking. Just what they expected.

The difficulty that a person with a drinking problem may encounter when seeking employment has just been instanced, and the example shows how stigmatization may compound the objective difficulties. The varieties of adverse influence that excessive drinking may have on work performance are many and costly (Jones, Casswell & Zhang, 1995; Romelsjö, 1995). The impact is not limited to any one level of seniority in the employment hierarchy, and drinking problems are as likely to be found in the boardroom as on the shop floor.

Drinking can be particularly destructive in work settings and professions in which the lives and well-being of others are in the problem drinker's hands. For the bus or train driver, the airplane pilot (Holdener, 1993), or the ship's officer on the bridge, intoxication carries enormous dangers for the public. In senior positions in industry or the armed services, in the diplomatic service or in the legal profession (Goodliffe, 1994), drunken indiscretion, irascibility or bad judgement at a crucial moment can have far-ranging repercussions. Legal authorities recognize the tremendous damage alcohol dependent physicians can do, which is why extensive disciplinary and monitoring procedures are quite rightly called into action if a doctor's drinking comes to official attention (DuPont et al., 2009). For teachers and clergy, the hint of scandal may be specially damaging, although it is surprising how tolerant or blind-eyed those in the individual's environment often appear to be. These more dramatic examples may not be relevant to many cases, yet they serve to underscore that, whoever the individual we are trying to assess and help, the analysis of their alcohol-related social complications requires a job-specific enquiry.

A social complication of drinking that deserves greater note is the long-term handicap that results when an educational or training opportunity is partly wasted or totally lost. Being sent down from university, failing to complete a postgraduate degree, the abandonment of an apprenticeship because of a drinking problem, may all have serious long-term consequences.

Violence and other crime

Multiple relationships

The relationship between crime, violence and heavy drinking is as complex as with any other social complications of alcohol. Simple, direct and one-way causality is seldom a sufficient analysis and various models of understanding have been proposed (Graham & West, 2001; Graham et al., 1998; Zhang et al., 1997). Personality, background and social circumstances which predispose to crime may as much and independently predispose to drinking. Genetic influences may need to be considered. A drinking problem may also in passing affect dedicated professional criminals, perhaps at a later stage of their careers. Alternatively, one may see the person who is alcohol dependent and who at a much later age than the usual 'first offender' falls foul of the law, or is caught up in a flurry of recidivism. Sometimes the person is seen who suddenly shifts from a circulation around the prisons to a hospital and voluntary agency circuit: their drinking remains much the same, but they have learnt to present themselves and their problems differently. The offence may by definition involve the actual intoxication itself: for instance, 'the drunkenness offender' and/or the person caught 'driving while intoxicated' (Greenfield & Weisner, 1995). The drunkenness offender overlaps with the vagrant drinking population. Social context may be very important in determining whether a drunken assault will occur or a drunken driver take off in their car, and certain kinds of poorly ordered public drinking places may engender particularly high risk (Stockwell et al., 1992).

The variations on the alcohol–crime connection are legion. There is no type of offence that will not sometimes be related to drinking, and many types of offence that will often be so related. The problems load at the petty end of the spectrum: petty theft, minor assault, travelling on public transport without a ticket, failing to pay for the meal in the cheap café, urinating in the subway, aggressively panhandling. The person with a drinking problem may know that when they are drunk (and only when they are drunk), they are apt to engage in their own particular offence; for example, taking cars and driving them away, 'going burgling' in a clumsy sort of fashion or passing dud cheques. Drinking may be the story behind an embezzlement.

The link between drinking and violence is equally complex. Often drinking seems to be responsible for disinhibition and release of violent or sexually violent behaviour. A skid row drinker hits a fellow member of a bottle-gang on the head with an iron bar; a man follows a woman out of a pub and rapes her in the car park; three drunken yobs brutally assault and rob the owner of a liquor store.

Although to the courts and the ordinary citizen it may appear evident that alcohol causes or considerably contributes to the genesis of these kinds of serious crime, researchers have repeatedly pointed out the dangers in assuming an identity between correlation and causality in this arena (Graham & West, 2001; Shepherd, 1994). Many studies have shown a high frequency of intoxication among violent offenders at the time of the criminal act (McLellan & Teplin, 2001), but that does not prove that the drinking *caused* the crime. People bent on violence may coincidentally choose to drink, drinking can be a mere adjunct to intrinsically dangerous situations and confrontations, and alcohol may be used as an excuse.

Further light has, however, been thrown on an issue where everyday experience and rational analysis have previously sometimes seemed to be at odds, by research which explores the correlation over time in national per capita alcohol consumption and rates for assault or homicide (Babor et al., 2003, 2010; Edwards et al.,1994; Lenke, 1990). For some, but not all, countries the correlations are positive. Other research has looked specifically at the relationship between drinking and offending among juveniles and has shown that with correction for shared risk factors there is, in this age group, a significant association between drinking and violent offending (Fergusson et al., 1996).

A rather similar literature has been developing on the relationship between drinking, self-harm and suicide (Murphy & Wetzel, 1990; Rossow, 1996). That a true causal link exists here of some significance is becoming increasingly evident.

The individual's drinking and their risk of being a victim of crime

There is a positive relationship in the general population between the quantity an individual drinks and the likelihood of being assaulted (Babor et al., 2003, 2010; Edwards et al., 1994; McLellan & Teplin, 2001). A grossly intoxicated person will easily fall prey to having their pockets turned out, or be deprived of capacity to resist rape or other forms of violence. Thus, victimization is a common social complication of heavy drinking. Clinically, this information can have significant motivating power for problem drinkers.

Drink-driving offenders

The bulk of drink-driving offences are committed by the generality of the drinking population rather than 'alcoholics', and it is to that broad target that counter-measures should predominantly be directed (Babor et al., 2003, 2010; Edwards et al., 1994). The factors that predict involvement in this kind of offence include not only drinking behaviour (quantity and frequency of drinking) but also other groups of variables such as socio-demographic factors, drinking behaviour and psychological characteristics (National Institute on Alcohol Abuse and Alcoholism, 1996).

Estimates for the proportion of subjects among drink-driving offenders variously defined as 'alcoholics' or 'problem drinkers' have varied from 4% to 87% across samples and jurisdictions, with prevalence rates influenced by operational definition and tending to be lower when definitions are more tightly drawn. The higher the measured blood alcohol content at arrest, and the greater the number of previous offences, the more likely that someone arrested for drink driving is alcohol dependent (MacDonald & Pederson, 1990). Multiple offenders are not only likely to have alcohol as an associated factor but also to show wider personality and background disturbance.

From the clinical angle the conclusion must be that enquiry into driving behaviour and drink-driving offences should be an integral part of any assessment. Not everyone who has been convicted of driving while intoxicated will have an otherwise manifest drinking problem (Gruenewald et al., 1990), but among clinical populations there will be a significant proportion of individuals whose driving poses a threat to themselves and other people, with that fact putting distinct responsibility on the clinician.

Financial and housing stability

An awareness of the possible financial complications of drinking problems and of the family's financial position is necessary for any complete case assessment. To maintain a major drinking habit is expensive and large additional sums are often spent without the drinker knowing how the money has gone – rounds purchased for friends, drinks grandly offered to strangers, meals out and taxis home, coins and bills that fall unnoticed as keys are fumbled for, massive cigarette consumption, gambling and so on. As with housing problems and many other social complications, the well-moneyed will be better protected for a longer time.

The financial balance is determined not only by the cost of the drinking and associated spending, but also by whether drinking affects the inflow of cash. Demotion, sickness and unemployment add to the stringencies. Complicated and devious stratagems may be engaged in to maintain income. 'Moonlighting' or the second job is common (often in a bar so as further to aid the drinking), loans are negotiated on preposterous terms, possessions are pawned, houses remortgaged. The employee 'works a bit of a racket' and a load of bricks disappear from the builder's yard. It becomes vital to evade income tax and to defraud Social Security. The rent is not paid and credit card payments fall behind.

The family may have reached the stage where financial chaos has become the central and pressing pain. From the social-work angle, sorting out that chaos may be the necessary first-aid, but it will be a very temporary aid if the drinking problem is not radically met.

When financial complications are extreme, they may result in a substandard housing situation or, indeed, no housing at all. Cases are frequently encountered where drinking is leading directly to a housing problem. In this latter type of instance, the patient's claim that they are 'drinking because of their unsatisfactory surroundings' has a hollow ring – theirs is the only house in the street that is shabby and unpainted and with an old sofa lying in the front garden. Housing problems of this kind will be more acute the more marginal the family's income. Bad relationships with neighbours, gross evidence of poor house maintenance, failure to meet the rent, services cut off, eviction, the sojourn in 'temporary accommodation' and multiple changes of address are familiar elements in the housing history as the drinking problem becomes more extreme.

Literal homelessness due to problem drinking tends to result from a combination of financial distress as well as exhaustion of family and social supports (i.e. the drinker is kicked out of the house and has become so intolerable that no one else will take him in). Heavy drinking is a lifestyle among a subgroup of homeless people, and entry into this social environment may reinforce continued heavy consumption, particularly of the binge variety. On the other hand, those homeless problem drinkers who can be helped into 'sober housing', meaning a setting in which continued housing is contingent on abstinence and alcohol is not available, can evince remarkable turnarounds in their life situation.

References

Babor T, Caetano R, Casswell S, et al. (2003) *Alcohol: No Ordinary Commodity: Research and Public Policy.* Oxford: Oxford University Press.

Bear Z, Griffiths R, Pearson B (2000) Childhood sexual abuse and substance abuse. *Executive Summary* 67, 1–4.

DuPont R L, McLellan A T, White W L, Merlo L J, Gold M S (2009) Setting the standard for recovery: physicians health programs. *Journal of Substance Abuse Treatment* 36, 159–171.

Edwards G, Anderson P, Babor T F, et al. (1994) *Alcohol Policy and the Public Good.* Oxford: Oxford University Press.

Fergusson D M, Lynskey M T, Horwood L J (1996) Alcohol misuse and juvenile offending in adolescence. *Addiction* 91, 483–484.

Goodliffe J (1994) Alcohol and depression in England and American lawyer disciplinary proceedings. *Addiction* 89, 1237–1244.

Graham K, Leonard K E, Room R, et al. (1998) Current directions in research in understanding and preventing intoxicated aggression. *Addiction* 93, 659–676.

Graham P, West P (2001) Alcohol and crime: examining the link. In *International Handbook of Alcohol Dependence and Problems,* N Heather, T J Peters, T Stockwell (eds). Chester, UK: John Wiley & Sons, pp. 439–470.

Greenfield T K, Weisner C (1995) Drinking problems and self-reported criminal behavior, arrests, and convictions: 1990 US national and 1989 county surveys. *Addiction* 90, 361–374.

Griffin M L, Amodeo M, Fassler I, Ellis M A, Clay C (2005) Mediating factors for the long-term effects of parental alcoholism in women: the contribution of other childhood stresses and resources. *American Journal on Addictions* 14, 18–34.

Grucza R A, Bucholz K K, Rice J P, Bierut L J (2008) Secular trends in the lifetime prevalence of alcohol dependence in the United States: a re-evaluation. *Alcoholism: Clinical and Experimental Research* 32(5), 763–770.

Gruenewald P J, Stewart K, Klitzner M (1990) Alcohol use and the appearance of alcohol problems among first offender drunk drivers. *British Journal of Addiction* 85, 107–117.

Holdener F O (1993) Alcohol and civil aviation. *Addiction* 88(7), 953–958.

Hurcom C, Copello A, Orford J (2000) The family and alcohol: effects of excessive drinking and conceptualizations of spouses over recent decades. *Substance Use and Misuse* **35**, 473–502.

Jones S, Casswell S, Zhang J-F (1995) The economic costs of alcohol-related absenteeism and reduced productivity in the working population of New Zealand. *Addiction* **90**, 1453–1462.

Lenke L (1990) *Alcohol and Criminal Violence – Time Series Analyses in a Comparative Perspective.* Stockholm, Sweden: Almqvist and Wiksell.

MacDonald S, Pederson L L (1990) The characteristics of alcoholics in treatment arrested for driving while impaired. *British Journal of Addiction* **85**, 97–105.

McCrady B S, Hayaki J, Epstein E E, Hirsch L S (2002) Testing hypothesized predictors of change in conjoint behavioral alcoholism treatment for men. *Alcoholism: Clinical and Experimental Research* **26**, 463–470.

McLellan G M, Teplin L A (2001) Alcohol intoxication and violent crime: implications for public health policy. *American Journal on Addictions* **10**, 70–85.

Moos R H, Finney J W, Cronkite R C (1990) *Alcoholism Treatment: Context, Process and Outcome.* New York: Oxford University Press.

Murphy G E, Wetzel R D (1990) The lifetime risk of suicide in alcoholism. *Archives of General Psychiatry* **47**, 383–392.

National Institute on Alcohol Abuse and Alcoholism (1996) Drinking and driving. *Alcohol Alert* **31**, 1–3.

Orford J, Natera G, Davies J, et al. (1998) Tolerate, engage or withdraw: a study of the structure of families coping with alcohol and drug problems in South West England and Mexico City. *Addiction* **93**, 1799–1813.

Orford J, Natera G, Mora J, et al. (2005) *Coping With Alcohol and Drug Problems: The Experiences of Family Members in Three Contrasting Cultures.* Hove, UK: Routledge.

Romelsjö A (1995) Alcohol consumption and unintentional injury, suicide, violence, work performance and intergenerational effects. In *Alcohol and Public Policy: Evidence and Issues*, H D Holder, G Edwards (eds). Oxford: Oxford University Press, pp. 114–142.

Rossow I (1996) Alcohol and suicide. Beyond the link at the individual level. *Addiction* **91**, 1413–1416.

Shepherd J (1994) Violent crime: the role of alcohol and new approaches to the prevention of injury. *Alcohol and Alcoholism* **29**, 5–10.

Steinglass P, Bennett L A, Wolin S J, Reiss D (1987) *The Alcoholic Family.* London: Hutchinson.

Stockwell T, Somerford P, Lang E (1992) The relationship between license type and alcohol-related problems attributed to licensed premises in Perth, Western Australia. *Journal of Studies on Alcohol* **53**, 495–498.

Velleman R, Orford R (1999) *Risk and Resilience: Adults Who Were the Children of Problem Drinkers.* Amsterdam: Harwood.

West M O, Prinz R J (1987) Parental alcoholism and childhood psychopathology. *Psychological Bulletin* **102**, 204–218.

Zeitlin H (1994) Children with alcohol misusing parents. *British Medical Bulletin* **50**, 139–151.

Zhang L, Wieczoreix W F, Welte J W (1997) The nexus between alcohol and violent crime. *Alcoholism: Clinical and Experimental Research* **21**, 1264–1271.

5 Physical complications of excessive drinking

The physical element is an important part of a comprehensive approach to drinking problems. Helping services should be organized to cope effectively with diagnosis and treatment in the physical domain and, whatever the particular professional affiliation of the person who is working with the problem drinker, there is need for an alertness towards possible physical pathologies. Social workers in a counselling service are, of course, practising their own special types of skill, and no-one would suggest that they should also cultivate highly specialized knowledge of liver pathology. It is, however, a reasonable expectation that they should know enough about the liver to understand the significance to their client of a diagnosis of cirrhosis, rather than their being mystified by this term and consequently deflecting that client from talking about something of vital importance. A polite conspiracy can be set up in which both parties pretend that the body does not exist.

Why physical complications matter

Excessive alcohol consumption is a major contributor to mortality and ill health and 'has been shown to be causally related to over 60 different medical conditions' (British Medical Association Board of Science, 2008, p. 28) (Table 5.1).

Burden of disease is quantified in terms of disability adjusted life years (DALYs), a summary measure that combines years of life lost to premature death with years of life lost due to disability. Males have a higher alcohol-related disease burden than females. There are large variations in the alcohol-attributable disease burden in different regions of the world, with injuries accounting for a higher proportion of the burden in lower income countries and cancers accounting for a higher proportion in higher income countries. For any given level of pattern of drinking the harm is greater in poorer societies than in more affluent ones.

Alcohol is the third largest risk factor for mortality in developed countries after tobacco and hypertension and accounts for 9.2% of DALYs lost. This compares with figures of 12.2% and 10.9% for tobacco and hypertension respectively (Rehm et al., 2004; World Health Organization, 2007).

Although physical complications are common in any population of heavy drinkers, early detection and cessation of drinking can lead to recovery from the medical co-morbidity. Continued drinking, on the other hand, is likely to exacerbate the alcohol-related problem and may seriously threaten life. Physical complications impinge upon all aspects of the problem drinker's life and it is unrealistic to compartmentalize psychological, social and physical disability.

Often physical complications are the main reason for seeking help. If information about the physical symptoms is imparted clearly, so that the patient can understand their significance, this information can be used to consider their position. Thus, an understanding of the physical symptoms may have the potential to influence drinking behaviour. As ever, the therapist is the

Table 5.1. Major disease and injury conditions related to alcohol and proportions attributable to alcohol worldwide (%).

	Men	Women	Both
Malignant neoplasms			
Mouth and oropharynx cancers	22	9	19
Oesophageal cancer	37	15	29
Liver cancer	30	13	25
Breast cancer	N/A	7	7
Neuropsychiatric disorders			
Unipolar depressive disorders	3	1	2
Epilepsy	23	12	18
Alcohol use disorders	100	100	100
Diabetes mellitus	−1	−1	−1
Cardiovascular diseases			
Ischaemic heart disease	4	−1	2
Haemorrhagic stroke	18	1	10
Ischaemic stroke	3	−6	−1
Gastrointestinal diseases			
Cirrhosis of the liver	39	18	32
Unintentional injury			
Motor vehicle accidents	25	8	20
Drownings	12	6	10
Falls	9	3	7
Poisonings	23	9	18
Intentional injury			
Self-inflicted injuries	15	5	11
Homicide	26	16	24

Source: Room, Babor & Rehm (2005).

informant, the person who brings up the issue, and who shares and reflects the patient's feelings and concerns, rather than the disembodied pronouncer of facts. The way in which information on physical problems is presented to the patient can be part of therapy. Here are two dialogues which illustrate different ways in which the patient's concern over his physical health can be met at interview. Firstly, and very briefly, a dialogue which is not to be dismissed as caricature:

PATIENT: What does the doctor mean when he said my liver had been hit by the drinking?

COUNSELLOR: You will have to ask the doctor to explain.

PATIENT: But he never explains anything.

COUNSELLOR: Well, he's the person to ask.

Secondly, and more constructively:

PATIENT: What did the doctor mean when he said my liver had been hit by the drinking?

COUNSELLOR: 'That's something pretty important to talk about. What did you think he meant?'

PATIENT: 'I suppose I was dead scared. Not sure I believe him, though. He may just be trying to put the frighteners under me. But if what he's really saying is that I'm going to die of cirrhosis, I'll go out on the crest of the all-time greatest booze-up.'

COUNSELLOR: 'I don't think anyone wants to scare you in a horror-story sort of way, but it's your own liver and you have a right to know about it.'

PATIENT: 'So what's the score?'

COUNSELLOR: 'I spoke to your doctor on the phone. You have undoubtedly done your liver some harm, and if you go on drinking you would be risking cirrhosis, and that's a miserable way to die. If you stop drinking, your liver disease will not progress and may improve. You've a right to know all the facts. It's reasonable to be anxious, but at least there is something positive you can do towards repairing the damage – stop drinking.'

PATIENT: 'When I was getting that pain, I guessed it must be my liver, but I suppose I have been shutting my eyes, doing the 'it can't happen to me' trick.'

The vital question is what any information on physical consequences means to the patient. Patients and their families are concerned about their physical health, and deserve to be given the facts. Explaining and talking through this information is an opportunity for the therapist to facilitate behavioural change in the patient.

Some patients stop drinking abruptly when persuaded that alcohol is posing a tangible threat to their physical health. Even if the news of physical damage constitutes the turning point, in reality this is only the final event to tip a decision where the moment for change has been set up by many previous happenings. But using the results of the physical examination or the laboratory tests for crude scare-tactics is likely to be counter-productive. Patients may dismiss what they are being told simply because the information is too frightening to accept, or they may decide that all is lost and that they may as well drink themselves to death.

Physical complications

The medical conditions associated with alcohol consumption can be classified into three categories: those directly due to alcohol and those due to acute and chronic conditions to which alcohol is a contributory factor (British Medical Association Board of Science, 2008). Physical conditions directly attributable to alcohol include alcoholic polyneuropathy, alcoholic gastritis, alcoholic liver disease and ethanol toxicity. Acute conditions to which alcohol is a contributory cause include road injuries (drivers and pedestrians), injuries from falls, fires, drownings, occupational and machine injuries, other accidents, suicide and assault. Chronic alcohol-attributable conditions include various cancers, liver cirrhosis, acute and chronic pancreatitis, spontaneous abortion and psoriasis (British Medical Association Board of Science, 2008).

Heavy drinking in pregnancy can lead to fetal alcohol spectrum disorders (British Medical Association Board of Science, 2007). Heavy drinking in adolescents and young people affects brain development. In some conditions, both the toxic element and disturbance of nutritional status may be implicated as a cause of damage at the same time. Less is known about the risks associated with different beverage types although it has been suggested that the risk of developing certain physical disorders is higher for spirit drinkers (Chou, Grant & Dawson, 1998).

What level of alcohol intake constitutes a threshold for physical dangers? The answer must vary according to the particular condition, but in general the evidence points to a dose–response relationship, with higher consumption being associated with a higher risk of disease. Even individuals who drink 'socially' but above the daily guidelines are at risk.

Binge drinking puts individuals at higher risk of developing alcohol dependence syndrome, injuries and brain trauma. Paradoxically, light or moderate drinking of one or two drinks per day is associated with a lower risk of coronary heart disease (CHD) in men over 45 years and post-menopausal women. The issue of level of consumption and risk of physical harm is complex and does not allow for an easy calculation of a 'safe' level. There is considerable individual variation in the effects of alcohol consumption: not every chronic heavy drinker develops liver cirrhosis.

However, whatever the risks at the relatively lower ranges of intake, by the time someone is drinking in the fashion characteristic of the dependence syndrome, the question of whether their level of intake carries dangers hardly needs to be asked. The answer is resoundingly 'yes' for nearly every tissue of the body. And, quite apart from any specific tissue damage discussed in this chapter, it should be remembered that as a consequence of heavy drinking and dietary neglect, almost every aspect of the body's chemistry may in some circumstances be put out of balance; even such seemingly obscure aspects as serum zinc or magnesium levels may be disturbed.

The physical complications that can result from excessive drinking will now be described. As far as possible, technical language is explained, but as noted in the Introduction, this is a chapter where the non-medical reader will have to show some forbearance. In Table 5.2 we list the major alcohol-related health conditions contributing to morbidity and mortality. The presence of these conditions should alert the clinician to the possibility of an underlying drinking problem. In any case, basic enquiry into the patient's drinking history should be absolutely routine in medical practice.

Table 5.2. Major alcohol-related disorders.

- **Acute intoxication**
- **Cancers:** head and neck cancers, cancers of the gastrointestinal tract, liver cancer and female breast cancer
- **Cardiovascular disorders:** arrhythmias, ischaemic heart disease, cardiomyopathy, cerebrovascular disease
- **Gastrointestinal disorders:** alcoholic liver disease, acute and chronic pancreatitis, gastritis and peptic ulceration, Mallory–Weiss syndrome
- **Endocrine and metabolic disease:** type II diabetes, alcohol-induced pseudo-Cushing's syndrome, male hypogonadism, hypoglycaemia, alcoholic ketoacidosis, gout, hyperlipidaemia
- **Immune system**
- **Alcoholic muscle, bone and skin disease**
- **Respiratory disease:** respiratory tract infection; acute respiratory distress syndrome (ARDS)
- **Haematological effects:** anaemia, macrocytosis, iron deficiency, neutropaenia, thrombocytopaenia
- **Accidents**
- **Surgery**
- **Neurological disorders:** alcohol withdrawal seizures, peripheral neuropathy, alcoholic cerebellar degeneration, Wernicke–Korsakoff syndrome, alcoholic pellagra encephalopathy, alcohol-related brain damage, central pontine myelinolysis, Marchiafava–Bignami disease, alcohol amblyopia, hepatic encephalopathy
- **Fetal alcohol spectrum disorders (FASD)**

  All patients, whatever their presentation, should on first contact with medical services be asked about their drinking

Acute alcohol intoxication and coma

The effects of intoxication vary according to a number of factors including the amount of alcohol consumed, how rapidly it has been consumed, whether the drinker has a degree of tolerance to alcohol or is young and rarely drinks. A life-threatening overdose with alcohol is unlikely to occur in the alcohol-dependent person, both because of their experience in handling their drinking and their raised tolerance: that is not to deny the possibility of such a patient at times getting very drunk, or drinking to unconsciousness. Drinking to the point of collapse and 'passing out' is more likely to be the result of a casual drinking binge, or a Saturday night celebration, and it is this type of patient who is the familiar late-night visitor to the Accident and Emergency Department (Emergency Room). Drug overdoses are often taken in the context of intoxication, intentionally or otherwise. Occasionally a child will overdose accidentally with alcohol: this is discussed in relation to hypoglycaemia (see Hypoglycaemia, below).

Intoxication can usually be dealt with on a sensibly conservative basis and patients left to sleep off their binge, with due care taken to ensure that they do not inhale their vomit: examination must of course also ensure that there is no other cause for the unconsciousness. A stomach wash-out may sometimes be indicated. With higher levels of intoxication there is a risk of respiratory depression and death. The blood alcohol concentration (BAC) likely to be associated with such a tragedy will vary with the individual but a BAC of 400 mg/100 ml is usually quoted as the threshold for very serious danger. Because of the occasional risk of death from respiratory paralysis, the more common danger from inhaled vomit, and the many possibilities of being unwarily caught out by some underlying or complicating condition (head injury, hypoglycaemia, ketoacidosis, systemic infection, overdose of other licit or illicit drugs, for example), the problem set by alcoholic overdose and by the often rather unwelcome visitor to the Accident and Emergency Department (Emergency Room) should not be too casually dismissed as 'routine'. When coma is thought to be due to alcohol, it is important that a high alcohol concentration is shown by measurements of breath or blood alcohol. Skull radiography, neuroimaging and urine toxicology are other fundamental investigations. Alcoholic coma has a mortality rate of approximately 5%.

Acute poisoning with methyl alcohol (methanol) is a rarer and a much more threatening condition than intoxication with ordinary beverage alcohol. There are substantial risks of blindness or death and intensive emergency medical care will be required, possibly with dialysis.

Cancers

Evidence has mounted over recent years implicating alcohol consumption as a contributory factor in a number of cancers (Bofetta & Hashibe, 2006; International Agency for Research on Cancer, 1998; World Cancer Research Fund/American Institute for Cancer Research, 2007). There is clear evidence linking alcohol consumption with an increased risk of cancers of the mouth, pharynx, larynx and oesophagus (gullet), colorectum (men) and breast (women). Alcohol consumption is also a probable cause of colorectal cancer in women and of liver cancer. There appears to be 'no safe threshold below which no effect on cancer risk is observed' (British Medical Association Board of Science, 2008, p. 29) .

Cardiovascular disease

Alcohol-related arrhythmias

Arrhythmias, or disturbances of the normal heart rhythm, can occur as a result of episodic heavy drinking (binge drinking) and heavy consistent alcohol use, and are often called 'holiday heart' because of their association with binge drinking at weekends and holidays. The mildest presentation is that of palpitations, caused by a few extra and irregular beats (extra-systoles). Palpitations can also be caused by an alcohol-induced tachycardia (fast heart rate): either atrial fibrillation or atrial flutter or a supraventricular tachycardia. Atrial fibrillation is the most common arrhythmia associated with alcohol use. These arrhythmias typically resolve with abstinence, but some individuals will require anti-arrhythmic medication. Ventricular arrhythmias have also been reported.

Several studies have now documented an association between alcohol use and sudden coronary death in both heavy drinkers and occasional drinkers, even in people without any evidence of pre-existing heart disease (Mukamal et al., 2005a).

Hypertension

Alcohol raises blood pressure and increases the risk of hypertension in a dose-dependent manner in both men and women, independent of age, body weight and cigarette smoking (Corrao et al., 1999). Consumption exceeding 30 g per day is associated with higher blood pressure, and binge drinking may be particularly implicated (Beilin & Puddey, 2006). Intervention studies indicate that persistent heavy drinkers who cut down on their alcohol consumption, or who abstain, lower their blood pressures (Stewart et al., 2008). Individuals presenting with hypertension to a general practitioner or physician should always have an alcohol history taken, together with appropriate laboratory investigations, and should be advised to reduce their alcohol consumption.

Cerebrovascular disease

There are two broad categories of stroke. These are *haemorrhagic stroke*, due to ruptured blood vessels on the surface of the brain (subarachnoid haemorrhage) and in the substance of the brain (intracranial haemorrhage), and *ischaemic stroke*, due to blockage of brain blood vessels by clot formation or emboli to the brain from the heart or elsewhere, or blockage of blood vessels outside the brain (mainly the carotid arteries). Alcohol increases the risk of haemorrhagic stroke in a dose-dependent fashion (Corrao et al., 1999). Episodic heavy drinking is a risk factor for both haemorrhagic and ischaemic stroke, particularly in adolescents and people under the age of 40 years. The risk of heavy drinking leading to ischaemic stroke is moderated by a gene that influences high density lipoprotein (HDL) cholesterol, one of the mediators of the cardio-protective effect. In the absence of this effect there is no statistical relationship between alcohol consumption and risk of ischaemic stroke. When it is present, alcohol consumption increases the risk of ischaemic stroke (Mukamal et al. 2005b).

Coronary heart disease

Regular light drinking is associated with a lower risk of coronary heart disease (CHD) in men over 45 years and in post-menopausal women (Gunzerath et al., 2004). The reduced risk for CHD occurs at alcohol consumption levels of as little as 10 g (1 drink) per day or every second day. Beyond 20 g (2 drinks) of alcohol per day the risk of coronary heart disease increases, exceeding that of an abstainer beyond 80 g per day. However, heavy drinking bouts are associated with increased rates of heart attacks. The number of years of life lost, attributable to drinking, outweighs the years saved, attributable to protective factors.

The 'cardio-protective' effect appears to derive from alcohol itself rather than any specific beverage type. Alcohol may have a partial inhibitory effect on atherosclerosis by increasing levels of HDLs, which carry cholesterol to different parts of the body. This is because HDLs are associated with a reduced risk of coronary heart disease and are thought to protect the arteries from a build-up of cholesterol. Alcohol also reduces platelet stickiness and aggregation, lowers plasma fibrinogen and increases fibrinolysis.

Cardiomyopathy

Chronic excessive alcohol consumption (over 90 g per day for 5 years or more) can lead to cardiomyopathy (Rubin & Urbano-Marquez, 1994). This appears to occur as a result of the toxic action of alcohol on heart muscle, although a genetic predisposition may also be an important factor. Alcoholic cardiomyopathy was formerly attributed to thiamine deficiency, but this is probably not the case because it occurs in heavy drinkers who are well nourished. The disorder usually manifests itself between the ages of 30 and 60 years. Although commoner in men, due to their heavier consumption, women seem to be particularly vulnerable (Urbano-Marquez et al., 1995).

Alcoholic cardiomyopathy is characterized by an enlarged, hypertrophied heart. The left ventricle is dilated and there is dysfunction in cardiac contractility, leading to a depressed output (ejection fraction). In the early stages of hypertrophy and dilatation, there may be few symptoms. However, as the disorder progresses, patients develop arrhythmias, including atrial and ventricular tachyarrhythmias and atrioventricular conduction defects. Congestive cardiac failure is another typical form of presentation (breathlessness on exertion, breathlessness at night and peripheral oedema).

Subclinical forms of alcoholic cardiomyopathy can be identified in problem drinkers, using non-invasive procedures such as echocardiography. Early detection and abstinence may halt or reverse the progress of this disorder.

Gastroenterological disorders

Alcoholic liver disease

Alcohol misuse is the commonest cause of liver damage in the UK, Europe, the USA and Australia. Rates vary enormously from country to country but appear to be highest in the wine-growing countries where alcohol consumption is highest. Many studies suggest that women are at greater risk than men for a given level of alcohol consumption.

The liver is vulnerable to alcohol-related injury because it is the primary site of alcohol metabolism. Three types of alcoholic liver disease have been described – fatty liver, alcoholic hepatitis and alcoholic cirrhosis. All three may coexist. Fatty liver is present in up to 90% of persistent heavy drinkers at some time. Alcoholic hepatitis is seen in approximately 40% of individuals with a history of persistent heavy drinking. Despite the fact that that there is a strong correlation between the risk of developing cirrhosis and a long history of daily heavy drinking, only about 20% of people with alcohol dependence develop liver cirrhosis (Thun et al., 1997). Some individuals appear to be more susceptible. Genetic factors that increase the oxidation of alcohol to acetaldehyde, or reduce the rate of acetaldehyde clearance, will increase acetaldehyde levels in the liver and cause greater injury. Women develop cirrhosis at lower levels of alcohol consumption than men. In women, a reduced 'first pass' metabolism of alcohol in the stomach, by gastric alcohol dehydrogenase (ADH), leads to increased blood alcohol levels. The ratio of water to fat is lower in women than in men. Alcohol is distributed in water, so for a given body weight the concentration of ethanol in water, and thus the blood stream, tends to be higher in women than in men. Alcohol dependent individuals with hepatitis C infection develop liver injury at a younger age and at a lower cumulative dose of alcohol than those without hepatitis C. Continuing heavy alcohol consumption is associated with accelerated progression of liver disease associated with cirrhosis and a higher risk of hepatocellular carcinoma in patients with hepatitis B and C. Cigarette smoking and coffee consumption also appear to increase the risk of developing cirrhosis in alcohol dependent individuals, although

Table 5.3. Alcohol and the liver.

- Fatty liver rarely causes illness and is reversible with abstinence
- Alcoholic hepatitis may be fatal but can be reversible with abstinence
- Alcoholic cirrhosis is often progressive and fatal but can stabilize with abstinence
- Abstinence is the single most important component of treatment for alcoholic liver disease

the reasons for this are not known. Smoking more than 20 cigarettes per day and drinking 4 or more cups of coffee per day is associated with a greater risk. The main features of alcoholic liver disease are summarized in Table 5.3.

Fatty liver

The first histological change seen in persistent heavy drinkers is deposition of fat. While this is usually asymptomatic, patients may present with non-specific symptoms such as malaise, tiredness, nausea, an enlarged tender liver or abnormal liver function tests. Occasionally very severe fatty liver can lead to jaundice (obstructive jaundice), liver failure or death due to a fatty embolism (globules of fat getting into the circulation and obstructing arteries to the brain). Fatty liver is reversible with abstinence.

Alcoholic hepatitis

Minor degrees of alcoholic hepatitis may be asymptomatic and clinically indistinguishable from fatty liver. More severe episodes reflect inflammation and destruction of liver tissue. Scar tissue may begin to replace liver tissue. This process is called fibrosis. Symptoms of alcoholic hepatitis include loss of appetite, abdominal pain, nausea, weight loss, jaundice and fever. Severe alcoholic hepatitis has a mortality of about 60% during the first 6 weeks after hospital admission. Corticosteroids, which suppress the inflammation process, may improve survival in the early stages, but abstinence is the best 'treatment', and is essential for long-term survival. Abstinence leads to reversal of the histological changes, but alcoholic hepatitis almost always progresses to cirrhosis in women, even following abstinence.

Alcoholic cirrhosis

Cirrhosis may arise de novo in some cases, without passing through the intermediate state of hepatitis. Here, liver tissue becomes scarred by the development of fibrous septa which link the hepatic veins to portal tracts. This scarring, together with the regeneration of liver tissue, disturbs the normal liver architecture, and the consequences are two-fold. Firstly, the actual loss of functioning liver tissue causes a range of metabolic disturbances and ultimately liver failure may occur. Secondly, and very importantly, the scarring and disorganization lead to the squeezing and blocking off of blood vessels. This physical damming causes a build-up of pressure in the portal venous system (the veins which carry blood from the alimentary tract to the liver), called portal hypertension. This can, in turn, cause bleeding from veins at the lower end of the oesophagus (oesophageal varices), and this bleeding can be severe and fatal.

Cirrhosis can exist in degrees. If the condition is not too advanced, abstinence may lead to stabilization and enhance life expectancy. From the patient's point of view, they may know nothing of this insidious condition until they suddenly become jaundiced, find their abdomen swelling up with fluid (ascites) or have a massive bleed. More often, the diagnosis is picked up at an earlier stage on clinical examination and liver toxicity tests, with confirmation coming from various special investigations. Ultrasound scanning is a relatively easy and non-invasive investigation.

Treatment for cirrhosis is largely directed at relieving symptoms and complications. Liver transplantation is increasingly being used as a treatment for end-stage alcoholic cirrhosis, and outcomes are as good as for other liver disease. Psychiatric and specialist alcohol assessment has become an important element of the screening process in many transplant centres, because of the risks of anxiety, depression and relapse to drinking in the post-operative period. If drinking is reinstated it is usually at lower levels than previously.

Patients with alcoholic liver disease may develop Zieve's syndrome, characterized by a combination of cholestasis, haemolysis (breakdown of red cells) and gross hyperlipidaemia (rise in blood fats).

Acute pancreatitis

Alcohol misuse and biliary disease are the two main causative factors in acute pancreatitis. Individuals with acute alcoholic pancreatitis are likely to be young men, drinking in excess of 80 g of alcohol per day. The most common form of presentation is a sudden onset of severe upper abdominal pain, typically penetrating through to the back, associated with vomiting. The pain lessens in severity over the first 72 hours. Patients with severe acute pancreatitis may be feverish, hypotensive, have rapid breathing and suffer with acute ascites, pleural effusions and paralytic ileus (paralysis of the intestines). The diagnosis is usually made from the clinical presentation and confirmed by gross elevations of amylase and lipase in the blood. The mortality rate is between 10% and 40%.

> A businessman aged 52 had a long history of alcohol dependence. On occasion he would stop drinking for a few months, but was never willing to consider long-term abstinence as the goal. One weekend he relapsed once more into drinking with a very heavy binge. On the Sunday night he was admitted as an emergency to his local hospital with appalling abdominal pain radiating through to the back. A raised serum amylase confirmed the diagnosis of acute pancreatitis. Despite the hospital's best efforts, he died in shock 36 hours later. Post-mortem showed extensive necrosis of the pancreas and some old scarring. There was also evidence of early liver cirrhosis.

Chronic pancreatitis

Heavy drinking is the most frequent cause of chronic pancreatitis in adults, particularly the calcifying form. It mainly affects men aged 40–50 years, who have been drinking heavily. Although the quantity and duration of alcohol consumption are related to the development of this condition, it rarely occurs alongside cirrhosis. The main presenting symptom is severe dull epigastric (abdominal) pain radiating to the back, which may be partly relieved by leaning forward. The pain is often associated with nausea and vomiting. Steatorrhoea (fat in the faeces making them pale, loose and difficult to flush away), diarrhoea and weight loss also occur. These symptoms occur when over 90% of the functioning exocrine tissue (the tissue which secretes digestive enzymes) is destroyed. Damage to the Islets of Langerhans, with consequent failure of insulin secretion and diabetes mellitus occurs more slowly. Treatment is focused on the management of acute attacks of pain, and the other complications such as diabetes mellitus and fat malabsorption. Abstinence from alcohol is the mainstay of treatment, and essential if attacks of pain are to be stopped. Severe and intractable pain may lead to opiate use with a high risk of dependence.

Gastritis, peptic ulceration and intestinal symptoms

Alcohol stimulates gastric juice secretion and increases mucosal permeability. It can cause acute erosive ulcers in the stomach. Chronic heavy alcohol use favours colonization by

Helicobacter pylori, which produces ammonia and contributes to chronic gastritis. Heavy alcohol consumption is also thought to contribute to the development of gastric or duodenal ulcers.

Patients presenting to alcohol services commonly suffer from intestinal symptoms, such as diarrhoea and malabsorption. The general malnutrition and weight loss seen in these patients are usually due to dietary neglect. Alcohol dependent individuals are therefore at risk of vitamin deficiencies (especially of folic acid, B_1/thiamine and B_{12}). Deficiencies of minerals and trace elements (zinc, selenium) are also possible, again as a result of malabsorption and malnutrition.

Mallory–Weiss syndrome

This syndrome is associated with heavy alcohol consumption and alcohol dependence, and occurs as a result of acute intense vomiting which leads to a build-up of pressure within the oesophagus. This, in turn, causes a longitudinal tear in the mucosa at the gastro-oesophageal junction, with consequent vomiting of blood.

Endocrine and metabolic disorders

Type II diabetes

Alcohol consumption is associated with type II diabetes in a J-shaped fashion, low doses (10–20 g per day) decreasing the risk relative to abstainers, and higher doses increasing the risk (Rehm et al., 2004). This is probably due to the fact that alcohol increases insulin sensitivity in low doses.

Alcohol is a source of calories, each gram being equivalent to 7.1 kcal (Lieber, 1988). Why then are alcohol dependent individuals not all overweight? It would appear that, in alcohol dependence, this excess energy is largely used by the induced microsomal ethanol-oxidizing system (MEOS). Alcohol dependent people also tend to neglect their diet, so the two factors, taken together, mean that the excess energy does not translate into weight gain.

Alcohol-induced pseudo-Cushing's syndrome

Alcohol-induced pseudo-Cushing's syndrome is a term used to describe heavy drinkers who present with a clinical picture similar to that seen in Cushing's syndrome, i.e. truncal obesity with thin extremities, ruddy appearance, 'moon-face', bruising, striae (stretch marks), muscle wasting and hypertension. Biochemical abnormalities include elevated urinary and plasma cortisol levels (the latter failing to suppress with dexamethasone) and reduced circadian rhythm of plasma cortisol, and normal or suppressed adrenocorticotropic hormone (ACTH). The biochemical abnormalities rapidly revert to normal with abstinence from alcohol. The mechanism of this disorder is poorly understood.

Male hypogonadism

Alcohol causes a lowering of plasma testosterone concentrations through a direct toxic effect on the Leydig cells in the testis where testosterone is synthesized. This effect occurs independently of liver disease and may be related to the total lifetime dose of alcohol consumed.

Hypoglycaemia

Alcohol-induced hypoglycaemia (lowering of the blood sugar) can occur as a result of alcohol intoxication or after a modest intake of alcohol in individuals who are malnourished or fasting. Clinically the patient may present as flushed and sweaty with a rapid pulse and the appearance of being 'drunk' and inco-ordinated. An alternative presentation is in coma and hypothermic, without obvious features of hypoglycaemia. Children and adolescents are particularly susceptible to alcohol-induced hypoglycaemia, and the condition is much more dangerous for them than for adults (Lamminpaa, 1995).

Alcoholic ketoacidosis

This is a rare condition, which usually arises when an episode of heavy drinking has been followed by vomiting or cessation of eating. Patients can present in a drowsy and collapsed state, with a blood alcohol level of zero. Metabolic acidosis is a more typical presentation: this responds to rehydration and glucose. A metabolic alkalosis may also be evident if there has been vomiting.

Gout

Gout is a metabolic disorder characterized by episodic painful swelling of peripheral joints, especially the fingers and toes. Individuals with gout have high levels of uric acid, which is deposited in the joints causing inflammation and swelling. Most gout occurs in middle-aged men, who often have a family history of the disorder and drink heavily (Choi et al., 2004). Beer is particularly liable to produce hyperuricacidaemia, because of its high purine content. Other conditions predisposing to gout include obesity, hyperlipidaemia and hypertension, all of which are independently associated with heavy drinking. Heavy drinking can bring out a latent tendency towards gout or aggravate established gout.

Hyperlipidaemia

Heavy drinking is associated with a rise in circulatory blood fats (serum triglycerides). This will only be picked up by laboratory tests, but probably carries implications for enhanced risk of arteriosclerosis.

The immune system

Chronic excessive alcohol use is associated with suppression of the immune system, leading to high rates of infectious disease in this group (Estruch, 2001). Autoimmunity is also triggered by heavy alcohol consumption, contributing to organ damage such as alcoholic liver disease and skin disorders.

Heavy drinkers are at particular risk of respiratory infections and pneumonia (see Respiratory disease, below), tuberculosis (TB) (Cook, 1998) and possibly infection with HIV. They are also vulnerable to septicaemia secondary to pneumonia, urinary tract infections, bacterial peritonitis and biliary infections. Tuberculosis has long been the scourge of the chronic heavy drinker. The combination of alcohol dependence and HIV/AIDS puts individuals at particular risk for TB. Unfortunately, there has been a rise in drug-resistant strains of *Mycobacterium tuberculosis*. Further work needs to be done to elucidate the interaction between alcohol use and HIV/AIDS.

There is some evidence that alcohol dependence predisposes individuals in some way to develop hepatitis C infection, the increased incidence being in the order of 10%. This might reflect an increased susceptibility to hepatitis C in this group, increased risk behaviours or both.

Although alcohol dependent individuals have increased serum immunoglobulins they are immunodeficient; this increase is due to an abnormal regulation of the synthesis of antibodies (Estruch, 2001). They have reduced cell-mediated immunity. Lymphocyte (white cell) numbers are reduced in those with liver disease; although numbers are normal in those without liver disease, alterations in the percentage of various types are seen. B cells are normal or slightly reduced, and natural killer cells show reduced functional activity.

Alcoholic muscle, skin and bone disease

Effects of alcohol on skeletal muscle

Acute myopathy, produced by alcohol poisoning, is a condition occurring in less than 5% of alcohol misusers. It is characterized by severe pain, tenderness, swelling and weakness of the skeletal muscles. In its severe form, acute rhabdomyolysis is associated with myoglobinuria, renal damage and hyperkalaemia (raised potassium levels). Alcohol consumption reduces the normal metabolic responses of skeletal muscle to the action of insulin by causing acute insulin resistance.

Chronic alcoholic myopathy occurs in up to 60% of individuals with long-standing alcohol problems and is easily overlooked or misattributed to poor nutrition. As is the case with alcoholic liver disease and brain damage, women are more susceptible than men. Individuals typically present with proximal muscle weakness, pain and abnormal gait, and show evidence of atrophy and loss of muscle fibre in the shoulder and pelvic girdle region. Histology reveals a reduction in the diameters of white (fast-twitch) fibres. The weakness and atrophy tend to improve with abstinence or a substantial reduction in consumption.

Here is a case abstract that illustrates a fairly typical picture.

> A 45-year-old storekeeper who was severely alcohol dependent came along to complain that he had developed 'terrible rheumatics'. There was severe pain and some tenderness and swelling of both upper arms, and he could no longer lift his stock down from the shelves. It took about 2 months for him to make a reasonable recovery.

Effects of alcohol on skin

Heavy drinkers and individuals misusing alcohol are prone to a variety of skin disorders including psoriasis, discoid eczema and superficial cutaneous fungal infections, such as tinea pedis and pityriasis versicolor. Rosacea and acne may be exacerbated by alcohol.

Psoriasis is an alcohol-related skin condition that deserves special note. The daily alcohol consumption of men with psoriasis is higher than in men with other skin diseases, and heavy drinking appears to be related to the severity of the disease. In heavy drinkers, psoriasis mainly affects the palms of the hands and the soles of the feet. Alcohol-induced psoriasis responds poorly to treatment unless the patient stops drinking.

Effects of alcohol on bone

Individuals misusing alcohol have increased rates of osteoporosis (reduction in the amount of bone per unit volume without a change in its composition), osteopenia, an increased frequency of fractures and avascular necrosis. The association between alcohol consumption and osteoporosis is dose-dependent and independent of nutritional status (Preedy, Mantle & Peters, 2001). There is some evidence that the association between alcohol consumption and decreased bone mass is less prevalent in women than in men.

The reduced bone density in individuals with alcohol dependence is thought to arise as a result of impaired bone formation (reduced osteoblastic function) and increased bone resorption (increased numbers of osteoclasts). These effects of alcohol on bone metabolism appear to be reversible with abstinence. Heavy drinkers are therefore at risk of fractures, even after minimal trauma. Symptoms of back pain indicative of osteoporosis and possible vertebral collapse should not be overlooked, particularly as these patients are also likely to develop dependence on opiate-based analgesics. Post-menopausal women may be particularly susceptible to the effects of alcohol on bone.

Respiratory disease

Respiratory tract infection

Heavy alcohol consumption is associated with defects in the body's immune responses, and clinically this is reflected in an excess of lower respiratory tract infections with *Streptococcus pneumoniae*, *Mycobacterium tuberculosis* and *Klebsiella pneumoniae*. Self-neglect and the associated way of life, particularly in skid row drinkers, are also important factors predisposing to infections. Because heavy drinkers may both vomit and become stuporose, they are prone to inhale material into their lungs and hence develop lung abscesses or bronchiectasis (dilation and infection of the smaller bronchi).

Many problem drinkers also smoke heavily. A carcinoma of the lung is not, therefore, an uncommon coincidental finding, sometimes confusing the diagnostic picture. What is thought to be an alcoholic 'dementia' turns out, for instance, to be a secondary cancer of the brain, or a severe 'alcoholic' peripheral neuropathy turns out to be a cancer-related (carcinomatous) neuropathy. The simple message is that if a problem drinker presents for an assessment and has not had a recent chest X-ray, such an examination should be arranged.

Adult respiratory distress syndrome

Adult respiratory distress syndrome (ARDS) is a severe form of lung injury that results from blood infections, trauma, pneumonia and blood transfusions. Alcohol predisposes the lung to the inflammatory stresses of infection and trauma.

Haematological effects

Problem drinking gives rise to anaemia, macrocytosis, simple iron deficiency, neutropaenia and thrombocytopaenia.

Anaemia

Anaemia is common in problem drinkers and can be caused by a variety of factors including malnutrition, chronic blood loss, liver disease, malabsorption, chronic infections and the direct toxic effect of alcohol on the bone marrow.

Macrocytosis

Macrocytosis (enlarged red blood cells) is also common in problem drinkers and an unexplained macrocytosis should always alert clinicians to the possibility of an alcohol problem. If nutrition is adequate, it is probably caused by the direct toxic action of alcohol on the bone marrow. Folate deficiency in malnourished problem drinkers can give rise to a megaloblastic anaemia. However, alcohol may interfere directly with folate metabolism.

Iron deficiency

Iron deficiency among heavy drinkers will probably reflect a poor diet or chronic blood loss due to gastritis or bleeding varices. It may be associated with folate deficiency.

Neutropaenia and thrombocytopaenia

Heavy drinking may cause a neutropaenia (lowering of white cells), either by a toxic effect on the bone marrow or as a result of folate deficiency, and thereby render patients susceptible to infections. Alcohol may also interfere with neutrophil function. Thrombocytopaenia (decrease in platelets) is frequent in heavy drinkers and can account for a susceptibility to bruising. The platelet count usually returns to normal with abstinence.

Accidents/trauma

Alcohol is an underlying and frequently overlooked risk factor for accidents in the general population, not just in individuals with alcohol problems or alcohol dependence. Ingestion of alcohol causes diminished co-ordination and balance, slower reaction times and impaired attention, perception and judgement, all of which increase risk of accidental injury. Road traffic accidents in which alcohol is implicated are more serious than accidents in which it is not, and the risk of being involved in an accident rises as a function of the increased BAC. Approximately one third of pedestrians killed in road traffic accidents by day have measurable BACs. Although the literature on alcohol-related accidents has historically been focused largely on road traffic accidents and drink-driving, accidents in the home, workplace and civil aviation, and also leisure accidents such as drowning, now receive more prominence. The consumption of more than 60 g of alcohol within a 6-hour period is associated with a significant risk of injury. Alcohol consumption may put women at particular risk for injury because of the greater physiological impact of a given dose of alcohol (McLeod et al., 1999).

Studies from various countries suggest that drinking is involved in 26–54% of home and leisure injuries (Babor et al., 2003, 2010). It is particularly associated with violent family incidents and is implicated in child abuse. Positive blood alcohol levels have been obtained in 40% of fatal industrial accidents and 35% of non-fatal work-related accidents.

Surgery

Heavy drinking is associated with an increased risk of post-operative complications. This risk is evident in consumption levels of about 5 drinks ($\geq$60 g) per day (Tønnesen, 1999). Complications include prolonged hospital stay, the need for further surgery, infections, cardiopulmonary insufficiency and bleeding. A Danish study has shown that a period of pre-operative abstinence lasting for 1 month (treatment with disulfiram 800 mg twice weekly) reduced post-operative complications in heavy drinkers with colorectal disease (Tønnesen et al., 1999).

It is worth entering a brief general reminder as to the potential importance of the patient's heavy drinking to the work of the anaesthetist both operatively and post-operatively. Emergency surgery may in particular run into difficulties if intoxication is overlooked and recovery complicated by a seizure or by other unexpected withdrawal symptoms. Tolerance to alcohol may result in cross-tolerance to certain anaesthetics, notably thiopentone.

Neurological disorders

Alcohol withdrawal seizures

Alcohol withdrawal seizures occur in about 2–5% of alcohol dependent individuals, approximately 7–48 hours after cessation of drinking. The seizures are generalized, tonic-clonic (*grand mal*), and are thus associated with a loss of consciousness, followed by convulsive movements in all four limbs. During a particular withdrawal episode the patient may have only one seizure, but more commonly there will be three or four seizures over a couple of days. Very rarely status epilepticus will supervene. This is a continuous run of seizures, one merging into another, which is associated with risk to life. Alcohol withdrawal seizures have sometimes been termed 'rum fits', but they are not associated with any one type of beverage.

Predisposing factors to alcohol withdrawal seizures include hypokalaemia, hypomagnesaemia, a previous history of withdrawal seizures and concurrent epilepsy. An EEG is generally unhelpful but a brain scan will help to rule out intracranial lesions.

Alcohol dependent individuals who have experienced seizures due to alcohol withdrawal may be more prone to developing further seizures in future withdrawal episodes. Any proposed detoxification for this group should therefore be carried out in an in-patient setting. Patients at risk of alcohol withdrawal seizures should be advised not to stop drinking suddenly, but to continue at the same level of consumption until admission, or to institute an extremely slow reduction.

Tragedies have sometimes occurred when a severely dependent patient has stopped drinking on their own initiative and sustained a withdrawal seizure, which has led to an accident. For example, the driver of a heavy goods vehicle had, after a long period of sobriety, relapsed into dependent drinking, but after 2–3 months he determined abruptly to put a stop to his drinking. He had a seizure, his truck went out of control and mounted a pavement and killed a woman who was standing by a bus stop. There are therefore a number of reasons for taking withdrawal seizures and the risks of such seizures very seriously.

Seizures of other origin

A number of other possible reasons for seizures in patients with drinking problems must be borne in mind, as well as the fact that seizures may be entirely coincidental. Heavy drinking may, for example, lower the threshold in a person with an underlying epileptic tendency of any origin. A patient with epilepsy who is being treated with anticonvulsants may simply forget to take his or her tablets when he or she goes on a drinking binge. Heavy drinking can also, as a result of liver enzyme induction, lead to increased metabolic clearance of anticonvulsant medication.

Heavy drinkers are often heavy cigarette smokers, and a seizure may on occasion be the first and tragic signal of the secondary spread to the brain (metastases) from a carcinoma of the lung. Problem drinkers are prone to accidents and a seizure may be symptomatic of an old or more recent head injury. Alcoholic 'dementia' may sometimes be accompanied by seizures. A rather common cause of seizures is coincidental withdrawal of sedative or hypnotic drugs, particularly benzodiazepines. Rarer causes include alcohol-related hypoglycaemia (lowered blood sugar; see Hypoglycaemia, above) and fatty emboli lodging in the brain.

Peripheral neuropathy

Alcoholic peripheral neuropathy is a sensorimotor neuropathy detectable to some degree in approximately 10% of chronic heavy drinkers. The main causal factors are thought to be vitamin B deficiency and the toxic effect of alcohol. The lower limbs are more frequently affected than the upper limbs, and the typical presentation is with an insidious onset of weakness, pain, parasthesiae and numbness in the feet, which progresses proximally and symmetrically in a 'glove and stocking' distribution. Bilateral foot drop and weakness of the small hand muscles and finger extensors may occur. Distal reflexes are usually absent. Treatment includes B-group vitamins and abstinence. Recovery is usually slow and incomplete, with residual sensory loss.

Alcoholic cerebellar degeneration

The cerebellum is a part of the brain concerned with balance and motor integration, and it is sometimes the focus for alcohol-related brain damage. Alcoholic cerebellar degeneration usually develops insidiously and is characterized by ataxia of gait (unsteadiness) and incoordination of the legs. It is thought to be due to thiamine deficiency but alcohol neurotoxicity may also be an important factor. Abstinence and treatment with thiamine (vitamin B_1) may halt the progress of the disorder, but the patient may still be left with a disabling condition.

Wernicke–Korsakoff syndrome

Although Wernicke's encephalopathy and Korsakoff's psychosis were originally described as different entities (in 1881 and 1887 respectively), both are caused by thiamine (vitamin B_1) deficiency and show the same underlying pathological lesions in the periventricular and peri-acqueductal grey matter (Victor, Adams & Collins, 1971). Cortical abnormalities have also been reported in a proportion of cases. Prevalence rates of the Wernicke–Korsakoff syndrome vary, with autopsy studies reporting rates of about 1.5% (Cook, Hallwood & Thomson, 1998). The condition is commoner in autopsy studies of 'alcoholics'. Incidence rates are reported to have increased in Scotland over recent years (Ramayya & Jauhar, 1997). Wernicke's encephalopathy is the acute or subacute manifestation of the syndrome and Korsakoff's psychosis the chronic form.

Wernicke's encephalopathy

Wernicke's encephalopathy occurs in individuals with alcohol misuse and dependence, and in a variety of other disorders associated with a poor intake or absorption of thiamine. These other disorders include gastric carcinoma, other malignancy, hyperemesis in pregnancy, anorexia nervosa and haemodialysis. In alcohol dependent individuals, Wernicke's encephalopathy is often precipitated by alcohol withdrawal or the stress of an intercurrent illness. Some individuals may have a particular susceptibility to developing the condition.

The encephalopathy usually has an abrupt onset, although it may take a few days for the full picture to develop (Lishman, 1998; Thomson et al., 2008). Mental confusion or staggering, or unsteady gait, are often the first features to be seen. The patient may be aware of ocular abnormalities – they complain of wavering vision or double vision on looking to the side. The classic triad of confusion, ataxia and ocular abnormalities (nystagmus, an oscillatory movement of the eyeballs; and ophthalmoplegia, a paralysis of the eye muscles that might cause a squint) is diagnostic. However, these symptoms and signs may only be present in part, or not at all, and the diagnosis is often missed in life. There must always, therefore, be a high index of suspicion, particularly in cases of unexplained confusion. Other common features include anorexia, nausea and vomiting (Thomson et al., 2008). There is usually a degree of memory disorder. Lethargy and hypotension have also been described. Rarely, the disorder presents with hypothermia, stupor or coma. About 17–20% of sufferers die in the acute stage (Cook, Hallwood & Thomson, 1998).

Given the difficulties in making a definitive diagnosis, there should be a low threshold for making a presumptive diagnosis.

Wernicke's encephalopathy is a medical emergency. Treatment with high-dose parenteral thiamine should be given promptly to offset the risk of death or irreversible brain damage. Parenteral thiamine is itself associated with a small risk of anaphylactic reactions and should only be given when appropriate resuscitation facilities are available. Up to 1 g of thiamine may be needed initially to achieve a clinical response. Thereafter, 500 mg of thiamine should be given once or twice daily for 3–5 days (Thomson and Marshall, 2006) (see Chapter 12).

Hypomagnesaemia may impair the clinical response to treatment, and it is therefore worth checking serum magnesium levels. Electrolyte imbalance and dehydration must be avoided, and any intercurrent infection treated. Oral B vitamins are usually continued for several weeks.

Ocular abnormalities usually recover quite quickly (days–weeks) and the ataxia usually responds within the first week, but takes about 1–2 months to resolve (Lishman, 1998). Some patients are left with a residual nystagmus and ataxia. Improvements in acute confusion or delirium usually occur within 1–2 days. Global confusion begins to improve after 2–3 weeks, but may take 1–2 months to clear. As it improves, so the amnesic (memory) defects become more obvious.

A milder, subclinical form of Wernicke's encephalopathy exists in which patients do not manifest the clinical signs and symptoms outlined above. Undiagnosed and untreated episodes are experienced, resulting in chronic pathological changes at autopsy. The existence of subclinical Wernicke's encephalopathy has important implications for the prophylactic use of high-dose parenteral vitamin B therapy.

Korsakoff's syndrome

Korsakoff's syndrome often emerges as a chronic disorder following an episode of Wernicke's encephalopathy. It can, however, develop insidiously, with no clear prior history of a Wernicke episode. The main defect in Korsakoff's syndrome is in recent memory (Lishman, 1998; Kopelman et al., 2009). New learning is impaired. In some instances there is no new learning and an anterograde amnesia is evident (this is an inability to lay down new memories). However, the immediate memory span is unimpaired, so performance on a test of digit span (ability to repeat a list of numbers) is usually normal. Some retrograde amnesia (loss of memory for events occurring before the onset of the syndrome) is usually evident and this may be of long duration. Individuals with Korsakoff's syndrome also manifest a disturbance in time sense; for instance, some recent memory is allocated to the past, or a past event is brought up as a recent happening. Remote memory for matters beyond the retrograde gap is better preserved, but may also be impaired. Confabulation (the fabrication of ready answers and fluent descriptions of fictitious experiences compensating for gaps in memory) has been described. However, it is more likely that patients produce false memories without realizing this (Knight, 2001). Confabulation may come and go and seems to be commoner in the early stages (Lishman, 1998).

Other cognitive functions may appear to be superficially intact, but are often found to be impaired when examined carefully. These individuals therefore find it difficult to sustain mental activity, have an inflexible set and a reduced capacity to shift attention from one task to another. Their thinking is often stereotyped, perseverative and facile (Lishman, 1998). There are marked disturbances in personality, with a degree of apathy and self-neglect. Some patients are chatty, but the content of the conversation is superficial and repetitive. They often lack interest in their surroundings and may show little interest in alcohol. They show a remarkable lack of insight, with few realizing that they have memory deficits.

In Korsakoff's syndrome the pathology at the base of the brain is usually associated with cortical shrinkage and dilatation of the cerebral ventricles. It is likely that Korsakoff's syndrome is misdiagnosed in clinical practice and that there is some overlap between it and 'alcoholic dementia'. Neuroimaging studies report a range of subcortical lesions and cortical atrophy. Functional imaging studies report impaired frontal cortical blood flow. Neuropsychological studies also reveal frontal lobe deficits, which could explain aspects of the syndrome such as lack of insight and apathy.

The amnesia of Korsakoff's syndrome does not generally respond to treatment with thiamine. This raises the question that thiamine deficiency may not be the sole factor contributing to the development of the disorder. Alcohol neurotoxicity must also be considered, either alone, or in association with thiamine deficiency.

These rather strange-sounding eponyms should not deflect the non-specialist from trying to understand what is being talked about, and the following case abstract illustrates both how the acute element can present very suddenly and the type of chronic disorder that may occur when the Wernicke–Korsakoff syndrome supervenes.

> A woman aged 48, who had been drinking a bottle of whisky each day for 10 or more years, was admitted to a psychiatric hospital for detoxification. It was noted that she was suffering from severe peripheral neuropathy (weakness, tingling and pain in the legs). On the evening of admission, she was found to be rather confused, to be complaining of double vision and to be staggering. By the next evening, she was stuporose, and her eye movements were unco-ordinated (external ocular palsies). At this stage, and much too late, she was started on massive doses of thiamine – the classical picture of confusion, staggering gait and ocular palsies should have alerted the staff to the dangerous onset of Wernicke's encephalopathy. After 5 days of the acute illness, the confusion cleared and the patient was then found to have a grossly impaired memory for recent events, a tendency to make things up to fill her gaps in memory (confabulation) and very little ability to remember new information, as witnessed by her difficulty in finding her way around the ward. This amnesic syndrome (Korsakoff's syndrome), showed little recovery over the ensuing months, and arrangements had to be made for the patient's transfer to long-term residential care.

This is a story of a tragedy which might have been averted, and there is a good argument for giving thiamine prophylactically to any patient who is in danger of this sort of complication.

Alcoholic pellagra encephalopathy

This is caused by a deficiency of the B vitamin, nicotinic acid, and its precursor tryptophan in association with chronic alcohol misuse. It is rarely reported in the British and American literature, perhaps because of the routine use of parenteral multivitamin therapy (Lishman, 1981). However, this may be due to under-diagnosis, because it is still evident in other countries, such as Japan. Clinical features include a fluctuating confusional state with global memory loss, visual hallucinations, restless alternating with apathy and other neurological signs including myoclonic jerks and hyper-reflexia. Differential diagnosis can be difficult and it can be misdiagnosed as delirium tremens. Treatment with thiamine and pyridoxine can aggravate the condition. The condition responds to treatment with nicotinic acid.

Alcohol-related brain damage

The mechanisms underlying alcohol-related brain damage are complex (Marshall, 2009). Poor nutrition and diminished vitamin reserves predispose to thiamine and nicotinic acid depletion. Alcohol is neurotoxic and acetaldehyde, its main metabolite, may have a similar action. Metabolic factors resulting from acute and chronic intoxication and withdrawal, such as hypoxia, electrolyte imbalance and hypoglycaemia, are also important, as are alcohol withdrawal seizures, hepatic encephalopathy, subarachnoid haemorrhage, haemorrhagic stroke and head injury.

Many individuals with a history of chronic alcohol misuse have mild to moderate impairment in short and long-term memory, learning, visuo-spatial organization, visuo-perceptual abstraction, maintenance of cognitive set and impulse control. Performance on neuropsychological testing improves with abstinence, but some impairment may still be evident even 5 years later. With the advent of CT scanning, cortical shrinkage (particularly in the frontal area) and ventricular enlargement were confirmed in about two thirds of 'alcoholics' compared with age-matched controls (Lishman, 1998). Abstinence was shown to lead to reversal of brain shrinkage, particular in younger individuals and in women. Magnetic resonance imaging (MRI) confirms cortical atrophy and mild ventricular enlargement, also volume reductions in various parts of the brain. Functional imaging studies suggest a reduced cerebral blood flow within the medial

frontal cortex. Implications of alcohol-related brain damage for the treatment of alcohol dependence are discussed in Chapter 8.

Neuropathological studies have shown that in comparison with controls, brain weight is
significantly reduced in heavy drinkers at autopsy with selective neuronal loss.

Cognitive deficits likely represent one possible factor contributing to poor treatment outcome. Therapeutic programmes may be too complex for these individuals to grasp. Clinicians
should therefore be familiar with the risk factors and early signs of cognitive impairment in
their patients. Simple objective feedback about neuropsychological test results and neuroimaging of the brain may help to motivate the patient to abstinence. Patients with moderate to
severe brain damage who appear cognitively intact may not be able to understand the principles of motivational interviewing, cognitive behavioural therapy and relapse prevention
(see Chapter 13). Their initial needs are more basic and likely to include good nutrition, treatment with parenteral and oral thiamine and residential placement in a supervised setting. The
repetitive structure and routine of Alcoholics Anonymous is well suited to those with mild
to moderate brain damage. Alcoholics Anonymous, of course, also has within it much complexity, but the cognitively handicapped patient will perhaps be able to focus on the simpler
aspects of the AA programme.

Central pontine myelinolysis

This is a rare disorder of cerebral white matter in the brain stem, which is usually seen in
alcohol dependent individuals, but can also occur in malignancy, non-alcoholic liver disease,
chronic renal disease, rapid correction of hyponatraemia, hypokalaemia and other debilitating diseases. Clinical features include a pseudobulbar palsy and spastic or flaccid quadriple-
gia, which evolves over a few days or weeks, often resulting in coma or death. Lesions are often
picked up on MRI scans. Post-mortem examination reveals demyelination of the pons.

Marchiafava–Bignami disease

This rare disorder of the corpus callosum and adjacent white matter is not confined to problem drinkers. A nutritional deficiency or a contaminant of alcohol have been postulated as
causes. Presentation can either be acute with agitation, apathy, hallucinations, epilepsy and
coma, or insidious with dementia, spasticity, dysarthria and inability to walk. Lesions can be
visualized on brains scans, but the diagnosis is usually made only at post-mortem.

Alcohol amblyopia

This uncommon condition presents as a gradual bilateral blurring of vision in association with
alcohol misuse. It can be accompanied by difficulty in distinguishing red from green. Most
patients are also smokers. Testing reveals a central blind spot (scotoma), with the peripheral
field of vision intact. The most likely cause is a deficiency of both thiamine and vitamin B_{12}. It
responds to treatment with thiamine and B-complex vitamins. The same picture sometimes
occurs as 'tobacco amblyopia'.

Hepatic encephalopathy

In heavy drinkers with alcoholic liver disease, the predominant clinical picture can be that of
hepatic encephalopathy. This is a chronic organic reaction with psychiatric and neurological
abnormalities which come and go and are extremely variable. The typical features include
impaired consciousness (ranging from hypersomnia to coma), delirium, impaired recent
memory, mood swings, a flapping tremor, muscular inco-ordination, foetor hepaticus (a
characteristic smell on the breath), upgoing plantar responses and hypoactive or hyperactive

reflexes (Krige & Beckingham, 2001). Liver function tests are usually abnormal, and an EEG shows a picture which can be extremely helpful in diagnosis (initially slowing of the alpha rhythm, followed by appearance of 5–7 per second theta waves, and later theta replacing the alpha activity). Hepatic encephalopathy is a sign of deteriorating liver function. It can be precipitated by alcohol withdrawal and benzodiazepine use.

Fetal alcohol spectrum disorders

That the mother's drinking could cause damage to the unborn baby was widely believed in the nineteenth century, but was later to be forgotten or dismissed as temperance scaremongering. It is only over the last four decades or so that firm evidence has accumulated for the reality of the danger, and even so there are questions remaining as to the level of maternal drinking that carries risk. There is currently no reliable evidence on the incidence of fetal alcohol spectrum disorders (FASD) in the UK as, in England and Scotland, data are only collected on fetal alcohol syndrome (FAS), not the full spectrum of disorders (British Medical Association Board of Science, 2007). In the USA, the incidence estimates for FAS range from 0.5 to 2.0 per 1000 live births (Abel & Sokol, 1991; British Medical Association Board of Science, 2007). Rates of FASD vary with ethnicity, socio-economic and medical status. Nutrition, licit and illicit drug use and smoking all contribute to variability in studies. Some populations are more likely to have children affected by these disorders, particularly indigenous populations in Australia, the USA and Canada.

Diagnostic criteria for FAS are well established. The fully developed picture includes: (1) prenatal and postnatal growth retardation; (2) craniofacial abnormalities of the face and head (a small head, shortened eyelids, underdeveloped upper lip and flattened wide nose); and (3) central nervous system dysfunction. Associated abnormalities include limb deformities and congenital heart disease. As they grow up, these children remain small for their age and often have significant cognitive impairment. Cognitive deficits, together with concentration, attention and behavioural problems, may handicap education or employment.

The clinical features of partial fetal alcohol syndrome (PFAS), alcohol-related birth defects (ARBD) and alcohol-related neurodevelopmental disorders (ARND) are less well defined (British Medical Association Board of Science, 2007). Children with PFAS usually have minor facial anomalies, intellectual deficits, hyperactivity with attention deficit, impulsivity, short attention span and developmental delay. Children with ARND typically have prominent neurocognitive deficits but do not have facial anomalies or growth problems. Children with ARBD are characterized by behavioural problems or structural abnormalities; these children lack the facial anomalies (British Medical Association Board of Science, 2007).

Evidence from animal studies indicates that the critical periods of exposure occur during the first and third trimesters in humans. The very early stages of embryogenesis are critical periods for damage to the developing brain and development of craniofacial anomalies. Prenatal alcohol exposure during the third trimester is associated with damage to the cerebellum, hippocampus and prefrontal cortex (British Medical Association Board of Science, 2007).

The crucial public health question relates to what is meant by 'heavy drinking' in this context. It is not known what levels of prenatal alcohol exposure produce what intensity of developmental problems. However, there is no doubt that a woman who is drinking at a level that implies her having developed alcohol dependence is at risk of damaging her baby. Heavy-dose binge drinking in pregnancy is particularly associated with FAS. For any alcohol treatment service the practical message must be that a woman of child-bearing age who has a serious drinking problem requires very special counselling, and should be discouraged from having a baby until the drinking has been dealt with successfully. One has to think not only of the potential damage to an unborn child, but also of the lifetime guilt of the mother should an affected child be born.

What is the safe upper limit of drinking for a pregnant woman or a woman intending to have a child? The British Medical Association report recommends that pregnant women or women considering pregnancy should abstain absolutely from alcohol (British Medical Association Board of Science, 2007). The National Institute for Health and Clinical Excellence (NICE) advises that women should not drink any alcohol during pregnancy (National Institute for Health and Clinical Excellence, 2008). If women must drink, NICE advises that they should not do so in the first 3 months of pregnancy, and should then limit their consumption to 1 or 2 units once or twice a week for the rest of the pregnancy. Binge drinking should be avoided completely. Women trying to conceive are advised to limit their alcohol consumption to no more than 1–2 standard drinks once or twice per week. It might be sensible for them to consider abstinence. In the USA, the advice from the Surgeon General to pregnant women has been to abstain from alcohol during pregnancy.

Women who drink heavily during pregnancy also have increased rates of complications of pregnancy and delivery, of spontaneous abortion, preterm delivery and stillbirth.

The need for two kinds of alertness

This chapter started with the plea that everyone working with problem drinkers should be more aware of the physical element within the assessment and treatment plan. It should similarly be pleaded that everyone who works in the medical field be vigilant to the possibility of an undeclared drinking problem being behind any one of a host of clinical presentations.

Medical problems sometimes emerge during abstinence and the clinician should be alert to this reality. When patients finally stop drinking they often become aware of lingering injuries, pains, tiredness and a host of other problems. What they perceive as 'depression' may, in fact, be hypothyroidism. The wise clinician will keep a watchful eye on the newly abstinent patient and will not attribute every symptom and sign to alcohol.

References

Abel E L, Sokol R J (1991) A revised conservative estimate of the incidence of FAS and its economic impact. *Alcoholism: Clinical and Experimental Research* **15**, 514–524.

Babor T, Caetano R, Casswell S, et al. (2010) *Alcohol: No Ordinary Commodity*, 2nd edn. Oxford: Oxford University Press.

Beilin L J, Puddey I B (2006) Alcohol and hypertension: an update. *Hypertension* **47**, 1035–1038.

Bofetta P, Hashibe M (2006) Alcohol and cancer. *Lancet Oncology* 7, 149–156.

British Medical Association Board of Science (2007) *Fetal Alcohol Spectrum Disorders – A Guide for Healthcare Professionals*. London: British Medical Association.

British Medical Association Board of Science (2008) *Alcohol Misuse: Tackling the UK Epidemic*. London: British Medical Association.

Choi H K, Atkinson K, Karlson E W, Willett W, Curham G (2004) Alcohol intake and risk of incident gout in men: a prospective study. *Lancet* **363**, 1277–1281.

Chou S P, Grant B F, Dawson D A (1998) Alcoholic beverage preference and risks of alcohol-related medical consequences: a preliminary report from the National Longitudinal Alcohol Epidemiologic Study. *Alcohol: Clinical and Experimental Research* **22**, 1450–1455.

Cook C C H, Hallwood P M, Thomson A D (1998) B vitamin deficiency and neuropsychiatric syndromes in alcohol misuse. *Alcohol and Alcoholism* **33**, 317–336.

Cook R T (1998) Alcohol abuse, alcoholism, and damage to the immune system – a review. *Alcoholism: Clinical and Experimental Research* **22**, 1927–1942.

Corrao G, Bagnardi V, Zambon A, Arico S (1999) Exploring the dose-responsive relationship between alcohol consumption and the risk of several alcohol-related conditions – a meta analysis. *Addiction* **94**, 1551–1573.

Estruch R (2001) Nutrition and infectious disease. In *International Handbook of Alcohol Problems and Dependence*, N Heather, T J Peters, T Stockwell (eds). Chichester, UK: John Wiley & Sons, pp. 185–204.

Gunzerath L, Faden V, Zakhari S, Warren K (2004) National Institute on Alcohol Abuse and Alcoholism report on moderate drinking. *Alcoholism: Clinical and Experimental Research* **28**, 829–847.

International Agency for Research on Cancer (1998) *IARC Monographs on the Evaluation of Carcinogenic Risks to Humans*, Vol. 44. *Alcohol Drinking*. Lyon, France: International Agency for Research on Cancer.

Knight R G (2001) Neurological consequences of alcohol use. In *International Handbook of Alcohol Problems and Dependence*, N Heather, T J Peters, T Stockwell (eds). Chichester, UK: John Wiley & Sons, pp. 129–148.

Kopelman M D, Thomson A, Guerrini I, Marshall E J (2009) The Korsakoff syndrome: clinical aspects, psychology and treatment. *Alcohol and Alcoholism* **44**, 148–154.

Krige J E J, Beckingham I J (2001) ABC of diseases of liver, pancreas and biliary system. Portal hypertension – 2. Ascites, encephalopathy, and other conditions. *British Medical Journal* **322**, 416–418.

Lamminpaa A (1995) Alcohol intoxication in childhood and adolescence. *Alcohol and Alcoholism* **30**, 5–12.

Lieber C S (1988) The influence of alcohol on nutritional status. *Nutrition Review* **46**, 241–254.

Lishman W A (1981) Cerebral disorders in alcoholism. *Brain* **104**, 1–20.

Lishman W A (1998) *Organic Psychiatry. The Psychological Consequences of Cerebral Disorder*, 3rd edn. Oxford: Blackwell Scientific Publications.

Marshall E J (2009) Alcohol-induced dementia (alcohol-induced dementia; alcohol-related brain damage). In *The New Oxford Textbook of Psychiatry*, 2nd edn, M G Gelder, J J Lopez-Ibor, N Andreasen (eds). Oxford: Oxford University Press, pp. 399–402.

McLeod R, Stockwell T, Stevens M, Phillips M (1999) The relationship between alcohol consumption patterns and injury. *Addiction* **94**, 1719–1734.

Mukamal K J, Chung H, Jenny N S, et al. (2005b) Alcohol use and risk of ischaemic stroke among older adults: the cardiovascular health study. *Stroke* **36**, 1830–1834.

Mukamal K J, Tolstrup J S, Friberg J, Jensen G, Gronbaek M (2005a) Alcohol consumption and risk of atrial fibrillation in men and women: the Copenhagen City Heart Study. *Circulation* **112**, 1736–1742.

National Institute for Health and Clinical Excellence (2008) *National Collaborating Centre for Women's and Children's Health. Antenatal Care: Routine Care for the Healthy Pregnant Woman*, 2nd edn. London: RCOG Press. http://www.nice.org.uk/CG62.

Preedy V R, Mantle D, Peters T J (2001) Alcoholic muscle, skin and bone disease. In *International Handbook of Alcohol Problems and Dependence*, N Heather, T J Peters, T Stockwell (eds). Chichester, UK: John Wiley & Sons, pp. 169–184.

Ramayya A, Jauhar P (1997) Increasing incidence of Korsakoff's psychosis in the east end of Glasgow. *Alcohol and Alcoholism* **32**, 281–285.

Rehm J, Room R, Monteiro M, et al. (2004) Alcohol use. In *Comparative Quantification of Health Risks: Global and Regional Burden of Disease Due to Selected Major Risk Factors*, Vol. 1, M Ezzati, A D Lopez, A Rodgers, C J L Murray (eds). Geneva: World Health Organization, pp. 959–1109.

Room R, Babor T, Rehm J (2005) Alcohol and public health. *Lancet* **65**, 519–530.

Rubin E, Urbano-Marquez A (1994) Alcoholic cardiomyopathy. *Alcoholism: Clinical and Experimental Research* **18**, 111–114.

Stewart S, Latham P K, Miller P M, Randall P, Anton R (2008) Blood pressure reduction during treatment for alcohol dependence: results from the Combining Medications and Behavioural Interventions for Alcoholism (COMBINE) study. *Addiction* **103**, 1622–1628.

Thomson A D, Marshall E J (2006) The natural history of Wernicke's encephalopathy and Korsakoff's psychosis. *Alcohol and Alcoholism* **41**, 151–158.

Thomson A D, Cook C C H, Guerrini I, et al. (2008) Wernicke's encephalopathy: 'Plus ca change, plus c'est la meme chose'. *Alcohol and Alcoholism* **43**, 180–186.

Thun M J, Peto R, Lopez A D, et al. (1997) Alcohol consumption and mortality among middle-aged and elderly US adults. *New England Journal of Medicine* **337**, 1705–1714.

Tønnesen H (1999) The alcohol patient and surgery. *Alcohol and Alcoholism* **34**, 148–152.

Tønnesen H, Rosenberg J, Nielsen H J, et al. (1999) Effect of preoperative abstinence on poor postoperative outcome in alcohol misusers: randomised controlled trial. *British Medical Journal* **318**, 1311–1316.

Urbano-Marquez A, Estruch R, Fernandez-Sola J, et al. (1995) The greater risk of alcoholic cardiomyopathy and myopathy in women compared with men. *Journal of the American Medical Association* **274**, 149–154.

Victor M, Adams R D, Collins G H (1971) *The Wernicke–Korsakoff Syndrome*. Philadelphia, PA: F A Davis.

World Cancer Research Fund/American Institute for Cancer Research (2007) *Food, Nutrition, Physical Activity, and the Prevention of Cancer: A Global Perspective*. Washington DC: American Institute for Cancer Research.

World Health Organization (2007) *WHO Expert Committee on Problems Related to Alcohol Consumption. Second Report*. WHO Technical Report Series 944. Geneva: World Health Organization.

Further reading

Strategy Unit (2003) *Alcohol Harm Reduction Strategy for England: Interim Analytical Report*. London: Department of Health.

Drinking problems and psychiatric disorders

Anyone working in the field of drinking problems must cultivate an awareness of the range of psychiatric disorders that may result from, or lie behind, the drinking. Very serious issues will otherwise be overlooked. Psychiatric disorders occur more commonly in individuals with drinking problems (and substance use disorders) than in the general population. Although the term 'dual diagnosis' is sometimes used to describe such individuals, they often have multiple problems; for example, alcohol and drug use; one or more psychiatric disorders; physical health, behavioural, forensic and social problems.

The aetiology of co-morbidity is most likely to be multi-factorial and due to an interaction between biological (genetic), psychosocial, environmental and personality factors. Alcohol problems and dependence can put individuals at increased risk for developing a secondary psychiatric disorder such as major depression (Ferguson et al., 2009). Psychiatric symptoms experienced by alcohol dependent individuals may be related to the experience of intoxication and withdrawal. On the other hand, individuals with primary psychiatric disorders may be vulnerable to developing a secondary alcohol problem or drug use disorder. Some individuals may drink to cope with symptoms of anxiety, social phobia or psychosis and this may, in time, lead to a secondary alcohol problem. It is also possible the drinking problem and the psychiatric disorder may co-occur independently. Co-morbidity complicates treatment and prognosis and these individuals make heavy demands on mental health services. It is important that clinicians focus on the needs of the patient, not the disorder.

Clinical samples have higher prevalence rates of co-morbidity than community samples, because the presence of the co-morbid disorder increases the likelihood that they will seek help. Studies exploring co-morbidity have tended to use clinical samples during the first few weeks of abstinence, and this does not allow an appreciation of how the various syndromes wax and wane over time.

Epidemiology

Epidemiological studies indicate that individuals with a lifetime history of an alcohol use disorder (AUD) have a higher risk of a mental health disorder and vice versa. This was the case in the US National Co-morbidity Survey (NCS) (Kessler, Crum & Warner, 1997; Kessler et al., 1994) (Table 6.1).

The evidence for lifetime co-morbidity was stronger for alcohol dependence than for alcohol 'abuse', and co-morbidity was more likely to occur in women than in men. The predominant co-morbid disorders among men were substance use disorders, conduct disorder and antisocial personality disorder. Anxiety and affective disorders were the main contributors to co-morbidity in women. The more recent National Epidemiologic Survey on Alcohol Problems and Related Conditions (NESARC) in the USA found that among individuals with

Table 6.1. The US National Co-morbidity Survey. The lifetime co-occurrence of psychiatric disorders with alcohol dependence.

Psychiatric disorder	Individuals with alcohol dependence			
	Men		Women	
	(%)	OR	(%)	OR
Anxiety	35.8	2.2**	60.7	3.1
Mood	28.1	3.2**	53.5	4.4**
Drug dependence	29.5	9.8**	34.7	15.8**
Antisocial personality	16.9	8.3**	7.8	17.0**

**Odds ratios (OR) significantly different from 1 at 0.05, 2-tail test.
Source: Kessler, Crum & Warner (1997).

Table 6.2. Prevalence of psychiatric disorder types among non-dependent and nicotine, alcohol and drug-dependent populations.

	Non-dependent population with a disorder (%)	Nicotine-dependent population with a disorder (%)	Alcohol dependent population with a disorder (%)	Drug-dependent population with a disorder (%)
No disorder	87.5	77.0	69.4	52.9
Mixed anxiety disorder	6.2	10.2	9.9	16.3
Generalized anxiety disorder	2.4	4.1	5.3	7.3
Depression	1.2	3.7	7.3	9.1
Phobia	0.8	1.5	1.0	5.4
Panic disorder	0.5	1.5	2.7	2.5

Adapted from: Farrell et al. (2003).

AUDs seeking treatment, 40.7% had at least one recurrent independent mood disorder and 33% had at least one current independent anxiety disorder (Grant et al., 2004).

The British Psychiatric Morbidity Survey (Farrell et al., 2003) showed that individuals with nicotine, alcohol and drug dependence had an increased risk of psychiatric morbidity compared with the non-dependent population (Table 6.2) .

There are two broad categories of co-occurring psychiatric problems: firstly, alcohol-induced disorders such as hallucinations, delirium and delusions; and secondly, common co-morbid diagnoses such as depression, anxiety disorders and the like. These will be discussed in turn. Alcohol-related brain damage and the Wernicke–Korsakoff syndrome are discussed in Chapter 5.

Alcohol-induced disorders

Transient hallucinatory experience

Transient hallucinatory experience deserves note for two reasons. Firstly, it may herald the onset of delirium tremens (DTs) or alcoholic hallucinosis, and can often give early warning of the likelihood of these much more serious illnesses. It may therefore be viewed as continuous with those states, rather than an altogether discrete clinical entity. Secondly, it is important to be aware that transient hallucinations may occur without the illness progressing to either of the major presentations. The diagnostician who is unfamiliar with these transient phenomena may be tempted to record incorrectly that the patient has 'suffered from DTs' when this was not the case.

The essence of this condition is that the patient fleetingly and suddenly experiences any one of a variety of perceptual disturbances, often very much to their surprise and consternation, and with the episode then immediately over. These occurrences may be experienced during periods of continued, heavy and chaotic dependent drinking or during withdrawal. There is no delirium or evidence of severe physiological disturbance as seen in DTs. Here are some examples of how patients described such experiences.

> I would be driving along the road and suddenly something would run across in front of the car – a dog, a cat, I couldn't be sure – and I would slam on the brakes. A real fright. And then I'd realize there was nothing there.

> I would be walking down the road and, ZOOM, a car would come up behind me and I'd jump on the pavement. Frightened out of my life. But it was all imagination.

> What used to happen was that I would turn around thinking someone had called my name.

The degree of insight is often characteristic; the patient immediately disconfirms the reality of the hallucination. A relatively stereotyped and limited kind of hallucinatory experience is also typical; for one patient it is nearly always the car coming up from behind, for another a pigeon flying into the room. It is important to realize that some patients can experience such discomforting happenings for many months without progressing to a major disturbance. The meaning and significance of 'continuity' will immediately become clear as we go on below to discuss DTs and alcoholic hallucinosis.

Delirium tremens

The clinical picture

Delirium tremens (DTs) is a short-lived toxic confusional state that usually occurs as a result of reduced alcohol intake in alcohol dependent individuals with a long history of use (World Health Organization, 1992). It can produce a range of clinical pictures, but it is best viewed as a unitary syndrome with a continuum of severities and a variation in symptom clustering. The disturbance is often fluctuating, with the patient's condition worsening in the evening or when the room is unlit and shadowy. The classical triad of symptoms includes clouding of consciousness and confusion, vivid hallucinations affecting any sensory modality and marked tremor. Delusions, agitation, sleeplessness and autonomic arousal are frequently also present.

Symptoms of delirium usually occur from about 24–150 hours after the last drink (within this band earlier rather than later onset is more typical), peaking between 72 and 96 hours. Prodromal symptoms are usually evident, but may be overlooked. The onset is often at night with restlessness, insomnia and fear.

Delirium

The patient is more or less out of contact with reality, and potentially disorientated as to person, place and time. For instance, they may believe that they are cruising on a liner, mistake the nurse for a steward and order a drink, but 5 minutes later know that they are in hospital and correctly identify the people around them.

Hallucinations and illusions

Hallucinations and illusions are characteristically vivid, chaotic and bizarre and occur in any sensory modality – the patient may see visions, hear things, smell gases or feel animals crawling over them. The classical visual hallucinations are vivid and horrifying, and typically include snakes and rats and other small animals which may appear to attack the patient as they lie in bed. They may also take a 'microscopic' form (small furry men dancing on the floor), but any type of visual hallucination can occur. Patients often become completely preoccupied by, and interact with, the hallucinated objects. Thus, they feed the dogs or argue with the little men.

Hallucinatory voices or bursts of music may be heard, or the threatening screams of animals. Hallucinations are often based on a ready tendency to illusional misrepresentation: the wrinkles in the bedclothes become snakes, patterns in the wallpaper become faces.

Tremor

As the illness develops the patient becomes anxious and more fearful and develops tremor. At worst they may be shaking so severely that the bed is rattling, but, as with other symptoms, there can be a continuum of severity and the tremor may not be very noticeable unless the patient is asked to stretch out their hands.

Fear

The patient may be experiencing extremes of horror in reaction, for instance, to the snakes which writhe all over their bed, but on other occasions the hallucinations appear to be enjoyable or entertaining, and the patient is perhaps happily watching a private cinema show.

Paranoid delusions

The illness often has a degree of paranoid flavouring: enemies are blowing poisonous gas into the room, assassins lurk at the window and there is a nameless conspiracy afoot. The mood can in fact be paranoid, with every happening and stimulus being misrepresented as it comes along, but the patient's mental state is too muddled for the delusional ideas to become systematized.

Occupational delusions or hallucinations

The barman, for instance, may believe that he is serving in his cocktail bar and pour out imaginary drinks, or the bricklayer may be building an imaginary wall.

Restlessness and agitation

Partly as a consequence of the fearfulness of the hallucinatory experiences, the patient is often highly restless, clutching and pulling at the bedclothes, starting at any sound, or attempting to jump out of bed and run down the ward. This over-activity, when combined with a degree of weakness and unsteadiness, can put the patient seriously at risk of falls and other accidents.

Heightened suggestibility

The patient who is suffering from DTs can show a heightened susceptibility to suggestion, which occasionally becomes evident spontaneously but may only come out on testing. The older textbooks often mention such stories as the patient agreeing to deal from an imaginery pack of cards or 'drinking' from a proffered but empty glass.

Physical disturbances

Heavy sweating is typical, with risk therefore of dehydration. Appetite is usually lacking, the pulse is rapid, the blood pressure is likely to be raised and the patient feverish. If the illness continues over many days, the picture gradually becomes that of dehydration, exhaustion and collapse, with the possibility of a sudden and disastrously steep rise in temperature.

Aetiology and course

Delirium tremens is today generally viewed as essentially an alcohol withdrawal state, although it is conceded that other factors such as infection or trauma sometimes play an ancillary role. The withdrawal state precipitating the attack may have been occasioned by admission to hospital, arrest and incarceration, or a self-determined effort to give up drinking. Often, though, there is no history of abrupt withdrawal and the illness starts while the patient is still drinking, but there has probably been at least partial withdrawal. In some instances the patient seems to have hovered on the brink of DTs for many preceding weeks, with much evidence of transient hallucinatory experience, whereas in other instances the illness has a more explosive onset. It is unusual for a patient to experience DTs without a history of at least several years of severe alcohol dependence and many years of excessive drinking, but an attack may occur even after 1 or 2 weeks if a previously abstinent patient rapidly reinstates dependence. Recurrent attacks are common once a patient has had one such episode.

The condition usually lasts for 3–5 days, with gradual resolution. On rare occasions the illness drags on for some weeks, fluctuating between recovery and relapse. The possibility of severe physical complications has been mentioned, and before the advent of antibiotics, intercurrent chest infection or pneumonia constituted serious risks. Reported mortality rates have varied from centre to centre and even with skilled care a degree of risk remains, with death occurring in about 5% of admissions (Chick, 1989). Death is typically due to cardiovascular collapse, hypothermia or intercurrent infection.

Possibilities of diagnostic confusion

It might be supposed that DTs would give a picture so vivid and distinct as to make diagnostic mistakes unlikely. There is always the possibility that an underlying condition, which is contributing to the picture, is being overlooked. Liver failure, pneumonia and head injury should always be borne in mind. Confusion may also occur when the possibility of DTs is entirely overlooked, although in retrospect the diagnosis was plainly evident. This is often the case in the setting of a general hospital ward, where the patient is noted to be suffering from 'confusion', to be 'rambling a bit' or trying to get out of bed at night. In this situation the condition may be put down to the non-specific effects of infection, trauma or an operation. The diagnosis is at times overlooked in the psychiatric hospital setting when it may be misdiagnosed as an 'acute schizophrenic reaction'; for instance, when the acutely disturbed person with DTs has florid paranoid ideas and is found running up the street with a knife in their hand and presents as an emergency admission from the police.

The treatment of DTs is outlined in Chapter 12.

A 65-year-old widower was admitted to a general hospital via ambulance following a period of heavy drinking. On admission he was written up for one dose of chlordiazepoxide (25 mg orally). A reducing dose was not commenced, even though the nursing and medical staff were aware that he had an alcohol problem. During the first 2 days of admission he was 'pleasantly confused'. On the third day he went into the nursing office where he saw a nurse 'organizing patients into groups'. He suddenly realized that this meant everyone had to be evacuated because of a bomb scare. He left the ward in his pyjamas and bare feet, walked out of the hospital into a busy street, 'shouting vividly' that the hospital was in danger. He was duly found, returned and reassured by nursing staff. Ten days later he had a hazy recall of the event: 'I knew it wasn't true, and yet I experienced a mounting and inexplicable fear and I knew that I had to escape. Since then nothing extraordinary has happened'.

Alcoholic hallucinosis

The term alcoholic hallucinosis is used to describe auditory or visual hallucinations that occur either during or after a period of heavy alcohol consumption (Glass, 1989a, 1989b; Tsuang et al., 1994). The hallucinations are vivid, of acute onset and typically occur in the setting of clear consciousness (World Health Organization, 1992). They may be accompanied by mis-identifications, delusions, ideas of reference and an abnormal affect. Alcoholic hallucinosis typically resolves over a period of weeks, but can occasionally persist for months. Delirium tremens and psychotic disorders must be ruled out before diagnosis of alcoholic hallucinosis can be made.

In alcoholic hallucinosis the auditory hallucinations may consist of unformed noises or snatches of music, but usually take the form of voices. These voices may be talking to the patient directly, but more often take the form of a running commentary about them. Sometimes there is only one voice but often several engage in discussion, and the same voice may come back again on different occasions. The commentary may be favourable and friendly, or accusatory and threatening. Sometimes the voices command the patient to do things against their will and this may result in acting-out behaviour or a suicide attempt. There is a lack of insight and the voices are considered as real, but the patient will seldom elaborate any complex explanation as to the supposed mechanism by which the voices are reaching them. The voices may come and go or haunt the patient more or less incessantly.

There is little evidence to support the view that alcoholic hallucinosis is a form of latent schizophrenia. Nevertheless it may superficially resemble acute paranoid schizophrenia and the differential diagnosis may be difficult. The delusions associated with alcoholic hallucinosis are usually attempts to explain the hallucinations. There is no evidence of a complicated delusional system, schizophrenic thought disorder or incongruity of affect, and insight is regained as the voices diminish (Lishman, 1998).

While these guidelines provide useful indications, it can still in practice be difficult to make the distinction, and in such circumstances the sensible course of action is to admit the patient to hospital, withdraw them from alcohol and observe what happens. Remission may take place abruptly, but more often there is a slow fading of the symptoms. The voices become less persistent, do not make such an urgent demand on attention and their reality begins to be doubted. The possibility that the illness will finally declare itself to be schizophrenia has, of course, to be borne in mind, and if symptoms have not ceased within a couple of months, the latter diagnosis becomes more likely, although it has been reported that alcoholic hallucinosis may sometimes require even 6 months for complete recovery. Some drug intoxications, including most noteably amphetamine psychosis, can also result in a picture mimicking alcoholic hallucinosis and with a presentation of this sort it is always wise to carry out urine testing for drugs.

When a patient has experienced one attack of alcoholic hallucinosis they are at risk of recurrence of this condition if they drink again, although such a recurrence is not inevitable.

Alcohol-induced psychotic disorder with delusions

The category *alcohol-induced psychotic disorder with delusions* has been included in DSM-IV and DSM-IV-TR (American Psychiatric Association, 1994, 2000) and deserves mention here. Although few studies have systematically focused on this clinical condition, it has been reported in the literature for at least 150 years. Such patients typically develop paranoid or grandiose delusions in the context of heavy drinking, but remain alert and do not display any confusion or clouding of consciousness. Although psychiatric hospitalization may be required, the prognosis is generally good, and the delusional syndrome clears within days to weeks of abstinence. As with alcoholic hallucinosis, there appears to be no association with schizophrenia.

'Pathological intoxication'

Pathological intoxication, sometimes referred to as *mania à potu*, is a term used to describe a sudden onset of aggressive and often violent behaviour, not typical of the individual when sober, and occurring soon after drinking small amounts of alcohol that would not produce intoxication in most people (Coid, 1979). There is classically amnesia for the event and witnesses typically report that the aggressor (i.e. the drinker) was in a trance state or displaying automatism. The episode is usually followed by a long sleep. There may be an association with EEG abnormalities and other signs of brain damage, particularly frontal lobe dysfunction.

Pathological intoxication is an ill-defined entity and it is doubtful whether such a distinct entity deserves recognition. Clearly a relationship between drinking and aggression does exist (see Chapter 4), and the aggressor in such circumstances often manifests an alcohol-induced amnesia if there has been a high blood alcohol level at the time of the offence. Careful questioning will usually reveal that the amount of alcohol ingested was more than a 'small amount' and that there has been previous evidence of propensity to violence. Other instances of supposed pathological intoxication may be attributable to alcohol-induced hypoglycaemia, organic brain damage or personality disorder.

Here is an account of the type of case which frequently comes before the courts.

> A young man aged 23 had a pattern of frequent but intermittent heavy drinking. At his brother's wedding he became very drunk and argumentative. The best man tried to quieten him down but a quarrel ensued, and without warning this young drinker picked up a knife and stabbed a bystander, narrowly missing the victim's heart. The assailant said that he had 'only taken a drink or two', but this was clearly untrue. He displayed a patchy amnesia for the surrounding events. Further enquiry revealed that he had, on several previous occasions, been involved in dangerous fights, both when drunk and when sober.

It can hardly be doubted that this young man's intoxication contributed to his loss of impulse control, and it was probably the crucial additional factor that sparked off his violence, given also the background importance of predisposition and circumstance. The position taken here is not that intoxication is irrelevant to understanding such events, but rather that it is unproductive to segment cases into those due to 'intoxication', as opposed to instances where 'pathological intoxication' is deemed to be the cause. This distinction is encouraged by legal systems which give simple drunkenness no standing, and therefore lead defence lawyers to search for a medical basis on which to argue that their client's intoxication was a disease manifestation. From the strictly medical point of view 'pathological drunkenness' is a very uncertain concept.

Alcoholic blackouts (alcohol-induced amnestic episodes)

The widely used but somewhat confusing lay-term 'alcoholic blackout' refers to transient memory loss which may be induced by intoxication. There is no associated loss of consciousness.

Clinicians should not enquire simply whether the patient has had a blackout and leave it at that. It is preferable to ask: 'Have you ever forgotten things you did while drinking?' Although such occurrences are reported in some two thirds or more of alcohol dependent individuals, alcoholic memory blackouts are also relatively common in social drinkers after incidents of heavy indulgence. Approximately one third of young men in the general population are likely to have experienced memory blackouts (Goodwin, Crane & Guze, 1969a). Thus, while they are an important warning sign of problem drinking, they are not necessarily pathognomonic of alcohol dependence.

Blackouts have been described as being of two types (Goodwin, Crane & Guze, 1969a, 1969b). The en bloc variety is characterized by a dense and total amnesia with abrupt points of onset and recovery, and with no subsequent recall of events for the amnesic period, either spontaneously or with prompting. This period may extend from 30 to 60 minutes up to as long as 2 or 3 days. In contrast, 'fragmentary' blackouts or 'greyouts' are patchy episodes of amnesia, with indistinct boundaries and islands of memory within these boundaries. They are often characterized by partial or complete subsequent recall, and usually extend over a shorter period than the en bloc variety. In reality, alcoholic memory blackouts can occur with every degree of gradation, and although it is useful to recognize the two types, the experience of each patient has to be described separately.

Blackouts may begin to occur at a late stage in a career of excessive drinking or never at all. Once they start to be experienced with any frequency, they tend to recur, and a patient may often be able to identify the phase at which they 'began to get bad blackouts'. The reason for such varied susceptibility to the disorder is unknown, but blackouts are associated with an early onset of drinking, high peak levels of alcohol and a history of head injury. Concurrent use of sedatives and hypnotics may increase the likelihood of amnesia. Blackouts are not predictive of long-term cognitive impairment.

During an alcoholic blackout the individual can engage in any type of activity. To the observer the drinker will not obviously be in an abnormal state of mind (other than being intoxicated), although a spouse or someone else who knows them well, may claim to recognize subtle changes – for instance, 'they get that glazed look'.

The journey syndrome

Patients sometimes report that during an alcohol blackout period they wandered away from home, later 'waking up' in a strange place. Here is an example.

> When I came round I was sitting in a barber's chair having a shave. Hadn't a clue where I'd got to this time, terribly embarrassed, didn't like to ask. I had to go outside and look at the shop signs until I found the answer, and then to my amazement I discovered I was in this town 150 miles from home. To this day I don't know how I got there. That was the worst experience of this kind, but time after time I woke up in strange places or found myself sitting on a train going to the coast.

Blackouts and their significance to the patient

One patient may mention their blackouts only on direct questioning and appear not to be at all worried about such experiences, while another patient may see such experiences as a leading reason for seeking help. Blackouts for that type of patient are often a matter of dread with, for instance, recurrent anguished fear that they may have hurt or killed someone while driving home; they do not remember getting their car into the garage the previous night, and they go out in the morning fearfully to check the paint work.

Co-morbid disorders

A number of co-morbid disorders will now be considered: depressive disorder, suicide, bipolar disorder, anxiety disorder, post-traumatic stress disorder (PTSD), personality disorder, eating disorders and psychosis. In this section the emphasis will be on clinical presentation. Alcohol services should be in a position to assess mood and anxiety co-morbidity and signpost individuals to appropriate treatment. Specialist alcohol services will usually be in a position to offer treatment or to work in a co-ordinated way with other specialist services.

Depression

Depression is common amongst individuals with drinking problems and may be the decisive factor in seeking treatment. However, the nature of the relationship between the two is still poorly understood. What seems, on the surface, to be a simple association, is in fact extremely complex. Part of the problem is a lack of clarity in terminology. The word 'depression' has a variety of meanings and a distinction has to be made between the experience of being depressed and depressive illness.

Depressive illness

Depression as a psychiatric illness must be distinguished from feelings of sadness and unhappiness that can occur as a normal reaction to adversity. The essential feature of a depressive episode is a period of at least 2 weeks during which there is depressed mood and loss of interest or pleasure in nearly all activities. The mood disturbance is often worse at a particular time of day, usually the morning. Loss of energy, fatigue and diminished activity are common, as is marked tiredness after slight effort. Other symptoms include reduced concentration and attention, reduced self-esteem and self-confidence, ideas of guilt and unworthiness, bleak and pessimistic views of the future, disturbed sleep and early-morning wakening, diminished appetite and weight loss, and ideas of self-harm and suicide (World Health Organization, 1992). Sexual interest is reduced or lost. Somatic complaints, rather than feelings of sadness may be emphasized and the patient thinks that they are physically ill. There is often increased irritability, an impaired ability to think or make decisions and poor concentration. The patient may be agitated or slowed down. Psychotic symptoms such as delusions, hallucinations or depressive stupor can occur in a severe depressive episode.

Depressive illness exists in degrees, and there are many variations in which symptoms cluster and present. No one description can do justice to the true variety of presentations. The picture will be influenced by culture and the patient's age and personality. There have been many attempts to typologize this disorder – endogenous versus reactive, 'neurotic depression' versus true depressive illness and so on. Current diagnostic classification is set out in the ICD and DSM manuals. A distinction is made between unipolar affective disorder and bipolar affective disorder, the latter characterized by repeated episodes in which the patient's mood and activity levels are significantly disturbed, sometimes in terms of elevation of mood (elation), increased energy and activity (mania or hypomania) and at other times by episodes of depression.

Deciding whether a person is just miserable or, on the other hand, ill with depression can be extraordinarily difficult when they are drinking, and there is the ever-looming possibility of suicide as the price of a mistake. Depressive illness is often over-diagnosed in problem drinkers, with consequent needless prescribing of drugs, while on other occasions the diagnosis may be overlooked. This is an instance where correct diagnosis will speak very importantly to appropriate management. If the patient is suffering from non-specific unhappiness rather than a depressive illness, that aspect of their situation may require skilled help, but not the same type of help as would be indicated for the undoubted illness. A picture of drinking problems together with a complaint of depression is illustrated by the following case abstract.

> A married woman aged 35 had been drinking excessively for 3 or 4 years. When a social worker visited the patient at home, the house was in a terrible state and the children much neglected. The patient herself was dishevelled, obviously rather drunk and declaring in a maudlin fashion that she was no good and that the family might as well be rid of her.

How should the social worker respond to this situation? Quite certainly an entirely inadequate course of action would be simply to arrange for a prescription of antidepressant drugs, and let the patient mix these drugs with the drinking. Treatment cannot be intelligently and usefully started until it is known what there is to treat. The obverse approach, and one as misguided as the ill thought out use of pharmacotherapy, is to assume that all problem drinkers can be a bit maudlin at times, and to dismiss this woman's complaint as 'just the alcoholic miseries' – later perhaps to hear that she killed herself.

How, in practice, does the clinician decide whether such a patient is suffering from a depressive illness? Assessment of the history is very important – a history of depressive illness, an event such as childbirth or bereavement which might have precipitated the illness, a sense of some more or less demarcated point where 'things changed' and the patient knew that whatever the previous ups and downs of mood, something was now being experienced which was fixed and of different degree. A family history of depression can also be an important indicator of potential vulnerability. With the history has to be integrated what details can be observed of present behaviour and mental state. But it is also true that many problem drinkers will, when drinking, show emotional lability, will cry easily, will talk of the hopelessness of their lives. To leap to an immediate diagnosis of depressive illness in all such instances, would result in a great deal of over-diagnosis. The dilemma can be very real, and even experienced clinical judgement may be unable to resolve this diagnostic question while that patient is intoxicated. The patient's account may be inconsistent, it may seem to be over-dramatized, the immediate life situation may be distressingly fraught and chaotic, but it is still unclear whether or not behind this drinking lies a depressive illness.

In such circumstances the sensible rule is to admit that diagnosis cannot be made in the presence of drinking. Stopping drinking is the prerequisite to a resolution of the diagnostic difficulty. In most individuals depressive symptoms resolve following 2–3 weeks of abstinence. Alternatively, it may become very apparent that a classical depressive illness now stands out as certainly as a rock left by the tide. Sometimes, however, even after a period of in-patient observation and continued sobriety, it may be difficult to know whether what is emerging is a depressive illness, or a personality chronically prone to unhappy feelings and explosive declarations of misery. The ultimate resolution of the diagnostic problem might, for instance, be that the woman described above had always been a rather unhappy and insecure person, that in this setting and to relieve these feelings she had gradually started to drink and had been drinking heavily for 5 or more years, but that against all this background she had undoubtedly a year previously and following childbirth developed a true and severe depressive illness which had been untreated. The unravelling of such a story may require a lot of time, but arriving at a proper understanding is no optional extra if the depressed drinker is effectively to be helped.

Drinking problems and depression: their relationship

In most cases depression is secondary to the alcohol problem (Table 6.3). However, a proportion of problem drinkers have primary depression, which may predispose them to the direct development of an alcohol problem or exacerbate it once it has developed. It is worth noting that depression more commonly predates alcohol problems in women than in men (Helzer & Pryzbeck, 1988).

Depression is commoner in women drinkers and in problem drinkers who have a family history of alcohol problems, an earlier onset of heavy drinking, are divorced and are of lower social status (O'Sullivan et al., 1983). Other predisposing factors include a history of anxiety, other drug misuse and previous suicide attempts (Roy et al., 1991). A history of recent, particularly 'negative', life events and a family history of depression appeared to be risk factors for secondary depression in male 'alcoholics' (Roy, 1996).

Depressive symptoms are common during alcohol withdrawal, particularly following a period of heavy consumption. Clinically significant levels of depression are found among in-patients with drinking problems during the early stages of admission and alcohol withdrawal, but in most people these symptoms improve after 2–3 weeks of abstinence. However, depressive symptoms may persist, or even emerge during abstinence and the astute clinician should always be on the look out for this. Long-term follow-up studies suggest that depressive experience usually declines with continued abstinence.

In the clinical situation it may be helpful to differentiate between alcohol-induced depressive syndromes and independent depressive episodes. Major depressive episodes occurring during a period of active alcohol dependence are considered to be alcohol-induced. Independent major depression is defined as an episode that occurred either before the onset of alcohol dependence, or during a period of 3 or more months of abstinence.

Depression and drinking problems: the practical importance of the diagnostic question

There are several reasons why it is important to determine whether a patient with a drinking problem is also suffering from a depressive illness. If such an illness exists, it of course deserves treatment as well as whatever psychological or social help may be necessary: the illness may respond to cognitive behavioural therapy (CBT) or to an antidepressant drug. The second important reason for believing that every effort must be made not to miss this diagnosis is that, if depression is untreated, any attempts to treat the drinking problem will be grossly handicapped. A depressed patient may find it extremely difficult to stop drinking, and untreated depression can on occasion run on for 2 or 3 years, or even longer, perhaps then with partial remissions and further relapses making the time course even more blurred and extended. Another important reason for taking the diagnostic question extremely seriously is the issue of suicidal risk (see below). Problem drinkers who are not suffering from depressive illness may kill themselves, but the risk is certainly enhanced if this illness is present.

Table 6.3. Drinking problems and depression.

- Drinking problems are a major cause of depression
- Abstinence from alcohol alleviates depression
- A small proportion of problem drinkers will benefit from antidepressants but the alcohol problem must be tackled first

Knowledge that there has been a depressive illness has a bearing on long-term management, and this must be openly discussed with the patient. Once someone has suffered from one such illness they are at some risk of developing depression again at some point, and if they can recognize early signs and seek appropriate help a lot of trouble may be averted. An episode of depression is not an uncommon cause of relapse into drinking after a longish period of sobriety. Paradoxically, the development of an underlying depression may be the reason for a drinker eventually seeking help. It may be an expression of their depressive illness when they say they 'can't carry on any more', start to blame themselves rather than others for their drinking or make the suicidal gesture which gets them into hospital.

> A 35-year-old woman with her own home-based design consultancy was narrowly saved by her partner from death by hanging. Her family history showed a heavy loading both with depressive illness and alcohol dependence, and she undoubtedly was suffering from both problems. She responded well to a maintenance antidepressant and accepted that she had to stop drinking.

Summing the matter up, it is fair to say that an awareness of the significance of depressive illness is so essential to working with problem drinkers that anyone who is going to take a close interest in drinking problems will also need to develop a good understanding of depression and how best to treat it. If, in relation to this question, there exists a golden rule, it is that when a drinker is suffering from depressive illness, the therapeutic priority is to aid and persuade that patient first to stop drinking (offering perhaps immediate admission to achieve this purpose). Treating the depression is then the second phase of help and the immediate follow-through. It is generally messy and ineffective to try to treat a depressive illness when the patient is still drinking.

Suicide

The lifetime risk of suicide in 'alcoholics' was previously estimated to be 15% (Murphy & Wetzel, 1990), but this figure was challenged by a meta-analysis of mortality studies which calculated a lifetime risk of 7% (Inskip, Harris & Barraclough, 1998). When national suicide rates are taken into account, it is likely that the lifetime risk is somewhere in the region of 2.5% and 7% (Jenkins, 2007). A 25-year follow-up study of almost 50 000 Swedish male conscripts, born in 1950 and 1951, showed that those who had abused alcohol had a highly elevated risk of suicide attempts (odds ratio of 27.1) and of completed suicide (odds ratio of 4.7) (Rossow, Romelsjö & Leifman, 1999). The odds ratios remained elevated when the data were adjusted for psychiatric co-morbidity (8.8 and 2.4 respectively). Intoxication was considered to be the main component in non-fatal suicide behaviour. The role of hazardous and harmful use in suicidal behaviour, particularly in male adolescents and young men, has been highlighted in a number of other studies (Fombonne, 1998; Pirkola et al., 1999; Vassilas & Morgan, 1997).

Stressful life events are key contributors to suicide in individuals with alcohol problems. Other factors include isolation, lack of social support, unemployment, co-morbid disorders, such as anxiety, depression and personality disorder, and medical problems. Close attention to these factors may help in the assessment of suicidal risk in such individuals when they present to the emergency services and to other healthcare professionals. Their suicidal ideation should be taken seriously, their drinking and co-morbid disorders assessed carefully and appropriate treatment instituted (Brady, 2006; Foster, 2001; Pirkola, Suominen & Isometsa, 2004) .

Bipolar disorder

Hypomania

Pathological elevation of mood is not so common a condition as pathological depression, and when it occurs does not carry a particularly high risk of being associated with drinking. Occasionally the hypomanic patient finds that alcohol can help to relieve unpleasant elements in their feelings: accompanying the basic elevation of mood, the hypomanic state may be characterized by considerable admixture of anxiety, irritability and suspiciousness. Mixed affective illnesses exist where the patient is both excited and tearful, with a confusing presentation that moves within minutes from elation to depression. A patient with repeated hypomanic bouts may give the appearance of 'bout drinking'. In an attack they are likely to lose their social judgement, and to spend large sums of money and live things up, and this general disinhibition, as well as the more specific seeking of relief from unpleasant feelings, may contribute to the drinking. The treatment is primarily that of the underlying illness.

> A 40-year-old lawyer was persuaded by his colleagues to seek help because they thought his excessive drinking was making him unpredictable and bad-tempered. At interview it became clear that he was in the hypomanic swing of a bipolar illness. His generally heavy background drinking was apt to go out of control during this kind of episode. With lithium instituted and his own decision that drinking was 'best cut out', he returned to practice.

A more difficult diagnostic problem arises when there is a suspicion that the patient's mood may phasically become slightly elevated but with the condition not approaching a hypomanic illness in severity. This slight elevation and disinhibition may appear to be sufficient to spark off some weeks of drinking, and on occasion this is a plausible explanation of 'periodic drinking', although there are many other explanations for such a drinking pattern. What is being discussed here is a mood disturbance, which would usually be seen as a character trait (cyclothymic personality) rather than as an illness, but there is no absolute demarcation between this sort of state and hypomania. In turn, hypomania merges with mania, with the latter term indicating a state of appalling over-excitement, or the traditional picture of 'raving madness'. A patient with fully developed mania is far too disordered to be other than rapidly admitted to hospital, and drinking as a complication of this illness is not a question which arises other than in the very short term.

Anxiety

Symptoms of anxiety are particularly prominent after a bout of heavy drinking and during alcohol withdrawal. Alcohol withdrawal symptoms can mimic anxiety and panic disorder, and it is possible that a common neurochemical process underlies both. Individuals with alcohol dependence and anxiety disorder have been found to experience more severe alcohol withdrawal symptoms than a non-anxious control group, even though the two groups had similar drinking histories (Johnston et al., 1991). Anxiety symptoms diminish in the early stages of abstinence and continue to improve with prolonged abstinence.

Here is a case example illustrating one kind of possible clinical relationship between alcohol and anxiety.

> A woman aged 50 was admitted to hospital with a long history of drinking. She worked as an office cleaner, so rose early. She would have a drink at 6 o'clock before leaving the house, and would then put a couple of bottles of wine into her bag. Information from her case notes revealed that when she had first attended the clinic many years previously, her presenting complaint was agoraphobia and difficulty in leaving her house. Careful questioning revealed

that phobic anxiety symptoms still very much persisted, although alcohol dependence had now developed as a problem in its own right.

The ideal clinical approach when a problem drinker appears to be suffering from an anxiety state would be to arrange hospital admission, both for purposes of diagnosis and of treatment. It is difficult to assess the true severity or fixedness of anxiety symptoms until the patient has been completely off alcohol for about 4 weeks, and sometimes a longer period of observation is required. What may then happen is that seemingly rather severe anxiety symptoms fade away following detoxification, and in the event there is no anxiety to be treated. The symptoms were part of general 'bad nerves' related to alcohol dependence.

If, however, severe anxiety symptoms persist, an effort must be made to treat them. Treatment of the underlying condition requires sobriety. Any attempt to treat these symptoms when the patient is still drinking is likely to be a hopeless undertaking. Treatment will usually involve the planned application of cognitive behavioural therapy (CBT). The response is often excellent provided that the patient can maintain abstinence and co-operate with treatment, that the background level of anxiety is not too high and that the phobic situations are not too universal. It would be optimistic to suppose that CBT is a panacea because such favourable conditions do not always exist.

What about the use of medication? This is primarily an adjunctive treatment, and should be used in the context of a comprehensive treatment programme incorporating a range of interventions such as psychosocial support, CBT, coping skills training and educational strategies. Pharmacological treatments that have been used in this context include benzodiazepines, antidepressants (tricyclics, selective serotonin reuptake inhibitors [SSRIs] and selective noradrenaline reuptake inhibitors [SNRIs]), buspirone and anticonvulsants, among others (see Marshall, 2007). Benzodiazepines should only be used with extreme caution, because alcohol dependent individuals are at increased risk of developing a super-added benzodiazepine dependence. Indeed, by the time the problem drinker with a co-morbid anxiety disorder presents for treatment, it is not uncommon to find that they also have a medically induced drug problem, as well as alcohol dependence.

John was a 41-year-old divorced teacher who presented to the in-patient unit for treatment. He had been alcohol dependent for about 15 years but had never sought any specialist alcohol treatment. However, he had been receiving treatment for anxiety and depression for about 20 years, having first presented to psychiatric services following an overdose. During his admission he successfully completed a medically assisted withdrawal from alcohol and then had a full psychiatric assessment. This revealed social anxiety and lack of confidence, difficulties relating to others, chronic depressive features and feeling of inadequacy, all rooted in early childhood experiences.

Following discharge from hospital, he attended a 12-step day programme and had 16 sessions of CBT with a clinical psychologist. He continued to attend his psychiatrist who helped to monitor progress and liaised with the psychologist and general practitioner. He took to the cognitive model very well and found it quite revelatory in terms of his ability to focus on and identify aspects of his difficulties of which he had not previously been aware. After seven sessions he was less depressed and more optimistic, but continued to experience significant social anxiety and still felt 'socially inadequate'. However, after a further 9 sessions (and 6 months later) there had been an improvement in his anxiety symptoms, which were now within the normal range. It was clear that he had used alcohol to cope with his social anxiety and feeling of social inadequacy. By this time he was back at work and feeling satisfied with the changes that he had been able to achieve. In the early days of abstinence he attended AA nightly. A year later he was still abstinent and attending AA twice a week. He concluded the CBT with the psychologist but continued to see his psychiatrist for a number of years, latterly about twice a year.

Post-traumatic stress disorder

Post-traumatic stress disorder (PTSD) is an anxiety disorder that develops following exposure to an extremely traumatic stressor considered to be exceptionally threatening or catastrophic in nature (American Psychiatric Association, 1994). Characteristic symptoms include persistent re-experiencing of the traumatic event, persistent avoidance of stimuli associated with the trauma, numbing of general responsiveness and persistent symptoms of hyper-arousal. Post-traumatic stress disorder may exist with major depressive disorder, may present as a combination of the above symptoms and typical grief and often leads to drug and alcohol misuse.

Several hypotheses have been proposed to explain the link between PTSD and alcohol misuse; notably that these patients may drink to cope with their symptoms (Khantzian, 1990). However, other studies have shown that alcohol misuse may precede the onset of PTSD symptoms (Cottler et al., 1992). It may be that early substance misuse occurs in the context of other 'high-risk' behaviours, which increase the likelihood of exposure to potentially traumatizing events and hence the likelihood of developing PTSD. Additionally, individuals who begin using alcohol at an early stage may also be susceptible to the development of PTSD following traumatic exposure because they have historically relied on alcohol as a way of combatting stress and have failed to develop more effective stress reduction strategies. In the clinical setting it is helpful to differentiate between experiences of childhood and adult trauma and to assess how these experiences have affected the individual.

The association between PTSD and alcohol misuse or dependence is particularly strong for women, and this is associated with the higher incidence of childhood physical and sexual abuse in women. Early experiences of physical and sexual abuse put individuals at a greater risk of developing PTSD symptoms following traumatic events in adulthood (Breslau et al., 1999).

In an ideal world, individuals with alcohol dependence and PTSD should be enabled to tackle both problems simultaneously. Therapeutic strategies help them to cope with the trauma and situations that remind them of the event or events. They learn how to control or avoid such situations. However, this is not always possible, and 'therapy' may, in some individuals, be so traumatic as to cause relapse to heavy drinking, as is illustrated in the following case example.

A 36-year-old man was referred to a specialist PTSD clinic. He had a long history of alcohol dependence and PTSD, secondary to childhood sexual abuse. Now abstinent from alcohol for 1 year, he was motivated to engage in treatment for his PTSD. Unfortunately he relapsed to dependent drinking after only four treatment sessions, during which he had been 'exposed' to the traumatic memories, and encouraged to relive them as vividly as possible. His wife then left him because he was repeatedly violent to her while intoxicated. She was also worried that he might repeat the pattern of sexual abuse with their two children. There followed a number of admissions to an alcohol unit but he was unable to sustain any substantial period of abstinence over the next 5 years, despite in-patient and out-patient treatment, CBT and pharmacotherapy for alcohol dependence and depressive illness. He now lives on his own, continues to drink, and has lost custody of his children whom he rarely sees. He is 'obsessed' with the man who sexually abused him as a child.

Personality disorder

It is impossible to work with drinking problems without becoming aware of the relevance of personality to an understanding of the genesis of drinking and the treatment of excessive drinking and dependence. Patients with drinking problems are sometimes, and to various degrees, angry, unhappy, non-conformist, rule-breaking, aggressive and handicapped in their ability to deal with social demands and expectations. It can be difficult to determine how much such seeming disturbances are cause, and how much are the consequences of excessive drinking. Personality disturbance can make treatment difficult and has to be dealt with therapeutically as a significant issue.

Studies in population and clinical settings show a higher prevalence of personality disorder among people with AUDs (and drug use disorders) than among the general population, with antisocial and borderline personality disorder being particularly prominent. Borderline personality traits have been shown to predict later alcohol use problems (Stepp, Trull & Sher, 2005). Specialist alcohol services are accustomed to dealing with people with personality disorder, especially antisocial and borderline personality disorder. These patients should not be excluded from standard treatment programmes as they are as likely to benefit from treatment as those without a personality disorder. The key to treatment in this group is longer-term support.

Pathological jealousy

Jealousy is a normal human emotion, and it is not easy to set a cutting point between the normal and the pathological. At one end of the spectrum there is, however, a group of people whose lives are plagued and corrupted by their jealous feelings, and who make life miserable for the objects of their jealousy. This condition is likely to be met quite frequently in the treatment of drinking problems, and one should know how to recognize its features.

> A 34-year-old garage owner said that he had been painfully jealous ever since his adolescence. His jealousy was now threatening to break up his marriage. He would repeatedly charge his wife with infidelity, taunting her and threatening her, as well as accusing her. There would then be explosive rows, and sometimes violence resulted. Later he would be desperately sorry and transiently realize the falseness and cruelty of his accusations. But very shortly worrying doubts would again return. He would come home secretly and keep watch on the house, and sometimes he would follow his wife down the road. His wife's handbag was regularly searched, and he checked on her underclothes for seminal stains. Recently he had thought of hiring a detective. He remained sexually potent, and wanted to keep his wife pregnant so as to make her uninteresting to other men. His drinking appeared to be inextricably mixed with the jealousy story, but his jealousy only came to light when his wife was interviewed.

The essential characteristics of this syndrome suggest that it may sometimes parallel an obsessional disorder, although this is not a view of the condition that finds approval in the standard psychiatric texts. The constant rumination, the fact that there is frequent (if only short-lived and partial) realization of the falseness of the belief, the unpleasantness of the associated feelings, the compulsive need to check and the transient relief from the active checking, are features very reminiscent of obsession. But it seems certain that pathological jealousy cannot be related to any one all-embracing psychiatric diagnosis, and underlying the common presenting features may be any one of several psychiatric disorders, including paranoid schizophrenia.

Attention deficit hyperactivity disorder

Attention deficit hyperactivity disorder (ADHD) is an early-onset neurobehavioural disorder characterized by symptoms of inattention, hyperactivity and impulsivity, which affects between 4% and 7% of children (Spencer, Biedernman & Mick, 2007). Children with the disorder typically have trouble concentrating and staying still, and this can lead to problems at school. Several studies have shown that ADHD is a risk factor for the development of psychiatric co-morbidity in childhood, adolescence and adulthood; problems include mood and anxiety disorders, alcohol, nicotine and drug use disorders (Spencer, Biedernman & Mick, 2007). Adolescents with ADHD are at increased risk for nicotine dependence and alcohol misuse during adolescence. It is likely that they use nicotine and alcohol to cope with their symptoms (Ohlmeier et al., 2007). Individuals with ADHD can present to alcohol services as adolescents or adults. It is worth bearing this diagnosis in mind when seeing patients with multiple co-morbidities. Early diagnosis and treatment of the ADHD may help to reduce the onset of other addictions (Ohlmeier et al., 2007).

Psychosis and schizophrenia

Prevalence studies suggest that approximately 40–50% of schizophrenia patients have a lifetime history of substance use disorders (Menezes et al., 1996; Weaver et al., 2001). Cannabis and psychostimulants (amphetamine, methamphetamine and cocaine) are the drugs most commonly implicated. Early cannabis use in individuals with a genetic predisposition and environmental vulnerability to psychosis may act as a final trigger factor to the development of a psychotic illness.

High rates of alcohol problems have been reported in individuals with schizophrenia (22.1%; Duke, Pantelis & Barnes, 1994) and psychosis (31.6%; Menezes et al., 1996). Alcohol use may be an added risk factor for the development of tardive dyskinesia in some schizophrenics (Duke, Pantelis & Barnes, 1994).

Alcohol consumption is a risk factor for violence in individuals with schizophrenia (Fazel et al., 2009; Lindquist & Allebeck, 1989). Violence may be associated with intoxication or withdrawal effects, and their impact in mentally ill individuals, or with personality changes associated with prolonged use of substances. Antisocial and personality traits and brain damage are also important risk factors for violence.

> A dentist aged 35 came to disciplinary attention because he had been found to be injecting himself with diazepam obtained from his practice. Assessment revealed a long-standing alcohol problem. He then began to talk about 'hearing voices'. Over the next few months it became evident that he was developing a schizophrenic illness. The clinical course was stormy, with continued drinking. He had to cease practising.

Eating disorders

The most common disorders of body weight that result from excessive drinking are obesity, due to the high calorie content of alcohol, and the loss of weight and general malnutrition, which are consequences of the dietary neglect that frequently accompanies heavy drinking. However, a small proportion of people approaching alcohol services also have anorexia or bulimia nervosa (Goldbloom, 1993). The research evidence suggests that the co-morbidity of alcohol dependence and eating disorders occurs against the background of other psychiatric disorders (Sinha & O'Malley, 2000). Individuals with eating and alcohol use disorders may also have a predisposition towards other 'impulse' disorders such as self-harm and misuse of illicit or prescribed drugs.

Damage to the tissue of the brain

The question often arises as to whether the patient with a drinking problem is suffering from brain damage. If the damage is gross there will be no diagnostic difficulty, but the diagnosis (and significance) of lesser degrees of damage commonly set problems.

The most familiar picture is that of alcohol-related brain damage, and this condition is discussed more fully in Chapter 5 in relation to the physical damages that can result from drinking. Much the same sort of picture is to be seen when the patient is developing a dementia for any other reason (pre-senile dementia, for instance, or senile or multi-infarct dementia). The patient with alcoholic dementia will typically give a history of many years heavy drinking with ultimate development of brain damage. With non-alcoholic dementia the sequence of events is the other way round: the patient develops dementia and, as a result of the ensuing disinhibition and personality deterioration, becomes involved in drinking.

The fact that brain damage can be cause as well as consequence of drinking needs to be written into any diagnostic check-list. Besides brain damage due to degenerative processes such as those already mentioned, the significance of a history of brain injury should be specially borne in mind. Instances occur where personality change as a sequel to head injury is disproportionate to any fall-off in intellectual functioning, and this type of personality change may, for instance, result in drinking problems as a late sequel of a road accident. The following brief case extracts show some of the many possible organic relationships which should be on that check-list.

> A woman civil servant aged 50, of previously unblemished record, suffered a subarachnoid haemorrhage (a bleed into the space around the brain). The leaking blood vessel was operated on and she 'recovered completely', but she had, in fact, sustained a degree of brain damage. Work habits, which had for a lifetime been almost over-meticulous, now deteriorated, and she was found to be drinking secretly in the office.

> A man aged 40 suffered from crippling obsessional symptoms, and a leucotomy was performed. His obsessional symptoms were relieved, but although up to the time of his operation he had been a very moderate drinker, he now rapidly developed alcohol dependence.

> A woman of 60 presented with alcohol dependence, seemingly of recent onset. She was found to have a brain tumour.

Some of these case histories illustrate only rather rare associations, and the precise part that brain damage played in the aetiology of the drinking is in some instances difficult to establish. However, the general picture, which is being built up by listing these diverse cases, is valid and important. Some associations between brain damage and alcohol dependence are relatively common (personality deterioration following head injury, for example), while others, such as tumour, are rare, but the general message that no diagnostic assessment is complete without thinking about the possible significance of brain involvement has to be stressed. Alcohol dependence can also supervene as a complication of learning disability of any origin.

Whatever the underlying brain syndrome associated with alcohol dependence, the clinical features can be grouped under a number of headings. There are, of course, firstly the primary symptoms of the brain damage itself. Features of the drinking problem will also stand in their own right, but it is the interaction of the underlying brain damage and the drinking which gives these cases their colouring. Personal and social deterioration may seem to be disproportionate to the drinking, or suddenly to have accelerated. Drunken behaviour where there is underlying brain damage often appears to be particularly heedless of consequences or antisocial. There are increasing episodes of violence or the patient sets their lodgings on fire. There is also an increased sensitivity to alcohol; the patient gets drunk on less drink, and with relatively little alcohol becomes disinhibited or begins to fall about.

Given proper alertness to the possibility of such underlying problems, what are then the practical implications? If brain involvement is in any way suspected, it usually constitutes an indication for hospital admission so that appropriate neurological and psychological investigations can be carried out with a sober patient. The sad fact is that most of the possibly relevant brain conditions are going to prove more diagnosable than treatable, but even so an accurate diagnostic formulation is the necessary basis for working out what is best to be done. If, for instance, an individual with alcohol dependence is severely brain damaged, the only kind and safe policy may be to propose long-term hospital care, or care in a supportive residential community. If there is milder damage, the patient will be able to keep going outside an institution, but brain damage can adversely affect the course of alcohol problems, and relapse and further troubles are probably to be expected. The continuing treatment policy must be set up so as to be able to meet these sorts of eventuality, and to be designed to support the family in what may well be a difficult situation. The emphasis may sometimes have to be on rather directive intervention, such as ensuring that money is properly handled or that the local publicans will not serve drinks. But even here there is no cause for absolute pessimism, for sometimes a patient with brain damage will be able to stop drinking, the progression of such damage will be arrested and the patient's behaviour will improve. Treatment implications are discussed in Chapter 14.

Psychiatric disorder: the general implications

The account that has been given in this chapter of the many types of psychiatric disorder which can be associated with excessive drinking, and of the nature of those possible relationships, must not be interpreted as meaning that only the psychiatrist can treat the problem drinker. Neither does the fact that psychiatric treatment or admission to a psychiatric hospital may be indicated for some of these patients mean that the treatment of alcohol problems is a psychiatric preserve. However, what must be evident is that psychiatry may quite often have a part to play, and that a working liaison with psychiatric services should be available to anyone helping with drinking problems. An awareness of this psychiatric dimension must, moreover, be important, whatever the therapist's professional discipline.

References

American Psychiatric Association (1994) *Diagnostic and Statistical Manual of Mental Disorders*, Fourth Edition. Washington DC: American Psychiatric Association.

American Psychiatric Association (2000) *Diagnostic and Statistical Manual of Mental Disorders*, Fourth Edition, Text revision. Washington DC: American Psychiatric Association.

Brady J (2006) The association between alcohol misuse and suicidal behaviour. *Alcohol and Alcoholism* **41**, 473–478.

Breslau N, Chilcoat H D, Kessley R C, Davis G C (1999) Previous exposure to trauma: results from the Detroit Area Survey of Trauma. *American Journal of Psychiatry* **156**, 902–907.

Chick J (1989) Delirium tremens. *British Medical Journal* **298**, 3–4.

Coid J (1979) 'Mania a potu': a critical review of pathological intoxication. *Psychological Medicine* **9**, 709–719.

Cottler L B, Compton W M, Magger D, Spitznagel E L, Janca A (1992) Post-traumatic stress disorder among substance users from the general population. *American Journal of Psychiatry* **149**, 664–670.

Duke P, Pantelis C, Barnes T R E (1994) South Westminster Schizophrenia Survey. Alcohol use and its relationship to symptoms, tardive dyskinesia and illness onset. *British Journal of Psychiatry* **164**, 630–636.

Farrell M, Howes S, Bebbington P, et al. (2003) Nicotine, alcohol and drug dependence, and psychiatry morbidity – results of a national household survey. *International Reviews in Psychiatry* **15**, 50–56.

Fazel S, Långström N, Hjern A, Grann M, Lichtenstein P (2009) Schizophrenia, substance abuse and violent crime. *Journal of the American Medical Association* **301**, 2016–2023.

Ferguson D M, Boden J M, Horwood J (2009) Tests of causal links between alcohol abuse or dependence and major depression. *Archives of General Psychiatry* **66**, 260–266.

Fombonne E (1998) Suicidal behaviours in vulnerable adolescents. *British Journal of Psychiatry* **173**, 154–159.

Foster J (2001) Dying for a drink. *British Medical Journal* **323**, 817–818.

Glass I (1989a) Alcoholic hallucinosis: a psychiatric enigma – I. The development of an idea. *British Journal of Addiction* **84**, 29–41.

Glass I (1989b) Alcoholic hallucinosis: a psychiatric enigma – 2. Follow-up studies. *British Journal of Addiction* **84**, 151–164.

Goldbloom D S (1993) Alcohol misuse and eating disorders: aspects of an association. *Alcohol and Alcoholism* **28**, 375–381.

Goodwin D W, Crane B J, Guze S B (1969a) Phenomenological aspects of the alcoholic 'blackout'. *British Journal of Psychiatry* **115**, 1033–1038.

Goodwin D W, Crane B J, Guze S B (1969b) Alcoholic 'blackouts': a review and clinical study of 100 alcoholics. *American Journal of Psychiatry* **126**, 191–198.

Grant B F, Stinson F S, Dawson D A, et al. (2004) Prevalence and co-occurrence of substance use disorders and independent mood and anxiety disorders: results from the National Epidemiologic Survey on Alcohol and Related Conditions. *Archives of General Psychiatry* **61**, 807–816.

Helzer J E, Pryzbeck T R (1988) The co-occurrence of alcoholism with other psychiatric disorders in the general population and its impact on treatment. *Journal of Studies on Alcohol* **49**, 219–224.

Inskip H M, Harris E C, Barraclough B (1998) Lifetime risk of suicide for affective disorder, alcoholism and schizophrenia. *British Journal of Psychiatry* **172**, 35–37.

Jenkins R (2007) Substance use and suicidal behaviour. *Psychiatry* **6**, 19–22.

Johnston A L, Thevos A K, Randall C L, Anton R F (1991) Increased severity of alcohol withdrawal in in-patient alcoholics with a co-existing anxiety diagnosis. *British Journal of Addiction* **86**, 719–725.

Kessler R C, McGonagle K A, Zhad S, et al. (1994) Lifetime and 12-month prevalence of DSM-III psychiatric disorders in the United States: results from the National Comorbidity Survey. *Archives of General Psychiatry* **51**, 8–19.

Kessler R C, Crum R M, Warner L A (1997) Lifetime co-occurrence of DSM-III-R alcohol abuse and dependence with other psychiatric disorders in the National Comorbidity Study. *Archives of General Psychiatry* **54**, 313–321.

Khantzian E J (1990) Self regulation and self medication factors in alcoholism and addictions: similarities and differences. In *Recent Developments in Alcoholism*, Vol. 8, M Galanter (ed.). New York: Plenum Press, pp. 255–269.

Lindquist P, Allebeck P (1989) Schizophrenia and assaultive behaviour: the role of alcohol and drug abuse. *Acta Psychiatrica Scandinavica* **82**, 191–195.

Lishman W A (1998) *Organic Psychiatry*, 3rd edn. Oxford: Blackwell Scientific Publications.

Marshall E J (2007) Medical management of anxiety and substance use disorders. In *Comorbid Anxiety and Substance Use Disorders*, S H Stewart, P J Conrod (eds). New York: Springer, pp. 221–238.

Menezes P, Johnson S, Thornicroft G, et al. (1996) Drug and alcohol problems among individuals with severe mental illness in South London. *British Journal of Psychiatry* **168**, 612–619.

Murphy G G, Wetzel R D (1990) The lifetime risk of suicide in alcoholism. *Archives of General Psychiatry* **47**, 383–392.

Ohlmeier M D, Peters K, Kordon A, et al. (2007) Nicotine and alcohol dependence in patients with comorbid attention-deficit/hyperactivity disorder (ADHD). *Alcohol and Alcoholism* **42**, 539–543.

O'Sullivan K, Whillans P, Daly M, et al. (1983) A comparison of alcoholics with and without co-existing affective disorder. *British Journal of Psychiatry* **143**, 133–138.

Pirkola S, Marttunen M J, Henriksson M M, et al. (1999) Alcohol-related problems among adolescent suicides in Finland. *Alcohol and Alcoholism* **34**, 320–329.

Pirkola S P, Suominen K, Isometsa E T (2004) Suicide in alcohol-dependent individuals: epidemiology and management. *CNS Drugs* **18**, 423–436.

Rossow I, Romelsjö A, Leifman H (1999) Alcohol abuse and suicidal behaviour in young and middle-aged men: differentiating between attempted and completed suicide. *Addiction* **94**, 1199–1207.

Roy A (1996) Aetiology of secondary depression in male alcoholics. *British Journal of Psychiatry* **169**, 753–757.

Roy A, DeJong J, Lamparski D, George T, Linnoila M (1991) Depression among alcoholics. *Archives of General Psychiatry* **48**, 428–432.

Sinha R, O'Malley S (2000) Alcohol and eating disorders: implications for alcohol treatment and health services research. *Alcoholism: Clinical and Experimental Research* **24**, 1312–1319.

Spencer T J, Biedernman J, Mick E (2007) Attention-deficit/hyperactivity disorder: diagnosis, lifespan, comorbidities and neurobiology. *Journal of Pediatric Psychology* **32**, 631–642.

Stepp S D, Trull T J, Sher K J (2005) Borderline personality features predict alcohol use problems. *Journal of Personality Disorders* **19**, 711–722

Tsuang J W, Irwin M R, Smith T L, Schuckit M A (1994) Characteristics of men with alcoholic hallucinosis. *Addiction* **89**, 73–78.

Vassilas C A, Morgan H G (1997) Suicide in Avon. Life stress, alcohol misuse and use of services. *British Journal of Psychiatry* **170**, 453–455.

Weaver T, Rutter D, Madden P, et al. (2001) Results of a screening survey for co-morbid substance misuse amongst patients in treatment for psychotic disorders: prevalence and service needs in an inner London borough. *Social Psychiatry and Psychiatric Epidemiology* **36**, 399–406.

World Health Organization (1992) *The ICD-10 Classification of Mental and Behavioural Disorders.* Geneva: World Health Organization.

Background to understanding

Alcohol and other drug problems

Alcohol is often used with other drugs, ranging from simple combinations, such as alcohol and nicotine at one end of the spectrum, to multiple combinations at the other end. Drugs may be used concurrently with alcohol or as a substitute for it. In the clinical situation, one often sees alcohol dependent patients who report that they have been abstinent from alcohol for some considerable time, but this 'abstinence' has only been achieved by substituting with another drug such as benzodiazepines or cannabis, or both. The patterns of relationship that can exist between the uses of different types of drugs are myriad, and the following case extract illustrates one variation on this theme.

> The patient was a successful and wealthy entrepreneur aged 35. His working day was lived at a great pitch of tension, and every evening he would go out to restaurants and nightclubs and get through a lot of alcohol. He would on average drink a couple of bottles of wine and up to six double vodkas before becoming, in his terms, 'pretty incoherent'. He was beginning to feel 'dreadful, sick, sweaty' on most mornings, and would often be unable to remember how he had reached his bed. Cocaine then began to be available in his social circle and before long he discovered that this drug appeared to provide an antidote to some of the unwanted effects of alcohol. For instance, if he snorted (sniffed) cocaine a few times during the evening, 'it lifted me up, I could go on drinking, it stopped me passing-out with the alcohol'. He also found that a snort or two of cocaine helped to alleviate the unpleasant early-morning symptoms caused by the previous night's drinking. Within a few months he progressed from snorting to free-basing (inhaling) cocaine, and his cocaine use rapidly and disastrously went out of control. His problem came to attention when a club was raided and he was arrested for possession of cocaine. Seen by a doctor at the request of the defence solicitor this man said: 'OK, I'm addicted to cocaine but let's not keep on about the alcohol'.

What this patient's history illustrates is that another drug often lies behind the immediately presenting drug. It would be unprofitable in such circumstances to debate whether alcohol or cocaine was the 'real' problem. This man's problem was his tendency to misuse substances. Both the alcohol and cocaine aspects of his history have to be taken seriously, but what the patient himself and those who are seeking to help him need to realize is that dependence can often resemble the many headed Hydra of mythology: one head can be lopped off and two grow in its place. Unless with such a patient there is a focus on the central issue of his tendency to develop dependence on substances, the story will all too probably progress in terms of a further switching or mixing of different substances – in terms perhaps of tranquillizers or sleeping tablets then being added to alcohol.

This chapter will describe some of the more frequently encountered connections between alcohol and other drug use. It will also consider the general implications both for prevention and for clinical practice that stem from the realization that alcohol and other drug problems

Table 7.1. Drug problems and alcohol problems: key issues.

- Polydrug use is common
- Alcohol is almost always implicated in polydrug use
- Other drugs are not always implicated in alcohol misuse
- Polydrug use is associated with significant physical and psychosocial morbidity
- Clinicians and treatment services need the skills to meet mixed problems

potentially constitute one continuous domain rather than two distinct problem areas. The main points are summarized in Table 7.1.

Polydrug use

Polydrug use has become increasingly prevalent over recent decades. It occurs in the general population and is not confined to individuals heavily involved in the 'drug scene' or in contact with treatment services. Many factors are implicated in the initiation and perpetuation of drug use in people whose problem is primarily one of alcohol, and these can be considered under general headings such as psychological, socio-economic, pharmacological and genetic–environmental. Such factors do not occur in isolation but are often multiple and interrelated.

Polydrug use has been defined by the World Health Organization as the consumption, by an individual, of more than one psychoactive drug or drug class at the same time (concurrent use) or in succession (sequential use) (World Health Organization, 1994). Research has focused on concurrent polydrug use (CPU), that is, the use of multiple drugs over a given time period such as 1 month or 1 year. However, simultaneous polydrug use (SPU), the use of alcohol and other drugs in combination or on the same day, is a major problem in a number of drinking populations, including those with alcohol use disorders (AUDs), adolescents, rave and nightclub attendees and users of other drugs (Barrett, Darredeau & Pihl, 2006; Grant & Harford, 1990; Martin et al., 1996).

Polydrug use serves a number of purposes (Leri, Bruneau & Stewart, 2003). It can enhance the effect of a drug or drugs, counteract or attenuate negative effects or substitute for another drug when it is not available. For instance, alcohol can enhance the effects of stimulants such as cocaine and amphetamines, and also the effects of benzodiazepines and volatile solvents. Alcohol can also reduce the jittery feelings associated with stimulant use and moderate the symptoms of the withdrawal phase or 'crash'. A heroin user may substitute with alcohol, cannabis or benzodiazepines, either alone or in combination, to tide them over until heroin is again available.

Combinations and patterns of polydrug use vary according to the characteristics of users, the availability of drugs, peer influence and fashion, the context of drug use and prescribing practices (European Monitoring Centre for Drugs and Drug Addiction, 2009). Particular combinations of drugs are not taken in a haphazard fashion. It is likely that the order in which they are taken and the relative doses used are related to the desired effects. When alcohol is used in a polydrug context, there is a tendency for it to be taken first, before the other drugs. It may increase the probability that other drugs will be used and is likely to have effects on the pharmacokinetic properties of other drugs, e.g. augmenting plasma concentrations (Barrett, Darredeau & Pihl, 2006).

Polydrug use is associated with significant medical, neuropsychological and psychosocial complications, and thus has a significant impact on public health. It is associated with increased risk-taking behaviours and with outcomes ranging from road traffic accidents to contracting HIV/AIDS. Most drug-related attendances at Accident and Emergency Departments (Emergency Rooms) involve polydrug use, in particular the combination of alcohol and prescription drugs (McCabe, Cranford & Boyd, 2006). Polydrug users are more likely to have psychiatric co-morbidity (Regier et al., 1990) (see Chapter 6). The interaction of alcohol with drugs such as opioids, cocaine, benzodiazepines and ecstasy (MDMA) is potentially a dangerous one, with death from an accidental overdose being a real risk.

Who is at risk of polydrug use and what drugs are used in combination with alcohol?

There are two main groups of polydrug users: younger non-dependent recreational users, and older alcohol and drug-dependent users.

Adolescents

The initiation of substance use in adolescents is largely determined by environmental factors such as availability, price, the social situation, peer group usage and fashion (Han, McGue & Iacono, 1999). Adolescents are prone to risk-taking and experimenting behaviour. In moderation, this is part of healthy development. Indeed, adolescents who experiment a little are better adjusted as adults than are those who abstain completely. However, adolescent substance use is a powerful predictor of substance use disorders in adulthood (Grant & Dawson, 1997), and those with psychological traits such as impulsivity, alienation and distress may be more vulnerable. Rates of cigarette smoking and alcohol and illicit drug use increase in the teenage years. Young people using one or more of these substances, especially alcohol, are more likely to use the other substances subsequently. Teenagers with heavier drinking and smoking patterns are at greater risk of later drug use and dependence. Family 'moral–religious' influences may help to attenuate a genetic predisposition to substance use. Drug fashions come and go, but alcohol is almost always implicated in the shifting picture of multiple substance use.

Recreational polydrug use is common in younger people in dance-club settings (the 'clubbing scene') and the drugs used here are typically alcohol, cannabis and stimulants (European Monitoring Centre for Drugs and Drug Addiction, 2009). One European study of drug use in nightclubs found that the combination of cannabis and alcohol was the most common, followed by alcohol and ecstasy, and cannabis and ecstasy (Calafat et al., 1999). Nicotine is an almost inevitable part of the mix.

Many people entering treatment for alcohol problems typically use one or more other drugs at the same time as alcohol. The most common two-drug combinations are alcohol with cocaine, cannabis, opiates and sedatives (Kedia, Sell & Relyea, 2007; Martin et al., 1996; Staines et al., 2001; Substance Abuse and Mental Health Services Administration, 2002). As previously mentioned, alcohol/drug combinations are not used in a random way, but rather in a consistent temporal pattern suggesting that particular effects are being sought, such as a heightened experience of subjective intoxication on the one hand or the modulation of withdrawal symptoms on the other.

Other drugs used in combination with alcohol include over-the-counter (OTC) medicines, which include analgesics such as paracetamol (acetaminophen) and non-steroidal anti-inflammatory drugs (NSAIDs) such as ibuprofen. Antidepressants are also used, as is methadone and certain cough mixtures (codeine linctus). Prescription drugs are increasingly available via the Internet and are typically used without prescription, in a manner not intended by the prescribing doctor: this is termed non-medical use of prescription drugs (NMUPD). Problem or dependent drinkers often use OTC or prescribed drugs to obtain relief from chronic conditions such as insomnia, pain and perceived stress. Benzodiazepines or the 'Z' drugs (zopiclone; zolpidem) may help with insomnia in the short term, but cross-tolerance means that there is a risk of dependence. Analgesics (pain-killers) may help to relieve head-ache, musculo-skeletal pain or pain associated with pancreatitis or gout but, after a time, simple aspirin and paracetamol (acetaminophen) may not afford adequate pain relief so the drinker progresses to stronger analgesics, such as NSAIDs, codeine or di-hydrocodeine. High doses of analgesics can lead to both liver and renal problems, so the clinician should try to intervene before their patient, who may already have a compromised liver, ends up in inten-sive care with liver and renal failure.

Drinkers with chronic pancreatitis typically experience severe incapacitating pain and often seek opiate analgesia from their family doctor or hospital specialist. If these drinkers are economical with the truth, their doctor may be unaware that they are obtaining prescriptions for opiates from a variety of sources. There is a real risk that when individuals with chronic pancreatitis or other chronic pain syndromes finally manage to become abstinent, they find that they are dependent on opiates.

Many drinkers complain of non-specific pain in their joints, arms and legs. It is important to take a history as the pain may have its origin in injuries sustained in road traffic or other accidents, a fight or a fall or following an alcohol withdrawal seizure. They may have little memory of the episode, relating, for instance, how 'I woke up in intensive care with a mangled shoulder/leg/arm'. At this point they usually pull up a shirt sleeve or a trouser leg to show the injury. The perceived pain from such injuries can be compounded by long periods of self-neglect, poor diet and lack of exercise, and also alcohol-induced myopathy.

Perceived stress is another reason why drinkers use OTC and other drugs. Healthcare professionals are particularly at risk here because of their privileged access to drugs, either on the hospital ward or in the clinic.

Specific combinations

Alcohol and nicotine

About 80% of alcohol dependent men and women smoke regularly (Hughes, 1996) and there may be a common genetic vulnerability (Daeppen et al., 2000). Alcohol dependent individ-uals are often heavy smokers, have difficulty quitting smoking, and when they stop drinking may compensate by an even heavier use of cigarettes (Hays et al., 1999). Nicotine depend-ence is associated with a greater severity of alcohol dependence and alcohol-related problems. 'Alcoholics' who smoke have high rates of tobacco-related disease, and they are more likely to die from tobacco-related disease than from their alcohol dependence. Both alcohol and nicotine dependence are associated with mood disorders.

Cigarette use is strongly associated with alcohol and other drug use in adolescence. Adoles-cents who smoke and drink have an increased risk of having difficulties at school, delinquency and use of other drugs (Myers & Kelly, 2006). Young people who are treated for alcohol and other drug use are typically heavy smokers, and smoking tends to persist after treatment.

Several psychological and neuropharmacological models have been proposed to explain the association between AUDs and cigarette smoking. The overlap between the two substances suggests that there are many shared cues. Theoretically, then, it might be more difficult to stop using either alcohol or nicotine than to quit both substances at the same time. Despite the fact that alcohol and nicotine are commonly used together, the feasibility of quitting smoking at the same time as drinking has largely been unexplored. Nevertheless, the implications for counselling problem drinkers to quit smoking are persuasive. Alcohol dependent individuals are open to advice on smoking (Harris et al., 2000). Counselling is safe even in the early stages of recovery, and it may have a positive effect on drinking outcomes at 6-month and 12-month follow-up (Martin et al., 1997). Smoking cessation programmes in residential alcohol treatment units have shown good outcomes for nicotine abstinence. Many in-patient units are now smoke-free and nicotine replacement therapy (NRT) can be offered during the course of the medically assisted withdrawal programme and thereafter.

Bupropion, an atypical antidepressant recently licensed in the USA as an aid for smoking cessation, has been shown to be effective in a sample of smokers with a former history of major depression and alcoholism (Hayford et al., 1999). Varenicline, another drug recently approved as a smoking cessation medication, may also have the potential to help people with alcohol dependence (Steensland et al., 2007) .

Alcohol and cocaine

The combination of alcohol and cocaine is an increasingly familiar pattern of polydrug use. Alcohol is typically used during a cocaine binge in order to prolong the euphoriant effects of cocaine, to diminish the unpleasant experiences associated with cocaine use, such as agitation and paranoia, and to ameliorate the dysphoria associated with acute abstinence from cocaine (the 'crash'). When the two drugs are used simultaneously, alcohol is used in greater quantities than when it is used alone (Barrett, Darredeau & Pihl, 2006). Indeed, cocaine appears to attenuate the intoxicating effect of alcohol, thus allowing drinkers to tolerate considerable quantities of alcohol with becoming obviously intoxicated. The Friday night drinking session can be extended over a weekend, and only comes to an end on Sunday night, as the working week looms nearer. Once regular cocaine and alcohol use is established, it may be difficult to give up one substance without giving up the other, as alcohol can become a powerful conditioned cue for cocaine. Cocaethylene, a pharmacologically active metabolite, formed when cocaine and alcohol are taken together, enhances and extends cocaine-induced euphoria.

For many people treatment of the cocaine problem may lead to an improvement in the alcohol problem. However, the presence of alcohol problems and dependence in treated cocaine users is associated with more severe dependence, poorer retention in treatment and a poorer outcome compared with either disorder alone (Brady et al., 1995; Carroll et al., 1993; Carroll, Rounsaville & Bryant, 1993). Treatment with disulfiram for 12 weeks was associated with better treatment retention and abstinence, particularly when combined with 'active' out-patient psychotherapy (cognitive behavioural coping skills and therapy) and 12-step facilitation (TSF) (Carroll et al., 1998). This disulfiram treatment effect persisted at 1-year follow-up (Carroll et al., 2000).

Alcohol and cannabis

Simultaneous use of alcohol and cannabis is common in adolescents, and is of concern as it may lead to higher absorption rates of delta-tetrahydrocannabinol (THC), have a detrimental effect on healthy brain development and possibly predispose to more severe cannabis- or alcohol dependence symptoms (Smuker Barnwell & Earleywine, 2006). Simultaneous use can sometimes be unpleasant, with individuals experiencing nausea, vomiting, dizziness and sweating. This most likely occurs because alcohol speeds up the absorption of THC, leading to a stronger cannabis effect. Alcohol and cannabis are often used when 'coming down' from ecstasy.

Alcohol and opioids

Here is a typical story of early heavy drinking in a setting of multiple substance use. This youthful pattern of mixed use may lead to a dominant use of heroin, with recovery from heroin dependence being followed a few years later by a plunge into alcohol.

> A 34-year-old unemployed man was referred for assessment of his heavy drinking and depression. He had experienced extreme emotional deprivation in childhood and had been in care. At 14 he began to drink beer and to smoke cannabis 'for comfort'. He soon began to use amphetamines and diazepam, and his daily alcohol consumption gradually increased to 3–4 cans of strong lager. He first smoked heroin in his early 20s and very soon switched to intravenous use, sharing needles. He also snorted cocaine on a regular basis, injecting it on occasion. Other drugs use included LSD intermittently, 'mushrooms' and ecstasy. When he was 30 he entered a residential rehabilitation unit and gave up all illicit drug use. However, his alcohol consumption escalated and 4 years later, at the time of referral, his drinking was out of control. He was also experiencing a marked craving for heroin and cocaine and was worried that he would begin to use them again.

Problematic use of alcohol is a common problem in opioid users. Alcohol consumption typically precedes first use of heroin in the early career of heroin addicts, but levels of alcohol use tend to drop off when regular opioid use is established. However, the impact of treatment of opioid dependence on alcohol use is uncertain, some studies finding that rates of alcohol misuse remain constant or decline and others reporting that treatment entry is associated with increased alcohol use. The theme that emerges from these studies is that alcohol problems frequently predate opioid use, and when one dependence has developed, a variety of drugs will be misused.

Two general patterns of drinking have been recognized in heroin-dependent subjects during and following treatment: *concurrent* use while on a methadone programme; and use of alcohol as *a substitute for* opioids. Benzodiazepines and stimulants are usually part of the mix. Methadone is known to block the intoxicating effect of opioids and some addicts respond by looking for another intoxicating substance. Between a quarter and a half of patients in methadone maintenance programmes drink in a hazardous or harmful manner (Otomanelli, 1999). Yet numerous studies also report that methadone maintenance often produces reductions in drinking relative to baseline levels.

Alcohol problems may substitute for opioids when heroin users attempt to detoxify on their own, or in a treatment programme or during prolonged periods of abstinence. A seemingly promising recovery from a drug problem is then brought down by alcohol. Treated opioid addicts who go on to develop alcohol problems are more likely to have had disruptive childhoods, more legal problems and polydrug use, more problems with social functioning and higher rates of psychiatric disorders than 'non-alcoholic addicts'.

Alcohol and benzodiazepines

Benzodiazepine misuse is associated with illicit drug use, particularly opiates. It occurs much less frequently in individuals with alcohol problems and does not appear to increase the risk of alcohol misuse or relapse.

Benzodiazepines were introduced to clinical practice in 1960 and soon became widely used in the treatment of anxiety and insomnia. They are also accepted as the treatment of choice for alcohol withdrawal symptoms. A wide variety of benzodiazepines have been marketed, and Table 7.2 lists the commoner substances, giving both their official and trade names. In many countries, including the UK, prescriptions for benzodiazepines as anxiolytics have fallen over the past two decades whereas prescriptions for their use as hypnotics are little changed.

Drugs within the benzodiazepine group have many properties in common. Important differences exist, however, in relation to the duration of action either of the drug itself or of its active metabolite. Lorazepam, oxazepam and temazepam are all relatively short acting; chlordiazepoxide and diazepam are long acting, while the other substances listed in Table 7.2 produce an action of intermediate duration.

Long-term, continuous use of benzodiazepines carries a risk of dependence. This is most evident for high doses, but dependence can develop in patients who take therapeutic doses for as little as 6 weeks. The relatively short-acting compounds may have a greater dependence potential than the long-acting compounds. The proportion of patients taking therapeutic doses of benzodiazepines at risk of developing dependence is not known. Neither is there enough information other than in broad terms to identify the level of exposure (dose and duration) associated with an increased risk of dependence. New prescriptions of benzodiazepines should be restricted to approximately 2 weeks, and certainly no longer than 4 weeks.

Patients with alcohol problems should not generally be given benzodiazepines, except for treatment of acute alcohol withdrawal, and then only on a careful and time-limited basis. Patients with a concurrent anxiety disorder should be referred for cognitive behavioural therapy (CBT) (see Chapter 6). A selective serotonin reuptake inhibitor (SSRI) or other antidepressant can also be prescribed. The use of benzodiazepines as a hypnotic in alcohol dependent individuals should be avoided.

Dependence is not the only potential problem encountered with benzodiazepine use. Ataxia, falls, confusion, depression and irritability are all significant effects of long-acting compounds, with the elderly being at particular risk. Short-acting benzodiazepines at high doses are associated with amnesia. Benzodiazepines and alcohol are important factors in fatal overdose.

Table 7.2. Some common benzodiazepines.

Non-proprietary name	Proprietary name	Active metabolites	Approximate duration of action	Approximate equivalent dose (mg)
Diazepam	Valium	Several	2–4 days	5
Chlordiazepoxide	Librium	Several	2–4 days	15
Nitrazepam	Mogadon	None	12–24 hours	5
Clonazepam	Rivotril	Several	1–2 days	0.5
Lorazepam	Ativan	None	8–12 hours	0.5
Temazepam	Normison	None	8 hours	10
Oxazepam	Oxanid	None	8–12 hours	15

Sources: British National Formulary (2010); Brunton, Lazo Parker (2006).

Alcohol and non-medical use of prescription drugs (NMUPD)

Research in the USA has shown that non-medical use of prescription opioids, stimulants, tranquillizers and sedatives is more prevalent among individuals with AUDs (McCabe, Cranford & Boyd, 2006). Most of this polydrug use is 'simultaneous use'. Young adults (18–24 years), particularly those with a history of binge drinking or alcohol dependence, showed higher prevalence rates of past-year NMUPD than adults over 25 years of age. Clinicians should ensure that when young people with alcohol problems present for treatment, a thorough drug history is taken, and they should be assessed for NMUPD. Further work is needed to understand the associated individual and situational risk factors.

'A web of dependence'

Polydrug use raises fundamental questions about the nature of dependence (Gossop, 2001; West, 2001). Should dependence be viewed as a condition that spans more than one substance, rather than multiple substance-specific conditions residing in the same person (West, 2001)? This has profound implications for treatment. For instance, should we routinely be trying to help alcohol dependent individuals in recovery to quit smoking too?

Alcohol and other drugs as one domain: the practical implications

Several of the most immediate implications of this perspective have already been discussed in earlier sections of this chapter. At this point it may, however, be useful to bring together the core implications, and in Table 7.3 we draw attention to some matters of special clinical relevance.

Implications for training and service organization

Anyone taking professional responsibility for treatment of alcohol problems should recognize that polydrug use is pervasive and possess a good working knowledge of drug problems (and vice versa). There may be a continuing place for specialized drug or specialized alcohol treatment services, but the intensity of specialization must not be of such a degree as to be out of tune with clinical realities. For many problem drinkers who enter treatment, their medical and psychosocial co-morbidity cannot be understood on the basis of their alcohol consumption/dependence alone. Clinical assessment must take into account the complexities of any polydrug use and the treatment intervention tailored accordingly. Many of these individuals also have anxiety, depression, post-traumatic stress disorder (PTSD) and other psychiatric disorders, and may present, in the first instance, to general psychiatric services. Psychiatric services should also be able to assess individuals with polydrug use and factor this into their treatment programmes. Working with polydrug users requires cross-discipline liaison and collaboration. Complex patients with complex problems do not always respect specialist

Table 7.3. Tips for therapists.

- Have a good working knowledge of alcohol and drugs
- Always take a complete alcohol and drug history
- Update history regularly
- Organize spot urinary drug screens where indicated

demarcations. Inadequate training may mean that individuals with combined drug and alcohol problems, particularly those who also have psychiatric co-morbidity, find it difficult to obtain treatment, are incompletely evaluated and treated, and effectively abandoned, because they don't meet rigid criteria for treatment services. However, this is a 'cop-out' for services. Treatment services wishing to face the challenge of polydrug use successfully must develop the capacity to integrate alcohol, drug and psychiatric treatment, in order to meet the needs of these complex individuals.

A prime responsibility for prevention

Therapists who treat patients with drinking problems have a special responsibility not to do their patients damage by careless prescription of sedatives and minor tranquillizers. It is likewise important that anyone treating opioid-dependent patients should offer counselling on the use of alcohol and the dangers of alcohol dependence. At the very least, it is important to provide alcohol and drug users information on the effects of specific drugs and combinations of drugs and, in particular, how to manage emergencies (European Monitoring Centre for Drugs and Drug Addiction, 2009).

Diagnosis and screening

With a patient whose presenting problem is with one type of substance, an open eye should be kept on the possible existence of problems with other drugs. It is, for instance, less than useful to concentrate exclusively on a patient's drinking while failing to detect the fact that massive quantities of benzodiazepines or cannabis are being consumed.

A complete alcohol and drug history should be obtained. This means charting as necessary the evolution of use and dependence for every drug taken, as well as for alcohol. In this way the sequence and pattern of alcohol and drug use can be mapped out; for example, solvents as a child, alcohol and later amphetamines in the teenage years, cocaine and heroin as an adult. A history of combinations of drugs used should be taken (alcohol and cannabis; alcohol and cigarettes; alcohol and cocaine and so on). It will be helpful to work out whether the scale of drug(s) used amounts to dependence or not. Polydrug users who are dependent on one or two drugs may use other drugs in a problematical but non-dependent way. They are usually very clear in their minds as to which drugs are currently posing the greatest problems and, when asked, are able to rank them in a hierarchical fashion. Indeed, they are the 'experts' on their own drug use, and sensitive clinical engagement will use their insights to map out a workable treatment plan.

Many clients presenting to alcohol services may have a past history of intravenous drug use and will need assessment of risk behaviour and counselling with respect to testing for hepatitis B and C and HIV status. Routine urine testing should be more widely employed. The history should be updated at regular intervals.

Treatment goals

Polydrug use is more difficult to treat than an uncomplicated AUD. Staff should be trained to deal with polydrug users and their problems, and services should focus on behaviour rather than on substances. Although there is little research on what treatments are effective, therapists working within treatment programmes that take the concept of chemical dependence as a central tenet would probably advise a patient who has encountered difficulties, with either alcohol or other drugs, to avoid all mood-altering chemicals for ever after. For many patients this is the best advice, although it is unlikely to be acceptable for all (some former heroin addicts may, for instance, later use alcohol moderately and safely). The insistence that patients should be made aware of the dangers of crossing over from one substance to another is very generally appropriate. It should also be recognized that some patients may not want to tackle the totality of their polydrug use. For those individuals, it is important to set out the risks and to continue to work with them so that they are in the best position to take responsibility for their drug use, to the point where they may agree ultimately to come off everything.

A constant two-way vigilance

When seeing a patient or client for the first time, when planning and carrying through a treatment programme and when assessing success, the patient and therapist should be thinking in terms of drugs and alcohol and not just alcohol or just drugs.

References

Barrett S P, Darredeau C, Pihl R O (2006) Patterns of simultaneous polysubstance use in drug using university students. *Human Psychopharmacology: Clinical and Experimental* 21, 255–263.

Brady K T, Sonne E, Randall C L, Adinoff B, Malcolm R (1995) Features of cocaine dependence with concurrent alcohol use. *Drug and Alcohol Dependence* 39, 69–71.

Brunton L L, Lazo J, Parker K L (eds) (2006) *Goodman and Gilman's: The Pharmacological Basis of Therapeutics*, 11th edn. New York: McGraw Hill.

Calafat A, Bohrn K, Juan M, et al. (1999) *Night Life in Europe and Recreative Drug Use*. Valencia: IREFREA and the European Commission.

Carroll K M, Power M-E D, Bryant K, Rounsaville B (1993) One-year follow-up status of treatment-seeking cocaine abusers. *Journal of Nervous and Mental Disease* 181, 71–79.

Carroll K M, Rounsaville B J, Bryant K J (1993) Alcoholism in treatment seeking cocaine abusers: clinical and prognostic significance. *Journal of Studies on Alcohol* 54, 199–208.

Carroll K M, Nich C, Ball S A, McCance E, Rounsaville B J (1998) Treatment of cocaine and alcohol dependence with psychotherapy and disulfiram. *Addiction* 93, 713–728.

Carroll K M, Nich C, Ball S A, et al. (2000) One-year follow-up of disulfiram and psychotherapy for cocaine-alcohol users:

sustained effects of treatment. *Addiction* 95, 1335–1349.

Daeppen J-B, Smith T L, Danko G P, et al. (2000) Clinical correlates of cigarette smoking and nicotine dependence in alcohol dependent men and women. *Alcohol and Alcoholism* 35, 171–175.

European Monitoring Centre for Drugs and Drug Addiction (2009) *Polydrug Use: Patterns and Responses*. Luxembourg: Publications Office of the European Union, pp. 1–29.

Gossop M (2001) A web of dependence. *Addiction* 96, 677–678.

Grant B, Dawson D (1997) Age at onset of alcohol use and its association with DSM-IV alcohol abuse and dependence: results from the National Longitudinal Alcohol Epidemiologic Survey. *Journal of Substance Abuse* 9, 103–110.

Grant B, Harford T (1990) Concurrent and simultaneous use of alcohol with sedatives and tranquillisers. Results of a national study. *Journal of Substance Abuse* 2, 1–4.

Han C, McGue M K, Iacono W G (1999) Lifetime tobacco, alcohol and other substance use in adolescent Minnesota twins: univariate and multivariate behavioural genetic analyses. *Addiction* 94, 981–993.

Harris J, Best D, Man L-H, et al. (2000) Change in cigarette smoking among alcohol and drug misusers during in-patient detoxification. *Addiction Biology* 5, 443–450.

Hayford, K E, Patten C A, Rummans T A, et al. (1999) Efficacy of bupropion for smoking cessation in smokers with a former history of major depression or alcoholism. *British Journal of Psychiatry* **174**, 173–178.

Hays J T, Schroeder D R, Offord K P, et al. (1999) Response to nicotine dependence treatment in smokers with current and past alcohol problems. *Annals of Behavioural Medicine* **21**, 244–250.

Hughes J R (1996) Treating smokers with current or past alcohol dependence. *American Journal of Health Behaviour* **20**, 286–290.

Leri F, Bruneau J, Stewart J (2003) Understanding polydrug use: review of heroin and cocaine co-use. *Addiction* **98**, 7–22.

Kedia S, Sell M A, Relyea G (2007) Mono- versus polydrug abuse patterns among publicly funded clients. *Substance Abuse Treatment, Prevention and Policy* **2**, 33. http://substanceabusepolicy.com/content/2/1/33.

McCabe S E, Cranford J A, Boyd C J (2006) The relationship between past-year drinking behaviours and non-medical use of prescription drugs: prevalence of co-occurrence in a national sample. *Drug and Alcohol Dependence* **84**, 281–288.

Martin C S, Clifford P R, Maisto S A, et al. (1996) Polydrug use in an inpatient treatment sample of problem drinkers. *Alcoholism: Clinical and Experimental Research* **20**, 413–417.

Martin J E, Calfas K J, Patten C C A, et al. (1997) Prospective evaluation of three smoking interventions in 205 recovering alcoholics: one-year results of project SCRAP-Tobacco. *Journal of Consulting and Clinical Psychology* **65**, 190–194.

Myers M G, Kelly J F (2006) Cigarette smoking among adolescents with alcohol and other drug use problems. *Alcohol Research and Health* **29**, 221–227.

Otomanelli G (1999) Methadone patients and alcohol abuse (review). *Journal of Substance Abuse Treatment* **16**, 113–121.

Regier D A, Farmer M E, Rae D, et al. (1990) Comorbidity of mental disorders with alcohol and other drug use. *Journal of the American Medical Association* **264**, 2511–2518.

Smuker Barnwell S, Earleywine M (2006) Simultaneous alcohol and cannabis expectancies predict simultaneous use. *Substance Abuse Treatment, Prevention and Policy* **1**, 29.

Staines G L, Magura S, Foote J, Deluca A, Kosanke N (2001) Polysubstance use among alcoholics. *Journal of Addictive Disorders* **20**, 53–69.

Steensland P, Simms J A, Holgate J, Richards J, Bartlett S E (2007) Varenicline, an $\alpha_4\beta_2$ nicotinic acetylcholine receptor partial agonist, selectively decreases ethanol consumption and seeking. *Proceedings of the National Academy of Sciences of the United States of America* **104**, 12518–12523.

Substance Abuse and Mental Health Services Administration (SAMHSA) (2002) *The DASIS (Drug and Alcohol Services Information System) Report: Polydrug Admissions – 2002*. Rockville, MD: Office of Applied Studies.

West R (2001) Multiple substance dependence: implications for treatment of nicotine dependence. *Addiction* **96**, 775–776.

World Health Organization (1994) *Lexicon of Alcohol and Drug Terms*. Geneva: World Health Organization.

Background to understanding

Various presentations

This chapter describes a varied set of clinical presentations identified in Table 8.1. These pictures are selected arbitrarily from a much wider gallery, and anyone who practises in this field will soon themselves begin to identify additional headings. To keep a mental card index, which allows one to see patterns of presentation and use the last such case to illuminate understanding of the next, will add to the reward and interest of therapeutic work. The only proviso to be borne in mind is the latent danger of forcing people into pigeon-holes. Management of the next elderly patient will be helped by thinking through one's previous case experience with individuals in this age group, but each new patient is unique in some respects.

The young drinker

In many countries a common experience over recent years has been the increasingly frequent presentation of young people (including young women) with drinking problems. 'Young' may in extreme instances mean the early teens, but the particular focus of this discussion will be on patients in the late teens or early 20s. More significant than the exact boundaries of chronological age is the fact that these are people who in an important sense see themselves as *not adult,* and who have not yet made the social transition from adolescent to adult self-image. The therapist is encountering a person who is still finding a way through adolescent conflicts and who has not resolved fundamental questions about the balance between dependence on others and independence. For the anxiety, anger and despair which may be generated by these frustrations, alcohol can be a panacea. It temporarily relieves a painful confusion of feelings, provides at the same time a 'high' of optimism and excitement, while in a state of intoxication the aggressive feelings can be liberated and acted out, and with the natural energy and physicality of this age adding intensity to the chaos. Moreover, drinking can give companionship and the approbation of peers.

As for the pattern of alcohol use itself, in most instances the young person will not have had a drinking history of sufficient duration for established alcohol dependence. The picture is of repeated drinking to the point of intoxication, often with experience of amnesias. Other drugs are usually part of the mix (see Chapter 7) .

Possibilities for growth

There is a common perception that personality disorder is likely to be associated with a drinking problem of early onset, and a diagnosis of underlying personality disorder is readily pinned on the patient. But, paradoxically, the mutable nature of personality at this age can itself bear witness to the potential for growth. A uniformly pessimistic attitude towards the prognosis of the young drinker is therefore unjustified, even when their behaviour is flagrantly disturbed. Here is a brief case history of one such young person whose story typifies this kind of presentation.

Table 8.1. The range of clinical presentations.

- The younger person with a drinking problem
- The person who is drunk and violent
- A patient on a general hospital ward
- The pregnant drinker
- A combined problem with alcohol and drugs
- The patient with cognitive impairment
- A drinking problem in later life
- Cultural differences
- The family member making contact
- The very important patient
- When a child is at risk

A 22-year-old man was referred to a counselling centre by the court. He had been charged with assault after a pub fight, and he had also broken a few windows. There had been several suicide gestures. He had been working in a garage but had been sacked. His drinking involved his becoming explosively and obstreperously drunk whenever he had money in his pocket. He had been forced to leave his parental home because of his rowdy drunkenness at the age of 19, and his respectable parents did not want him back. Five years after being seen at the counselling centre he had a steady job in the Post Office and was happily married. He now drank occasionally and moderately. He looked back on his past as distant, and saw it in terms of: 'I was all messed up at that time'.

What needs to be emphasized is that while pessimism is often self-fulfilling, a treatment approach that responds to the needs for growth may catch a moment of possibility. There is no one recipe for treatment for the younger drinker, and the basic approach will have much in common with what is done to help the patient of any age. This young man discovered a capacity to talk about his problems and was helped by a counsellor who was able to arrange her schedule so that she had time to see him whenever he dropped in for an hour's talk – he needed to do a lot of talking. During the first 2 years he was a keen Alcoholics Anonymous attendee. He also benefited from a 6-month residence in a 'drug' hostel and from a set of friendships which developed from that stay. Later, he was lucky to meet the right partner. In essence, what these various relationships offered, each in their own way, was a series of experiments in facets of growing up.

If there are common ingredients in such stories of therapeutic success they lie in the qualities of the therapist – someone who is specially and evidently warm, who will be able to tolerate projection of unworked-out feelings towards parents, but who will not be manoeuvred into treating the patient as a child. There is also often a need to find a way of helping the young person pull out of a pattern of living (or pattern of drifting) which is a series of makeshifts rather than anything that offers either real demands or real rewards.

Special difficulties

Having taken as illustration a case with a happy outcome, it is also necessary to look at reasons why the story may on other occasions be turbulent or marked by nothing but defeat. One reason may be that the personal handicaps are already more fixed, a matter of psychological damage rather than of frustrated growth. There may be a history of genetic predisposition and early-onset antisocial behaviour. Family risk factors, such as physical and sexual abuse, family breakdown and parental substance use, may be present. Peer influence and the availability of alcohol and other drugs are also likely to be in the frame. A detailed assessment will include information on the above, together with a collateral history from parents, family members and school. If the history is not taken carefully the alcohol problem may obscure important underlying issues. The young man or woman who is profoundly anxious, restless and irritable, who cannot easily use or tolerate a relationship of any kind, who will not stay in a job and who is likely to move around the country is going to be difficult to help. Even so, it is worthwhile holding out the availability of friendship, with the modest expectation of working for small immediate gains and taking a very long-term view.

Another reason for special difficulty, grossly evident or only revealed by assessment, is when excessive drinking in someone of this age is symptomatic of learning difficulties. In this situation it is important to take a good history from the parents. Is there a history of birth trauma, meningitis, encephalitis or head injury? Have there been behavioural problems since birth or are they of more recent onset? Is there a history of school failure?

A further common diagnostic perplexity is the interpretation to be made when a client in this age group reports 'being depressed'. Most often this complaint is to be understood in terms of the general lability of mood which so often accompanies problems in development. It is a mistake to over-diagnose depressive illness or inappropriately to prescribe antidepressant drugs. On the other hand, there are cases where recurrent depressive illness may first declare itself at this age, and where this distress leads to use of alcohol as self-medication. Suicide and suicidal behaviour are closely linked with substance use and psychiatric disorders.

Yet another type of story is that of the young man or woman who is referred to an alcohol clinic because drinking has been seen as the exclusive problem. It then becomes apparent that one is dealing with a major psychiatric illness, the exact nature of which is perplexingly difficult to diagnose. The picture shifts perhaps from that of depression to a presentation that looks worryingly like schizophrenia. The excessive use of alcohol is no more than a confounding factor in a very complex disturbance.

Taking the problems of the young drinker very seriously

With these young patients there are a number of reasons for arguing with special force the general position that earlier rather than later intervention is to be preferred. They should be helped before dependence supervenes. The young drinker who is left to run deeper into trouble is in danger of becoming increasingly unemployable. It must also be remembered that it is particularly among young drinkers that mortality rates are elevated, often as a consequence of accident or violence. There are, therefore, good reasons for taking the young drinker very seriously.

It is often difficult to engage young people in therapy, so flexibility in setting up appointments and home visits, co-ordinated multi-agency intervention and other forms of outreach are essential components of the treatment package. Motivational, cognitive behavioural and family-based treatment approaches are often combined in multidimensional family therapy (MDFT) and multisystemic therapy (MST) (Tober, 2007). Pharmacotherapy should be used in the context of a comprehensive treatment plan (Dawes & Johnson, 2004; Marshall & Mirza, 2007) (see Chapter 14).

The patient who is drunk and violent

The general issue of the relation between drinking and violence is discussed elsewhere in this book (see Chapter 4). Every now and then a therapist will be faced by the worrying problem set by the patient who repeatedly turns up drunk and violent, and demanding to be seen. The safety of staff and other patients may be at risk, and an enormous amount of anxiety can be engendered. If an alcohol treatment service is coexisting closely with other facilities, it will acquire a bad name if disruption is allowed to get out of hand.

> A 40-year-old man after a long drinking history had been thrown out of his home, and was now drifting around temporary accommodation or sleeping rough. Over a period of 6 months he was twice admitted to hospital but on each occasion came back drunk onto the ward, assaulted the nurses and smashed the furniture. A few days after his last discharge, he came up to the hospital late at night and got into a fight with a porter. He then arrived at out-patients drunk and demanding admission, with threats of further violence if admission was not granted.

In such circumstances, there are two courses of action that are anti-therapeutic and should not be followed. The first of these is to tolerate further violence or the threat of violence. The patient will not be helped, the morale of the treatment service will be torn apart and staff may indeed be hurt. The second non-answer is to ban the patient from the hospital. Even if the banning is successful, it will only transfer the problem of violence onto someone else's doorstep, and things will not look too good if a week later the man is on an assault charge with the court told that a hospital had abrogated its responsibilities. The principle guiding the therapeutic response to this kind of patient is the realization that violence is often triggered by contextual cues which provoke that reaction (Graham et al., 1998).

Such a problem is dealt with more easily by a treatment service than by anyone working in isolation. A hospital, for instance, ought to be able to meet this type of problem, and the general practitioner and other local services will not be grateful if the hospital seeks to pass the buck. What is needed is a firm treatment policy drawn up for the individual, one that sets explicit limits but which, nonetheless, is a treatment rather than a mere containment policy. It must reward constructive behaviour and in no way reinforce unacceptable behaviour, and it must be communicated fairly and openly to the patient themselves, put at the front of the case notes (or prominently in the electronic record) and a copy given to the patient and to all staff who may be involved. It is useful to hold a staff meeting for formulation of the care plan so that things go forward by agreement, with everyone fully in the picture. It may be wise to ensure that the treatment centre administrative staff are consulted and supported, and a legal opinion obtained if necessary.

On the basis of consultation, a memo such as the following might be drawn up for the man whose story has just been sketched.

Mr Smith: agreed treatment plan

> So that we can go on helping this patient within a treatment programme, the following guidelines have been agreed by the treatment team, and we would be grateful if everyone will give this plan support.

1. Mr Smith will only be seen by appointment, and if he comes up without an appointment he should be asked to leave.
2. He will then only be seen at the appointment if he is not intoxicated. If there is any suspicion of intoxication, he will be asked to leave without being seen further.
3. If Mr Smith refuses to leave when asked, or if he threatens or offers violence, help should be summoned through the hospital's usual emergency system and the police should be telephoned. The number is ... and the police station has been alerted. On no account should an individual staff member attempt to argue with this patient.

4 Mr Smith has been told that if he commits any chargeable offence on the hospital premises, the hospital will not hesitate to press charges.

5 These ground rules have been explained to Mr Smith personally, and they have been set up not only to protect the staff but also so as to make it possible for us to go on working with this patient within a constructive treatment plan.

Contained within those seemingly harsh guidelines is a plan designed to enable the team to go on offering help to a man who would probably be rejected by many centres as unhelpable. In practice, this drawing of limits is reassuring to the patient himself. A disorganized and inconsistent response, which may even involve a sort of complicity with his violence, is likely to exacerbate anxiety and violence, whereas a firm policy often results in the patient showing a capacity to go along with constructive expectations. They are able to come to appointments sober, and make a new and positive therapeutic engagement. Things do not, however, always run smoothly, and if the patient does turn up drunk and tries to hit someone, a charge may have to be brought, for otherwise no learning can take place. To be able to use the police in support of the treatment plan requires careful liaison.

With the immediate threat of violence contained, it should be possible to get down to an individually planned and positive treatment programme. Violence is then no longer the central issue, and the patient's reputation should not be allowed to overshadow therapeutic dealings. There will be need to talk about the violence, and the patient has to come to terms with the full implications of the fact that alcohol, for them, releases violent feelings.

Another problem is how the stated rules are to be interpreted flexibly in certain difficult circumstances. For instance, if there is anxiety about the possibility of head injury, deterioration in the patient's physical condition, or concern as to whether underlying mental illness is now hidden within the picture, appropriate help should be obtained. Therefore, there has to be an understanding that individual clinical judgement allows a flexible response to an emergency, but the team should, whenever possible, be brought into the decision or promptly informed as to what has been done. There are some patients who pose extreme dangers of violence, and staff and public safety should then be the paramount consideration without prevarication or apology.

A presentation on a general hospital ward

This is an account of a late-night happening on a surgical ward.

> A woman had been admitted 3 days earlier with an abdominal emergency. A diagnosis of acute pancreatitis had been made and the patient had spent the first 2 days in intensive care. With her physical condition stabilized, she was back in a surgical bed. That evening at about midnight she pulled out her intravenous line, made for the door of the ward and said she was going home in a taxi. She drifted into the belief that she was in a hotel, but then suggested that her husband was hiding in a gas cylinder.

Delirium tremens (see Chapter 5) is not infrequently precipitated by a medical or surgical event with consequent admission to hospital, and abrupt withdrawal of alcohol. The condition is often satisfactorily treated in that kind of general ward setting, but sometimes there are difficulties. The case history outlined above reflects a situation where a surgical team is suddenly faced by a dangerous alcohol-related emergency. It is a danger that needs to be emphasized. If she is allowed to run off the ward, she may get lost in the hospital grounds and die of exposure, or walk into traffic and be killed. If the patient is brought back onto the ward without a safe nursing environment established and appropriate medication given, there is a danger of a fall from a window or other accident.

When a surgical or medical team is confronted by this kind of presentation there are three golden rules. Firstly, the patient must by all means possible be kept on the ward and their physical safety ensured. Secondly, advice from the consultation–liaison psychiatry team should immediately be obtained. Thirdly, adequate and appropriate medication should be given to bring the disturbance under control as quickly as possible, but with care taken not to induce overdose. A later response may need to be a review of staff training and procedures.

The pregnant drinker

Pregnancy is an opportunity for women to reflect on their alcohol consumption. Those who have consumed alcohol in the very early stages of pregnancy, before finding out that they that they were pregnant, may feel guilty and should be reassured that stopping at any stage will have positive benefits for them and their unborn child. Others will feel guilty that they have continued to drink during their pregnancy and may require considerable support. Any advice given to pregnant women during their first contact with a healthcare professional should be imparted in a non-judgemental and supportive way, as it is important that women remain in contact with prenatal services throughout their pregnancy.

Because there is no evidence for a safe level of drinking in pregnancy, most health messages now emphasize abstinence. The UK lagged somewhat behind the USA, Canada, Australia and other countries in adopting the abstinence message (Mukherjee et al., 2005), but recent guidelines from the Department of Health (England) and the National Institute for Health and Clinical Excellence (NICE) (England, Wales and Northern Ireland) are now in line with other countries (National Institute for Health and Clinical Excellence, 2008). In general, women are advised not to drink any alcohol during pregnancy. Alcohol should be avoided during the first 3 months of pregnancy, because it may be associated with an increased risk of miscarriage. Women choosing to drink during pregnancy are advised to drink no more than 1–2 UK units once or twice a week for the remainder of the pregnancy and should not drink to intoxication.

Even women who drink heavily can engage successfully in interventions to reduce their drinking during the course of their pregnancy. Brief interventions for the non-dependent pregnant drinker are considered in Chapter 10. Medically supervised withdrawal of the alcohol dependent pregnant woman should be carried out in an in-patient setting, to allow close supervision both of the woman in withdrawal and the developing fetus (see Chapter 12) (Guerrini, Jackson & Keaney, 2009). See Chapter 5 for an account of the effects of alcohol exposure on the pregnant women and on the developing fetus.

A combined problem with drink and drugs

A woman aged 26 had been given an assessment appointment at the request of her lawyer. She was a single parent, her 6-year-old son had been taken into care, and she wished to contest the decision and regain custody.

> The patient arrived with a half-consumed can of lager in her hand, and despite requests not to smoke, she repeatedly lit up a cigarette. She was so excited, irritable and importuning as to make it impossible to proceed with the interview. A few days later she came back in a more co-operative mood and apologized for her previous behaviour – 'Sorry, I'd been snorting cocaine'. Her story was of previous use of injected heroin (she was now on methadone maintenance), intermittent use of cocaine, heavy current use of cannabis and diazepam swallowed like sweets.

Mixed with all this, intermittent heavy drinking was occurring to the point of gross intoxication. She was beginning to experience alcohol withdrawal symptoms. Clearly, it was impossible to support this woman's wish immediately to have her child returned to her care. After some further out-patient visits, she was, at her request, admitted to hospital – 'I can't do it by myself, give me a break'. Six weeks later she came out of hospital off all drugs other than the prescribed oral methadone and 30 cigarettes a day. Social Services were, as a preliminary, happy for her to make supervised visits to her son.

Here are some principles which may guide the therapeutic approach to someone exhibiting this sort of chaotic combined use of drugs and alcohol:

1 Alcohol and other drugs all need to be responded to with equal and concomitant seriousness. There is a danger that drug treatment services will ignore the alcohol (and perhaps also the diazepam), with risks of fatal overdose from methadone taken in combination with these cerebral depressants (Advisory Council on the Misuse of Drugs, 2000). The drinking cannot safely be regarded as an optional therapeutic target to be left over for a later day.

2 Admission to hospital may be needed not once but on a repeated, low-threshold basis for detoxification, renewed goal-setting and another start.

3 Treatment goals need to be unambiguously defined. Abstinence from alcohol and all other psychoactive drugs other than the prescribed methadone is likely to be the only feasible long-term goal. Tolerance of setbacks and failure, a willingness to accept achievable intermediate goals and policies for harm minimization need to be combined with the maintenance of the long-term effort to help the patient towards being 'clean and sober', with accompanying positive life changes. Therapeutic drift is sadly likely to see death by overdose, hepatitis C, liver damage exacerbated by the drinking or death by alcoholic cirrhosis 20 years on. The need to deal with the nicotine dependence should not be ignored (Breslau et al., 1996).

The needs of a patient like the young woman described here may pose a considerable challenge to services.

The patient with cognitive impairment

A description of the brain pathologies which can result from excessive use of alcohol was given in Chapter 5. Here, discussion will focus on the everyday clinical implications of the fact that brain damage will, in some patients, compromise the ability to respond to and engage in the usually available treatment programmes. The following passage gives a nurse's report on a 50-year-old man with a long history of alcohol dependence.

He gets everyone else irritated in the group. He doesn't seem to listen to what other people say and then bats in with his own views, saying exactly the same as he said yesterday and the day before. Things like: 'If you keep yourself tidy and clean you've got no problem'. I don't think that after 3 weeks he even knows anyone else's name.

That observation might be evidence of a particular patient's habitual conversational style, but it must also raise a warning flag as to the possibility of brain damage. Subsequent psychological testing with this patient revealed short-term memory impairment and evidence of frontal lobe impairment.

Gross brain damage is not likely to set difficulties in recognition. What has to be cultivated is an alertness to lesser, but still clinically important, degrees of cognitive impairment. The problem can present with various severities, but the picture given by the patient who was having difficulties functioning in the ward group is fairly typical. There is often a sense of the patient's social awareness being blunted, of their not being good at taking in new ideas or information, of their memory for newly learnt material being impaired (hence that patient's difficulty with remembering names), and there may also be difficulty in sustaining concentration.

Ward observation and watching the patient's behaviour in groups can be helpful diagnostically, as can an assessment of daily living report from an occupational therapist. In many instances, some recovery in functioning takes place over weeks or months, and serial assessments are therefore needed. Testing carried out immediately after detoxification can give misleadingly pessimistic results. Beyond the ward observation and routine mental state examination (simple tests of memory and concentration), a full assessment will involve skilled psychological testing and neuroimaging.

If neuropsychological testing and an MRI scan confirm the presence of significant impairment and damage, and if repeated assessment demonstrates that recovery is likely to be incomplete, the implications for clinical management must be considered. A patient who is experiencing cognitive difficulties will become frustrated by a demanding therapeutic regime: the best therapeutic programmes involve a great deal of new learning, emotional awareness and social interaction, and it is in exactly the skills needed to engage successfully in those types of experience in which the cognitively impaired patient may be deficient. If sympathetic note is not taken of their special needs and handicaps, the patient will either go through the programme without benefit or, more probably, they will break therapeutic contact.

A programme that acknowledges the needs of this type of patient cannot be formulated on a one-off basis but must be designed by interaction with the patient concerned. Would it be helpful for them to have individual discussions which identify the core simplicities of their personal recovery programme? Would they be helped by written material or by making out check-lists?

On return to their own home from the ward, thought must be given to the special aftercare needs of such a patient and their family. The programme should put therapeutic emphasis on management of external and situational factors, such as arranging how money is to be controlled, how time is to be spent, how work or sheltered employment is to be found and how the local liquor stores are to be persuaded to be proscriptively helpful.

Alcohol problems in later life

A long-standing history of excessive drinking continuing into old age may often be marked by brain damage, and other physical complications and nutritional neglect are common. The drinking pattern may have become fragmented compared with previous years, and loss of tolerance to alcohol is a frequent manifestation (see Chapter 1).

In contrast is the elderly patient who began excessive drinking as a response to a problem, or a cluster of difficulties, that he or she only recently encountered. Widowhood, retirement, insomnia, the physical complications of ageing and a general loss of purpose in life are often important factors in the onset of a drinking problem at this age. Possible underlying brain disease or depressive illness should also be considered as causes of a late-onset problem.

The division of the drinking problems that occur in this epoch of life into those of early and late onset is clinically useful and carries implications for management of the problem. A not unusual story is of the seemingly late-onset condition being found, on closer enquiry, to have a much longer background history. Many of the basic features can, however, be the same whether the onset of the problem was remote or recent, and one should be aware of elements which can very generally colour the presentation at this age. For instance, there is often the likelihood of social isolation. Delirious states are common in the elderly, and at this time of life depression and a degree of brain impairment often go together. Elderly people are more likely than younger people to be taking prescription medication. There are often multiple physical pathologies.

Help for the older patient

Basic principles have to be borne in mind, but for patients in this age group special skills are needed to design a treatment plan which effectively responds to their situation in life (Dar, 2006; O'Connell et al., 2003). This implies knowledge of the local resources that are available to help the elderly, including clubs, day centres, home helps, community nurses and so on. Mobilizing whatever family support is available can also be important. The patient may be ambivalent about surrendering independence, but sheltered accommodation can provide companionship and enable better adjustment than continued isolation. Initial hospital admission may be needed for diagnosis, but it should not be too prolonged. The sensitivity of the ageing nervous system to drugs should be borne in mind, with tranquillizers or sedatives used only in the short term and with caution. Disulfiram is too dangerous at this age, but acamprosate may be helpful (see Chapter 14). Some older people will join Alcoholics Anonymous, but that kind of group experience can be difficult to utilize at that age.

Whatever the specifics of therapy, the non-specifics are again important, including the warmth, the hopefulness and the goal-setting. An old person may need things explained slowly, positions explored and solutions negotiated at an acceptable pace. Abrupt and clumsy interference will be met deservedly with tetchiness, and there will be no therapeutic gain.

The approach to old-age drinking problems still tends sometimes to be negatively influenced by a gulf in understanding: 'Well, drink is all she's got, and if she drinks herself to death . . .' Such attitudes are unjustified. Elderly people with drinking problems can be helped, with a large benefit in terms of health, enjoyment of life and dignity.

The patient from a cultural background other than the therapist's

'I don't understand him at all', said the Community Psychiatric Nurse (CPN) who was reporting on a visit to her patient's home. 'He's a Pakistani man who owns a fruit shop, aged about 60, very much the head of the family, with two grown-up sons who help in the business and take orders from their father. He and his wife have only a rather poor understanding of English. He has a bottle of whisky at the back of the shop, and he swigs at it steadily throughout the day. When I went round I was treated with kindness, loaded with presents of fruit and met with massive denial. He says that he uses a little whisky now and then for medicine'.

The CPN had the openness to admit that she did not understand this patient's cultural position, and no doubt the shopkeeper was puzzled as to the role, credentials and purpose of this person whom his doctor had asked to call.

The cultural meaning of the drinking itself can be puzzling. What does 'normal' drinking mean within a particular culture, and how are religious prohibitions in practice interpreted? What are the legitimate functions of alcohol and its symbolism? What are the culturally determined ideas that define 'drinking too much', and, if there is a concept equivalent to 'alcohol dependence', with what adverse connotations is that idea loaded? The questions that relate to difficulties in understanding the drinking itself constitute only a small part of the total cross-cultural puzzle. The essential background problems relate to such issues as an understanding of personality, family and family roles, religion, social class and status, and who has a right to say what to whom (Galvan & Cactano, 2003; Heim et al., 2004; Lee, Law & Eunjoo, 2003; Rao, 2006). Different cultures will carry different assumptions as to what constitutes 'treatment', the primacy given to the prescription of medicines or the degree of directiveness which is expected (Edwards & Arif, 1980).

The case of the shopkeeper is one example of the many and varied cross-cultural problems in understanding that can be met whatever the country in which the therapist is practising. The presentation may be the recently immigrated family; the postgraduate student from abroad; the immigrant labourer, who is today part of the workforce in many parts of the world; the refugee; or the patient of the therapist's own culture but with regional or social class identity different from the therapist's. The problems set by the extreme cases of cultural difference can, in fact, serve as useful reminders of the need for a more general awareness of culture clash, which is often present in many 'ordinary' therapeutic encounters.

There is no one formula for dealing with such situations. It is important to be alert to the need for understanding, and hence, to avoid those clumsy errors which come from assuming that everyone else is like us, or that there is something odd about others if they do not comply with our own, parochial expectations. Treatment services are still often too ethnically insensitive.

Every such case has to be seen as an exercise in building bridges. With the fruit-shop owner it may, for instance, be possible to find a second generation member of the family who can be a broker in understanding. The patient's son may identify the key figures within the extended family network that have a right to advise and intervene. It may also be possible to find a professional within the local agencies or hospitals who speaks the language and understands the culture, and who can help with an assessment or perhaps take over the case.

The family member as intermediary

Anyone working in this field will, from time to time, receive the following type of letter or a phone call of similar nature.

> I wonder whether you can possibly help. It's not about me but my daughter who needs assistance. She won't take any notice of me, but I know she's an alcoholic.

The letter may be from a mother about her son or daughter, a husband about his wife, a divorced wife about her ex-husband, or reflect any one of a wide range of other possible combinations. The common theme is that a concerned family member is seeking help on behalf of someone who is not themselves at that moment of a mind to do so.

Helping agencies ought to have the capacity to meet such requests, at least by offering a preliminary evaluation session. The principle, which guides the response to this type of proxy consultation, is that there may be fruitful possibilities of working with the person who is actually in the room (the intermediary), rather than the therapist being lured into the impossible position of trying to find instant solutions for the person who is absent (the problem drinker).

For instance, the mother who has come to talk about her daughter's drinking may in fact be wanting to talk about her own sense of guilt, anger or frustration; or about her need to control; or her difficulty in 'letting go'. More than one session may be required. Information about Alcoholics Anonymous (AA) can be timely.

Secondly, there are possibilities of the encounter with the intermediary leading to help for the individual who is drinking. Information can be passed on about treatment services and AA, or an open and unthreatening invitation can be offered for the drinker to come along to discuss whether there is anything to talk about. Beyond that level of information-giving, there may also be indirect ways of working with the drinker through changing the behaviour, attitudes and level of confidence of a key family member. In terms of family systems theory (Bennett & La Bonte, 1993), one is introducing movement into a system which is otherwise going to maintain the drinking. One should also be aware that this kind of approach can at times be manipulative and an attempt to establish blame, and one does well not to be lured into secret contracts.

The 'very important patient'

Frequently, and despite every supposed personal advantage, the man or woman with a large public reputation is the person whose alcohol problem is likely to be mishandled. Because of the aura of prestige, no-one quite dares make the diagnosis or take a firm line. Phone calls are made in the middle of the night, and a quick visit is demanded to a hotel room. Instead of a full history, there is a superficial and interrupted conversation, and everything is a whispering game. The therapist may need considerable confidence to stand their ground when dealing with the demands and expectations of the tycoon, the politician, the famous actress, the judge or the distinguished surgeon, but unless they are willing to hold to a therapeutic position their patient will not be well served. Paradoxically, the rich and famous may be as much at hazard of receiving inadequate treatment as the drinker on skid row.

The key to dealing with such problems is to act with awareness that this person, as much as the vagrant or any other patient who comes one's way, is indeed to an extent a 'special case'. But, at the same time, one has to hold to the commonalities and the basic working rules of the therapeutic approach. These two ideas need to be discussed briefly and separately.

Firstly, as regards the 'specialness' of this type of patient, the situation may be clouded by fear of public revelation. For instance, the politician will be concerned about the damage to their reputation and electoral chances from any rumour that they are an 'alcoholic'. Advice that they should attend AA where their face will be recognized may in these circumstances be impractical, and anxiety about the dangers of 'the newspaper getting hold of things' may consequently so dominate their thinking as to block every effort to help them. The truth of the matter may be that their drinking habits are already public knowledge and a known embarrassment to their colleagues – and news that they are getting help can only do good not harm. The extent to which it is possible for someone in this position to admit publicly that they have had to deal with a drinking problem must vary from country to country and across professions. In the USA, for example, such openness is increasingly and beneficially possible (Hughes, 1997).

There are certain other rather typical features. The pressure under which such people are living and working can be extreme and engender a great deal of tension, with alcohol used as self-medication. Fear of failure may be potently linked to this stress, with an uncertain personal sense of worth and security despite every public success. The lifestyle may involve frequent entertaining and thus pressures to drink. Marriages are often under strain.

With this kind of patient there may sometimes be difficulty in initiating effective therapy because the patient claims that they are too important to waste their time on treatment: there is a film to make, a business meeting to be attended on the other side of the world, an invitation to Downing Street which must take priority.

So much for a brief consideration of what may be 'special'. It must, however, be obvious that what has been instanced as 'special' could be turned around and argued the other way. There is nothing unique about the fear of public exposure, and it may affect the driver of the company car as well as the company president, while stress and fear of failure are common themes whatever the stratum from which patients are drawn. Although it is necessary to be alert to the intensity and clustering of certain factors that affect the 'special' patient, one is soon brought back to the need to hold onto the basics of the therapeutic approach. A full assessment must, for instance, be carried out, rather than the argument accepted that the patient is too busy for proper time to be given to this task. The formulation has to be discussed, the diagnosis agreed and goals appropriately set. And, as always, the quality of the relationship is fundamental. At one level the encounter may be between public figure and psychiatrist or counsellor, but more fundamentally it is between a patient or client with a drinking problem and a person seeking, as best possible, to offer help.

A child at risk

Over recent years there has been a sharp increase in public anxiety about the risks children may be subjected to as a result of parental violence or sexual abuse. Such anxieties provide the context within which Social Services departments deal with sensitive problems which arise when a parent's drinking appears to put a young child's safety at risk.

> Mr and Mrs B had met when they were both patients in an Alcohol Treatment Unit. He was aged 35, she 30, and they had both experienced deprived childhoods and chaotic adult life histories. In their recovery they gave each other a great deal of mutual understanding, and they started to live together. Seen 3 years later they reported much improvement but they would still periodically relapse into short bouts of drinking. At these times they were sometimes violent to each other, and the police had been called on several occasions. They now had an 18-month-old daughter and the neighbours had reported their concern about the safety of this child to the Social Services.

The issues being dealt with in this section overlap with the discussion of the patient who was drunk and violent (see earlier in this chapter), but a new and worrying element is introduced when a child is at risk (Sher et al., 1991). Every such case must be approached differently, but guidelines can be helpful.

The child's safety and welfare must come first

In any decision-making around this case that simple rule of priority must never be lost from sight.

Do not panic, but err on the side of caution

No one would wish, on reflex, to put every child into care where there is a history of parental drinking. But, at the same time, it would be culpable to engage in an extended process of leisurely assessment, rather than taking firm emergency action, in those instances where the safety of the child requires immediate placement in care.

Try to work with, rather than against, the parents

This advice will seem obvious to the experienced case-worker. The parents may feel guilty about and frightened by their own behaviour and their failure adequately to care for a child who is precious to them. Any threat of having that child taken away is likely to cause a reaction not only in terms of self-blame but of angry projected blame of other people. The parents need therefore, so far as possible, to be helped into a position where they can accept that everyone is working constructively together for a resolution of the problem.

Assess the total background family situation and interactions rather than focus only on the drinking

In the case outlined above, there is evidence that when both parents were sober they cared for their child lovingly and competently. When sober, the relationship between the parents was also a happy one, and whenever they could obtain a baby-sitter they went to AA meetings together. There was no suggestion of violence other than in the setting of drunkenness.

Assess the parental drinking history and the likely consequences of the drinking for the child

Drinking bouts in this family tended to last about 3–5 days, with one parent's drinking sparking off drinking in the other partner, although sometimes one would drink and the other stay sober. There was evidence that several months (sometimes as long as 6 months) could elapse without a bout occurring. There had never been any indication of intentional violence to the child, but she had on one occasion been accidentally knocked to the floor. She had also been left neglected and crying in a bedroom when both parents were drinking and rowing. Drunken driving may also cause concern if the child is at risk as a passenger.

Examination of the child

Assessment is not complete without a physical and developmental assessment of the child. This is usually best conducted by a child psychiatrist or a paediatrician. A social worker will also usually be involved in assessing the child and the family situation. In the case we are describing the little girl showed no abnormalities.

Setting up an appropriate level of safeguard and monitoring

The appropriate level of safeguard must depend on the individual situation and can range from the emergency decision to take a child into care, to putting that child on the 'at risk' register, or even some lesser level of intervention. In the present circumstances, it was felt that there was a small but real danger of the child coming to accidental harm if the parents continued to drink and fight in this explosive fashion. They agreed to strict supervision, and each decided to take disulfiram and attend a hospital out-patient group. It was agreed that their ability to look after their child would have to be viewed as dependent on their continued sobriety. Twelve months later they had remained abstinent and made good therapeutic progress.

Not every such story has a happy outcome. Circumstances may arise when a child has to be taken into care, but the hope may then still be that a constructive and monitored programme can be set up which allows the parents access and the opportunity to work towards getting their child back.

This discussion has been in terms of a situation where both parents have a drinking problem. Situations also arise when only one parent is drinking or where there is drinking and a single-parent family.

All presentations are special presentations

Every presentation sketched out in this chapter might be met any day in clinical practice. We are not describing the exotic, but the extraordinary texture and variety of the common and ordinary. Good clinical practice in this arena is rooted in the capacity to respond flexibly to a vast spectrum of presentations with the response fitted to very different needs and circumstances – one formula will never do.

References

Advisory Council on the Misuse of Drugs (2000) *Reducing Drug-related Deaths*. London: The Stationery Office.

Bennett L A, La Bonte M (1993) Family systems. In *Recent Developments in Alcoholism*, Vol. 2, M Galanter (ed.). New York: Plenum, pp. 87–95.

Breslau N, Peterson E, Schultz L, Andreski P, Chilcoat H (1996) Are smokers with alcohol disorders less likely to quit? *American Journal of Public Health* **86**, 985–990.

Dar K (2006) Alcohol use disorders in elderly people. *Advances in Psychiatric Treatment* **12**, 173–181.

Dawes M, Johnson B A (2004) Pharmacotherapeutic trials in adolescent alcohol use disorders: opportunities and challenges. *Alcohol and Alcoholism* **39**, 166–177.

Edwards G, Arif A (eds) (1980) *Drug Problems in Socio-cultural Perspective*. Geneva: World Health Organization.

Fitzgerald J L, Mulford H A (1992) Elderly vs younger problem drinkers' 'treatment' and recovery experience. *British Journal of Addiction* **87**, 1281–1291.

Galvan F H, Caetano R (2003) Alcohol use and related problems among ethnic minorities in the United States. *Alcohol Health and Research World* **27**, 87–94.

Graham K, Leonard K E, Room R, et al. (1998) Current directions in research on understanding and preventing intoxicated aggression. *Addiction* **93**, 659–676.

Guerrini I, Jackson S, Keaney K (2009) Pregnancy and alcohol misuse. *British Medical Journal* **338**, 829–832.

Heim D, Hunter S C, Ross A J, et al. (2004) Alcohol consumption, perceptions of community responses and attitudes to service provision: results from a survey of Indian, Chinese and Pakistani young people in greater Glasgow. *Alcohol and Alcoholism* **39**, 220–226.

Hughes H (1997) Journal interview. *Addiction* **92**, 137–149.

Lee M Y, Law P F M, Eunjoo E (2003) Perception of substance use problems in Asian American communities by Chinese, Indian, Korean and Vietnamese populations. *Journal of Ethnicity in Substance Abuse* **2**, 1–30.

Marshall E J, Mirza K A H (2007) Pharmacological treatment of adolescent substance use disorders. In *Clinics in Developmental Medicine No 172: Alcohol, Drugs and Young People*, E Gilvarry, P McArdle (eds). London: MacKeith Press, pp. 197–216.

Mukherjee R A S, Hollins S, Abou-Saleh M, Turk J (2005) Low level alcohol consumption and the fetus. *British Medical Journal* **330**, 375–376.

National Institute for Health and Clinical Excellence (2008) *Ante-natal Care: Routine Care for the Healthy Pregnant Woman*, 2nd edn. London: National Institute of Health and Clinical Excellence. http://www.nice.org.uk/CG62.

O'Connell H, Ai-Vym C, Cunningham C, Lawlor B (2003) Alcohol use disorders in elderly people – redefining an age old problem in old age. *British Medical Journal* **327**, 664–67.

Rao R (2006) Alcohol misuse and ethnicity. *British Medical Journal* **332**, 682.

Sher K J, Walitzer K S, Wood P K, Brent E E (1991) Characteristics of children of alcoholics: putative risk factors, substance abuse and psychopathology. *Journal of Abnormal Psychology* **100**, 427–448.

Tober G (2007) Psychosocial interventions for young people with substance misuse disorders. In *Alcohol, Drugs and Young People: Clinical Approaches*, E Gilvarry, P McArdle (eds). London: MacKeith Press, pp. 176–184.

Section 2

Treatment: context and content

Treatment: context and content

Introduction, settings and roles

The preceding chapters of this book provide the background information for the following chapters that will describe the actual 'treatment of drinking problems'. Historically, there has been a tendency to focus on the specialist field of treatment – 'alcoholism hospitals', 'addiction treatment clinics' and the like – but only a small minority of those with drinking problems are actually in contact with these sorts of services (Substance Abuse and Mental Health Services Administration, 2007). We take a far broader view in this book of where problem drinkers may find help (Figure 9.1).

The outermost layer of Figure 9.1 comprises informal influences on problem drinkers: the work colleague who advises that a career may be damaged if drinking is not stopped; the husband who supports his wife as she tries to get away from the bottle; and the friends who praise or mock a newly abstinent chum's lifestyle. These influences were addressed primarily in Section 1, though their role is felt in Section 2 in that informal influences often spur help-seeking from formal sources of help, as shown in Figure 9.1's inner two circles.

The medium tinted area of Figure 9.1 is the non-specialist sector, those agencies that may offer support or apply pressure (or both) to problem drinkers even though their *raison d'être* is not related to alcohol. The hidden majority of problem drinkers daily 'rub shoulders' with fellow members of their community in these settings; for example, when they consult their primary care doctors or have the misfortune to attend the Accident and Emergency Department (Emergency Room). Therefore, any approach to the treatment of drinking problems must consider the many different settings in which these develop and present. These settings are described in detail in Chapter 10.

Finally, the innermost circle of Figure 9.1 is the specialist sector, namely professional services (see Chapters 13 and 14) and self-help programmes (see Chapter 15) with the explicit purpose of helping problem drinkers. Its location at the centre of the diagram is not professional narcissism: most drinkers who get better do so without ever accessing this sector. Rather, it reflects that this is where a small minority of all drinking problems is handled.

Trajectories of help-seeking and progress or regress in the drinking problem

The help-seeking pathway of most individuals will not be straightforward but in fact rather 'messy', as they will derive varying degrees of parallel support from informal, non-specialist and specialist sources that vary over the time course. Whilst it is recognized that multiple sources of treatment can be accessed simultaneously, the position of the treatment arrow on Figure 9.1 highlights the treatment source that is 'making the running' at any one particular time. The temporary or sustained treatment goal is depicted by the star, and many

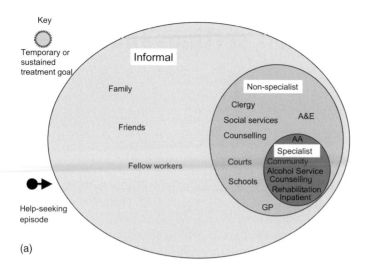

Key

Temporary or sustained treatment goal

Help-seeking episode

(a)

Figure 9.1. Treatment Influences and trajectories. The light-tinted area represents the informal influences on problems drinkers, the medium-tinted area is the non-specialist sector and the dark-tinted innermost circle is the specialist sector. Different treatment trajectories are depicted (a–c) on and between these treatment settings. AA, Alcoholics Anonymous; A&E, Accident and Emergency Department (Emergency Room); GP, general practitioner.

treatment paths may not terminate in one. Furthermore, there are multiple permutations of these treatment trajectories that occur in various combinations, with associated gaps, pauses and delays. Whilst the treatment arrows build into a trajectory that is unique for that individual, characteristic patterns may also be recognized.

Many will manage their drinking problem without accessing specialist or non-specialist services, using the informal support of family and friends to achieve their goal, either rapidly as shown in Figure 9.1b by trajectory 1 or over a longer period as depicted in trajectory 2. Others will approach non-specialist services, such as their practice nurse, who may assist by using a brief intervention (trajectory 3). An example of the stepped care model is presented in trajectory 4, in which specialist alcohol treatment is reserved for those who do not respond to simpler approaches (Bower & Gilbody, 2005). In this example, concerned relatives advise the individual to cut down, and when this fails for the second time, the individual consults their general practitioner who provides community detoxification. Several weeks later they relapse and the individual drinks during a second community detoxification. The general practitioner then refers them to the specialist services, and following detailed assessment, in-patient detoxification is arranged followed by residential rehabilitation, and the individual successfully maintains a prolonged period of abstinence with the support of Alcoholics Anonymous. Some see stepped care as providing specialist input to those who have 'failed' at other approaches, thereby delaying access to the needed treatment. Therefore, an important aspect of stepped care is a mechanism for self-correction, which monitors progress and provides for the 'stepping up' of treatment as required. In addition, accurate assessment in the early stages of presentation is vital as this can identify an individual who needs direct access to specialist care; thereby preventing the delay and negative impact associated with multiple failures at lower intensity interventions. Indeed, in trajectory 5 in Figure 9.1b, a friend at work who has experienced a drink problem, advised the individual to attend the open-access assessment clinic with the local community alcohol team, who recommend a course of individual counselling. An early accurate assessment enabled the appropriate specialist treatment for this individual to be identified and recommended.

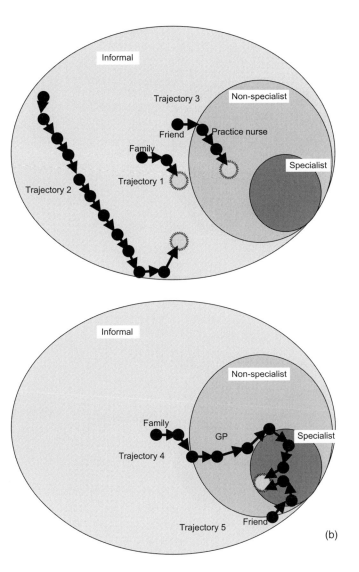

Figure 9.1 (Continued).

(b)

The 'messy' treatment of drinking problems

The majority of treatment trajectories will not be joined up, direct or efficient, and many will represent 'messy treatment'. For example, in trajectory 6, in Figure 9.1c, the individual experienced multiple inputs from informal sources, including family, friends, the local church and work colleagues, before presenting to their general practitioner and undergoing several community detoxifications. They were eventually referred to the local specialist alcohol team where they underwent multiple rounds of in-patient, group and individual treatment before they finally achieved abstinence. This trajectory includes zigzag patterns, during which the individual goes backwards and forwards between services: this is sometimes termed 'ping-pong' therapy. There are also loops in which they repeatedly circulate between services: these

Figure 9.1 (Continued)

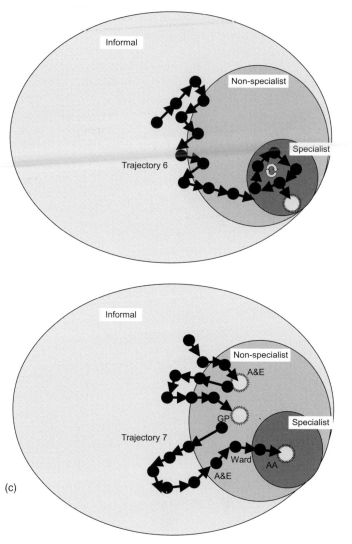

people are sometimes labelled 'revolving-door' patients. In this case, the individual finally broke out of the 'revolving-door' loop and achieved their treatment goal of stable abstinence. But this is not always the case, and some may access different levels of treatment throughout their lives. As such, therapists may maintain their enthusiasm for this work by hoping that this occasion might be the one in which the individual finally succeeds. A further common complication is the changing of goals as treatment progresses. In trajectory 7, in Figure 9.1c, the person initially wishes to pursue controlled drinking and, after presenting to the local Accident and Emergency Department (Emergency Room), they achieve this following a brief intervention by the alcohol liaison worker. Subsequently, they lose their job; the drinking escalates and it can no longer be reined in. Further attempts at controlled drinking, through their general practitioner, fail and they disengage. They do not attend the practice for several months, finally presenting again, but on this occasion with features of physical dependence upon alcohol. This time they reluctantly recognize that they cannot control their alcohol consumption and opt for community detoxification, which they complete, only to relapse after several weeks. A year later they present again in the Accident and Emergency Department (Emergency Room) with a head injury. Fortunately, the drinking history is noted, and they undergo medically assisted detoxification following which they achieve stable abstinence for several months with the support of Alcoholics Anonymous.

It is worth taking a moment just to imagine different patterns that can exist and to identify individual treatment trajectories of those people who have shared their treatment histories with you. It is important to recognize that for many the treatment path or trajectory will be 'messy' and complex; at times simultaneously accessing support across the informal, non-specialist and specialist domains whilst at others a single source may be the most helpful. The pathway may be punctuated with pauses by the individual or waits, and specific patterns can be discerned as the drinking problem unfolds and suitable treatment is sought and delivered. Retrospectively, the presentation of the drinking problem and consolidation of the previous treatment experience can be plotted on the individual's life map. The chapters that follow explore the various components of these different treatment trajectories that together make up the breadth of the 'treatment of drinking problems'.

References

Bower P, Gilbody S (2005) Stepped care in psychological therapies: access, effectiveness and efficiency. Narrrative literature review. *British Journal of Psychiatry* **186**, 11–17.

Substance Abuse and Mental Health Services Administration (2007) *Results of the 2006 National Survey on Drug Use and Health.* Rockville, MD: The Office of Applied Statistics.

10

Non-specialist settings

It may, at first, seem odd that a book on the 'treatment of drinking problems' would venture outside the familiar confines of specialist alcohol treatment programmes. But, for three key reasons, it can benefit individual clients as well as public health generally for problem drinking interventions to cast a wider net.

Most drinking problems are not encountered in specialist care

Every survey of the question conducted has confirmed that the proportion of all people with drinking problems dwarfs the number receiving specialist alcohol treatment. In the USA, for example, the ratio of those meeting diagnostic criteria for alcohol abuse/dependence to those who receive treatment is typically around 10 to 1 in any given year (see, e.g. Substance Abuse and Mental Health Services Administration, 2007). Yet most of these individuals still go to see their general practitioner, work or attend school or college, or access the Accident and Emergency Department (Emergency Room). All of these sites thus provide opportunities for intervention.

Many interventions outside of specialist care fail in their intended purpose due to the unappreciated influence of drinking problems

Alcohol misuse is a causal or exacerbating factor in countless problems that come to the attention of health and social service professionals: unhappy marriages, family violence, unemployment, anxiety disorders, injuries, college failure and cardiovascular illness, to name but a few (see Section 1). When the drinking problem is not addressed, the attempts to tackle the presenting problem may be ineffective, or even cause harm. The 'depression' will not respond to the prescribed antidepressant, a peptic ulcer will fail to heal, a family's situation will deteriorate and the helping professional is left puzzled and frustrated.

Non-specialist settings provide the chance to influence low-level problems before they become serious

Specialist alcohol services in most countries tend to serve individuals with quite severe drinking problems (Humphreys & Tucker, 2002). In many cases, this end state could have been forestalled by intervention earlier in the life course/drinking career. A serious discussion with a guidance counsellor when college drinking has just started to harm academic performance, advice to cut down from a physician at the first report of occasional tiredness after an evening's drinking, support from an employee assistance programme after a few late arrivals to work on Monday may only nudge the life course slightly. But even a small intervention made early enough can have a pronounced long-term impact, akin to how a small turn of an ocean liner's wheel as it leaves Boston Harbour can make it arrive in Liverpool rather than Brest.

Non-specialist settings in which drinking problems are prevalent

Table 10.1 lists eight settings in which drinking problems tend to be prevalent, if not necessarily recognized. We include on the list the special case of general psychiatry services, in which drinking problems are overlooked despite the capacity to treat them. Each setting is described in more detail below.

Criminal justice

In many cities, the majority of individuals arrested are intoxicated with a substance at the time. Domestic violence, reckless driving and child abuse are just three of many crimes strongly associated with drinking problems (see Chapter 4). The criminal justice system is thus de facto among the largest handlers of alcohol-involved individuals. Assessment of the use of alcohol and other drugs is therefore an essential part of any psychiatric consultation in the criminal justice system, including competency assessments, child custody hearings and evaluations of dangerousness.

The workplace

The emergence of in-house 'employee assistance programmes' was both a reaction to and an illuminator of the high prevalence of alcohol problems in many companies. Alcohol is the hidden factor behind many cases of absenteeism, job conflicts and worksite accidents. Workforces with particularly high prevalence of alcohol problems – and therefore particular opportunity for intervention – include the military, law enforcement and the alcohol industry itself.

Schools/colleges/universities

Educational institutions at all levels are profoundly affected by drinking problems. In primary school, a drinking problem in the family may be the force driving the child who is chronically late, anxious, socially rejected or physically aggressive. In adolescence and young adulthood, problem drinking by students themselves is frequently commingled with problems of academic achievement and social behaviour.

Table 10.1. Non-specialist settings in which drinking problems are prevalent.

- Criminal justice system
- Workplace
- Schools/colleges/universities
- Primary care
- Accident and Emergency Departments (Emergency Rooms)
- Obstetrics/gynaecology clinics
- Elderly care settings
- General psychiatry/mental health clinics

Primary care

Within the healthcare system, the primary care setting is probably the greatest missed opportunity to address drinking problems, which are in some way implicated in perhaps 25% of all visits. Yet recognition of drinking problems is often not given priority, and it is even less frequently the subject of intervention.

Accident and Emergency Departments

The other critical opportunity for intervention in the healthcare system is the Accident and Emergency Department (Emergency Room) (Crawford et al., 2004; Havard, Shakeshaft & Sanson-Fisher, 2008). A growing body of work has documented that drinking problems are prevalent among individuals injured in a range of accidents, including, but not limited to, road traffic accidents. The shock of the injury can provide a 'teachable moment' during which long-ignored pleas for attention to drinking are finally heard.

Obstetrics/gynaecology clinics

As the prevalence of heavy alcohol consumption among young women has risen, so has the level of alcohol problems encountered in prenatal clinics. A night's heavy drinking is often behind an unintentional pregnancy, as well as contraction of a sexually transmitted disease. These risks arise in consensual sexual relationships when condoms or other forms of contraception are forgotten or simply disregarded. They are also prevalent in sexual assaults, for which intoxicated females may be targeted by perpetrators. Intervention for women in these settings is important not only for the women themselves, but also in cases of pregnancy for the developing fetus (see Chapters 5 and 8).

Elderly care settings

One less appreciated effect of the ageing of the baby-boom generation is a rise in elderly people who have substance misuse problems. Such problems can be the source of presenting complaints of confusion and poor memory in the Old Age Psychiatry Clinic, or of depression or agitation in a nursing home. Addressing alcohol problems in this population assumes particular importance in those cases where the individual is taking a prescribed medication that interacts with alcohol.

The special case of general psychiatry/mental health services

> I was in psychoanalysis for depression 3 days a week for 20 years. I killed a pint of bourbon almost every night throughout it, but my analyst never even asked me about my drinking.

> There is no point addressing symptoms without getting at their root cause. That's why I don't get distracted by how much patients drink. Once their emotional conflict is resolved in therapy, they won't need to self-medicate their pain any more and the drinking will stop on its own.

These comments, the first by an elderly psychiatric patient, the second by a young psychiatry resident, illustrate a sad reality in many mental health settings not specifically dedicated to alcohol treatment: despite the presence of trained psychiatrists, psychologists, social workers and counsellors, drinking problems are often completely ignored. The reasons for the oversight are partly ideological and partly practical.

Freudian theory, which remains influential with many mental health professionals, considers that heavy drinking is not a problem per se, but a side-effect of a psychodynamic conflict. Freud himself conveyed great scepticism about whether alcoholics could ever form a therapeutic alliance that would promote change. This combination of dismissing the importance of drinking on the one hand and being nihilistic about the prospects of intervention on the other has been absorbed into much of the mental health field and remains a considerable barrier to intervention in some settings.

At a practical level, training in psychiatry, psychology and allied fields often devotes little attention to drinking problems, despite their prevalence in psychiatric settings. Many mental health professionals thus feel incompetent to address problem drinking and hence never broach the subject with patients.

More positively, once drinking is recognized and taken seriously, virtually everything that can be done in a specialist alcohol clinic can be accomplished in a general mental health programme. This would include, for example, all those therapeutic processes and tactics described in Chapter 13.

Key differences between non-specialist and specialist settings

Alcohol problems are not inherently recognized in non-specialist settings. It goes without saying that a patient in an alcohol treatment programme has a drinking problem. Yet the same patient may never even be asked about drinking in another programme with a different mission. For example, only about 2% of people with alcohol use disorders have their drinking problem recognized by their general practitioner. In primary care the rate of detecting problem drinkers at the dependent end of the continuum is higher in absolute terms (4.5%), but this still reflects missing more than 19 out of every 20 cases (Cheeta et al., 2008). Even in the hospital setting, where one might imagine more time was available for enquiry and investigation, the problem often goes unrecognized (Canning et al., 1999).

Even when a drinking problem is identified in a non-specialist setting, both the patient and the staff may take the view that, 'Yes, the drinking is unfortunate, but it's not what I am here about'. The clinician may consider that drinking problems are someone else's job, and the patient is often happy to play along with the implication that the drinking problem bears no relationship to the problem for which he or she is seeking help.

A final key difference is that, in most non-specialist settings, the resources available for focusing on problem drinking are less than those available in specialist care. In a worksite employee assistance programme, it may be three or four 30-minute therapy sessions; in the primary care setting, a single 15-minute intervention followed by a phone call a month later; and in the Accident and Emergency Department (Emergency Room), 3 minutes of discussion after which the provider and patient will never see each other again. The interventions described later in this chapter thus assume greater time constraints than will the chapters of the book devoted to specialist care.

Case-finding and detection

As previously mentioned, outside of alcohol treatment programmes a drinking problem will not be assumed and may not be detected. If the element of drinking is allowed to remain hidden, it will defeat efforts to help the patient, client, student or employee. This section starts with a review of clinical strategies for enhancing detection of problem drinking, followed by a review of biological assays and standardized screening questionnaires.

The use of disarming questions

It is useful to have a few disarming questions about drinking problems which can be fed into any assessment in an almost throwaway fashion. The scene is often best set by a casual introductory remark such as, 'I always ask everyone about drinking – it can be important to feel that one can talk about one's drinking without being got at'. This implies that questions in this area are routine rather than the patient being singled out as a special case, and this is coupled with an immediate indication that anything the patient reveals will be sympathetically heard. The questions that follow are then usually best phrased in very open terms; for instance, 'Have you ever been worried about your drinking? For example, has it led to any rows or troubles at home or at work ... or any health troubles? Have you ever thought you ought to cut down? Has anyone criticized your drinking?'

Questions that feel out the possibility of worry or trouble are more likely to provide a way into fruitful dialogue than mechanistic questions along such lines as, 'How much do you drink?' The latter type of interrogation does not immediately reach across barriers towards what the patient is feeling and experiencing. It is too readily deflected by a bland answer, such as 'Just socially'.

Remembering who may be especially at risk

To bear in mind a list of who may be especially at risk is useful, provided the clinician does not become blinkered to the wider truth that drinking problems can affect both sexes and, either directly or indirectly, people of any age and every occupation. With that proviso, an awareness of a particular occupational hazard is then important (see Chapter 3). The single, separated or divorced person, those considered to be at risk of suicide, the recently bereaved and certain ethnic groups also go in this 'at risk' list. The person who is homeless and drifting is also very likely to have a drinking problem.

Common social presentations

One should always be on the look out for a hidden drinking problem with the client or patient who is frequently changing house, jobs or relationships. Family presentations are common – marital disharmony or family violence, the wife presenting with depression or the children with truanting, school failure, antisocial behaviour or neurotic symptoms. Criminal offences also suggest the need to ask about drinking.

Common psychiatric clues

Here the essential background list derives from Chapters 6 or 7. In particular one should be alert to the possibility of a drinking problem when the patient or client complains rather non-specifically of 'bad nerves', insomnia or depression. Phobic symptoms, paranoid symptoms and dementia or delirium may all at times be alcohol-related. A drug problem may also often be associated with a drinking problem. A suicidal attempt or gesture always demands enquiry into drinking.

Common medical clues

An account of the medical complications of heavy drinking is given in Chapter 5. In practical terms, one should be particularly alert if a patient repeatedly asks for a 'certificate', is a frequent visitor to the doctor's office on a Monday morning, is suffering from malnutrition, is complaining of any gastrointestinal disorder or liver problem, has otherwise unexplained heart trouble or is presenting with 'epilepsy' of late onset. Bruising may be a clue, or burns which resulted from a cigarette being dropped on the skin while the drinker was intoxicated. Accidents of any sort may be alcohol-related, and 20% of those involved in road traffic accidents may be classified as problem drinkers (Mayou & Bryant, 1995).

Not overlooking the obvious

The patient may declare the diagnosis by the smell of alcohol on their breath, by the bottle sticking out of their pocket, by their flushed face and bloodshot eyes or by their tremor, but even the fact that they are obviously intoxicated can be overlooked if the possibility of drinking is not held in mind. The patient who makes jokes about their drinking should have those jokes taken seriously. Similarly obvious presentations may be seen on a visit to the home: bottles and glasses lying around; decoration neglected and furniture reduced to a few sticks; the home may be a sad parody of a stage-set portraying decay. It would, however, be a mistake to think only in terms of such flagrant presentations and therefore overlook more subtle clues.

Having a word with the spouse or partner

If there is any cause to suspect excessive drinking, a word privately with the spouse is essential, particularly so if the patient says that 'the wife's too busy to come along'. It cannot be automatically assumed that the spouse will be ready and willing to talk about a family drinking problem; loyalty, fear of reprisal, embarrassment or a determined unwillingness to face up to the painful truth may all stand in the way. Much the same sort of tactful and open questioning may therefore be needed as with the partner who is drinking.

Laboratory tests

A number of laboratory tests are useful in the screening of populations for possible drinking problems – within, for instance, a routine medical examination when staff are recruited or undergo annual health checks. These tests can also be confirmatory in the individual case where excessive drinking is suspected but has not been admitted. No one test by itself is of as much value as a battery of investigations, and it seems likely that a properly chosen array of tests should nowadays detect over 90% of people with an, at least, moderately severe drinking problem (Niemela, 2007). A negative result does not rule out the possibility that excessive drinking has begun adversely to affect the individual's life, and false positives also occur. Laboratory tests, therefore, need to be interpreted shrewdly, and no test results stand by themselves; they can only be read in the context of all those considerations that have been listed above.

Sensitivity and specificity

Before listing the individual tests that may be used, it is helpful to identify two characteristics of such tests, which provide a guide to their usefulness in making a diagnosis. The *specificity* of a test is a guide to the extent to which a positive result is indicative of the condition of interest. In this case, the condition of interest may be heavy drinking, drinking problems or alcohol dependence, depending upon the circumstances and reasons for screening. A non-specific test for heavy drinking, for example, would show a positive result not just in heavy drinking but in a range of other unrelated disorders as well. The ideal test would be 100% specific, indicating that it only became positive as a result of heavy drinking. The *sensitivity* of a test indicates the extent to which it reliably detects every case of the condition of interest. For our present purpose, we would like a 100% sensitive test, which would always be positive in every case of heavy drinking, drinking problems or alcohol dependence (as appropriate).

To date, no one has devised a 100% specific and 100% sensitive test for heavy drinking, drinking problems or alcohol dependence. Different tests are more or less specific and sensitive and these parameters vary with the group under study, e.g. dependent or hazardous drinkers. The extent to which these tests will serve practical diagnostic needs depends upon the prevalence of heavy drinking, drinking problems or alcohol dependence in the population in which they are being used. In order to understand this better, let us consider a fictitious illustration.

A new test for heavy drinking, 'alcoholin', has 95% specificity and 60% sensitivity. It is used to screen 1000 apparently healthy employees at their annual medical review. Let us assume that 10% of these employees are actually drinking sufficient amounts of alcohol to be a cause for concern. How useful will the new test be?

Out of 1000 employees, 10% ($n = 100$) are drinking too much, and 60% of these ($n = 60$) will be correctly identified by the test as being 'heavy drinkers'. However, out of the whole group of 1000, 5% ($n = 50$) will be identified as positive due to non-specific (i.e. not alcohol-related) results of the test. Therefore, a total of 110 people will be identified by the test, and only 60 of these (55%) will actually be drinking too much. The 'alcoholin' test is therefore of limited usefulness, and must be followed by other tests and by more detailed enquiries, in order to confirm whether or not each of the individuals testing positive actually is drinking too much. Furthermore, 40 people who are drinking excessively will not be identified by the test.

The problems illustrated by this example become more severe as the ratio of those with versus without the disorder departs farther from 1 (i.e. as the base rate of disorder departs in either direction from 50%). Thus, if the prevalence of heavy drinking were only 1%, only 1 in 9 of those who tested positive with the same test would actually be heavy drinkers. Conversely, if used in a population where almost everyone had a drinking problem (say in an alcohol problems clinic), then more than 9 out of 10 of those who tested positive would be heavy drinkers.

Screening tests for heavy drinking

Let us now give consideration to the actual tests that are used to screen for heavy drinking in populations, as well as to monitor clinical progress in ongoing cases. The most useful tests are as follows.

Mean corpuscular volume

Mean corpuscular volume (MCV) is a measure of the size of red blood cells, which may increase in response to heavy drinking; due to a poorly understood mechanism affecting the developing cells. Sensitivity is 20–30% in hazardous drinkers and 40–50% in dependence, with a specificity of 64–100% (Conigrave, Saunders & Whitfield, 1995). In addition, the sensitivity in women is higher. The MCV, if it has been elevated as a result of heavy drinking, may remain raised for several months after a reduction or cessation of alcohol consumption. This is because of the relatively long life of red blood cells (about 120 days) and the average cell size reduces as those of normal size replace the large red blood cells. Other causes of a raised MCV that affect the specificity include vitamin B_{12} deficiency, folic acid deficiency, liver disease, blood disorders, hypothyroidism and smoking (Niemela, 2007).

Liver function tests

Serum gamma-glutamyl transferase (GGT) is an enzyme that the body produces in response to alcohol ingestion. However, it is also increased in liver damage, including that secondary to long-term heavy drinking. Serum aspartate aminotransferase (AST) and serum alanine aminotransferase (ALT) are also indicators of alcoholic hepatotoxicity, which may be elevated as a result of heavy drinking. Of these, GGT is generally considered to be the most useful as a screening test for heavy drinking. However, the sensitivity of 20–50% in hazardous consumption and 60–90% in dependence, along with a specificity of 55–100% (Conigrave, Saunders & Whitfield, 1995) has led to its value in this role being questioned. If GGT has been elevated due to drinking, it will fall again after abstinence is established. This occurs more rapidly than the restoration of MCV, with the level falling to approximately half after approximately 2 weeks of abstinence. It may still take several weeks to return to normal, depending upon the level to which it had been raised. Non-alcohol-related causes of a raised GGT include other liver diseases, with the greatest increases being associated with biliary obstruction (blockage of bile flow, from any cause), obesity, diabetes, pancreatitis, hyperlipidemia, cardiac failure, severe trauma, nephrotic syndrome, renal rejection and other drugs (e.g. barbiturates, anticonvulsants, statins and anticoagulants) (Niemela, 2007). With more serious liver damage other biochemical parameters, such as the albumin level, clotting factors and bilirubin, will also be altered, and in such cases there may be enduring abnormalities of some levels, even after prolonged abstinence.

Carbohydrate-deficient (desialylated) transferrin

Carbohydrate-deficient (desialylated) transferrin (CDT) is a variant of a serum protein that transports iron around the body. The usual transferrin molecule contains three or more sialic acid residues, a carbohydrate. Excessive alcohol consumption is associated, by reasons not clearly understood, with the 'stripping off' of some of these residues. Levels are increased in response to heavy drinking. Its sensitivity as a test of hazardous consumption is 26–62% and for dependence 65–95% with a specificity greater than 90% (Conigrave, Saunders & Whitfield, 1995). This is arguably better than most other tests, and it is now considered by some to be the best available screening test for heavy drinking. Similar to GGT, an elevated CDT takes approximately 2 weeks to fall to half its level on stopping drinking (Niemela, 2007).

Blood alcohol concentration

Blood alcohol concentration (BAC) returns to zero quickly with abstinence: in humans, the average rate of clearance of alcohol from the blood is 15 mg/100 ml per hour or, very approximately, 1 unit per hour. This results in a fairly low sensitivity when used as a screening test for habitual heavy drinking. Depending upon the time and context of testing, as well as the threshold alcohol concentration used to define a positive result, moderate social drinkers will also be detected, thus making BAC fairly non-specific as well. Blood alcohol (or breath alcohol as an indirect measure) is therefore not often used as a screening test in the way that GGT or CDT may be used. However, BAC is known to be related to impairment of psychomotor performance and therefore provides a particularly valuable measure in the workplace, or in other safety sensitive contexts, such as driving. The BAC may also have an underestimated utility as a screening test in the clinical setting.

Even if not used as a screening test, BAC may be a useful confirmatory investigation. A patient may, for instance, say that he 'only had a few drinks' the previous evening, but at 9 am the next morning he still has a blood alcohol level of say 60 mg/100 ml, suggesting much heavier consumption. In addition, the finding of a high BAC in the absence of evident intoxication suggests a high level of tolerance and is therefore important presumptive evidence for habitual heavy drinking.

Other potential biomarkers of alcohol consumption

Other biomarkers of alcohol misuse are currently being evaluated and may be introduced into future clinical practice. These include acetaldehyde adducts, phosphatidylethanol and sialic acid in blood along with 5-hydroxytryptophol and ethyl glucuronide in urine (see Niemela, 2007). Ethyl glucuronide can also be detected in other tissues, and this raises the possibility of new sampling methods to detect alcohol misuse using hair samples; an approach that has already been developed and adopted in the detection of drug misuse.

Laboratory tests: an overall judgement

It will be apparent that none of the tests mentioned above offers improvement over the fictitious 'alcoholin' test. In fact, 'alcoholin' could easily be GGT or CDT. All these tests are limited in their usefulness as screening instruments and in some circumstances standardized questionnaires, such as the AUDIT, may fare better (Drummond, Ghodse & Chengappa, 2007). However, the sensitivity and specificity of laboratory tests as screening instruments may be improved when they are used in combination. More generally, laboratory tests will be of greatest assistance to both clinician and patient if used in full awareness of the strengths and weaknesses of each; in this field of practice there are skills to be learnt in using this technology to best advantage.

Screening questionnaires

A number of screening questionnaires have been devised in recent years with the intention of detecting hazardous and harmful drinking, as well as dependence, in non-medical settings. In this context, the Alcohol Use Disorders Identification Test (AUDIT) is of interest. The AUDIT was developed by an international group of investigators, at the request of the World Health Organization (Babor & World Health Organization, 1992). It was designed for use by healthcare workers in both developed and developing countries. It shows good sensitivity and specificity and is useful in screening for hazardous and harmful drinking in non-treatment-seeking populations.

The AUDIT is administered as a brief (10-item) structured interview or self-report instrument and comprises questions about recent alcohol consumption (3 items, which, incidentally, should be adjusted to local standard drink definitions), alcohol-related problems (4 items) and alcohol dependence (3 items). A score of eight or above denotes hazardous drinking (or worse). The AUDIT is not in itself a diagnostic test, but it is the first step in the process of identifying, diagnosing and treating someone with an alcohol problem (Babor & Higgins-Biddle, 2001). Based on the score generated by the AUDIT, the associated manual provides guidance for the management of any identified alcohol problem.

The AUDIT is also available as an even briefer 5-item questionnaire, which has almost 80% sensitivity and 95% specificity in screening for hazardous alcohol intake and formal alcohol disorders (Piccinelli et al., 1997). Anyone scoring five or above should undergo further assessment. The AUDIT-C is another shorter version comprising the first three AUDIT consumption items: here a score of three should lead to further assessment (Bush et al., 1998) .

Other validated questionnaires include the Fast Alcohol Screening Test (FAST) and the Paddington Alcohol Test (PAT), both developed for use in the busy Accident and Emergency Department (Emergency Room) (Hodgson et al., 2002; Smith et al., 1996).

Older screening tools, including CAGE and the Michigan Alcoholism Screening Test (MAST), are better at picking up more extreme or dependent drinkers rather than hazardous or harmful drinkers (Mayfield, MacLeod & Hall, 1974; Selzer, 1971). CAGE is an acronym derived from taking the first letter from the keywords of each of the four items that comprise the CAGE questionnaire and it also acts as a handy mnemonic; Cut down, Annoyed, Guilty and Eye-opener. The MAST is a 24-item questionnaire also published in a 10-item brief form (BMAST; Pokorny, Miller & Kaplan, 1972). Both the CAGE and the MAST focus on lifetime experiences of alcohol use. The MAST, for instance, has among its items delirium tremens and hospital admission for drinking. However, they show remarkably good sensitivity and specificity, for 'excessive drinking' as well as 'alcoholism', and may be superior to laboratory tests when used as screening instruments (Bernadt et al., 1982) .

Two screening instruments have been developed for use with pregnant women, the T-ACE (Sokol, Martier & Ager, 1989) and the TWEAK (Russell, 1994). They each perform rather better than the CAGE and MAST, the 5-item TWEAK being more sensitive and less specific than the 4-item T-ACE.

Screening instruments are of value in hospital settings where there is a more or less captive population reasonably attuned to the idea of filling in questionnaires. Questionnaires may also be of value in primary care, although usefulness in this setting depends more on the characteristics of the panel for which the general practitioner is responsible (King, 1986). But, in general, these tests have found more application as research tools than in the front-line medical and social settings where a paper-and-pencil test provides no substitute for vigilance, sympathetic questioning and the very real skills needed for identifying drinking problems of all manner of degree, type and disguise.

Practical conclusions on case-finding

The relative utility of the various procedures described above, for detection and diagnosis of heavy drinking and drinking problems, is summarized in Table 10.2. To a large extent their utility for detection and screening is determined by their sensitivity, and their utility for diagnosis depends upon their specificity. However, both parameters are important in both contexts. Cost, convenience and flexibility are also important.

There is no substitute for careful clinical enquiry as a means for detecting heavy drinking, drinking problems or alcohol dependence, either in specialist practice or in primary care or other generalist settings. Information gained in this way may valuably be supported by the discerning use of appropriate laboratory investigations, breath alcohol testing and questionnaires.

Where a large, healthy population must be screened as, for example, in the occupational setting, even a brief clinical interview may not be possible and questionnaires are therefore

Table 10.2. Advantages and disadvantages of different screening procedures.

Procedure	Advantages	Disadvantages
Clinical interview	Flexibility	Subjectivity
	Potentially high specificity	Dependent upon clinical skill and time/trouble taken
	Potential to detect cases that laboratory tests or questionnaires will miss	Poor sensitivity if the subject is embarrassed or covering up
		Can be time-consuming
Laboratory tests	Objective	Limited sensitivity and specificity (CDT arguably best, but GGT not much worse)
	Quick and convenient for screening large numbers of subjects	CDT is expensive (GGT much cheaper)
	If positive, useful to monitor subsequent progress	Do not detect social/psychological problems
	Detect heavy use/some tissue toxicity (e.g. liver/blood)	
Breath alcohol estimation	Objective	Rapid clearance of alcohol from the blood/breath limits sensitivity
	Cheap and convenient	Detects alcohol use, not problems per se (i.e. poor specificity)
	Good for detecting drinking in safety sensitive context (e.g. drinking and driving)	
	Useful to confirm history and monitor progress	
Questionnaires	Standardized and more objective than clinical interview	Subject to honesty of the respondent
	Cheap and convenient	Limited sensitivity and specificity (but better than laboratory tests)

CDT, carbohydrate-deficient (desialylated) transferrin; GGT, gamma-glutamyl transferase.

advantageous. But, where the follow-through of detection includes disciplinary procedures or other adverse consequences, responses to questionnaires may not be reliable. In such circumstances, laboratory tests such as GGT, MCV or CDT can give useful information. Where the maintenance of a safe environment is of concern, such as drinking and driving or certain work settings, blood or breath alcohol testing may also be effective.

Triage and intervention once a case of drinking problems has been identified in a non-speciality setting

When a drinking problem has come to light, the helping professional must make a judgement as to whether the appropriate decision is to attempt to manage the problem on site or to link the problem drinker to specialist alcohol services. This section discusses this triage process and how to proceed in each of these situations.

How to determine whether the case will be handled in a non-specialist setting

From a clinical standpoint, the most compelling reason for handling someone with a drinking problem in a non-specialist setting is that therapeutic gains can be made with the more limited level of intervention that can typically be accomplished in such settings. There is no firm rule for making such judgements, but two general guidelines are supported both by research and by common sense. The lower the severity of the individual's drinking problem and the greater his or her social capital (e.g. a job, a marriage, a network of friends), the greater the likelihood that a modest intervention can nudge the course of drinking down a safer road (Moyer et al., 2002).

In cases where an advance judgement of whether specialist care is required is not easily made, the clinician should make the matter empirical: that is, provide the non-specialist interventions (described in the next section) and then assess the impact. If the drinking problem responds to the intervention, then so much the better; if not, the failure provides information for both the clinician and patient that the problem is too severe to respond to this level of care, and elevation to the next 'step' in the care system is the logical response. Indeed, from a public health viewpoint, it is probably a good strategy for all but the most obviously impaired problem drinkers to receive lower intensity interventions as a first step, such that specialist services are conserved for those who most need them.

The concept of stepped care being invoked here is a perfectly reasonable one that has long guided medical care and public health planning in many countries. In the alcohol field, however, it has faced some practical problems that have impeded its impact. Many non-specialist providers do not want to treat even minor alcohol problems, whether because they feel incompetent to do so, look down on patients with drinking problems or feel burned by prior experiences (in their clinical or personal life) with problem drinkers. This leads some of them to over-refer patients reflexively to specialist alcohol services the moment even a relatively minor alcohol problem comes to light. In addition to the problems this can create in overloading specialist services, it sends a potent meta-message to the patient: 'Your drinking problem is so severe or so shameful (or both), that while I, your doctor, can handle whatever other problems you have, at this I throw up my hands'.

Resistance to specialist referral can also come from the other end of the patient–doctor interaction. For most health conditions, referral to a specialist is experienced as a chance to get expert help and superior care. Few patients with a heart condition, for example, would react with anger if their general practitioner said, 'Just to be sure you get the care you need, I'm going to refer you to a cardiologist who has much more experience with your condition than I have'. Yet many people with drinking problems have no interest in specialist care. They may fear consequences to their reputation if they are seen entering the door of a 'rehab', turn up their nose at being in group therapy with 'chronic drunks', or simply may be unable to accept that their alcohol problem is indeed too severe to be handled by a non-specialist. In such cases, the clinician can still make efforts to manage the problem in the non-specialist setting, but should still communicate that a referral would be better in order not to collude with the patient in denying the severity of the problem.

The above hints at the other broad class of cases that may be treated in non-specialist settings, not because it is optimal but because needs must. In the hustle and bustle of the Accident and Emergency Department (Emergency Room), a one-time, brief chat may be all that can be done even with a severely dependent drinker. In the USA, a patient's health insurance may practically preclude specialist alcohol treatment, as can restrictions of distance and time. Again, there is little to be lost with trying a less involved intervention in such cases, as long as the clinician does not communicate false hope or implicitly minimize the severity of the problem.

Intervention within the non-specialist setting

The three mainstays of non-specialist intervention are the provision of information about safe drinking guidelines, brief motivational interviewing and medical management. Each can also be part of more comprehensive specialist treatment, but are discussed here because they are well suited to the constraints of most non-specialist settings (e.g. primary care).

Provision of information on safe drinking, with special attention to pregnant patients

Safe drinking guidelines were reviewed in Chapter 1, and need not be repeated here. As such, guidelines are simple and easy to convey and can motivate change; there is little excuse for a patient with a drinking problem leaving any of the settings discussed in this chapter without having been exposed to the guidelines, even if only in a handout.

In the special case of a pregnant patient, the usual drinking guidelines do not apply. On the positive side, a woman who is distressed because she became pregnant on a night of unusually heavy alcohol consumption (e.g. an anniversary party, New Year's Eve) will be reassured to learn that alcohol on the night of conception is cleared from the body prior to the time when the fertilized egg has implanted in the uterus.

On the more concerning side, alcohol consumption after this point can profoundly damage a fetus, as described in Chapter 5. Physicians and alcohol experts are divided as to the best advice for drinking limits during pregnancy. In the USA the typical advice is total abstention. Recent UK advice has been to avoid alcohol during the first 3 months and to limit consumption to 1–2 units once or twice a week during the rest of the pregnancy (see Chapter 8). The authors of this volume candidly do not know which advice is the best – the science does not permit such a simple judgement – but lean towards the US view. Even though a single drink a day is unlikely to damage a fetus directly, some evidence (British Medical Association Board of Science, 2007) has indicated that the developing brain may respond to alcohol by developing more receptors, potentially priming the brain to be more prone to alcohol problems in adulthood. Further, in our clinical experience, to some people 'a single drink' will mean 3 ounces of rye with ice in a tumbler, no matter what the guidelines define as standard. Lastly, given that the average woman in the UK and the USA is pregnant less than 2% of her adult lifespan, erring on the side of caution seems a small sacrifice when a long-term view of the mother and child is taken.

Brief motivational intervention

The term brief motivational intervention (BMI) is being used here as a 'grab bag' of techniques alternatively called brief intervention, motivational interviewing and brief motivational interviewing. These techniques were initially developed and tested in the UK, and are now employed in a wide range of developed and developing nations. All variants of these interventions assume that contact between the provider and the patient will be one to three in number, including instances in which the latter contacts are telephone calls from the clinician or someone else in his or her practice (e.g. a nurse).

In some respects, BMI is an attitude as much as a technique, being developed explicitly in contrast with the (albeit somewhat stereotyped) image of the alcoholism counsellor who labels every patient 'alcoholic', demands lifetime abstinence and accuses anyone who disagrees as being in denial. In BMI, rather than a making a moral judgement or being confrontational or hectoring, the clinician is concerned, warm and matter of fact. The patient's perceptions of the benefits of drinking are acknowledged rather than debated. The exchange is respectful and to the point, with the responsibility for making the ultimate decision about drinking placed explicitly on the patient. The patient is also responsible for setting change goals, with the clinician reinforcing small steps (e.g. avoiding drinking and driving, not drinking 2 days in a row, alternating soft drinks with alcoholic drinks during drinking sessions) rather than insisting on an all-or-nothing approach.

One helpful mnemonic for the components of BMI is '**FRAMES**' (Miller & Sanchez, 1993). Table 10.3 describes each technique in some detail. The rationale for each is discussed below.

Feedback can be powerful because heavy drinkers often underestimate the risks of their drinking, as well as how their drinking compares to that of the population. Normative feedback, for example noting that a patient's alcohol consumption is in the 90th percentile of the population, can be motivating insofar as many individuals dislike being outside socio-behavioural norms. Risk-related information can also enhance motivation, by inducing appropriate anxiety about possible harms.

Placing **responsibility** on the patient is partly an acknowledgement of reality (the patient is ultimately in the driver's seat) and partly a shrewd clinical tactic. When they feel pressed to change, many individuals will defend their drinking or otherwise engage in a power struggle with the clinician. Saying flat out, 'Of course whether you change is entirely up to you. I can

Table 10.3. The FRAMES mnemonic for brief motivational intervention.

Feedback: The clinician conveys in a factual, non-judgemental fashion the level of risk associated with the patient's drinking. Feedback may include the results of laboratory tests, including for medical problems upon which heavy drinking has an exacerbating effect (e.g. hypertension). In addition to oral feedback, written materials are commonly provided.

Responsibility of the patient: The clinician explicitly acknowledges that the patient has the power to change and that no one else can make him or her do so. Responsibility for goal-setting is also specifically allotted to the patient.

Advice to change: The clinician communicates concern about the current level of drinking and provides advice to reduce risk; for example, to avoid drinking in particular situations or to reduce or eliminate alcohol consumption.

Menu of change strategies: A range of options should be presented to the patient, including formal alcohol treatment, attendance at mutual-help groups and use of self-help manuals. For many patients, a range of interim goals the patient can attempt on his or her own can be useful; for example, keeping a diary of drinking, strictly limiting drinking to particular times of day (e.g. never before 6 pm) or days of the week (e.g. never the evening before a work or school day) and switching from regular to low-strength beer.

Empathetic counselling style: Confrontation and condemnation are completely avoided. The patient's emotions, including those that might mitigate against change (e.g. fear of failure, enjoyment of drinking), are respectfully acknowledged. The clinician reflects that patient's emotions in order to communicate understanding; for example, 'You would like not to deal with hangovers and vomiting in the mornings, but you also enjoy the way heavy drinking makes you feel while you are doing it'.

Self-efficacy enhancement: The clinician communicates confidence in the patient's abilities. To enhance motivation, the clinician specifically reinforces any verbal commitment to change; for example, 'You said you had been thinking of making a change and maybe this is the right time'.

Adapted from: Miller and Sanchez (1993).

provide advice but I can't decide for you', defuses any potential battles of this sort. Further, perception of having control enhances both motivation to change and sense of being able to accomplish it (Kanfer & Scheft, 1988).

Advice to change and the **menu** of alternative strategies must be offered completely in the spirit just described, with respect for the patient's autonomy. Thus, not, 'You must stop drinking right now!' but, 'I recognize that change is difficult, but I'd be failing in my job as your physician if I didn't advise you to take a hard look at your drinking before it destroys your health'. A menu of alternatives in some sense bridges advice provision with respect for autonomy, in that, although the patient is given a range of choices, all of them are aligned with the clinician's fundamental advice to recognize the current drinking as problematic and make some change in it.

The **empathic** style and enhancement of the patient's **self-efficacy** work together to reduce resistance to change and increase confidence that it can be accomplished. They also create a positive relationship between the clinician and patient that can facilitate future contacts.

Do such clinical tactics really work? BMI can be used in many contexts; for the present purposes, the question is how effective it is in non-specialist settings. A meta-analysis of 34 outcome studies conducted in such settings (typically primary care) found strong evidence of benefit, with significant reductions both in drinking-related problems and in alcohol consumption at follow-ups of less than 3 months, 3–6 months and 6–12 months (Moyer et al., 2002). And of course, whether a BMI succeeds or fails, the result will be informative as to what next steps, if any, are required.

Medical management

Medical management is a well-established model of care for many chronic illnesses. It does not compete with BMI as a strategy and indeed can follow after it. Care is ongoing in this model but, unlike with traditional alcohol treatment, the primary provider is a non-specialist (e.g. a general practitioner, nurse practitioner, physician's assistant) and the sessions are shorter. A manual describing this intervention in detail is available free of charge from the US National Institute on Alcohol Abuse and Alcoholism (Pettinati et al., 2004).

The initial session of medical management can last as long as 45 minutes and comprises a diagnostic interview, a review with the patient of the health and social effects of the drinking and a consideration of the medication options available (see Chapter 14). Follow-up appointments occur every week or two and are shorter in duration, perhaps 15–20 minutes. These are not psychotherapy sessions but a focused review of drinking since the last visit, medication compliance and side-effects and overall functioning. Concurrent involvement in mutual-help groups is encouraged but is not essential for medical management. If the drinking problem becomes more severe, the decision may be made to transfer the patient to the more extensive services available in a specialty alcohol programme.

A few comments on making the link to specialist care

Either based on the initial triage decision or in light of a poor outcome from non-specialist intervention, some patients will need to be transferred to a specialist setting. The clinician should be aware that this is a point at which many patients go missing. Sometimes this reflects an unwillingness to change, but in many cases it also reflects practicalities. In making the referral, it is therefore quite important for the clinician to explore the mundane questions with the patient: 'Are there alcohol services close to where you live?', 'Do you have a means to get there?; 'If it's a residential programme, is it possible for you to be away from work and family responsibilities?' As a general rule, the closer the programme is, the more rapidly it can accept the patient and the simpler the bureaucratic procedures (e.g. is there a mountain of new forms the patient must complete or can the patient's medical record simply be moved over to the new setting), the more likely the patient is to follow-through on the referral. Finally, as with all referrals to specialists, the clinician should stay in touch with the specialist rather than say, 'Out of sight out of mind'. For their part, specialists in the alcohol treatment programme have to keep the lines of communication as open as possible with the referring generalists and not become (as one referring physician put it) 'a black hole from which none of my patients ever returns'.

Summary

A care system that only provides help for drinking problems within alcohol treatment programmes will have a minimal impact on public health. Helping professionals who don't work in alcohol programmes can enhance public health and their own success by making alcohol intervention part of their work. A range of instruments is available to detect drinking problems in non-specialist settings, as are some evidence-based approaches for intervention. Particularly when drinking problems are at the lower end of severity, there is every reason to believe that non-specialists can make a very positive impact on the course of drinking problems.

References

Babor T F, Higgins-Biddle J (2001) Alcohol screening and brief intervention; dissemination strategies for medical practice and public health. *Addiction* **95**, 677–686.

Babor T F, World Health Organization (1992) *AUDIT: The Alcohol Use Disorders Identification Test: Guidelines for Use in Primary Health Care*. Geneva: World Health Organization.

Bernadt M W, Mumford J, Taylor C, Smith B, Murray R M (1982) Comparison of questionnaire and laboratory tests in the detection of excessive drinking and alcoholism. *Lancet*, **8267**, 325–328.

British Medical Association Board of Science (2007) *Fetal Alcohol Spectrum Disorders – A Guide for Healthcare Professionals*. London: British Medical Association.

Bush K, Kivlahan D R, McDonnell M B, Fihn S D, Bradley K A (1998) The AUDIT alcohol consumption questions (AUDIT-C): an effective brief screening test for problem drinking. *Archives of Internal Medicine* **158**, 1789–1795.

Canning U P, Kennell-Webb S A, Marshall E J, Wessely S C, Peters T J (1999) Substance misuse in acute general medical admissions. *Quarterly Journal of Medicine* **92**, 319–326.

Cheeta S, Drummond C, Oyefeso A, et al. (2008) Low identification of alcohol use disorders in general practice in England. *Addiction* **103**, 766–773.

Conigrave K M, Saunders J B, Whitfield J B (1995) Diagnostic tests for alcohol consumption. *Alcohol and Alcoholism* **30**, 13–26.

Crawford M, Patton R, Touquet R, et al. (2004) Screening and referral for brief intervention of alcohol-misusing patients in an emergency department: a pragmatic randomised contolled trial. *Lancet* **364**, 1134–1139.

Drummond C, Ghodse H, Chengappa S (2007) Investigations in alcohol use disorders. In *Clinical Topics in Addictions*, E Day (ed.). London: Royal College of Psychiatrists, pp. 113–129.

Havard A, Shakeshaft A, Sanson-Fisher R (2008) Systematic review and meta-analysis of strategies targeting alcohol problems in emergency departments: interventions reduce alcohol-related injuries. *Addiction* **103**, 368–376.

Hodgson R J, Alwyn T, John B, Thom B, Smith A (2002) The FAST Alcohol Screening Test. *Alcohol and Alcoholism* **37**, 61–66.

Humphreys K, Tucker J (2002) Towards more responsive and effective intervention systems for alcohol-related problems. *Addiction* **97**, 126–132.

Kanfer F H, Scheft B K (1988) *Guiding the Process of Therapeutic Change*. Champaign, IL: Research Press.

King M (1986) At risk drinking among general practice attenders: validation of the CAGE questionnaire. *Psychological Medicine* **16**, 213–217.

Mayfield D, MacLeod G, Hall, P (1974) The CAGE questionnaire: validation of a new alcoholism screening instrument. *American Journal of Psychiatry* **131**, 1121–1123.

Mayou R, Bryant B (1995) Alcohol and road traffic accidents. *Alcohol and Alcoholism* **30**, 709–711.

Miller W R, Sanchez V C (1993) Motivating young adults for treatment and lifestyle change. In *Issues in Alcohol Use and Misuse by Young Adults*, G Howard (ed.). South Bend, IN: University of Notre Dame Press.

Moyer A, Finney J W, Swearingen C E, Vergun P (2002) Brief interventions for alcohol problems: a meta-analytic review of controlled investigations in treatment-seeking and non-treatment-seeking populations. *Addiction* **97**, 279–292.

Niemela, O (2007) Biomarkers in alcoholism. *Clinica Chimica Acta* **377**, 39–49.

Pettinati H M, Weiss R D, Miller W R, et al. (2004) *Medical Management (MM) Treatment Manual*. Bethesda, MD: National Institute on Alcohol Abuse and Alcoholism.

Piccinelli M, Tessari E, Bortolomasi M, et al. (1997) Efficacy of the alcohol use disorders identification test as a screening tool for hazardous alcohol intake and related disorders in primary care: a validity study. *British Medical Journal* **314**, 420–424.

Pokorny A D, Miller B A, Kaplan H B (1972) The brief MAST: a shortened version of the Michigan Alcoholism Screening Test. *American Journal of Psychiatry* **129**, 342–345.

Russell M (1994) New assessment tools for risk taking during pregnancy: T-ACE, TWEAK and others. *Alcohol Health and Research World* **18**, 55–61.

Selzer M L (1971) The Michigan Alcoholism Screening Test: the quest for a new diagnostic instrument. *American Journal of Psychiatry* **127**(12), 1653–1658.

Smith S G T, Touquet R, Wright S, Das Gupta N (1996) Detection of alcohol misusing patients in Accident and Emergency Departments: the Paddington Alcohol Test (PAT). *Journal of Accident and Emergency Medicine* **13**, 308–312.

Sokol R J, Martier S S, Ager J W (1989) The T-ACE questions: practical prenatal detection of risk-taking. *American Journal of Obstetrics and Gynaecology* **160**, 863–870.

Substance Abuse and Mental Health Services Administration (SAMHSA) (2007) Results of the 2006 National Survey on Drug Use and Health. http://www.drugabusestatistics.samhsa.gov/nsduh.htm.

Treatment: context and content

Assessment as the beginning of therapy

Practically, the assessment process should explore what the individual wants or expects, provide the information based on which the drinking problem can be identified and explore any factors that may complicate the presentation and management, including the physical, psychiatric or social. On the basis of this assessment, a treatment approach can be recommended, and if this differs from that requested by the individual a mutually agreed treatment plan should be negotiated.

This chapter seeks to cover practical issues related to the art and technique of such history-taking. However, more research-orientated and structured approaches are provided by diagnostic instruments such as the Diagnostic Interview Schedule (DIS), the Structured Clinical Interview for DSM-III-R (SCID) and the Comprehensive International Diagnostic Interview (CIDI) (First, 1997; Robins et al., 1995; World Health Organization, 1993). The present chapter is cast in the form of a series of working guidelines. As such the framework builds on the general format for psychiatric history-taking (University of London, Institute of Psychiatry & Bethlem Royal Hospital and the Maudsley Hospital, 1987). History-taking is a rewarding aspect of therapeutic work, and the reader should not be daunted by the details of this presentation. In particular, anyone coming to this type of work for the first time should not attempt to absorb everything that is being said here at one sitting. Consequently, for those very much constrained by time, there follows a description of what might reasonably be achieved in a 15-minute assessment or even a mere 5 minutes. Then, having outlined the patient interview, the chapter will describe a parallel approach to history-taking from the partner or 'significant other'. Tables will provide a summary of the key points in history-taking, both for the person presenting with the problem and for the partner or 'significant other'. Finally, a scheme for the construction of a case formulation is provided.

Case history as initiation of therapy

Taking a history from an individual should not only be a matter of obtaining facts to be written down in the case notes. It is an interaction between two people, and it ought to be as meaningful for the person who answers the questions as for the questioner. The patient should be invited to use the occasion as a personal opportunity to review his or her past and present, and to make sense of what may previously have been a chaotic array of happenings. There is research evidence that demonstrates the potential power of the initial clinical encounter to change the drinker's attitudes, enhance commitment and clarify goals (Thom et al., 1992).

Assessment is therefore the beginning of therapy (Novey, 1968). The relationship between patient and therapist begins to be determined at this moment, and, if the occasion is mishandled, the patient may not attend for a second appointment. A positive relationship has been shown between the perceived quality of the initial assessment and client receptiveness with subsequent willingness to engage in treatment (Fiorentine, Nakashima & Anglin, 1999; Hyams, Cartwright & Spratley, 1996).

Setting the tone

Handling the initial contact with someone who has a drinking problem does not stand entirely apart from work with any other type of patient, but it may have been especially difficult for this person to get themselves so far as to recognize that they have a need for help, and then to keep the first appointment. To admit that they are not fully in control of their drinking can be felt by the patient as admitting failure, and they may be highly ambivalent about walking into the interview room.

It is therefore worthwhile for the therapist to ensure that they are not taking their own goodwill as self-evident. Special care must be put into showing ordinary courtesies; to introduce himself or herself, to walk up the corridor to the interview room with the patient rather than five paces in front, to take a coat and hang it up, to show that person towards a comfortable chair, turning off the mobile phone, are small but telling gestures. It may be useful to say, 'I'm glad you've decided to come, and I hope that this afternoon will be helpful for you'.

Case notes have to be recorded and a semi-structured approach is useful. There is a way of handling this procedure that makes it informal and unthreatening. The first question should always be something like, 'What can we do for you?' There should then be a willingness to listen to the answer, while looking at the person who is talking. The answer may be discursive or brief, may bear on the drinking or deal with other issues, but the patient is setting the scene in the way that he or she themselves finds helpful. It can be useful to explore the circumstances that have led to this appointment being made.

The therapist then has to introduce the fact that they are going to take a formal history. A statement such as the following can be made.

> 'I've listened to what you are saying carefully. If you don't mind, it would help if I asked you some questions and made notes. I'm going to assume that all your answers are as honest and as open as you can possibly make them. If there's anything too difficult to talk about, let me know, and I'll respect your feelings.'

This might seem to be emphasizing the ordinary assumption of the therapeutic position in a way which is overdrawn. But if history-taking is clumsily handled and the initial relationship not sympathetically established, the interview will be interpreted as an attack, and defences will rapidly be brought into play. The stereotype of the drinker as someone who 'never tells the truth' will have been confirmed. The disadvantages that stem from a neglect of the dynamic interactions of the initial interview are not only that the information obtained will probably be incomplete and inaccurate, but also that damage will be done to what should have been the initiation of therapy.

How much time for history-taking?

The scheme described in this chapter for the patient's history-taking envisages two parts to the reconstruction – the background history and the drinking history. To cover all of the matters which lie in either area, and to conduct the interview at a pace which allows useful pauses and human interactions, clearly means that the process cannot be accomplished in a few minutes. The general practitioner may know that 10–15 minutes is the most that can be allowed for a consultation. It could therefore seem impractical to lay out a scheme for history-taking which may on occasion require 2 hours for completion.

There are several reasons for believing that it is reasonable primarily to set things out in this way. There need be no apologies for the worth of investing time in thorough initial history-taking (especially if this is also seen as the start of therapy, and therapeutic time well-spent). The only problem is how that time is to be found. In some settings it may not be out of step with usual practices to expect that considerable time can be found for the initial history: a hospital in-patient unit, for instance. In other settings it may be feasible to take part of the history and then to ask the patient to come back so that the work can be completed. It is often possible to find a point at which the history-taking can temporarily be interrupted, and the patient may return for the second session with some reflective working-through accomplished meanwhile and an enhanced ability to join in the work of historical review.

Another consideration is the usefulness of extended history-taking for training. The process of taking, say, 5–10 histories at full-length with supervision and feedback, can mean the acquisition of very worthwhile skills. With trained practice an interview may then be conducted more quickly than had previously seemed feasible (and without undue sense of hurry). To acquire skill in handling such an enquiry, and then to design for oneself a shorter approach based on what has been learnt and the needs of a particular setting or agency, is better than to start out with a greatly abbreviated approach. Once familiar, the essential framework of this scheme is, moreover, not overwhelmingly complex.

With the reasons for setting out a full-length approach to history-taking thus stated, later in the chapter we also give as headings, 'What might go into a 15-minute assessment?', and 'What can be achieved in 5 minutes?' In the paragraphs that follow, the discussion will first focus on the meeting with the patient or client, and we will then turn to the interview with the partner or significant other.

Background history

It is assumed that anyone coming to this work will already have developed their own general style of case-taking, or that the agency in which they operate will have its preferred format. Emphasis will instead be placed on elucidating those features of background history which are likely to be especially relevant to the understanding of drinking problems.

Background history and drinking history are intimately related. In the *background* section, many matters are touched on which will inevitably elicit information on drinking and drinking problems, and such information should be jotted down, rather than discarded or ignored because it does not come tidily at the right moment. The *drinking* section, as well as eliciting further new information, then gives the opportunity to bring together and **explore the relevance of** the material which the patient gave earlier.

Family history

1   **For both parents.** Age, health (and mental health), occupation. Date and cause of death if deceased. Quality of relationships offered to patient in childhood; parents' drinking and drinking attitudes and drinking problems **and their use of drugs**; psychiatric illness. Present relationship with parents. Enquiry may also be needed into drinking problems and psychiatric illness in the wider family.

2   **Siblings.** Basic information; social and personal adjustment or maladjustment (including drinking **and use of drugs**); present contact with patient **and quality of relationship**.

3   **Childhood environment.** Reconstruction of the home atmosphere during childhood, and the social and cultural milieu to which this home related. Parental discord,

separation, divorce. Other important adult figures: step-parents, grandparents, aunts, uncles. History of trauma, including childhood sexual abuse.

The purpose of this section is to obtain a preliminary understanding of the crucial early relationships and experiences which may have contributed to the shaping of the individual's strengths or vulnerabilities, the possible dynamic meaning of alcohol (the meaning attached to alcohol because of parental drinking) and the individual's cultural symbolism of alcohol.

Personal history

1 **Birth.** Date of birth; any evidence of birth trauma which might have resulted in brain injury?
2 **Adjustment in childhood.** This assessment should include the psychological and social strengths of the individual, as well as any difficulties. For example, the good times of childhood, what gave them hope, their ability to make friends, signs of mastery, the proud moments and their sources of love. In addition, evidence should be sought of neurotic symptoms in childhood, difficulty in relating to other children, conduct disorder, dyslexia, trauma and childhood illness. Questioning around this area may help understanding as to whether the patient has exhibited lifelong traits of anxiety or difficulty in adjustment, and it is useful to go back to a period before their personality picture was overlaid by the drink.
3 **Education.** Information on schooling, with particular reference to social adjustment at school – how the patient got on with other children and with teachers, school refusal or truancy, whether they were bullied; literacy, exam certificates obtained. To ask, 'What were you best at?' will help confer a sense of self. Technical or university qualifications.
4 **Occupational history and present occupation.** Chronological information on jobs held; the alcohol-exposed nature of any occupation; problems caused by drinking.
5 **Sexual orientation and adjustment**, and the impact of drinking.
6 **Relationships and marriage**. Information should be gathered on previous relationships and marriages and whether there were any noteworthy reasons for breakdown.
7 **Children**. Dates of birth and sex; closeness of the patient to children and parenting abilities; perceived impact of drinking on the children and their reaction to the drinking.
8 **Finances and housing** and the impact of drinking.
9 **Leisure.** The way in which the person usually spends their leisure time, involvement of drinking in leisure pursuits, the degree to which leisure activities have been curtailed by drinking and how rewarding they find these activities.
10 **Religious affiliation and important beliefs.**
11 **Forensic history.** Enquiry should be made regarding public drunkenness offences, drink driving and all other convictions or pending court appearances. The relationship between the drinking and the offending may need to be explored.

Social support, friendship networks and the quality of life

The aim here is to let the patient sense and speak about the overall security, extent and satisfaction of their engagement with the social world around them. What other than alcohol makes their life rewarding? Do they have friends who are not drinking friends?

Previous illnesses

1   Physical illness, operations and accidents.
2   Psychiatric illnesses.

Information is needed under both subheadings, with emphasis on identification of alcohol-related health problems. Under the heading of *psychiatric illness*, specific enquiry should always be made for any history suggesting experience of depressive illness or pronounced mood swings, generalized or situational anxiety, obsessional disorder, post-traumatic stress disorder (PTSD), pathological jealousy, suicide attempts and drug-taking.

Personality

What is required here is a description of personality prior to drinking or in periods of sobriety – 'the real you'. Information is usefully elicited by open-ended questions such as:

What is the real you like?
Your good points?
Your bad points?
What do you want out of life?
What do you expect of friends?
What sorts of things worry or upset you?
What really makes you happy?

Prompts such as, 'Please tell me some more', will often give revealing information at a point where the patient at first believes that there is nothing more to add. An indication should be obtained on at least the following aspects of personality: self-esteem; ability to experience warm feelings and to relate to others; self-control, explosiveness, irritability; social conformity, rule-breaking, deviance; outgoingness, introversion; drive, ambition, passivity; habitual ways of coping with stress or adversity.

Drinking history

Evolution

It is unnecessary to obtain a detailed account of everything that has happened over a lifetime's drinking, but we are seeking here to understand the individual's drinking in longitudinal perspective. It is necessary to identify important milestones, and to understand the phases of the drinking career and the broadly related influences on it. This picture needs to be built up through exploring four different but closely related dimensions to the person's life, as follows.

The evolution of drinking

The task is to chart the major phases in drinking quantities and patterns, from first experiences of alcohol to the present. Useful questions may relate to such issues as:

First drinking other than the occasional sip in childhood?
First buying own drink?
First drinking most weekends?
First drinking spirits?
Any periods completely off drinking?
First drinking every day?

First drinking 8 pints of beer at a sitting or half a bottle of spirits?
First drinking in present pattern?

Evolution of drink-related problems

Apart from noting objective impacts on health and social functioning, there are two special questions which are often useful:

When did you yourself first realize drinking was a problem?
Looking back now with greater understanding, when in fact do you think drinking really became a problem?

With hindsight patients will nearly always distinguish between the first self-admission of there being a problem (precipitated perhaps by some catastrophic event) and an earlier date now recognizable as the period when drinking was undramatically beginning to, say, erode the happiness of a marriage or interfere with work.

Evolution of dependence

Here the task is to date the onset of a gradual or sometimes rather abrupt shift in the individual's overall relationship with alcohol, their realization that they could no longer control their drinking, that they were 'hooked'. Enquiry can then also be made as to the approximate date of onset for specific dependence symptoms, such as morning shakes or morning relief drinking.

Evolution of pressures and circumstances

The dimension which has to be charted under this heading is concerned with an understanding of the pressures and circumstances that have caused, contributed to or shaped the evolving drinking patterns, dependence and problem experience. Questioning has to sense out influences which were already operating when the patient began to drink (parental example, peer group pressures, cultural influence and so on), and then go forward to understand the subsequent impact of environment, life events, personal relations, mental state and other relevant factors. A few examples of questioning are these:

How did your drinking alter:
When you first left home?
At college?
When you were married?
After the children were born?
When the children left home?
When you were promoted to manager?
When you worked abroad?
After your partner left you?
After you developed depression?

The typical recent heavy drinking day

Review of the evolution in drinking history seeks to build an understanding which is *longitudinal* – the present is understood in its historical perspective. Reconstruction of the typical drinking day, on the other hand, focuses exclusively on the present, and the cross-sectional rather than the longitudinal view. The styles of enquiry are correspondingly different. When reconstructing the evolution of the problem it is the broad sweep which is important, and the reconstruction of how drinking has interacted with a life path. Analysis of the typical day requires in contrast a minute and focused enquiry directed at present behaviour. This understanding should be so exact that in the mind's eye it is possible to project a film of the patient's day.

Establishing the notion of 'typical'

Firstly, the concept which is involved has to be conveyed to the patient. He or she is asked to identify (1) *a recent period* when drinking was, in terms of their own definition, (2) *heavy*, with the drinking then of a kind which they would generally consider to be (3) *typical* of their recent drinking. The patient has to identify the exact period they have in mind – 'the way I was drinking until 2 weeks ago when I lost my job and had to cut down'. What has to be emphasized is the actuality, rather than any generalized abstractions which have no real time base. Most patients find it possible to identify such a period, but for others there is so much variability in their drinking pattern that what is typical is difficult to define, and this in itself is a reality which has to be described.

Waking and events around waking

Having explained the ground rules, it is necessary to establish at what time the patient usually wakes. Enquiry is then made as to the events immediately around the time of waking, for it is here that evidence will be obtained of withdrawal symptoms, withdrawal relief drinking and other signs and symptoms which help to elucidate the patient's degree of dependence.

Subsequent hour-by-hour timetabling

The patient is then taken through a reconstruction of the day, as follows:

1 *The background structure of daily activities.* For instance, what time they leave the house in the morning, what train they catch, what time they get to work, when they take their lunch break and so on.
2 *The timetabling of drinking.* With the framework now provided by the structure of the day, the next task is to fit in a full description of the day's drinking. What time does the patient take their first drink, how much do they drink and over what duration? This enquiry is then taken forward, step by step, through the day. In each instance, to a description of actual alcohol intake is added a note of where the drinking takes place and with whom (if anyone) the patient is drinking. Note also has to be made of the patient's ideas as to the determinants of each drinking occasion – whether to relieve or avoid withdrawal symptoms, to relieve anxiety or other unpleasant inner feelings, whether in the setting of business or for the companionship of the pub or for any other reason. A final aspect of drinking which has to be timetabled is the experience of intoxication, and whether at any point of the day the patient would consider that drink is interfering with ordinary functioning.

Influence of drinking on personality

Some patients are not aware that drinking alters their personality, while another will state that, 'I'm an entirely different person when I've been drinking – Jekyll and Hyde'. The issue has to be examined, both in terms of positive and negative effects. Positively, someone may, for instance, see themselves as more outgoing, confident and assertive when drinking. On the negative side, the effect may be irritability and loss of control over temper (including violence), suspiciousness, moroseness, self-pity or lack of feeling for others.

Probing and checking

The following dialogue shows how an important aspect of the drinking history can be elucidated by careful probing:

THERAPIST: All right, you say you have 3 pints of lager at lunch-time. How long do you spend in the pub at lunch time?

PATIENT: Noon till 2 pm, sometimes 3 pm.

THERAPIST: So, you are there until 2 pm or 3 pm?

PATIENT: Say, 2.30 pm.

THERAPIST: Three pints in two and a half hours seems quite slow drinking.

PATIENT: If I'm there 12 to 2.30, I suppose it would be 4 or 5 pints. I was thinking of when I have a short lunch break. It's more often a long liquid lunch these days.

THERAPIST: You say 4 or 5 pints – could it be more?

PATIENT: No, I'd get too bloated. I don't think I'd ever go above 5 pints.

THERAPIST: Anything else besides lager at lunch time?

PATIENT: I might have a couple of whiskies.

THERAPIST: Why 'a couple' – could it be more?

PATIENT: No, I'll have just a couple of whiskies to round things off when I've finished with the lager. Not more than a couple.

THERAPIST: Double or single measures?

PATIENT: Doubles.

THERAPIST: Ever leave out the whisky?

PATIENT: No, it's pretty regular.

Putting quantity consumed against time spent drinking, sometimes checking stated consumption against money usually spent, comparing reported alcohol consumption prior to attending with breathalyser readings, testing the stated upper limit by offering a higher or lower one, going through other alcoholic beverages than the one first named, relating the stated drinking to the company and other circumstances, all provide useful methods for checking which can help to build up a valid picture.

Totalling the daily intake

Information on quantity drunk throughout the day can be summed to total daily intake. Because of uncertainties in size of drink poured, broad variations in alcohol content for drinks within any beverage type (beer, wine or spirits) and international differences as to the size of a standard drink, the summated figure is at best an approximation rather than an exact index. For research purposes, the most satisfactory approach is to express the total in terms of grams absolute alcohol, but in the clinical setting the idea of *units or standard drinks* provides a useful basis (see Chapter 1) .

Bringing together the evidence for dependence

Much information relevant to establishing the degree to which the patient is alcohol dependent will have been obtained from questioning in the areas of *evolution* and *drinking day*. It is, however, necessary to have in the history a place where evidence on dependence is reviewed and brought together.

The picture of the alcohol dependence syndrome and its degrees of variation has been fully discussed in Chapter 1, and the headings used in that chapter to describe the core elements of the syndrome provide the framework for this section of the history-taking. Brief notes are added below on the practical approach to questioning in each instance.

Narrowing of the drinking repertoire

Useful questions relate to the sameness or otherwise of drinking during weekdays as opposed to weekends, or during the working year as opposed to holidays.

Salience of drinking

Reconstructing the evolution of the patient's drinking will have implicitly provided an account of the progressive importance of alcohol in their life, and their progressive ability to discount other considerations. Attempt should also be made to sense out with the patient how salient drinking has become in the here and now. Useful questions are, for instance:

> Just how important has drinking become for you?
> Is drinking more or less important for you than eating?
> Is drinking more important than people?

A particular phrase in the patient's answers may suddenly and empathetically convey the reality of their drink-centredness: 'When my husband said he would leave me if I went on drinking, I had the sly thought, well, if he leaves me, there will be more time and money for drinking'.

Here it is often useful to ask a question like, 'What are the good things that drinking does for you?' This way one gains a sense of the functional significance of alcohol for that patient; for example, whether they see themselves as drinking for company and the pleasures of the bar-room environment, or for the 'high' state and directly pleasurable effects of intoxication, or for relief of unpleasant feelings, or for a combination of these reasons. The dependent drinker may insist that they have ceased to get any pleasure out of drinking, or even say that they hate every drink – they are caught on a treadmill.

Increased tolerance (or evidence of decreased tolerance)

Most patients will say that they can, 'Drink a lot without getting drunk', and the quantity which is habitually taken is itself evidence of tolerance. If at a later stage in the drinking career a severe *decline in tolerance* is being experienced, this is often reported as a worrying happening (see Chapter 1) .

Withdrawal symptoms

Questioning has to deal with the frequency and intensity of the commoner withdrawal symptoms – tremor, nausea, sweating, mood disturbance. These symptoms may be experienced not only on waking but also with partial alcohol withdrawal during the waking day. Any history of subacute hallucinatory experiences, delirium tremens or withdrawal fits should also be noted.

Relief or avoidance of withdrawal symptoms by further drinking

Questioning must cover the frequency with which the patient drinks to relieve or avoid withdrawal, and the perceived urgency for such a drink.

Subjective awareness of compulsion to drink

Matters that may bear on assessment of subjective experience have again been discussed in Chapter 1. Craving may be most intense during withdrawal, but there may be rumination on drink and the need to protect the drink supply pretty well throughout the day.

Reinstatement after abstinence

Questioning should focus on the actualities of what happened on recent occasions when the patient was off drink and then went back to drinking again – when they came out of prison perhaps, or when they came out of hospital, or when after a period of involvement with Alcoholics Anonymous they 'had a slip'. How quickly were they again experiencing withdrawal symptoms or needing to take a morning drink?

Standard diagnostic systems for alcohol dependence

The DSM-IV-TR (American Psychiatric Association, 2000) and ICD-10 (World Health Organization, 1992, 1997) criteria for the classification of alcohol dependence are reproduced in Chapter 1 (Tables 1.3 and 1.4, respectively). These criteria are useful in standardizing diagnostic practice, nationally and internationally, and they carry authority. However, their drawback from the clinician's point of view is that they each picture dependence as an all-or-none rather than as a dimensional state. Categorical formulae are proposed at the cost of clinical subtlety. The DSM and ICD approaches are in many ways similar. In the text accompanying the ICD criteria, mention is made of the 'narrowing of the personal repertoire' and the 'subjective awareness of compulsion to use' (World Health Organization, 1992, p. 75–77), but these elements are not included in its diagnostic rubric. If a history has been taken in the detail outlined above, sufficient information will have been gathered to enable formal diagnostic decisions to be made within either official system.

Questionnaires for measuring dependence

Standardized instruments have been designed which can be used to rate the individual's degree of alcohol dependence, including the Alcohol Dependence Scale (ADS), Short Alcohol Dependence Data (SADD) questionnaire and the Severity of Alcohol Dependence Questionnaire (SADQ). The practitioner will do well to gain a working familiarity with just one such approach so that scores can be readily related to their clinical meaning. The SADQ has been widely employed both for clinical and research purposes. On the SADQ's 60-point scale, scores of around 20–30 suggest that the patient is entering a range of severe dependence (Stockwell et al., 1979; Stockwell, Murphy & Hodgson, 1983).

Bringing together the evidence for alcohol-related disabilities

Questioning in this section should be aimed at involving the patient themselves in an audit. Each relevant fact is adduced with the patient's exploration of its significance and the degree to which alcohol was involved. The list ends up as their audit, rather than it being the therapist's private clinical note.

Testing each item: the agreed audit

The introduction to this section of history-taking could be as follows:

> Let's try to bring together the ways in which alcohol may have been having any sort of effect on your life – on your physical health or your nerves, or your job, or your relationships, or anything else. You've already told me a lot about separate problems, but now let's try to make out the whole list.

If, for example, the impact of drinking on the patient's marriage were to arise in a particular case, the discussion might be as follows:

> THERAPIST: You told me that your wife walked out on you because of your drinking.

> PATIENT: If it hadn't been for the drinking we might have made a go of it. I'm not saying we *would* have made a go of it. We *might* have made a go of the marriage.

There is a question here which could be explored with this patient later at greater length, but for purposes of this initial history it is sufficient to establish that the patient accepts as a fair assessment that without the drinking he 'might have made a go of the marriage'. A clumsy interrogation that faced him with no more than a sort of yes/no alternative would not have given him an opportunity to convey and define in a personally meaningful way the impact of drinking on his marriage.

The patient should then be played back a summary of what seems to have been established – either fully established or accepted only with reservations. The summing-up has to be made with opportunity for interruptions and discussion.

Questionnaires for measuring intensity of problem experience and craving

The Alcohol Problems Questionnaire (APQ) is a standardized inventory, which exists in a fuller version that includes sections on marriage, children and employment, and in a shorter form that excludes these areas (Drummond, 1990; Williams & Drummond 1994). The APQ can make a useful contribution to the overall assessment with the meaning of any scored items discussed with the patient.

The Alcohol Use Questionnaire (AUQ) is a useful short questionnaire to measure craving, while the 36-item Desires for Alcohol Questionnaire (DAQ) gives scores within three sub-areas (Bohn, Krahn & Staehler, 1995; Love, James & Willner, 1998). An 'impaired control' scale is also available (Heather, Booth & Luce, 1998).

History of help-seeking for drinking problems and assessment of motivation

Enquiry should be made both about help sought by the patient in the past and help being given at present. It is then essential to understand the patient's reasons for coming to this present consultation – the pressures they see themselves as experiencing (a court order, or threats from a partner, for instance), what crisis may suddenly have precipitated the immediate help-seeking, or what inner sense of need is driving the motivation. Once more, the process of history-taking is an experience for the patient as well as it giving information to the therapist. The patient is exploring the question of why he or she is in this room and is trying to understand the ambiguous, confused or contradictory motivations that have brought them here. Such knowledge is an important basis for later work. The history has to be taken with awareness that motivation is often ambivalent: the patient both wants to go on drinking and wants to stop drinking. It is these conflicting forces that have to be identified, rather than the reality of conflict being evaded.

Physical examination and investigations

Physical examination and laboratory investigations will be part of the assessment routine in a medical setting. In a social work or probation office this aspect of assessment is not within expected practice, but there would be an advantage in such agencies in ensuring that the patient receives a physical examination from a doctor, with the results fed back. This insistence on the importance of making a medical connection may go against the usual working methods of some non-medical agencies and be seen as burdensome. However, the likelihood of physical disorder in the patient with a drinking problem puts that person in a different category from many other social work clients.

History-taking with the patient: the essential framework

In Table 11.1 the essential structure for history-taking is laid out. In the first column major areas of enquiry are tabulated, using the same headings employed previously. The second column seeks to help the practical business of history-taking by providing a few important reminders as to what has specially to be kept in mind during the process of interview – a series of working notes on technique. The third column provides reminders as to the purpose of the whole exercise and of individual sections. If the sense of purpose is lost, there is danger both of the history becoming inordinately long and, at the same time, of it failing in its essential goals.

What might go into a 15-minute assessment?

The way that short time is best used must be, to an extent, patient- and agency-specific. The following notes offer some general suggestions:

1 *Despite pressures of time, do not lose sight of the fact that assessment should be an indication of therapy.* Give the patient initial free time to talk, try to understand why this person has come to see you, respond to them positively and give encouragement, round off the interview and identify productive next steps.
2 *Concentrate on the present.* Try to get a sense of present drinking level, present and recent problems with drinking, present life situation and recent help-seeking.
3 *Estimate degree of dependence on alcohol.* Information on presence and intensity of withdrawal symptoms can provide a useful short-cut.
4 *Set proximate goals* in relation to moderation of drinking or abstinence.
5 *Always seek to identify any possibility of co-morbid diagnosis.* Concomitant depression, anxiety and drug-taking should always be on the check-list.
6 *In a medical setting* carry out blood tests (see Chapter 10). A quick physical examination may be needed.
7 *Make another appointment,* keep in touch, monitor progress, offer to see the partner, network with other agencies.

Table 11.1. Summary scheme for history-taking with the patient.

Area of enquiry	Matters to be kept in mind	Essential purposes
The whole exercise	History-taking is conducted within a patient–therapist *interaction*. The quality of this interaction must purposively be developed so as to *invite the surrender of defences*	
	A history must *serve the needs of both therapist and patient*	**For the patient**: *the initiation of therapy*, in terms of: (1) the accomplishment of a self-review which *factually arrays and inter-relates a wide variety of experiences* (with drinking and its impact placed in context); and (2) an *undefended exploration of the meaning of those facts*; together with (3) laying the *foundations of a therapeutic relationship*
		For the therapist: (1) the provision of initial understanding which will be the basis for *developing with this patient the treatment goals and treatment programme*; (2) building the relationship; and (3) a basis for *therapeutic training* and the continued *growth of awareness and skills*
		Overall: to provide: (1) essential understanding of *the person in their own right, of their present* as continuous with *their past*; and (2) the *context for understanding* the drinking history
Family history		
Both parents, childhood environment	*To search after* what the home felt like and looked like and who was there: 'the street in which it stood'	Preliminary understanding of crucial early relationships and experiences which may have contributed to the individual's strengths and vulnerabilities, the way they will relate to people and the dynamic and cultural meaning they will give to alcohol. Understanding of possible genetic influences
Personal history		
Birth, adjustment in childhood, schooling, occupational history, sexual adjustment, marriage, children, finances and housing, leisure, forensic history	… what it feels like to have lived this life …	Serving the overall purpose of this dialogue while, in passing, some information will be obtained on drinking and its consequences, which has later to be ordered
Previous illness		
Physical and psychiatric		Serves the overall purpose as above
Personality	… and to be this person	Crucial explorations to serve the overall purpose
Social support	Friendship networks, faith and belief	How does this person engage with life?

Table 11.1. (continued).

Area of enquiry	Matters to be kept in mind	Essential purposes
Drinking history	**Throughout**: put drinking against background history	
Evolution	Four strands of enquiry:	To sense the broad dynamic of an evolving story: *the longitudinal perspective*
	1 drinking pattern	
	2 dependence	
	3 drink-related problems	
	4 pressure and circumstances	
Typical recent heavy drinking day		
Waking and events around waking: the timetable of drinking, influence on personality, totalling the daily intake	**1** Establish the *notion* of the typical day	To understand the present in fine detail: *the cross-sectional view*
	2 The need to focus down on small actualities	
	3 The need to check and probe	
Bringing together the evidence for dependence		
	To look for *coherence*	
1 Narrowing of repertoire		
2 Salience of drinking		An understanding as to whether dependence is *present*, and if so its *degree*
3 Tolerance		
4 Withdrawal symptoms		
5 Relief or avoidance of withdrawal by drinking		
6 Subjective awareness of compulsion		
7 Reinstatement after abstinence		
Bringing together the evidence for alcohol-related disabilities		
Physical health, mental health, social functioning and functioning within the family	Testing each item for the patient's agreement	Building a broad and comprehensive picture of the way in which alcohol has adversely affected the patient's life – a *shared audit*
History of help-seeking for drinking problems: motivation		
Past and present	Motivation is a matter of ambivalence	To understand why the patient is in this room and the work on motivation that will have to be done

What can be achieved in 5 minutes?

The average general practitioner appointment lasts 7 minutes and, in many settings, time is of the essence and it is not possible to indulge in a protracted and relaxed full assessment of drinking problems. Brief screening for alcohol problems can be attempted by using a questionnaire like the Alcohol Use Disorders Identification Test (AUDIT), or routinely asking such questions such as 'When did you last have a drink?', or 'How many times did you drink last week?' Any answers suggesting possible alcohol problems should be followed by a more in-depth assessment and brief advice with written information, either at the time or at the earliest mutually convenient opportunity, as the 'teachable moment' can be short-lived. For example, one Accident and Emergency Department (Emergency Room) study demonstrated that delay in the appointment with the alcohol health worker was associated with a lower attendance and the rate fell to half after 2 days (Williams et al., 2005). The CAGE (Cut down, Annoyed, Guilty and Eye-opener) questionnaire (Table 11.2) is also wonderfully brief, easily remembered and performs well in the detection of more severe drinking problems (see Chapter 10).

Initial assessment with the spouse, partner or significant other

We now come to discussion of why it is important to interview the partner or significant other as part of the initial assessment procedures, how this interview is to be handled and its content. It is often helpful if the drinker can be interviewed by one member of the team, while the partner is being seen by another, with the information and perspectives then later brought together for joint appraisal and formulation. If that kind of support is not available, the therapist may decide to see both at this early stage in assessment. There can be advantages in seeing them separately rather than somewhat uncertainly fusing two accounts. Later, however, added insights may be gained through a joint interview.

An outline of the scheme is given in Table 11.3, and again the detail should not be allowed to intimidate the therapist who is working under extreme constraints of time. With practice, things are simpler than they first seem. Given that many of the issues discussed here parallel those considered earlier with the patient, the emphasis will be, so far as possible, on brevity.

Although this section deals primarily with the spouse or partner, the value of, at times, also obtaining a story from other informants should be remembered – from another family member, from a friend or from an employer. Permission always has to be obtained from the patient.

Making contact

The partner who is asked to come for interview may be glad to attend or may come along only with reluctance. One wife may have formed the view that her husband's drinking is in some sense a 'family problem', while another woman may see the problem as being solely in her husband's behaviour and be resistant to seeing herself as other than a passive victim. Before the therapist starts to guide

Table 11.2. The CAGE questionnaire.

1 Have you ever felt you should **c**ut down on your drinking?

2 Have people **a**nnoyed you by criticising your drinking?

3 Have you ever felt bad or **g**uilty about your drinking?

4 Have you ever had a drink first thing in the morning to steady your nerves or get rid of a hangover (**e**ye-opener)?

Source: Mayfield et al. (1974).

Table 11.3. Summary scheme for history-taking with the spouse or partner.

Area of enquiry	Matters to be kept in mind	Essential purposes
The whole exercise	Establishing the objective facts is important	*For the spouse or partner:*
		(1) the review of happenings and feelings in a way that begins to make sense and to have shape;
	Feelings and interactions also matter	(2) awareness of self as more than passive participant or victim;
		(3) laying the foundations for future therapeutic work
		For the therapist:
		(1) further understanding of the needs of the spouse;
		(2) further understanding of the marital interactions;
		(3) collateral information
Personal history of the spouse	A history has to be taken of this person in their own right; to know who this person is; where they are coming from, what is brought to the marriage	Understanding how these heritages interact with current problems and determine present needs
The drinking problem	The objective facts are only to be sensed through the colouring which this witness must bring to a situation in which he or she is personally involved	To sense the outlines and dynamics of the drinking story, the picture of the present drinking, and the extent of hardship
	The account given by the spouse of hardships experienced needs different headings than the patient's account of alcohol-related problems	To enable the spouse to express grief and anger and ambivalences of feeling, and to know that it is safe to share these experiences
Coping	The range and mixture of mechanisms which are being deployed	Understanding the stage of development in the marital interaction and possibilities for more constructive response

the discussion into a loosely formal structure, the spouse or partner should be given time to talk freely and to feel assured that their personal needs are going to be listened to attentively.

It is useful to be alert to some of the commoner ways in which the partner's account may deviate from anything that could fairly be considered the independent and objective truth. Some partners will, for instance, exaggerate their partner's drinking, and this is either because of a conscious wish to besmirch a reputation or because of a profound anxiety about drinking and drunkenness. At the other extreme, a wife or husband may, in the face of their partner's appalling and long-continued drinking, insist that all is well, either because they are frightened of the drinker's anger if they divulge the truth or because of shame or guilt. The more bizarre distortions are not common, but they can give rise to a great deal of puzzlement when they occur. It may be months before the treatment team tumbles to the fact that the client's plaintive insistence on their sobriety is valid, and the partner's account based on a desire to justify a divorce. But the importance of the issue being raised here is to be seen, not in terms of the extreme case, but in the reminder that with every case (and each partner) one is presented not with abstract chronicles but with accounts coloured by the active involvement in the story of the people who are talking.

Personal history of the spouse or partner

Family and personal history

The worth of routinely making such enquiry (and the handicap that results from not asking such questions) is illustrated by the following dialogue:

> THERAPIST: How much did your parents drink?

> WIFE: In childhood I went through everything I'm going through now. How my mother put up with it none of us ever understood. I'd say for years my father never came home sober, and my mother put up with it. He'd come home swearing and just looking for a fight, and my mother took it, year in and year out.

The extent to which this woman is acting out her mother's role is a question vital to any understanding of her (and her husband's) present position, and yet if no one bothers to ask about her parents, she may feel that it is not relevant to tell anyone about her childhood.

Spouse's account of the partner's drinking history

Evolution

The partner's picture of the evolution of the patient's drinking problem may be the same as the patient's account or they may be able to offer additional insights.

> He won't tell you this, but I've always felt that he's never liked the attention I've given to the children. I think it was soon after our first son was born that I noticed my husband's drinking. He didn't know how to fit back into the family. Sounds funny, but I've always thought *he* wanted to be the baby in the family.

Present pattern of drinking

To suppose that the partner can be the independent informant who can give a printout on the quantity and frequency of the patient's drinking is usually unrealistic. What the partner can, in fact, usefully describe is the frequency with which the patient behaves in a way that can be summarized as 'unacceptable'. A partner may be able to identify withdrawal symptoms and know that the patient is shaky and retching in the morning, or these symptoms may go unobserved.

Problems and hardships

The partner may or may not be in a position to know what alcohol-related problems the patient has experienced, but it is worthwhile to ask in outline about such matters as illnesses, accidents, lost jobs, debts, forensic involvement and so on. There are, however, a range of other matters relating to the patient's drinking that the partner may be uniquely well-equipped to speak about, and these concern the direct impact of the drinking on the family and the partner themselves – the *hardships* that are being experienced.

Here are some indications as to the areas of questioning which may be useful.

Has drinking made the patient unreliable?

The word 'unreliable' may, for the partner, exactly catch the frustration of what has been experienced, and a question phrased in this manner then leads directly into matters they want to talk about.

> Yes. That's it exactly. It's everything from you have the dinner ready and she's not there to eat it, to that dreadful time last year when we were all lined up for the summer holiday and she disappeared. You can never believe what she's telling you; never trust her to do what she says she is going to do.

'Rowing on and on'

Here the typical story is of the husband coming home after pub closing time, waking his wife up, and then embroiling her in a smouldering row which goes on for hours. She learns to expect these recurrent scenes in which he recapitulates all her faults and shortcomings, and with the wife knowing of no way to cut into or terminate these dreary replays. Jealous accusations are often part of the content.

'Turning nasty'

The partner may come to recognize that at a predictable stage of intoxication *bonhomie* suddenly passes over to a mood of anger or violence. They may know that in such moods the patient will start breaking up the furniture or assaulting the spouse or the children.

Money

Commonly the financial hardships and uncertainties experienced by the partner are part of the chronic strain of living with someone with a drinking problem. It may be a matter of taking money from a purse, the housekeeping money not being provided, of the bills not being paid. Possessions may have been sold or pawned.

'Useless in the evening'

The story here is of the drinker who gets home in the evening and who does not engage in arguing or violence, but who pushes aside the supper and then night after night slumps drunkenly asleep in an armchair. They may be found there in the morning.

Wetting the bed

Bed-wetting is a not uncommon feature of a drinking problem, and in an advanced stage the patient may soil themselves. Also, in a state of drunken confusion, they may get up and urinate in a corner of the bedroom.

Coping

The *coping mechanisms* which the partner may employ have been discussed in Chapter 4. Enquiry should be made into the ways in which the partner is dealing with the patient's drinking and the types of mechanism which they are deploying. It is useful to think in terms of different styles, such as circumvention, attack, manipulation, spoiling, constructive management and constructive help-seeking, although it is likely that in many instances some mixtures of styles will be perceived. This type of understanding can provide a useful basis for later therapeutic work. The partner begins to see patterns in their own behaviour, and to realize the degree to which they may be persevering in unproductive or counter-productive responses and the possibilities of a more constructive reaction.

Rounding off the interview with spouse or partner

It must be stressed again that any assessment interview is properly a therapeutic encounter, whether that interview is with the person with the drinking problem or with the partner. For the partner, the interview should be an opportunity to bring order and understanding to muddled and painful happenings, the chance to discover or express feelings and often a conflict of feelings, a confirmation of worth as an individual and a sensing of ways in which they may have compounded the problem. When this interview is being rounded off, it is necessary to show an empathetic response to the feelings that have been awakened.

Patient and partner: assessment as an asset

The assessment procedures, both with the patient and their partner, constitute a considerable investment of their time and that of the people conducting these procedures. Significant work has been accomplished in terms of building relationships and self-understanding, and the material gathered constitutes an essential base for planning and action. These initial assessments are designed to provide insights and information to be used and employed in guiding the practical next steps forward. A well-conducted assessment is an immensely valuable therapeutic asset on which to build further.

The case formulation

The diagnostic interview or interviews with the individual, interviews where possible with the partner or additional informants, reports from other agencies, the results of laboratory tests and any other enquiries will between them provide a mass of information. That information has to be synthesized into an initial case formulation. Lots of separate pieces may give many separate and partial insights, but it is crucial that the attempt should then be made to stand back and perceive the whole predicament. Formulation is the attempt to *understand*, and a well-constructed formulation is a creative act of empathy rather than just an ordering of information under headings.

There are several reasons for believing that this additional investment of time is worth the demand. The therapist is directionless until the formulation is made. Furthermore, even if after data-gathering has been completed and the therapist has a sense of understanding the person, when the notes are put aside for a few weeks and the individual re-attends, the freshness of understanding has often faded unless the formulation has been written. The original formulation will also be of great use if a case is reopened after a gap of a year or two, or if the patient is eventually taken over by someone else. Construction of a detailed formulation is invaluable as a training exercise.

Besides these various ways in which the formulation is of use to the therapist or therapeutic team, it is equally to be conceived as a basis for discussion with the individual and partner.

A formulation should not be of inordinate length or it defeats its purpose. The format proposed here is to be taken only as a starting point, to be amended or scaled down according to individual professional needs and feasibilities.

Headings for a formulation

Diagnosis

It is preferable that this heading should be taken as an invitation to a *full listing* of diagnoses rather than just a statement of 'the' diagnosis. The necessary subheadings are as follows:

1 *Alcohol diagnosis*: its presence or absence and, if present, its severity, with an outline of the supporting evidence.
2 *All alcohol-related disabilities* (medical, psychological and social).
3 *Ancillary diagnoses*, including underlying or accompanying psychiatric conditions and physical disorders.

Description of personality

It is preferable to attempt a brief description of personality, rather than to use such phrases as 'personality disorder' within the diagnostic listing above. The aim is to summarize provisional insights regarding both personal strengths and vulnerabilities.

Present social situation

1 Marital status or relationship, relationship satisfaction, partner's coping and role of children in the present situation.
2 Employment.
3 Accommodation.
4 Leisure.
5 Religious involvement.
6 Forensic status.

Drinking

1 *History of the drinking problem*. Synopsis.
2 *Aetiology of the drinking,* in terms both of more distant determinants and more recent influences.
3 *The typical drinking day.* Summary description and estimate of usual daily intake.
4 *The balance of present motivations.* Appraisal of patient's current losses and gains from drinking, and degree of motivation.
5 *History of help-seeking.*

The family's health and well-being

Problems currently affecting the partner or children.

Further information needed

A list, for instance, of what further information has to be sought from the patient, or other informants, other agencies to be contacted, specialist opinion to be obtained or specialized diagnostic procedures to be arranged.

Goals

On the basis of what has already been laid out in the preceding sections of the formulation it should be possible to set up a series of specific treatment goals. As with diagnosis, what is required is a list rather than a single monolithic statement. At least one goal should concern drinking behaviour, but other goals may be about other important life domains such as family and work.

Action steps

Under this heading, the steps that have to be taken to achieve the stated goals are set out in objective terms. The actualities should be listed, rather than any vague generalizations such as 'treat the alcoholism'. This is an aspect of the formulation that must be designed in co-operation with patient and family.

Prognosis

Prognosis should be written in terms of an informed, balanced and well-argued weighing of probabilities.

The formulation as shared exercise

Reference has already been made to the necessity of the formulation serving the needs of the patient as well as the therapist. Before making final notes on the formulation, there should have been an interchange in which the therapist says, 'What we have talked through is valuable ... I see it this way ... What we ought to do is perhaps this ... How do you see it? ... Can we agree then? ...' Such discussion ensures that not only is the therapist standing back from the data and gaining a whole view, but that the patient is doing the same and they are doing so together.

Formal communication of the formulation and treatment plan

As noted above towards the end of the assessment, the formulation and the individualized treatment plan should be reflected back to the patient, discussed and any changes accommodated. Depending on the local practice, and the individual's consent, the formulation and treatment plan may be summarized in a letter to the patient and copied to the referrer or vice versa, with the added corollary that if they do not feel that this is an accurate reflection of the meeting or if it raises any questions these should be discussed with the clinician.

Assessment: the essential business

Assessment is a process which if skilfully and humanely conducted should be both rewarding and challenging for the person who has come into the consulting room. It should allow patients to see the evolution of their drinking within their life course. It may illuminate problems that are serious, painful and/or embarrassing but it must at the same time give hope. Assessment is at best a small but important new step in a longer journey, but it should help the patient leave the room with the crucial sense that they are beginning to understand what needs to be done for them to make changes, and that change is possible.

References

American Psychiatric Association (2000) *Diagnostic and Statistical Manual of Mental Disorders*, Fourth edition, Text revision. Washington DC: American Psychiatric Association.

Bohn M J, Krahn D D, Staehler B A (1995) Development and initial validation of a measure of drinking urges in abstinent alcoholics. *Alcoholism: Clinical and Experimental Research* **19**, 600–606.

Drummond D C (1990) The relationship between alcohol dependence and alcohol-related problems in a clinical population. *British Journal of Addiction* **85**, 357–366.

Fiorentine R, Nakashima J, Anglin M D (1999) Client engagement in drug treatment. *Journal of Substance Abuse and Treatment* **17**, 199–206.

First M B (1997) *User's Guide for the Structured Clinical Interview for DSM-IV Axis I Disorders SCID-I: Clinician Version.* Washington DC: American Psychiatric Press, Inc.

Heather N, Booth P, Luce A (1998) Impaired Control Scale: cross-validation and relationships with treatment outcome. *Addiction* **93**, 761–771.

Hyams G, Cartwright A, Spratley T (1996) Engagement in alcohol treatment: the client's experience of, and satisfaction with, the assessment interview. *Addiction Research* **4**, 105–123.

Love A, James D, Willner P (1998) A comparison of two alcohol craving questionnaires. *Addiction* **93**, 1091–1102

Mayfield D, MacLeod G, Hall P (1974) The CAGE-questionnaire: validation of a new alcoholism screening instrument. *American Journal of Psychiatry* **131**, 1121–1123.

Novey S (1968) *The Second Look: The Reconstruction of Personal History in Psychiatry and Psychoanalysis.* Baltimore, MD: Johns Hopkins Press.

Robins L N, Cottler L, Bucholz K, Compton C (1995) *Diagnostic Interview Schedule for DSM-IV (DIS-IV).* St Louis, MO: Department of Psychiatry, Washington University School of Medicine.

Stockwell T, Hodgson R, Edwards G, Taylor C, Rankin H (1979) The development of a questionnaire to measure severity of alcohol dependence. *British Journal of Addiction to Alcohol and Other Drugs* **74**, 79–87.

Stockwell T, Murphy D, Hodgson R (1983) The Severity of Alcohol Dependence Questionnaire: its use, reliability and validity. *British Journal of Addiction* **78**, 145–155.

Thom B, Brown C, Drummond C, et al. (1992) Engaging patients with alcohol problems in treatment: the first consultation. *British Journal of Addiction* **87**, 601–611.

University of London, Institute of Psychiatry & Bethlem Royal Hospital and the Maudsley Hospital (1987) *Psychiatric Examination: Notes on Eliciting and Recording Clinical Information in Psychiatric Patients*, 2nd edn. Oxford: Oxford University Press.

Williams B T, Drummond D C (1994) The Alcohol Problems Questionnaire: reliability and validity. *Drug and Alcohol Dependence* **35**, 239–243.

Williams S, Brown A, Patton R, Crawford M J, Touquet R (2005) The half-life of the 'teachable moment' for alcohol misusing patients in the emergency department. *Drug and Alcohol Dependence* **77**, 205–208.

World Health Organization (1992) *The ICD-10 Classification of Mental and Behavioural Disorders: Clinical Descriptions and Diagnostic Guidelines.* Geneva: World Health Organization.

World Health Organization (1993) *Composite International Diagnostic Interview (CIDI): Interviewer's Manual.* Geneva: World Health Organization.

World Health Organization (1997) *The ICD-10 Classification of Mental and Behavioural Disorders: Diagnostic Criteria for Research.* Geneva: World Health Organization.

Treatment: context and content

Withdrawal states and treatment of withdrawal

Withdrawal in perspective

Different needs of differing patients

Many patients who have sustained serious problems as a result of their drinking have not contracted the dependence syndrome and will experience no significant physiological disturbance on withdrawal. A further important group of patients will show dependence to a slight or moderate degree, but will not suffer from withdrawal symptoms that are to any major extent debilitating. On the other hand there are patients who will feel wretched on withdrawal, and a small group for whom withdrawal will precipitate life-threatening disturbance.

Given diversity in possible withdrawal experience, it makes no sense to approach the treatment of withdrawal in terms of a fixed regime for all-comers. A spectrum of likely withdrawal experiences suggests the need for a spectrum of treatment approaches as corollary. Many patients will need no medication at all to help them come off alcohol while for many others withdrawal can be safely managed on an out-patient basis with minimum drug cover. In only the minority will withdrawal require admission to hospital, but for some of those patients the effective use of medication will be vital. The clinical significance of withdrawal is firstly, therefore, the demand it makes on the clinician to see the different needs of different patients and to manage minor withdrawal states without unnecessary fuss, while at the same time learning to recognize the necessity for very great care in treating the potentially dangerous situation. This chapter will discuss treatment in terms of different regimes for different intensities of need.

Significance of withdrawal as a barrier to 'coming off'

Some patients will present themselves as unable to come off alcohol because of their incapacity to cope with the withdrawal symptoms. This plea may be entirely genuine. A patient who has previously experienced an attack of delirium tremens ('the horrors') may know full well that when they are in a state of severe relapse there is a grave risk of precipitating a further attack of delirium if they attempt abruptly to stop drinking. Their pleas for admission should be heeded. On the other hand, there are patients with less severe degrees of dependence whose belief that they cannot stop drinking without coming into hospital should be kindly resisted. It is important for such patients to learn that they can cope with withdrawal at home, with minimal upheaval and without repeated admissions that reinforce the idea of incapacity to deal with relapse themselves. Unnecessary admissions, which engender sickness behaviour and time off work, must be avoided.

Withdrawal and team-work

Given that drugs may have to be prescribed for out-patient withdrawal, and given also the potential seriousness of the major withdrawal experience which demands in-patient admission, it is evident that the medical practitioner has an important role to play in the treatment of these conditions. If the patient is being handled primarily by non-medical staff, this implies the need for good medical liaison. The counsellor in a voluntary agency must, for instance, know when to make the quick out-patient/community alcohol team referral, or call on the advice of the general practitioner with whom there is a working relationship.

Withdrawal in context

Mere drying out is not by itself an effective way of helping a patient, and whatever is done about withdrawal only has its meaning within the context of other strategies for aiding the patient. When plans for withdrawal are being made at the same time as initial assessment and goal-setting, the withdrawal phase is easily placed within the wider frame. When, however, withdrawal is being dealt with in response to relapse and in an atmosphere of crisis, it is easy to react precipitously and forget the context within which decisions about withdrawal treatment ought to be made. Questions which should be asked in such circumstances centre on what *use* the patient is to make of this help (either as out-patient or in-patient), and what the patient's expectations are of this particular aspect of the contract to help. What plans has the patient got for the far side of withdrawal? Treatment of relapse is discussed in Chapter 13.

A check-list for managing alcohol withdrawal in the community

It should be possible safely and effectively to manage the majority of patients in the community (Collins et al., 1990; Stockwell et al., 1991). This section will consider the ways in which community or out-patient detoxification of the patient with mild to moderate alcohol dependence can be managed.

Does the patient want to come off alcohol?

To put this item first in the check-list may seem an overemphasis of the obvious, but it is not uncommon to see medical prescribing, which suggests a confusion of logic. The doctor has given the patient drugs to treat withdrawal because the doctor believes that the patient ought to come off alcohol, rather than because the patient seriously intends to come off alcohol. The patient leaves the interview with a prescription for a bottle of benzodiazepines, which they will use to supplement continued alcohol consumption.

Is it safe to conduct withdrawal in an out-patient/community setting?

This decision is made without difficulty when, as commonly happens, it is obvious that the patient has not got a severe dependence syndrome. They are, for instance, suffering from morning shakes of only moderate intensity, which have been present for not much longer than 6 months, and they came off alcohol for 2 weeks on their own initiative and without any untoward happenings a month ago. A brief review with the patient of such points as these will usually settle the question of whether out-patient withdrawal is appropriate. A similarly quick answer can be reached in the other direction if there is a previous history of major withdrawal experience and the patient has now reinstated dependence of serious degree. It is decisions in the middle ground which may call for the most experienced skill. Handling this problem will, as ever, depend on a relationship with the patient that allows open discussion of the issues involved. Such a patient may come into hospital for an admission of only 2 or 3 days 'to see how things go', or alternatively they may opt initially to try detoxification at home provided they have good support.

In addition to severity of dependence, a number of other specific pointers may offer further guidance regarding the safety of a community 'detox'. Has out-patient management failed previously and, if so, why? Is there any specific medical reason why community detoxification may be hazardous; for example, a history of delirium tremens or withdrawal seizures? Is the home environment sufficiently supportive, both in terms of family or friends who may summon help if needed and in terms of support for treatment of the drinking problem? This is discussed further, below.

A summary of the indicators that suggest detoxification might be more safely and effectively conducted on an in-patient basis is given in Table 12.1.

Are there likely to be withdrawal symptoms that require treatment?

If it is necessary to make sure that the patient is not so dependent as to preclude the out-patient approach, it is also necessary to ensure that they are indeed suffering from a dependence syndrome or from dependence of more than minimal degree. Otherwise, one may fairly talk about treatment of their drinking problem and the strategies they may apply for abstinence or ameliorated drinking, but there is no sense in setting up a withdrawal regime when there is no significant withdrawal disturbance to be treated. This might again seem a too obvious point if it were not common to find patients routinely being offered benzodiazepines without any enquiry being made into their true needs.

What is the best time?

It may be asking too much for a man or woman with a busy job to try to achieve successful withdrawal in the midst of engagements and in the full setting of usual drinking pressures. Discussion may suggest that the patient set aside a long weekend or take a holiday especially for this purpose. To suggest this degree of forward planning may usefully help to focus commitment.

Is there adequate support?

Although there are plenty of people who at some time in their lives have been so determined to deal with their drinking that they have come off alcohol in such adverse surroundings as a drink-ridden hostel for the homeless, it is always useful to think through with the

Table 12.1. Contraindications to a community detoxification.

- Severe dependence
- History of complicated withdrawal, delirium tremens or withdrawal seizures
- Previous failed community detoxification
- Lives alone or unsupportive home environment
- Medical and/or psychiatric co-morbidity
- Malnourished

patient how environmental supports may be deployed to maximize the chances of success. If there is a husband, wife or partner to give support, that person should be brought into the discussion and their active engagement may have benefit for both partners. This may also be the moment when a patient will be particularly able to accept the usefulness of Alcoholics Anonymous (AA): getting out perhaps to an AA meeting and hearing how others dealt with this problem; or a phone call from an AA member giving a feeling of contact and fellowship, with a follow-through to more continuing involvement. The hospital doctor should carry out a physical examination, organize blood tests and ensure that the general practitioner is kept in the picture. Support from the hospital or community alcohol team may imply the offer of daily appointments over the period of a few days or daily visits from a nurse. Staff should always be prepared to make a home visit if necessary. If there is no other social support available, day-patient facilities for a short period may be helpful.

Use of drugs

Some practical aspects for the use of drugs in out-patient withdrawal will be briefly discussed in this section, both so as to provide background information for the person other than the doctor who wants to understand this aspect of the patient's treatment, and so as to emphasize points of immediate medical concern.

Given that assessment suggests a major withdrawal state is not a risk but that there is reason to believe that some degree of withdrawal symptoms is going to be experienced, then most patients within this band of the dependence spectrum are going to require prescription of a minor tranquillizer. The same drug may be used for daytime and night-time sedation. Within this spectrum there will, however, be a range of severities, so therapy may involve a range of drug doses with the emphasis always on avoiding needless over-medication.

A drug of the benzodiazepine group should be considered as the first choice for treatment of alcohol withdrawal (see Lingford-Hughes, Welch & Nutt, 2004 for references). It is best for the individual doctor to become familiar with one drug from this group, so as to develop a sense of the likely needed dosages in particular circumstances, rather than switching from drug to drug. Among the benzodiazepines, chlordiazepoxide (Librium) may be prescribed in an initial dose of say 10–30 mg 3 or 4 times per day, but lower doses may be indicated. Local protocols are usually available and should be followed (Taylor, Paton & Kapur, 2009).

The dose and frequency of medication should be discussed with the patient and their partner and instructions written down explicitly. A prescription should not be given for more than 3–7 days, and prescribing should not be allowed to trail on unnecessarily once the patient has withdrawn. A community detoxification regime does not need to be longer than 1 week (Scottish Intercollegiate Guidelines Network, 2003). The patient should be cautioned against the risks of driving when under the influence of drugs.

Prescription of vitamins is not an absolute requirement of withdrawal treatment within this severity range, but oral supplements may be offered and may sometimes be specifically indicated on other grounds such as clinical evidence of malnutrition. Similarly, electrolyte disturbance is unlikely to be a major concern in this group. However, it should be remembered that serum potassium levels can fall, and oral potassium supplementation may be required, even in the relatively mild cases of alcohol withdrawal that are treated in the community (Burin & Cook, 2000).

A check-list for in-patient treatment of withdrawal (other than delirium tremens or withdrawal seizures)

In this section the treatment of the greater part of the spectrum of withdrawal states seen in the in-patient setting will be discussed, but treatment of delirium tremens and of alcohol withdrawal seizures will be held over for discussion in the next section. The check-list here bears on medical and nursing practice.

Remember that in the in-patient setting (as with out-patients) a wide range of withdrawal states will be encountered

It is inappropriate for a ward to operate in terms of any fixed drug regime. At the time of admission a patient-specific withdrawal regime has to be set up for each patient, and this regime must be flexible in response to unfolding events.

Monitoring is very important

Competent routine ward monitoring provides the basis for treatment that is alert, flexible and able to be rapidly escalated in case of need. There is much to be said for the use of standardized scales to facilitate this process, and a number of suitable instruments are available. The revised Clinical Institute Withdrawal Assessment for Alcohol Scale (CIWA-Ar; Sullivan et al., 1989) is a 10-item scale which can be completed in about 5 minutes. It scores the severity of nausea, tremor, sweating, anxiety, agitation, headache, orientation and sensory disturbances. An example of a briefer, 8-item, scale (Mainz Alcohol Withdrawal Scale; Banger et al., 1992) is given in Table 12.2. Careful monitoring, combined with supportive care, can reduce the need for medication (Shaw et al., 1981).

Table 12.2. Mainz Alcohol Withdrawal Scale (MAWS).

Item	Rating			
	0 None	1 Mild	2 Marked	3 Severe
Disorientation		Full orientation, but sluggish answers	Blurred orientation in at least one quality	Disorientation in at least one quality
Hallucinations		Occasional, distancing possible	Frequent, sometimes distancing still possible	Nearly permanently, no distancing at all
Inattentiveness		Slip of the tongue, misunderstanding	High suggestibility: string catching, reading	Spontaneous illusions
Disturbance of contact		Good contact with investigator, but not with environment	Sometimes poor contact with investigator	No contact with investigator
Agitation		Feeling nervous	Physical restlessness	Absolute psychomotor agitation
Tremor		Extended fingers	Extended hands	Tremor of hands or body when resting
Hyperhidrosis		Palpable on hands and forehead	Visible on hands and forehead	Visible on total body
Anxiety		Reported on questioning only	Expressed by behaviour	Panic

Source: Banger et al. (1992).

A sensible ward procedure may be for the nurses to make at least 8-hourly observations on all withdrawing patients for the first 3 days, but this may need to be more frequent during the first 24 hours. Observations may be discontinued with the senior nurse's approval if all areas are normal. Every now and then a patient who has given an incomplete history and who is expected to show only mild withdrawal will unexpectedly develop more severe symptoms. Routine observations over the first few days are therefore essential.

In addition to rating withdrawal symptoms, breath alcohol should be measured when the patient arrives on the ward, and again an hour or so later. This allows an estimation of the actual blood alcohol concentration and also confirms the rate of fall of blood alcohol. This is important for several reasons. Firstly, if estimated blood or breath alcohol is high, there may be a danger of interaction with prescribed medication during the first few hours of admission, and particular care must be taken with prescribing during this period. Secondly, if the patient has consumed a significant amount of alcohol immediately before admission, their blood alcohol levels may still be rising. This should generate even greater caution in the prescribing and administration of medication immediately after admission.

Environment

That the environment should be properly supportive is as important here as when the patient is detoxifying at home. General and psychiatric nursing skills have to be employed to help the patient through what may be a few unpleasant days, and the ability of the patient to tolerate this experience will depend in part on the sort of friendliness which they are being offered. To mobilize support from other patients and from visiting relatives can also be valuable.

Drug treatments

The possible use to be made here of a number of different drugs will be considered separately.

Benzodiazepines

Benzodiazepines can be prescribed as for ambulatory treatment, but in a setting that allows for close monitoring and where withdrawal symptoms are more severe, considerably larger doses may be required. There is an old saying that the proper dose of any drug is *enough*, and that certainly applies in these circumstances. The skilled use of a drug, with the intention of ameliorating severe withdrawal distress or aborting risk of delirium, is a matter of titrating the drug dose against the symptoms. The withdrawal symptoms occur because the level of alcohol in the brain is falling, and these symptoms will be ameliorated when the level of prescribed drug is high enough to compensate for the fall in alcohol. What one is in fact doing is substituting a monitored drug intoxication for an alcohol intoxication, and it is in those terms necessary and rational in the severe case to press the drug dose boldly.

Patients experiencing severe withdrawal symptoms may require quite large doses of a benzodiazepine; for example, chlordiazepoxide 40–60 mg 3 or 4 times a day, sometimes more, reducing over 7–10 days. Longer-acting benzodiazepines are helpful in preventing alcohol withdrawal seizures and delirium. If there is an immediate need to bring severe symptoms under control, then lorazepam may be given by intramuscular injection, with an initial dose of say 25–30 µg/kg. Alternatively, diazepam may be given by slow intravenous injection or per rectum (as a suppository or enema). A typical regime for individuals with less severe withdrawal symptoms might be 20 mg 4 times a day, reducing over 7 days.

Healthy older patients should be able to tolerate longer-acting benzodiazepines. However, they are more likely to experience concurrent physical illness, are at higher risk of developing medical complications (e.g. delirium) and are vulnerable to over-sedation. It may, therefore, be sensible to consider using short-acting benzodiazepines such as oxazepam or lorazepam to manage alcohol withdrawal in this age group (McKeon, Frye & Delanty, 2008).

Short-acting benzodiazepines should also be used in patients with alcohol-related liver disease. The extent of the elevation in biochemical markers (gamma-glutamyl transferase [GGT], aspartate aminotransferase [AST]) will help guide the decision as to the doses to be used.

Medically supervised withdrawal of alcohol dependent pregnant women is ideally carried out in an in-patient setting, with input from medical and obstetric services, as this maximizes the health and safety of both the mother and the fetus. Pregnant women with alcohol dependence are likely to present later in the pregnancy (e.g. mid-late second trimester) and may be using other drugs as well. A risk–benefit assessment of alcohol withdrawal symptoms versus the prescription of benzodiazepines should be carried out. This involves taking a comprehensive history of alcohol and drug use and of withdrawal symptoms, carrying out a physical examination and obtaining laboratory investigations. The trimester of pregnancy should be noted. The use of benzodiazepines should be avoided where possible. However, they are less teratogenic than anticonvulsants and are only needed for a short period of time. If they are required, it is probably wise to use a short-acting variety (Flannery, Wolff & Marshall, 2006; Substance Abuse and Mental Health Services Administration, 1993) .

It should again be stressed that what is 'enough' is determined by clinical observation of response, rather than by any rulebook. If the patient becomes excessively drowsy or if there is a large fall in blood pressure, drugs should be cut back or temporarily withheld. Such an approach is far more in the patient's interests than a blind reliance on heavy mixed drug schedules, which will be unnecessarily extreme in many instances and yet insufficient in other cases.

If it has been necessary in the acute phase to load the patient with a drug, one is then in effect subsequently carrying out a drug withdrawal rather than an alcohol withdrawal procedure. This implies gradually tailing off the drug dose at a rate that will not produce significant drug withdrawal symptoms. The rate of reduction must once more be patient-specific and in accord with monitored symptoms. On the other hand, there is evidence that few, if any, patients actually require medication with a benzodiazepine for more than 2 days (Saitz et al., 1994), and regimes of longer than 7–10 days are rarely if ever necessary for uncomplicated alcohol withdrawal.

Benzodiazepines can be prescribed in a number of ways. The most common mode of treatment is a tapering dose regime as outlined above. In patients without a history of complications, a symptom-triggered regime can be instituted whereby mediation is only given when symptoms emerge (Saitz et al., 1994). This requires skilled monitoring (Lingford-Hughes, Welch & Nutt, 2004). A third method is 'front-loading', which involves giving a loading dose of diazepam and following this with doses every 90 minutes or so, until the patient is lightly sedated (Sellers et al., 1983).

A number of other drugs have been used in the management of alcohol withdrawal including anticonvulsants. Studies of anticonvulsants have typically involved small numbers and heterogeneous populations, and so no definite conclusions about their effectiveness can be made (Polycarpou et al., 2009). Some anticonvulsants, including carbamazepine, topiramate and lamotrigine, have shown promise in reducing alcohol withdrawal symptoms. There is still insufficient evidence for the utility of other drugs in this class such as gabapentin and vigabatrin (McKeon, Frye & Delanty, 2008).

Vitamins

Patients who have been drinking heavily and neglecting their diet are at increased risk of acute Wernicke's encephalopathy developing with disastrous suddenness (see Chapter 5), and it is therefore a wise prophylactic measure to give thiamine (vitamin B_1) supplements. These may be given orally, for example in a dose of 100 mg daily, but there is evidence that absorption is particularly poor in this group of patients (Thomson, Baker & Leevy, 1970). Parenteral administration (either intramuscular or slow intravenous) is therefore essential where there is any specific cause for concern (Cook & Thomson, 1997; Thomson & Marshall, 2006). For example, in cases of malnutrition, peripheral neuropathy or signs and symptoms of Wernicke–Korsakoff syndrome, it is particularly important to employ this approach. Because the diagnosis of Wernicke's encephalopathy is easily missed, a presumptive diagnosis should be made, and treatment instituted, with a low threshold of suspicion (Cook, Hallwood & Thomson, 1998; Thomson et al., 2008). A presumptive diagnosis should be made in any patient undergoing alcohol withdrawal who shows signs of acute confusion, ataxia, ophthalmoplegia, memory disturbance, hypothermia or hypotension.

The correct dose of prophylactic thiamine is a subject of debate, but one pair of ampoules of high-potency parenteral B vitamins, administered intramuscularly once or twice daily for 3–5 days, is probably effective in preventing the onset of Wernicke–Korsakoff syndrome.[i]

Where Wernicke's encephalopathy is suspected, the treatment should be 2 pairs of ampoules of high-potency parenteral B vitamins 3 times daily for at least 2 days (Cook, Hallwood & Thomson, 1998; Thomson et al., 2008). Intravenous administration should be by infusion over 30 minutes. Parenteral thiamine should always be administered before an oral or intravenous glucose load. Thiamine is a cofactor for enzymes involved in glucose metabolism, thus there is a risk of precipitating Wernicke's encephalopathy if glucose is given before thiamine in at risk individuals.[ii]

Administration of parenteral vitamins has become much less popular following reports of very rare, but sometimes severe, adverse allergic reactions (O'Brien, 1995). However, it must not be forgotten that Wernicke's encephalopathy is potentially fatal and that the sequelae can be severely disabling (Day et al., 2008; Kopelman et al., 2009). In a properly supervised in-patient setting, where some patients may be at particular risk of Wernicke–Korsakoff syndrome, the balance of risks and benefits will usually be in favour of parenteral vitamin supplementation. However, parenteral administration of B-complex vitamins should only be given in circumstances that will allow emergency cardiopulmonary resuscitation to be offered if necessary.

Major tranquillizers

Phenothiazines and other major tranquillizers have no part to play in the treatment of this spectrum of withdrawal and only add to the risks.

---

[i] Pabrinex IM high-potency injection, 7 ml (2 ampoules) contains thiamine hydrochloride 250 mg; ascorbic acid 500 mg; nicotinamide 160 mg; pyridoxine hydrochloride 50 mg; riboflavin 4 mg.

[ii] Pabrinex IV high-potency injection, 10 ml (2 ampoules) contains thiamine hydrochloride 250 mg; ascorbic acid 500 mg; nicotinamide 160 mg; pyridoxine hydrochloride 50 mg; riboflavin 4 mg; anhydrous glucose 1 g.

Specific treatment to avert withdrawal seizures

The effective use of benzodiazepines, particularly long-acting preparations such as diazepam or chlordiazepoxide, should be sufficient to minimize the development of withdrawal seizures, and it is usually neither necessary nor useful to give additional medication for this purpose (Hillbom, Pieninkeroinen & Leone, 2003; Ntais et al., 2005) (also see below for further discussion of this matter). The use of an anticonvulsant in combination with a benzodiazepine does not appear to confer added benefit. Phenytoin does not prevent alcohol withdrawal seizures and is therefore not indicated (Hillbom, Pieninkeroinen & Leone, 2003). Anticonvulsants are not recommended as long-term treatment for alcohol withdrawal seizures.

The treatment of delirium tremens

This section deals with technical issues, which are mainly the concern of medical and nursing staff, but it may again be of interest to other professionals to acquaint themselves with at least the outlines of how such problems are handled. See Chapter 5 for a full discussion of the causes and clinical features of delirium tremens.

The best hope here is to prevent the onset of delirium by adequately treating severe alcohol withdrawal symptoms with benzodiazepines. If severe withdrawal is adequately managed with appropriate drug doses, the risk of delirium tremens will in many instances be aborted. However, despite the best efforts, hospital admission and alcohol withdrawal will sometimes precipitate delirium tremens, and cases of already established delirium will also sometimes present directly for admission. Once a fully developed attack of delirium tremens is underway, it is uncertain whether any treatment will actually shorten the course of the disorder, but there is persuasive evidence that the difference between competent and less competent treatment may be the survival as opposed to the death of the patient. The dangers of death from delirium tremens should not be exaggerated but they do exist.

Here is the list of matters to be kept in mind when treating this condition (and see also Table 12.3).

What setting for treatment?

Given the risks to life, patients suffering from this condition should have the benefit of being treated in a setting where the medical and nursing staff are as experienced as possible. When delirium tremens occurs on a psychiatric ward or in-patient alcohol unit there may be uncertainty as to whether the patient should remain on that ward or be transferred to a general

Table 12.3. Important requirements in the treatment of delirium tremens.

- In-patient environment, preferably with experienced staff
- Careful assessment and monitoring for co-morbid physical and psychiatric disorders – especially head injury, intercurrent infection, liver disease and hepatic coma, gastrointestinal bleeding and acute Wernicke–Korsakoff syndrome
- Chlordiazepoxide is the preferred drug treatment
- Careful monitoring of body temperature, fluids, electrolytes and blood sugar
- Parenteral vitamin supplementation
- Availability of emergency medical facilities

medical unit. The decision can only be made in the light of an appraisal of the skills and resources available in either setting.

Whatever the setting in which the patient is to be treated, the basic elements that must be provided are much the same. First-rate nursing is required, both for observation and for care. The situation must be one where a potentially disturbed patient can be cared for without staff becoming flustered, and there must be precaution against a patient sustaining accidental injury whilst in a state of confusion. A safe nursing environment must be established with no possibility of the patient falling out of the window or wandering off the ward. A patient who is only uncertainly in contact with reality is going to be helped by friendliness, reassurance and by good room lighting rather than a side room with shadowy corners.

Depending upon the mental health legislation of the country concerned, it may be necessary to consider formal admission if the patient refuses to stay in hospital. The risks to such a patient, should they be allowed to take their own discharge, would be considerable and there should be no hesitation to arrange an assessment for compulsory detention. In the UK, this would be under a section of the Mental Health Act (1983). Note that it is the delirium tremens, not alcohol dependence, which would justify detention against the patient's will.

What underlying or complicating conditions may be missed?

Those patients who die in delirium tremens perhaps most often do so as a result of a medical complication that has been overlooked. Such oversight, unless actively guarded against, can easily come about when all energies are being concentrated on dealing with the immediate and acutely worrying presentation. The patient is probably in no condition to give an accurate history or an account of other symptoms.

The conditions that may have to be recognized are many, and no check-list can substitute for full initial examination and subsequent continued watchfulness. But conditions particularly to be borne in mind include the possibility of head injury, intercurrent infection (particularly chest infection), liver disease and hepatic coma, gastrointestinal bleeding and the acute onset of the Wernicke–Korsakoff syndrome. The picture may also be complicated if the patient has been taking another depressant.

What drug to use for specific treatment?

Much the same considerations apply here as with choice of drugs for treatment of less severe withdrawal symptoms. A great deal of research has been aimed at determining which drug is likely to be most useful in treating delirium tremens. On the whole it seems best to employ a long-acting benzodiazepine. Chlordiazepoxide may be given in a dose up to 400 mg daily by mouth in divided doses. Where a rapid response is required, it may be necessary to supplement this with intramuscular, intravenous or rectal medication, as described above. As ever, an intravenous drug should not be used if avoidable. Phenothiazines and other major tranquillizers should not be used routinely as they have the potential to lower seizure threshold, and are associated with higher mortality and longer duration of delirium, when compared with other sedative-hypnotic agents (Mayo-Smith et al., 2004). They may, exceptionally, be used to reduce agitation, but only when a review of benzodiazepine dosage has been carried out.

Fluids and electrolytes

Patients who are over-active, sweating and feverish (and perhaps also suffering from gastro-intestinal disturbance) are candidates for serious disturbances in fluid and electrolyte balance, which must therefore be monitored. A dangerous fall in potassium level must be averted, and there have been suggestions that decreased magnesium levels are a particular likelihood in delirium tremens (Turner et al., 1989). Blood sugar levels should also be watched. Although an intravenous line may have to be set up, so far as possible fluid and electrolyte correction should be managed by oral administration: keeping an intravenous line in position with a delirious patient can set problems.

Vitamins

Given the dangers of Wernicke–Korsakoff syndrome, there can be no doubt that the patient with delirium tremens should receive appropriate doses of intravenous or intramuscular thiamine for several days. The British National Formulary advises intravenous infusion of 2–3 pairs of Pabrinex high-potency ampoules every 8 hours. With the virtual impossibility at an early stage of distinguishing the signs and symptoms of delirium tremens from those of Wernicke's encephalopathy, a presumptive diagnosis of the latter condition should be made, and treatment instituted accordingly (see above).

Life support

Emergency facilities must be available in the event of acute circulatory failure. A rare complication is hyperthermia with the temperature suddenly rising to 40.5°C or more. Hepatic coma is sometimes precipitated when the previously malnourished patient begins to take protein.

Alcohol withdrawal seizures

Seizures usually occur within the first 24 hours of admission (Turner et al., 1989) but they may also ensue during the course of delirium (see Chapter 5), or even while the patient is still drinking, if there is a rapid fall in blood alcohol concentration. They are less likely to develop if the patient has been adequately treated with long-acting benzodiazepines, particularly diazepam (Brathan et al., 2005; Ntais et al., 2005). Predisposing factors for alcohol withdrawal seizures include a history of such seizures, multiple detoxification episodes, concurrent epilepsy, hypokalaemia and hypomagnesaemia. Other contributing factors include head injury, hypoglycaemia and stroke. If a sequence of seizures occurs or status epilepticus develops (a run of seizures in continuous succession), intravenous medication will have to be given to bring the situation rapidly under control and the usual measures deployed as for any patient suffering from epilepsy.

A case history

A 33-year-old man, living alone, asked his social worker for help with 'coming off' alcohol. A previous episode of withdrawal, a year earlier, had failed because he recommenced drinking whilst still taking medication prescribed for his withdrawal symptoms. He therefore reluctantly agreed that on this occasion he would go into hospital for detoxification. On arrival on the ward he was intoxicated, with a BAC of 350 mg/100 ml. An hour later a repeat measurement indicated a decrease to 335 mg/100 ml, at which point the patient was starting to sweat and suffering from a coarse tremor. Regular observations of withdrawal symptoms were commenced using the CIWA-Ar and chlordiazepoxide was prescribed, commencing with a cautious dose of 25 mg in view of the high breath alcohol.

In view of the evidence of poor nutritional status, a high-dose B-complex vitamin preparation was prescribed, for intramuscular administration once daily for 5 days.

Over the first 24 hours, a total of 250 mg chlordiazepoxide was administered to the patient orally and this was effective in keeping him reasonably comfortable, albeit he was rather sleepless for the first night on the ward. Tapering doses of chlordiazepoxide were prescribed over succeeding days, and the drug was discontinued completely after 5 days on the ward.

The patient was discharged after 10 days. By this time, after encouragement and advice from the ward staff, he had made his own arrangements to be admitted to a residential rehabilitation facility in another part of the country. Arrangements had also been made, by the medical staff, for him to receive investigation and treatment for a suspected peptic ulcer. The ward Occupational Therapist had taught him some basic anxiety management techniques, as he had indicated that he often drank in response to symptoms of anxiety, due to various life stresses.

Withdrawal from drugs other than alcohol

Some patients may be dependent upon other drugs, in addition to their dependence on or misuse of alcohol (see Chapter 7). In these circumstances, appropriate medical management of withdrawal from drugs other than alcohol must be provided. It is not possible to describe here in detail the clinical management of withdrawal from all other types of drugs. However, a few comments may be in order in relation to dependence upon benzodiazepines and opioids, and the interested reader is referred to more detailed sources for further information in relation to these and other drugs (Taylor, Paton & Kapur, 2009).

Benzodiazepine dependence is usually best managed in the community, with gradual dose reduction being undertaken over a period of weeks or months (Higgitt, Lader & Fonagy, 1985; Lingford-Hughes, Welch & Nutt, 2004; Schweizer & Rickels, 1998). However, where concomitant alcohol withdrawal is involved, admission may be required in order to ensure appropriate monitoring and prescribing during the acute phase of alcohol and early benzodiazepine withdrawal. It is usually best to convert other benzodiazepines into the equivalent dosage of a long-acting preparation, such as diazepam or chlordiazepoxide, and then to adjust the dose of this single drug in accordance with alcohol withdrawal symptoms. Managing the doses of several benzodiazepines prescribed concomitantly can be confusing at best and dangerous at worst. Whereas benzodiazepines are usually discontinued after 7–10 days in cases of acute alcohol withdrawal alone, concomitant benzodiazepine dependence will usually require that the patient be discharged to the community on a lower dose, which is then gradually tailed off over a period of weeks or months. More rapid withdrawal can lead to prolonged symptoms of anxiety and a risk of benzodiazepine withdrawal seizures. Carbamazepine may be helpful in managing withdrawal from high doses of benzodiazepines.

Opioid dependence may be managed either by gradual dose reduction of the drug in question (e.g. methadone or codeine) or else by substitution with methadone or buprenorphine, and then a gradual reduction of whichever drug is used over a period of weeks or months (Lingford-Hughes, Welch & Nutt, 2004). Alternatively, other drugs may be prescribed in order to ameliorate symptoms of acute opioid withdrawal. Amongst the drugs used in this way are drugs such as lofexidine (Bearn, Gossop & Strang, 1996; Sheridan, Cook & Strang, 1999), which also have a reported benefit in the management of mild alcohol withdrawal (see, e.g. Cushman & Sowers, 1989).

Withdrawal symptoms in summary

From what has been said in this chapter, it must be evident that the clinical skills required effectively to respond to the range of alcohol withdrawal pictures that will be encountered, involve the ability to deploy a range of techniques apposite to varied presentations. The proper use of drugs can sometimes be very important, but this should not lead to any neglect of the importance of support and encouragement. The trust and the relationships established during the treatment of the crisis can be valuably carried through to the next phase of treatment.

References

Banger M, Philipp M, Herth T, Hebenstreit M, Aldenhoff J (1992) Development of a rating scale for quantitative measurement of the alcohol withdrawal syndrome. *European Archives of Psychiatry and Clinical Neuroscience* **241**, 241–246.

Bearn J, Gossop M, Strang J (1996) Randomised double-blind comparison of lofexidine and methadone in the in-patient treatment of opiate withdrawal. *Drug and Alcohol Dependence* **43**, 87–91.

Brathan B, Ben-Menachem E, Brodtkorb E, et al. (2005) *EFNS Guideline on the Diagnosis and Management of Alcohol-Related Seizures: Report of an EFNS Task force.* Vienna, Austria: European Foundation of Neurological Societies.

Burin M R M J, Cook C C H (2000) Alcohol withdrawal and hypokalaemia: a case report. *Alcohol and Alcoholism* **35**, 188–189.

Collins M N, Burns T, Van den Berk P A H, Tubman G F (1990) A structured programme for out-patient alcohol detoxification. *British Journal of Psychiatry* **156**, 871–874.

Cook C C H, Thomson A D (1997) B-complex vitamins in the prevention and treatment of Wernicke–Korsakoff syndrome. *British Journal of Hospital Medicine* **57**, 461–465.

Cook C C H, Hallwood P M, Thomson A D (1998) B vitamin deficiency and neuropsychiatric syndromes in alcohol misuse. *Alcohol and Alcoholism* **33**, 317–336.

Cushman P, Sowers J R (1989) Alcohol withdrawal syndrome: clinical and hormonal responses to a$_2$-adrenergic agonist treatment. *Alcoholism: Clinical and Experimental Research* **13**, 361–363.

Day E, Bentham P, Callaghan R, Kuruvilla T, George S (2008) *Thiamine for Wernicke–Korsakoff Syndrome in People at Risk from Alcohol Abuse. The Cochrane Collaboration.* Chichester, UK: John Wiley & Sons.

Flannery W, Wolff K, Marshall E J (2006) Substance use disorders in pregnancy. In *Psychiatric Disorders and Pregnancy: Obstetric and Psychiatric Care*, V O'Keane, T Seneviratne, M Marsh (eds). London: Taylor and Francis, pp. 197–222.

Higgitt A C, Lader M H, Fonagy P (1985) Clinical management of benzodiazepine dependence. *British Medical Journal* **291**, 688–690.

Hillbom M, Pieninkeroinen I, Leone M (2003) Seizures in alcohol-dependent patients: epidemiology, pathophysiology and management. *CNS Drugs* **17**, 1013–1030.

Kopelman M D, Thomson A D, Guerrini I, Marshall E J (2009) The Korsakoff syndrome: clinical aspects, psychology and treatment. *Alcohol and Alcoholism* **44**, 148–154.

Lingford-Hughes A R, Welch S, Nutt D J (2004) Evidence-based guidelines for the pharmacological management of substance misuse, addiction and comorbidity: recommendations from the British Association for Psychopharmacology. *Journal of Psycopharmacology* **18**, 293–335. Update pending: see http://www.bap.org.uk.

Mayo-Smith M F, Beecher L H, Fischer T L, et al. (2004) Management of alcohol withdrawal delirium: an evidence-based practice guideline. *Archives of Internal Medicine* **164**, 1405–1412.

McKeon A, Frye M A, Delanty N (2008) The alcohol withdrawal syndrome. *Journal of Neurology, Neurosurgery, and Psychiatry* **79**, 854–862.

Ntais C, Pakos E, Kyzas P, et al. (2005) Benzodiazepines for alcohol withdrawal. *Cochrane Database of Systematic Reviews* CD005063.

O'Brien P (1995) Parenteral vitamin therapy in alcoholism. *Psychiatric Bulletin* **19**, 788.

Polycarpou A, Papanikolau P, Ioannidis J P, Contopoulos Ioannidis D (2009) *Anticonvulsants for Alcohol Withdrawal. The Cochrane Collaboration.* Chichester, UK: John Wiley & Sons.

Saitz R, Mayo-Smith M F, Roberts M S, et al. (1994) Individualized treatment for alcohol withdrawal. A randomized double-blind controlled trial. *Journal of the American Medical Association* **272**, 519–523.

Schweizer E, Rickels K (1998) Benzodiazepine dependence and withdrawal: a review of the syndrome and its clinical management. *Acta Psychiatrica Scandinavica* **98** (Suppl 393), 95–101.

Scottish Intercollegiate Guidelines Network (SIGN) (2003) The Management of Drinking and Alcohol Dependence in Primary Care. A National Clinical Guideline. http://www.sign.ac.uk.

Sellers E M, Naranjo C A, Harrison M, et al. (1983) Diazepam loading: simplified treatment of alcohol withdrawal. *Clinical Pharmacology and Therapeutics* **34**, 822–826.

Shaw, J M, Kolesar G S, Sellers E M, Kaplan H L, Sandor P (1981) Development of optimal treatment tactics for alcohol withdrawal. I. Assessment and effectiveness of supportive care. *Journal of Clinical Psychopharmacology* **1**, 382–388.

Sheridan J, Cook C, Strang J (1999) Audit of the in-patient management of opioid withdrawal using lofexidine hydrochloride. *Journal of Substance Use* **4**, 29–34.

Stockwell T, Bolt L, Milner I, et al. (1991) Home detoxification from alcohol: its safety and efficacy in comparison with inpatient care. *Alcohol and Alcoholism* **26**, 645–650.

Substance Abuse and Mental Health Services Administration (SAMHSA) (1993) Pregnant, Substance-using Women. Treatment Improvement Protocol (TIP) Series 2. DHHS PublicationNo. (SMA) 95–3056. http://ncadi.samhsa.gov/govpubs/bkd107/2b.aspx.

Sullivan J T, Sykora K, Schneiderman J, Naranjo C A, Sellers E M (1989) Assessment of alcohol withdrawal: the revised Clinical Institute Withdrawal Assessment for Alcohol Scale (CIWA-Ar). *British Journal of Addiction* **84**, 1353–1357.

Taylor D, Paton C, Kapur S (2009) *The Maudsley Prescribing Guidelines*,10th edn. London: Informa Healthcare.

Thomson A D, Marshall E J (2006) The treatment of patients at risk of developing Wernicke's encephalopathy in the community. *Alcohol and Alcoholism* **41**, 158–167.

Thomson A D, Baker H, Leevy C H (1970) Patterns of 35 S-thiamine hydrochloride absorption in the malnourished alcoholic patient. *Journal of Laboratory and Clinical Medicine* **76**, 34–45.

Thomson A D, Cook C C H, Guerrini I, et al. (2008) Wernicke's encephalopathy: 'plus ca change, plus c'est la meme chose'. *Alcohol and Alcoholism* **43**, 180–186.

Turner, R C, Lichstein P R, Peden J G, Busher J T, Waivers L E (1989) Alcohol withdrawal syndromes: a review of pathophysiology, clinical presentation, and treatment. *Journal of General Internal Medicine* **4**, 432–444.

Further reading

National Institute for Health and Clinical Excellence (2010) Alcohol use disorders: diagnosis and clinical management of alcohol-related physical conditions. NICE Clinical Guideline 100. London: National Clinical Guidelines Center at the Royal College of Physicians. http://www.nice.org.uk.

Treatment: context and content

The basic work of treatment

What is meant by 'basic work'?

Therapeutic techniques, such as various psychotherapies, cognitive and behavioural therapy or the use of drugs, can all make contributions to an individual's treatment programme (see Chapter 14). These approaches are usually emphasized in the treatment literature, while the undramatic basics of the helping process tend to be passed by, or dismissed, as the background to the application of specialized techniques. It is, however, vital that attention should be given to the subtle and important range of happenings which occur whenever patient and therapist interact – the what, when and how of what is felt and said and done between them. Otherwise we are at risk of throwing out as packaging the essential content of the parcel. Here is how a patient saw what happened between him and a doctor.

> I remember when I first met that doctor. She seemed friendly but when I tried to con her, she laughed and told me to get my priorities right. Typical alcoholic thinking – just told myself that she didn't understand, and I didn't bother to turn up for the next appointment. What happened next? I get a letter, not one of those form-letters that hospitals send out, but a personal letter from this doctor saying something like, 'I know it's difficult. I don't want to push you into anything, but I'll be in the clinic on Friday afternoon if you want to talk about things further'. So I went back to tell her she didn't understand!

Concern for the impression made at the first encounter (Thom et al., 1992), the ability to combine being 'friendly' with confrontation, finding a phrase like 'priorities' to sort out complexity, the way a letter is written (Batel et al., 1995), these are examples which point to what is meant by 'basic work'.

Interventions are only likely to produce movement when in alignment with the real possibilities for change within the individual, the family and the social setting (Vaillant, 1983, 1995). The basic work of treatment is largely concerned with nudging and supporting movement along these 'natural' pathways of recovery. We need a more developed sense of people's innate capacity for recovery and the possible dimensions of recovery, rather than a belief that we can impose therapies on people who are to be marched along at our dictate. The clumsy therapist is like someone who tries to carve a piece of wood without respect for the grain. The basic work of treatment requires immense respect for that grain, and therapy must always be matched to individual needs.

This chapter will be written largely in terms of the patient or client who is aiming at abstinence rather than at modification of drinking. That latter question is dealt with in Chapter 17. However, much of what is said in this chapter is generally applicable, whatever the chosen goal.

Relationship and motivation

The typical chapter of this sort usually begins with a discussion of treatment techniques and therapeutic tactics. We will discuss such issues presently, but begin by emphasizing that *no technique is likely to be effective if there is a poor relationship between the patient and clinician, or if the patient's motivation to change is flagging or non-existent.* We therefore begin with the context in which all interventions are attempted, namely a particular relationship and a particular level of motivation. We advise also that whenever the clinician, the patient or both feel 'stuck' in treatment, the first two questions on the table should always be, 'What is the status of the therapeutic relationship?' and 'Does the patient really want to make a change?' Although we discuss each issue separately for ease of presentation, they are of course linked. A cold, distant or antagonistic therapeutic relationship is the enemy of motivation to change. In contrast, motivation to change and a positive, supportive, honest therapeutic relationship reinforce each other.

The therapeutic relationship

The relationship between patient and therapist is fundamental, both to what can be achieved in any one therapeutic session and to what changes can be won over time (Luborsky et al., 1985). It begins to be built at the first moment of contact, is developed during the assessment interview (or interviews), is vital to the effectiveness of the initial counselling and goal-setting and continues thereafter as an important component of therapy (Edwards, 1996). 'What is said' matters, but it cannot be abstracted from the feelings between the two people who are doing the saying and the listening. Take, for instance, the following remarks by a therapist which might be necessary at a certain point in an individual's treatment.

> You know that I believe you can stop drinking and make sense of your life, but things can't usefully just drag on. You've been coming up here regularly to talk about your problems for the last 6 months, and we are both aware that you're now becoming badly caught up in this business of, 'I'll start tomorrow ... the day after'. Here's a challenge. I'm not giving you an appointment for next week but instead am going to propose that you come back in 6 weeks and show me that by then you have stopped these binges and started instead to do some of those things with your family that you have been talking about. I want you to show yourself that you can succeed, and that will be a great feeling. It's time to make a start. You *can* make a start.

That same form of words may have three different types of impact. The impact may be negative, with the patient reinforced in their sense of hopelessness. The second alternative is for the patient in effect not to hear what is said, because no words spoken within a meaningless relationship can matter: if they bother to come back in 6 weeks' time, it will be with nothing having changed and with what was said in that previous session blandly neutralized. Lastly, there is the possibility that the challenge is taken and used as a turning point, but this outcome can only be expected when the relationship positively matters. At worst, the word 'relationship' is devalued into a catch-phrase of professional jargon, and yet every now and then one senses again the intensely important reality of what is being talked about.

Working with drinking problems requires an awareness of how relationships are made and used, but there is little which is unique to alcohol problems in this regard. The same basic skills are needed in any area of therapy but it may be worthwhile considering elements derived from psychotherapeutic principles (Luborsky & Crits-Christoph, 1990), which have to be thought through when working with drinking problems (Levin & Weiss, 1994). These issues are summarized in Table 13.1.

Table 13.1. The therapeutic relationship.

The quality of the relationship between therapist and client is fundamental to what can be achieved
• The ability to show empathy
• Avoiding possessiveness and the lure of directiveness
• Conferring worth and giving hope

Showing warmth and empathy

Warmth cannot be invented, and a show of pretended warmth will be transparent. When warmth is genuinely experienced, it still has to be conveyed in the voice, and there are skills in voice and gesture, as well as in learning how to convey warmth in words, which are not cloying.

Possessiveness and directiveness

Therapists must guard against taking up a 'parental' position in the therapeutic relationship as such a relationship is the antitheses of one which encourages growth towards autonomy. Directiveness may work in the short term, as the patient is carried along by the therapist's will and demand, but progress of that kind is unlikely to be sustained.

Conferring worth and giving hope

The way in which the patient's bad feelings about themselves are to be handled in the relationship is another question. Feelings of worthlessness, helplessness, pessimism and unresolved guilt are common in the person who has experienced years of excessive drinking, and can handicap the attempt at recovery. The therapist's job is not to give cheery and false comfort but to attempt by many small strategies to help towards better feelings.

Therapist characteristics

Certain characteristics of therapists seem to be associated with successful treatment outcomes and account for between 10–50% of the outcome variance. More effective therapists are empathic, supportive and also goal-directed (Najavits & Weiss, 1994; Raistrick, Heather & Godfrey, 2006). Being goal-directed bears special comment, in that the successful therapist is not the mushy stereotype of the clinician who approves of everything and sets no limits or change-targets in therapy. Rather, effective clinicians both take the work of change seriously while maintaining an attitude of respect and support toward the patient. The way in which therapists interact with patients may be at least as important as the specific approach used (Carroll, 2001; Connors et al., 2000) .

Motivation

Changing drinking behaviour is impossible without significant motivation on the part of the patient, and such motivation must be nurtured by the clinician before virtually any other therapeutic task. Even at its worst, problem drinking may include enjoyable elements that make patients ambivalent about change. Other patients may lack motivation simply because they feel defeated by alcohol. Motivation is a topic to which skilled clinicians will return again and again (Gerdner & Holmberg, 2000).

CLINICIAN: Robert, when you started treatment you told me how much you wanted to be a better father, and that you could see your drinking was getting in the way of that. Do you remember when we talked about that?

ROBERT: Of course. It's the only reason I came in.

CLINICIAN: Well, you stopped drinking for a month and I know you were proud of that. And you have every right to be. But since then you don't seem very engaged in our sessions together and you have missed others besides. I would really like to help you, but it's really up to you if you want to change. So I am just wondering, do you still feel that this a change you want to make?

ROBERT: Kind of. Well, I am less sure than I used to be. It's so boring in the evenings without my friends at the pub that I feel like I'm climbing the walls.

CLINICIAN: I see. You're missing some of the things about drinking that you liked, which is understandable. What about the reason you came in, your children?

ROBERT: That is going better. I see my son looking at me differently, with respect.

CLINICIAN: What is that like?

ROBERT: I feel so puffed up that my buttons are going to burst off my shirt.

CLINICIAN: So you miss one aspect of drinking but you have gained something from stopping that makes you feel wonderful. Since you can't have both things, this is a major choice for you. Tell me: what matters more to you?

The example above illustrates a number of therapeutic tactics that foster motivation, including communication of support, giving credit for steps taken, not arguing about the benefits of drinking and directing the conversation to the rewards of sobriety. And the clinical example ends with a critical therapeutic strategy, namely keeping the responsibility for change on the patient, rather than trying to rescue him or force him to become sober.

Readiness to change

As discussed in Chapter 11, a comprehensive assessment sets the scene for therapeutic work. Readiness to change should be considered alongside the particularities of the history and presenting circumstances, as all will inform the decision on the treatment goal. Abstinence may be the ultimate goal but it may not be immediately achievable. While the challenges ahead need to be acknowledged, the clinician does not want to overwhelm or scare the patient unduly at the outset. The first step is to facilitate engagement in treatment. This is done by creating a 'can do' atmosphere, deciding on achievable targets for the next appointment and setting out a timeline. The following is an example of how a clinician might summarize what has happened in the first session and the negotiation of the setting of an achievable target:

CLINICIAN: Thank you for coming. I think that we have achieved quite a lot in the session today. You are going to think about abstinence, but aren't very confident that you will achieve it immediately. I'd like you to come back to see me again next week, and in the meantime to keep a drinking diary. That way we can look at how much you are drinking over the week, and how it is affecting you, your relationships at home and at work.

JOHN: It's been very helpful to think about my drinking. I never meant it to get so out of hand. Yes I'll keep a diary.

CLINICIAN: I'd also like to organize some blood tests today. That should give us an idea of how your health has been affected. We can give you the results next week and have a chat about what they mean.

JOHN: I'd like that.

John leaves the appointment feeling encouraged and motivated. Before the appointment he thought that abstinence was impossible. Now he thinks that he might be able to do it with the help of the therapist, who had been warm and supportive and had listened carefully to him. Yes, he will keep the diary and will come back next week. If this appears to be an overly simplistic example, it should be remembered that 'mighty oaks from little acorns grow'. What we are doing in treatment is essentially harnessing an attitude – 'readiness to change' – to motivational forces that will help to effect lasting behavioural change.

Work with the patient: some guiding principles

What actually happens when, after the initial assessment, formulation and goal-setting, the client and therapist, on a series of later occasions, sit down together and talk? Here are some principles which can guide the work, and they are summarized in Table 13.2.

Maintain continuity of purpose

Both patient and therapist have to maintain a sense of progress and purpose and avoid confusion and drift. Recovery needs a maintained sense of direction. This is achieved in a number of ways:

1 Make use of the initial formulation and goal setting. The initial exercise in clarification of understanding and purpose should be referred to as the continued basis for action (see Chapter 11).
2 Emphasize what has been achieved. At each session, it is useful for the therapist to help the patient identify what has been achieved since the last meeting and thus reinforce the patient's own sense of achievement; for instance, a day or so or many days or weeks of abstinence, a difficult situation dealt with successfully, a new job started, an outing with the family or new aspects of self-understanding.
3 Set the next task for the short term. The meeting also has to identify what are to be the next steps, with the patient making a commitment to attempt these steps. The work plan is of no value if it is only in terms of generalities, such as, 'Getting some other interests going' or 'Trying to be more understanding of the wife's point of view'.
4 An eye on the slightly longer term. Although it is useful to concentrate on the short term (AA's 'day at a time'), patients will also, to a varying extent, want to see further ahead and be helped forward by thoughts of what things may look like in 6 months or a year hence. The person who thinks concretely will be happier to plan their steps in such visible terms as new possessions, while someone else may chart their progress in terms of personal changes and changes in relationships.

Table 13.2. Working with the patient: guiding principles.

- Seek to maintain continuity of purpose. Use the initial formulation and goal-setting, check on what has been achieved, set further goals in concrete terms
- Be flexible, listen to what the patient brings to the session, but identify leading issues for the session
- Be aware of what is happening in the therapeutic relationship
- Hold onto the family perspective
- Monitor progress and engage the patient in self-monitoring
- Keep a balance between dynamics and realities
- Maintain a balance of emphasis between drinking and other areas for work

Be aware of the relationship

The importance of the therapeutic relationship has already been noted, and continuing thought has to be given to what is occurring in this regard. Is the therapist, for instance, being edged into a too authoritarian role or being moved towards argument or sterile intellectual debate?

Hold onto the family perspective

Despite intentions, it is easy to become too focused on the individual and to discover after some months that the needs of the family and the relevance of the home situation have been allowed to slip from sight, with adverse consequences. If the patient has a family, what is happening within the family and within other close relationships has to be discussed and plans made for continuing work with the people involved.

Monitor progress

Implicit in the idea of commitment is the expectation that commitment will be met, but the process only works if the therapist checks on what is agreed. It is helpful for the patient to feel that their progress is being monitored, and periodic reporting to the therapist can be supported by an element of self-monitoring. The patient may, for instance, be asked to keep a daily diary, with headings to deal with such issues as drinking, craving, 'tricky situations' and the use of leisure time.

Maintain a balance between dynamics and realities

The treatment approach which is outlined in this chapter embraces a concern with psychodynamics, cognitive behavioural aspects and external realities. There is danger in putting too heavy an emphasis on one area while others are neglected.

Keep a balance between drinking and other issues

Each interview is likely to reinforce the agreed drinking goal and monitor progress along the drinking dimension. Work towards recovery also has to be planned, pursued and monitored along other dimensions, often bearing on enhancement of the quality of sobriety. It is when therapist or patient focuses too much on one sector to the cost of any other that things go wrong (see Chapter 18).

The therapeutic work

So much for a discussion of the general framework: with those headings in mind, we can now go on to look at some likely detailed content of the therapeutic work.

Working on the drinking problem

According to the phase of recovery to which the patient has progressed, this heading will have different meanings. It should again be emphasized that this discussion is worded in terms of the patient who is aiming at abstinence, although with due modification the same principles apply to work toward a controlled drinking goal. For instance, at the earliest stage the immediate question is how the patient who is aiming at abstinence is to come off drink and be helped where necessary with detoxification (see Chapter 12), while for the patient who has chosen the goal of controlled drinking the immediate task is to get the drinking under control. Whichever the chosen goal, the patient has to be presented with the unambiguous message that dealing with the drinking problem is a high priority.

In terms of Prochaska and DiClimente's 'Stages of Change' model (Prochaska, DiClemente & Norcross, 1992; Prochaska, Nacross & DiClimente, 1994), much of the initial work under this heading may be concerned with helping patients to move from 'precontemplation' to 'contemplation', 'preparation' and then on to 'action' and 'maintenance'. Many therapists find that this model provides them with a useful map for charting individual progress, although at the theoretical level there is debate as to the validity of this segmentation (Sutton, 1996). While the 'stages' tell us something about when people change, they do not explain *how* or *why* they change (Davidson, 1998). Self-efficacy, intention and motivation all appear to facilitate the change process. Some now argue for the model to be discarded and replaced by a model reflecting observations about behavioural change or, failing that, for a reversal to a 'common sense' approach (West, 2005). A further psychological approach relevant to this phase of work is that of *motivational interviewing* (Miller & Rollnick, 2002; Rollnick & Miller, 1995). Some patients may find a self-help manual useful (Heather, Kisson-Singh & Fenton, 1990).

When the patient is off alcohol – focusing again primarily in the present discussion on the abstinence goal – there is important work to be done on consolidation. The patient's basic understanding of the nature of their drinking problem (and the nature of dependence) has to be rehearsed and reinforced. This is not accomplished by the therapist giving a lecture, but by their pointing up a discussion: 'Just how do you *understand* this drinking problem?', 'How would you explain to another person what's different between your relationship with alcohol and their drinking?'. Work on ambivalence is also a continuing task rather than something ever settled once and for all: 'What would you lose now if you went back to drinking?', 'What so far looks like the best thing that's coming out of sobriety?'.

Discussion will usefully focus on questions such as the degree to which the patient is thinking about or craving for alcohol, the cues and circumstances which trigger these subjective experiences and the ways in which the patient copes with such feelings. Personal coping mechanisms must be identified, and it is important to teach patients to think in these terms and rehearse the strategies that are going to be employed in difficult situations. Much of the psychological underpinning of this phase of the work will come from a relapse prevention approach.

Motivational interviewing and cognitive behavioural techniques

Two broad psychosocial treatment approaches will be outlined briefly: motivational interviewing and cognitive behavioural therapy. No attempt will be made to go into details about the application of these strategies: anyone wanting to acquire the necessary specialist clinical skills will do best to train under the guidance of someone familiar with such methods.

Motivational interviewing

Brief motivational interviewing was described in detail in the chapter on non-specialist settings (see Chapter 10), where it is typically a stand-alone intervention. However, motivational interviewing techniques can be used at the beginning of specialist treatment; for example, to motivate entry into treatment and increase likelihood of retention. The tactics of motivational interviewing can also be incorporated into ongoing therapy, as described below.

In motivational interviewing the therapist does not assume an authoritarian role within the sessions but seeks to create a positive atmosphere conducive to change. The overall goal is to increase the intrinsic motivation of the patient, thus enabling them to take the responsibility for change themselves. The approach is underpinned by four broad principles: expressing empathy; developing discrepancy; rolling with resistance; and supporting self-efficacy (Miller & Rollnick, 2002). Rather than applying a confrontational stance, the therapist uses warmth and empathy to establish the therapeutic relationship. The patient is then helped to perceive a discrepancy between their present behaviour and where they want to be; this discrepancy is then amplified. The therapist seeks to be 'gently persuasive' and does not oppose resistance. When resistance is encountered the therapist shifts strategies and tries to use it to good advantage. Finally the therapist aims to impart a sense of hope and potential for change, supporting self-efficacy.

In the first phase the patient is encouraged to do most of the talking. The therapist asks open questions, affirms, listens reflectively and summarizes. Reflective listening is an active process on the part of the therapist, a way of checking out what the patient means. Summary statements are used to show the patient that the therapist has been listening, to link material that has been discussed or to move things on (a transitional summary). These techniques help to facilitate 'change talk'. Change talk, in turn, develops discrepancy and this helps to build intrinsic motivation.

The first phase of motivational interviewing may take much longer with some patients than with others. As patients come to the point where they are ready to change, but have not yet made a firm commitment, a plan is negotiated. This can involve setting goals and considering options for change.

Cognitive behavioural therapy

The cognitive behavioural approach to treatment is based on the assumption that it is the problem drinking which is to be treated, as opposed to the psychoanalytic view that the drinking is merely a symptom or symbol of an underlying psychodynamic conflict or neurosis. Implicit in this approach is the belief that problem drinking is mainly a learned behaviour and that treatment involves replacing the maladaptive pattern of drinking behaviour with more appropriate drinking or abstinence. Cognitive behavioural psychology also highlights the role of expectations about alcohol in the development of drinking and its consequences. Cognitive behavioural treatments are outlined in Chapter 14, and the interested reader should refer to that chapter's reference list for a fuller account.

Working on allied problems

Mental health

A patient will often bring up problems related to their 'nerves' – anxiety, phobic symptoms, irritability, jealousy, depression or difficulty in sleeping. During the initial weeks (or even months) of sobriety, these symptoms may still be related to withdrawal, and can therefore be expected gradually to clear. What at first appear to be handicapping phobic symptoms may, for instance, fade out with 2–3 months of sobriety. In practice the contribution made to the patient's 'nerves' by the biological processes of withdrawal will, over the initial period of sobriety, be inseparable from symptoms which may stem from the patient's rediscovery of what it is like to be their real self unshielded by alcohol. Their real self may be anxious and irritable, but for years alcohol has blotted out, exacerbated or confused these underlying propensities.

No matter which of the above factors may explain the patient's psychological discomfort, the best immediate response is not heedlessly to offer drugs but to employ a common sense and supportive approach. A reflex assumption which has been reinforced over many years' drinking has to be overcome: psychic distress may be part of the human condition and not something that has to be immediately and chemically ablated. The patient is, as it were, too anxious about being anxious.

The patient is then likely to be helped if, together with these basic messages, some ideas are offered as to how distress is to be ameliorated more constructively than by resort to tranquillizers. They may be helped by learning a relaxation technique, or by developing a variety of simple coping strategies such as listening to music, going for a walk or telephoning a friend. While the basic approach to many psychological problems is best made in this low-key fashion, the therapist must also keep an eye open for the presence of more serious disturbances (see Chapters 6 and 7), which may require very active attention.

Social and family adjustment

A wide range of problems may need to be discussed and monitored under this heading, as the patient works towards agreed goals. It may be wise for the therapist on each occasion to make at least a general enquiry as to what is happening within the family, how things are going at work (or as regards looking for a job) and how leisure time is being spent. Financial problems, housing or any court proceedings may also need to be checked on. Basic work with the family is discussed later in this chapter.

Physical health

Particularly in the early stages of sobriety, there may be problems in the patient's physical health that require attention or referral, and which must not be lost from sight because of all else that is on the agenda. A feeling of rediscovered physical well-being may be one of the prime rewards of sobriety.

Slotting in more specific treatments

The use of the more specific treatment approaches, which are discussed in Chapter 14, requires discretion and timing. Every session, besides its immediate contact, is also potentially a routing point.

Making the effort worthwhile

No one is likely to achieve long-term success in dealing with a drinking problem unless sobriety (or ameliorated drinking) proves to be a personally rewarding experience (Edwards, Oppenheimer & Taylor, 1992; Vaillant, 1983). If all that is won by the effort to stop drinking is a grey and empty existence, it will not be long before there is a relapse. When sobriety is unrewarding there is also the danger that alcohol will be substituted by uncontrolled gambling or by excessive use of tranquillizers or sedatives. Many patients move spontaneously towards the discovery of rewards, and two general patterns of development can often then be seen – either a wide new engagement in life or, alternatively, a much narrower substitute activity. The first of these two pathways – the wide new engagement – is in fact often a re-engagement in life than an entirely new series of moves, and is characteristic of the person who had a positive involvement in life before the emergence of the drinking problem overwhelmed these enjoyments. The second pathway – that of a narrower substitute activity – more often characterizes the recovery of the person who had never, at any previous period, achieved any great base of enjoyment. In this instance, it is not that a happy pattern of living was overwhelmed by drinking, but, on the contrary, that the drinking problem initially developed in the setting of unrewarding relationships and activities. Recovery may be marked by an almost frenetic commitment to one particular interest.

When no rewarding pattern of new involvement develops in the wake of sobriety and instead, as the months go by, there is a continued complaint that 'it was better when I was drinking', thought has to be given to what can be done to obtain constructive movement. The therapist's role is firstly that of identifying the problem and encouraging the patient to identify small real steps towards a solution and to take those steps. This is often a stage where the family again needs to be involved. Beyond common sense advice, there are various other lines of approach. For instance, the passivity and pessimism which stand in the way of a determined attempt to find rewards seem often to have the characteristics of a learnt expectation of failure – 'I just can't get on with people, I'm no good at anything'. Even one small limited success may begin to offer a new sense of possibilities – success generalizes.

On other occasions, the rewards of sobriety take a turn for the better after a major life change, which is either more or less accidental or very purposely brought about, such as a shift to a new locality, a new job, the break-up of a marriage or a new relationship. These are the kind of solutions that tend traditionally to be looked on with suspicion as 'geographical escape', with the problems in no way resolved but taken along to be acted out again in the new personal setting. Such strategies are, admittedly, in some instances no more than unprofitable escapism, but it is wrong automatically to take a negative view of what is likely to be achieved by these large shifts. At times the patient is precisely right in taking the bold and simple view that, 'What is wrong is living in this street'. The move to the new house, with the decorating, furniture buying and pride in ownership, the shared family involvement, the escape from the old social environment and all the drinking friends who used to knock on the door, can then mark the start of a new epoch.

The therapeutic use of the concept of alcoholism as a disease

A proportion of patients may find the concept of alcoholism as a disease (Edwards, 2000; Jellinek, 1960) helpful to recovery. Such a formulation can serve as an idea around which that patient organizes understanding of his or her condition and a personal programme of recovery. This concept is central to the philosophy of Alcoholics Anonymous (AA) (see Chapter 15).

The advantages inherent in such a simple definition of the problem can for many patients be considerable. There is comfort in the view that they are suffering from a condition that can be understood within much the same model as diabetes: guilt is relieved and acceptance of the inexorable fact that the only remedy for this disease is to stop drinking offers a clear personal goal. Seen in these terms, the disease is 'incurable', and recovery is a lifetime programme centred around vigilant avoidance of the first drink.

The disease concept is sometimes seized on as a revelation by a patient who has previously been thrashing around chaotically, with self-defeating attempts to 'control' their drinking. There are, however, therapists who are unhappy with this formulation or unwilling to work within its constraints. They see the disease concept as inviting the patient to avoid self-responsibility – 'It's a disease, I can't help it'. They may also see it as a formulation that detracts attention from the wider spectrum of drinking behaviours and alcohol-related problems and overemphasizes the dependence element.

From the therapeutic angle, the reasonable position to take must be that there are different ways of formulating problems which will be more or less helpful to different patients, and with which different therapists will be more or less comfortable. The patient can be rendered a disservice if the therapist insists on a dogmatic view of either kind. In reality the risk of damage is usually obviated by the patient shopping around until a model of understanding is found that suits that person best.

How to deal positively with relapse

Relapse is a common event. This statement will be interpreted pessimistically if one has misread the treatment of drinking problems as being only about rapid and maintained 'success'. More often, real success involves trial and error along the way. Dealing with and learning from relapse is part of the process of recovery, but such a view is not to be read as favouring a *laissez-faire* attitude. Relapse has to be taken seriously by the patient and therapist alike, but in another sense it has also to be demystified. It is a piece of behaviour to be objectively understood rather than a fall from grace.

Relapse can take many different forms. It may be precipitate and explosive, or it may be a matter of a slow slide; the pace of relapse is often directly related to the degree of dependence. The patient may then stay relapsed for months or years, and the AA member of 20 years' standing may seem tragically to have lost all their gains. On the other hand, relapse may be short-lived, with the patient pulling back after a day or two. Beyond the surface description of these different patterns, there is then the question of the cause and meaning of the occurrence, and it is these inner significances which, in the individual case, have to be examined if there is to be profit from the experience and recovery is to move forward.

Some of the commoner circumstances of relapse are set out below, but in reality the determinants are often likely to be multiple and will require varied responses (Carroll, 1996).

An initial and ambivalent sobriety overthrown

Here one is dealing with the patient who relapses in the early days of treatment because they have not as yet satisfactorily sorted out the balance of their motivations. They are as yet in two minds as to whether or not they want to stop drinking, and the relapse indicates that there is still important initial work to be done in sorting out these ambivalences. Motivation has got to be strengthened.

Insufficient coping mechanisms

Here the same surface picture has a different inner meaning and different therapeutic implications. This type of patient has, to a greater extent, overcome their ambivalence, but they are unskilled in defending their sobriety. They know what they want to do, but they are caught out and fail in their intentions. Effort has to be directed at better learning of coping mechanisms.

Failure to find sobriety rewarding

Sobriety has not been consolidated and no satisfactory substitutes have been found for drinking. This is the type of relapse that occurs after perhaps 6–12 months of uneasy sobriety. The need is to work again on the rewards of sobriety.

Disturbance of mood

Relapse is, in such instances, an indication that the patient has been unable to cope with an upset in mood. The patient may have experienced a transient patch of gloom, anxiety or irritability, which has overwhelmed their defences, or they may be prone to cyclical mood swings. Depressive illness is a not uncommon cause of relapse, and the possibility of hypomanic illness may also have to be considered.

Overcome by events

In such instances, an event or series of events proves too much for the individual's defences. Rather than drinking being a response to catastrophic happenings, the more usual story is of an event which, to the outsider, might seem trivial, or a cluster of seemingly minor troubles. For instance, the patient has had a row with her husband and, that same morning, the water tank in the roof has leaked, and the desire to bring back a bottle of gin from the supermarket is irresistible. To dismiss such a story as 'just a bundle of excuses' is unhelpful. Its analysis tells us that for this woman, ordinary marital discord gives rise to feelings of insecurity which are hard to bear, and that when subjected then to a little extra stress, she will be without any means of coping other than by resorting to drink.

Failure in vigilance

Sometimes it seems that the patient has been careless. They were half aware that it would be dangerous to go to that party, but such considerations were less important than the prospect of fun. They knew that it would be risky to start drinking in such a setting, but by the time the party was in full swing, they 'thought they could get away with it'. This lack of vigilance is often related to a fading of memory; the pains previously experienced with drinking are now rather distant, while the pleasure of a glass of wine is immediate.

Whether relapse is insidious or abrupt, it is a happening to be *used* in treatment. The usefulness of the experience is, however, lost if the incident is met inappropriately; for instance, if it is passed by as trivial and unimportant, interpreted as reason for pessimism and surrender of therapeutic effort or taken as occasion for abandonment of the patient's and family's active responsibility with an unnecessary retreat to hospital. Relapse is best met with no retreat from expectations of the patient's self-responsibility. That responsibility now includes getting out of the relapse, working out its meaning and setting things up so that further relapses are less likely.

Many relapses are short-lived, with the patient regaining sobriety before harm is done. It is potentially misleading to use the same word to describe the happenings when a patient takes a few drinks one evening and then stops drinking again completely, as opposed to their sliding into a rapid reinstatement of dependence and being once more in the grip of very threatening drinking. Some therapists therefore prefer to distinguish between 'lapse' (transient or minor) and 'relapse' (major and perhaps with reinstatement of dependence). A lapse may lead on to the relapse, but this is not the inevitable march of events. And what the therapist at first views as 'lapse' may be the patient's tentative move toward re-establishment of normal drinking.

As well as therapy seeking to enable patient and family to learn from the incident, there may be immediate actions needed to minimize the harm done by any such occurrence. The patient may, for instance, need to avoid losing their job and get back to work as soon as possible. Where there are particular dangers to physical health, such as may be present if the patient is suffering from pancreatitis or liver disease, then the sooner drinking is stopped the better. Relapse may sometimes pose dangers of suicide if the patient believes that 'the last chance has gone'.

Basic work with the family

The importance of the family dimension in the initial assessment and goal-setting and the value of the initial interview with the spouse have already been discussed (see Chapter 11).

Work with the spouse

The spouse's behaviour patterns may have become stuck in a rut and be producing no benefit, and sometimes just trying a change of tack can help. Constructive help-seeking and constructive management seem on the whole to be more effective than continued attack or manipulation (Orford & Edwards, 1977). It may generally be beneficial if the spouse can reach a decision as to what they definitely will not do and what are their limits. For instance, they may decide as an act of definite policy that they will abandon arguing and nagging, or that they will not give their partner money nor go out and buy them drink. It is the open identification of a set of intentions, the sense of something to do, the drawing up of a personal programme, which is useful in such a situation.

It is often helpful to hold a few joint sessions to try to ensure that mutual goals are understood and that there is shared commitment to constructive change. This can be used to give the sense of a new start, with an emphasis on the positive, on identifying what is good in the marriage, what each in practical terms wants from the other and what each will give to the other partner. There is no evidence that a routine, major therapeutic intervention with the spouse is of benefit.

Help for the children

The best help for the child is the restoration of happiness in the home. The fact of a previously alcohol dependent parent ceasing to drink, of rowing and violence no longer being the continuing experience, can be dramatically beneficial to the child's happiness and well-being (Lynskey, Fergusson & Horwood, 1994). Sometimes the changes are evident within a week. The teacher notices that the child is concentrating at school; the mother knows that a child has stopped bed-wetting or will say: 'It's lovely, they're talking to their dad again'. More often the changes are going to be seen over a longer period, and the restoration of confidence will take many months, with the previously drinking parent hurt and discouraged because their children have not sooner come towards them.

Given that help for the problem-drinking parent (and the partner) may be of indirect benefit to the children, other ways of aiding the children have also to be considered, especially where there is no immediate treatment response from the adult (Zeitlin, 1994). There can be instances where urgent thought has to be given to removal of the child from the home as an immediate measure of physical protection, or where high priority has to be given to social work supervision of an intensity that can monitor the child's safety (in Chapter 8 we give a case example of such a situation).

As regards individual help for the child remaining in the disturbed home, much the same range of approaches is applicable as with a child or young person facing any other disturbing home influence. The offer of a good and confident relationship is itself valuable, but with a child who is of an age to verbalize problems it is helpful to discuss directly the parent's drinking – to listen to and offer understanding of the child's distress, to find some more satisfactory way of looking at the parents and of coping with the anger and hurt, to offer straightforward information, to discuss the child's role within the family, what the child 'can do to help', and the limits of those possibilities, and to aid towards good friendships outside the home. Children too have their coping mechanisms, which can be adaptive or maladaptive.

There may be occasions when older children should be involved in family therapy in a formal sense, but the skills necessary to handle the interactions of children and parents in such a forum should not be underestimated. More often what is useful is the home visit or series of home visits where children can experience a family discussion in a natural setting, and where family members drop in and out as they feel like it. The role of Al-Ateen (a self-help group deriving from AA and Al-Anon) is discussed in Chapter 15.

The use of therapeutic groups

The place of group therapy as a special technique to be deployed at the stage when the patient is consolidating their recovery is discussed in Chapter 14. Alcoholics Anonymous and Al-Anon also provide group experience. But groups can also have their place in the basic work of treatment, and many therapists would see involvement in groups at an early stage of the treatment process as being useful for information-giving, shared solution of problems and support. There is no evidence that more intensive group work at these earlier stages brings special benefit.

Spacing of appointments

There is no one rule for the spacing of appointments, and some patients will need to be seen more frequently than others. In general, the emphasis on autonomy and self-determination is best supported by giving more spaced rather than more frequent appointments, with escalation into a modal routine of intensive intervention resisted. Much must depend on the thoroughness and purposeful nature of the initial assessment and exercise in goal-setting. It is better to put investment in that direction, with similarly purposeful but spaced follow-up, than to start from an incomplete assessment with a follow-through which lacks direction despite frequency of contact.

As for how long a session should last, this again must be individually determined. On many occasions, a 20-minute interview can give sufficient time for a focused monitoring of progress, while in other instances, it may be necessary to find 45–60 minutes for listening and detailed discussion.

The treatment organization should also have the capacity to respond to an emergency and to be able to see the patient who experiences a crisis between their fixed appointments. It will, however, be unhelpful to see a patient on a free-demand basis if their demands are witness to their over-dependence on other people. It would be better to encourage them to meet their own crises and keep to the schedule of appointments.

When a patient fails to keep an appointment there should be an administrative mechanism which ensures that they are not then lost from sight. A personal letter offering a further appointment should be written or a phone call made, and if contact is not re-established a home visit should perhaps be arranged. When all else fails the patient should still be left with the indication that the door remains readily open.

Duration and termination of treatment

The duration of treatment may be proposed by the therapist but it is effectively determined by the patient. There are patients who appear to have benefited from one or two sessions and who decide this is all they need, while at the other extreme there are those who want to maintain at least intermittent contact over years.

A fixed course of so many sessions over so many months cannot in reality meet the needs of an enormously varied patient population. Judgement needs to be made in terms of the patient's progress along a number of dimensions of recovery, the likelihood of further useful work, the timeliness of a move which further emphasizes the patient's ability to handle their own responsibilities and negotiation on timing between therapist and patient. Rather than there being a 'this is the end of your treatment' type of announcement, what is said might often be something like this:

'We've been meeting each month for the last 8 months, and you've achieved a great deal. If you agree, what I would now suggest is that we meet again just before Christmas – that's 5 months hence. But if for any reason you wanted to see me earlier, phone and let me know'.

The question arises in a different form when making this decision not in relation to the patient who has made substantial progress but in a case where after 6 months of work the drinking is continuing unabated. Does one 'terminate treatment' on the grounds that the patient is failing to benefit or show commitment to change? In general, rather than such a situation being an indication for termination of treatment, it more often suggests the need for reassessment of what is being done:

Basic work: bringing the ideas together

It would be misleading to present a carefully ordered flow chart or series of ordered steps to describe the basic work of treatment, for this would contradict the message that what is most required is the flexibility to meet the needs of the individual patient as their recovery evolves. But, with that caution in mind, it may be useful to have a check-list:

1   Assessment with patient and spouse is the initiation of therapy and a shared experience.
2   The case formulation orders the material obtained in the assessment and is again shared with patient and spouse.
3   Goal-setting must be negotiated in similar terms. Goals must be specific and cover non-drinking as well as drinking issues. There must be an invitation to a tangible commitment to working towards those goals.
4   The therapeutic relationship is important and must be skilfully fostered. The therapist must learn how to show warmth and give hope, but they should not be lured into over-directiveness either with the patient or spouse. Self-responsibility should be fostered.
5   Some basic therapeutic principles should be borne in mind: continuity of purpose and sense of movement must be maintained; salient questions must be identified at each interview, with the patient allowed to define what is of importance; and the family perspective must be maintained. Therapy requires continuous monitoring, and the patient may usefully engage in self-monitoring. Balances have to be struck both between focus on reality and dynamics and between drinking and other topics. Commitment may at various points need to be re-examined. An eye has constantly to be kept on the development of the relationship.
6   The actual content of the interview includes work on the drinking problem and attention to problems in the areas of mental and physical health and social adjustment.
7   Each interview, as well as being concerned with the continuing basics of treatment, is also an occasion for deciding whether it is timely to signpost the patient towards any more specialized type of help.

8   The effort towards recovery by patient and spouse has to be worthwhile. They must be helped to sense out the gains, and a sobriety that is only negative will not be maintained. The quality of sobriety is important. Strengthening of the patient's motivation is basic to therapy.

9   Relapse should not be considered a taboo subject. If relapse does occur, it should be possible to learn from the event. The many different patterns, causes and meanings of relapse must be understood.

10 Basic work with the family may also be needed. This includes meeting the immediate needs of spouse and children, as well as work which facilitates conjoint efforts towards the patient's recovery.

11 The pacing and intensity of help must be kept under review and ultimately tailed off, perhaps with the offer of an 'open door' rather than formal closure of the case. What must be guarded against is an automatic escalation into heavy intervention. Once there has been full assessment and careful and agreed goal-setting, often much may then be left to the patient and family with monitoring and encouragement and a little talking through.

12 Basic treatment is an alliance with the natural processes of recovery; it is a matter of discovering rather than imposing possibilities for change, a matter of teaching map-reading skills rather than pushing people along a path which we dictate.

References

Batel P, Pessione F, Bouvier A-M, Rueff B (1995) Prompting alcoholics to be referred to an alcohol clinic: the effectiveness of a simple letter. *Addiction* **90**, 811–814.

Carroll K M (1996) Relapse prevention as a psychosocial treatment: a review of controlled clinical trials. *Experimental and Clinical Psychopharmacology* **4**, 46–54.

Carroll K M (2001) Constrained, confounded and confused: why we really know so little about therapists in treatment outcome research. *Addiction* **96**, 203–206.

Connors G J, DiClimente C C, Dermen K H, et al. (2000) Predicting the therapeutic alliance in alcoholism treatment. *Journal of Studies on Alcohol* **61**, 139–149.

Davidson R (1998) The transtheoretical model: a critical overview. In *Treating Addictive Behaviours*, 2nd edn, W R Miller, N Heather (eds). New York: Plenum Press, pp. 25–38.

Edwards G (1996) Addictive behaviours: the next clinic appointment. In *Psychotherapy, Psychological Treatments and the Addictions*, G Edwards, C Dare (eds). Cambridge: Cambridge University Press, pp. 94–109.

Edwards G (2000) Calling alcoholism a disease. In *Alcohol the Ambiguous Molecule*. London: Penguin Books, pp. 93–102.

Edwards G, Oppenheimer E, Taylor C (1992) Hearing the noise in the system. Exploration of textual analysis as a method for studying change in drinking behaviour. *British Journal of Addiction* **87**, 73–81.

Gerdner A, Holmberg A (2000) Factors affecting motivation to treatment in severely dependent alcoholics. *Journal of Studies on Alcohol* **61**, 548–560.

Heather N, Kisson-Singh J, Fenton W (1990) Assisted natural recovery from alcohol problems: effects of a self-help manual with and without telephone contacts. *British Journal of Addiction* **85**, 1177–1185.

Jellinek, E M (1960) *The Disease Concept of Alcoholism*. New Brunswick, NJ: Hillhouse Press.

Levin J D, Weiss R H (eds) (1994) *The Dynamics and Treatment of Alcoholism: Essential Papers*. Northvale, NJ: Jason Aronson.

Luborsky L, Crits-Christoph P (1990) *Understanding the Transference*. New York: Basic Books.

Luborsky L, McLellan A J, Woody G E, O'Brien C P, Anerback A (1985) Therapist success and its determinants. *Archives of General Psychiatry* **42**, 602–611.

Lynskey T M, Fergusson D M, Horwood J (1994) The effect of parental alcohol problems on rates of adolescent psychiatric disorder. *Addiction* **89**, 1277–1286.

Miller W, Rollnick S (2002) *Motivational Interviewing: Preparing People for Change*, 2nd edn. New York: Guilford Press.

Najavits L M, Weiss R D (1994) Variations in therapist effectiveness in the treatment of patients with substance use disorders: an empirical review. *Addiction* **89**, 679–688.

Orford J, Edwards G (1977) *Alcoholism. A Comparison of Treatment and Advice, with a Study of the Influence of Marriage*. Maudsley Hospital Monograph No.26. Oxford: Oxford University Press.

Prochaska J O, Di Clemente C C, Norcross J C (1992) In search of how people change: applications to addictive behaviours. *American Psychologist* **7**, 1102–1114.

Prochaska J O, Nacross J C, DiClimente, C C (1994) Stages and processes of self-change of smoking: toward an integrative model of change. *Psychotherapy: Theory, Research and Practice* **19**, 276–288.

Raistrick D, Heather N, Godfrey C (2006) Review of the Effectiveness of Treatment for Drinking Problems. London: National Treatment Agency for Substance Misuse.

Rollnick S, Miller W R (1995) What is motivational interviewing? *Behavioural and Cognitive Psychotherapy* **23**, 325–334.

Sutton S (1996) Can 'stages of change' provide guidance in the treatment of addictions? A critical examination of Prochaska and DiClimente's model. In *Psychotherapy, Psychological Treatments and the Addictions*, G Edwards, C Dare (eds). Cambridge: Cambridge University Press, pp. 184–205.

Thom B, Brown D, Drummond C, et al. (1992) Engaging patients with alcohol problems in treatment: the first consultation. *British Journal of Addiction* **87**, 601–611.

Vaillant G E (1983) *The Natural History of Alcoholism*. Cambridge, MA: Harvard University Press.

Vaillant G E (1995) *The Natural History of Alcoholism Revisited*. Cambridge, MA: Harvard University Press.

West R (2005) Time for a change: putting the Transtheoretical (Stages of Change) Model to rest. *Addiction* **100**, 1036–1039.

Zeitlin H (1994) Children with alcohol misusing parents. In *Alcohol and Alcohol Problems*, G Edwards, T J Peters (eds). Edinburgh: Churchill Livingstone, pp. 139–151.

Specialist treatment

What treatments work?

In very general terms, about one third of individuals entering treatment for alcohol problems sadly derive little or no benefit. However, two thirds of patients do appear to benefit, and these patients fall into two groups of roughly equal sizes. The first group does very well during the first year following the treatment episode, and here improvement means abstinence, moderation of drinking and freedom from or a reduction in alcohol-related problems (Miller, Walters & Bennett, 2001). The second group continues to have periods of heavy drinking, but they drink less frequently and, when they drink, they consume less, so overall experience a reduction in alcohol-related health and social problems. A narrow focus on drinking outcomes will therefore miss the fact that treatment confers substantial benefits on patients. It is also likely that factors outside the treatment setting have a differential impact on the behavioural change process. It must be remembered, however, that there will always be a proportion of dependent drinkers who go on to kill or wreck themselves, despite treatment.

Our basic plea is that treatment choices should, wherever possible, be research based, while at the same time a spurious scientism should not be allowed to inhibit the efforts of the individual therapist who is trying to help the individual patient in difficult and unique circumstances. Table 14.1 summarizes the research evidence base for different treatments. No attempt will be made to go into details about the application of these strategies: anyone wanting to acquire the necessary specialist clinical skills would do best to train under the guidance of someone familiar with such methods.

Motivational interviewing

Brief motivational interviewing was described in detail in the chapter on non-specialist settings (see Chapter 10), where it is typically a stand-alone intervention. Motivational interviewing techniques can be used at the beginning of specialist treatment, for example to motivate entry into treatment and increase likelihood of retention (see Chapter 13), and are also helpful in sustaining ongoing therapy. Motivational interviewing is well supported by research (Burke, Arkowitz & Menchola, 2003; Burke et al., 2004).

Motivational enhancement therapy

Motivational enhancement therapy (MET) is an adaptation of motivational interviewing that has been evaluated in two large multi-centre trials, Project MATCH and the United Kingdom Alcohol Treatment Trial (UKATT).

Project MATCH found that MET, delivered over four sessions, was as effective on most outcomes as cognitive behavioural therapy (CBT) and 12-step facilitation (TSF) delivered

Table 14.1. Specialist treatments for drinking problems: an appraisal of their research underpinning.

- *Psychosocial treatments* including motivational interviewing, motivational enhancement therapy (MET), social behaviour and network therapy (SBNT), coping and social skills training, the community reinforcement approach (CRA), behavioural self-control, behaviour contracting. Well supported by research

- *Individual psychotherapies other than cognitive behavioural.* Little or no research support: deploy with discrimination

- *Group therapy.* Probably useful for basic support but efficacy as a treatment of choice not supported

- *Behavioural marital therapy.* Well supported by research

- *Alcoholics Anonymous (AA).* AA is an effective intervention for individuals who engage in the programme and attend mettings

- *Disulfiram.* Not without side-effects but useful in some circumstances

- *Anti-craving drugs* including naltrexone and acamprosate. Naltrexone and acamprosate supported by research

over 12 sessions. The exception was abstinence, which was consistently higher in the TSF condition. The improvements that occurred during the 12-week treatment period were still evident at 1-year and at 3-year follow-up (Project MATCH Research Group 1997a, 1997b, 1998a).

UKATT compared three sessions of MET with eight sessions of Social Behaviour and Network Therapy (SBNT) (UKATT Research Team, 2005a, 2005b). Both groups of subjects showed marked improvements at 3-month and 1-year follow-up, and there were no significant differences between the groups on alcohol-related measures. The evidence thus suggests that MET should be considered as the first step in a specialist treatment programme.

Cognitive behavioural therapy

The cognitive behavioural approach to the treatment of drinking problems is a structured, focused therapy that helps individuals to understand the environmental cues, thoughts, coping skills and behaviours that contribute to their drink problem. They learn to examine the sequence of events leading to their alcohol use and to identify the thoughts, feelings and circumstances associated with drinking. The therapist facilitates the recognition of risky situations that could potentially lead to relapse, and enables modification of thinking. In this section effective cognitive behavioural treatments are outlined.

Coping and social skills training

Some patients with drinking problems are handicapped by an underlying inability to function confidently in social situations and to manage everyday hassles. Coping skills training concentrates on developing interpersonal and communication skills and cognitive behavioural mood management (Monti et al., 1990, 1995). Social skills deficits are assessed and patients are then taught how to initiate social interactions and express their thoughts and feelings. This is typically done in a group setting where role-play and other behavioural methods can be used. For instance, the patient who is not assertive may find it difficult to say 'no' to an offered drink; one element in therapy may involve teaching them to rehearse saying 'no'. Social skills training, which includes assertiveness training, is an extremely effective method of treatment for alcohol problems (Holder et al., 1991; Miller et al., 1998). It can be delivered on an individual or group basis and is particularly suited to individuals with moderate alcohol dependence. It requires a certain level of cognitive functioning, and patients with neuropsychological impairment/alcohol-related brain damage are unlikely to benefit from this approach. Project MATCH included a form of CBT that was largely composed of coping skills training. Coping and social skills training is an effective treatment for those who are moderately dependent on alcohol (Raistrick, Heather & Godfrey, 2006; Shand et al., 2003; Slattery et al., 2003) .

Social behaviour and network therapy

Social behaviour and network therapy (SBNT) was developed for the UK Alcohol Treatment Trial (Copello et al., 2002, 2009). It acknowledges the role that the social environment plays in the addiction process and in treatment. Family members, friends and others from the client's social network are offered support and in turn are facilitated to help the client engage in treatment and change their drinking behaviour. Put another way, the social network mobilizes positive social support to change the drinking behaviour. The therapist thinks in terms of the social network and introduces topics such as communication, coping skills and the enhancing of the social support network. Non-judgemental listening, provision of information, exploration of sources of support and arrangement for other help if needed are all part of this very practical way of working with drinkers and their significant others.

The community reinforcement approach

The community reinforcement approach (CRA) is based on the principles of instrumental learning, and the emphasis is on manipulation of real-life rewards in the patient's environment. It focuses on altering reinforcement contingencies in the home environment, involves significant others and uses positive reinforcement. The family's positive reactions, aid with job-finding, membership of a social club and other social rewards are presented to the patient as contingent on treatment success, and the therapeutic team accepts responsibility to ensure that such rewards are in fact on offer. This technique was developed for in-patients by Hunt and Azrin (1973), but has evolved over time and is now used in out-patient/community treatment programmes (Azrin, 1976; Meyers & Miller, 2001). Treatment components include motivational counselling, drink-refusal training, communication skills training, problem-solving training, relapse prevention and disulfiram with monitored compliance. The CRA retains its focus on drinking behaviours, family and job-related problems. Early research found that married patients with family support did well using the stand-alone disulfiram component, whereas unmarried, unsupported patients only benefited from the full CRA package (Azrin et al., 1982). More recent research shows that CRA-based strategies are also effective when disulfiram is not used (Meyers & Miller, 2001). Although CRA is an effective treatment, particularly for drinkers with serious problems, it has never been widely adopted in clinical practice. This is surprising because the procedures are well specified and can be learned and applied successfully, even by novice therapists. The full package need not be time-consuming or expensive, and positive outcomes have been reported even after 5–8 sessions. It is more likely that CRA has not been disseminated distinctively or attractively enough to facilitate its transfer to routine clinical practice (Meyers & Miller, 2001) .

Behavioural self-control

Behavioural self-control training (BSCT) is particularly effective in helping individuals at the less severe end of the dependence spectrum to reduce their alcohol consumption. Initially the therapist and client negotiate sensible limits of alcohol consumption, and the client keeps a drinking diary or fills out a self-monitoring card to record all drinks taken. A craving diary or daily activity diary can also be helpful. Clients are then taught techniques for reducing the rate of drinking and are helped to identify triggers to drinking, in particular negative moods (boredom, anxiety, depression), positive moods (excitement, happiness) and external cues (meeting with friends, particular time of day, a particular place). Behavioural self-control training can be used in the individual or group setting and self-help manuals are available (Hester, 1995; Jarvis et al., 2005). It is an extremely effective treatment modality for individuals able to moderate their drinking (Raistrick, Heather & Godfrey, 2006).

Behaviour contracting

Behaviour contracting or contingency management involves the negotiation of an agreement between the patient and their significant others in relation to mutual expectations. This treatment modality rewards 'good behaviour' and is an integral component of treatment methods such as CRA and behavioural marital therapy.

Cognitive behavioural marital therapy

This effective treatment approach focuses on the patient's drinking behaviour and the quality of the marital relationship (O'Farrell et al., 1993). Behavioural and disulfiram contracts are used to address the drinking behaviour. The marital interventions focus on improving the relationship and resolving conflicts and problems. A stable relationship is clearly a prerequisite. Some programmes incorporate a disulfiram contract where the problem drinker takes disulfiram every day, observed by the spouse. Behavioural marital therapy has been shown to improve drinking outcomes at 18 months and to maintain marital stability and satisfaction (O'Farrell et al., 1993). Interactive couples' group therapy is another technique that shows promise (Bowers & Al-Rehda, 1990). Cognitive behavioural marital therapy is an effective treatment for individuals whose partners are willing to participate in treatment (Berglund, Thelander & Jonsson, 2003; Raistrick, Heather & Godfrey, 2006; Shand et al., 2003; Slattery et al., 2003).

Cue exposure

This approach is based on the principles of classical conditioning and borrows from a treatment strategy developed for phobias, obsessive-compulsive disorder and other anxiety disorders. The patient is exposed to conditioned stimuli or cues, which have previously precipitated craving or excessive drinking, and encouraged either not to drink or not to drink excessively. For instance, they may be asked to carry around with them a bottle of whisky and sniff at it without drinking, or the therapist may accompany them on outings to a bar, or they may be asked to take sufficient alcohol to activate craving and then desist from further drinking. Cue exposure reduces the likelihood that the stimulus will trigger a response in the future and improves the individual's self-efficacy. It can be combined with coping skills and communication skills (Monti et al., 1993; Rohsenhow et al., 2001) or incorporated into a relapse prevention programme (Drummond et al., 1995). It shows promise as a treatment method, especially when combined with coping and communication skills (Berglund, Thelander & Jonsson, 2003; Raistrick, Heather & Godfrey, 2006; Shand et al., 2003) .

Aversion therapy

Aversion therapy, based on the principles of classical conditioning, came to the fore in the 1930s and is of historical importance because it fostered an optimistic interest in 'alcoholism' treatment at a time when little else appeared to be promising. The act of drinking alcohol is paired with a variety of unpleasant experiences, and the individual should show an automatic negative response when later exposed to alcohol. Such counter-conditioning techniques have included chemically induced nausea (using emetine and apomorphine), apnoea (using intravenous succinylcholine), electric shock and covert sensitization (Miller et al., 1995). Although nausea aversion therapy has shown positive outcomes in a number of studies, aversion therapy has been abandoned and is not recommended.

Covert sensitization is the form of aversion therapy most commonly used. Here the patient is taught to associate the sight or taste of alcohol with unpleasant images, which they learn actively to conjure up (conditioned aversion). Covert sensitization is suited to an abstinence goal, and it is recommended for use on an individual basis as the best results appear to be achieved when the images are specific to the individual. Covert sensitization is an effective treatment (Holder et al., 1991), and its success can be predicted from the degree of conditioning established during treatment (Elkins, 1980).

Relapse prevention therapy

Some aspects of relapse have already been discussed in Chapter 13 in relation to the basic work of treatment. The term 'relapse prevention' refers to a wide range of techniques, many or all of which are cognitive or behavioural in their thrust. This approach has its origins within a theoretical model of relapse proposed by Marlatt and Gordon (1985). Within this perspective, relapse is not viewed as an inexplicable catastrophe but as an event that takes place through a series of cognitive, behavioural and affective processes. One of the main objectives of the relapse prevention programme is preventing a lapse from becoming a relapse. Relapse is viewed as an untoward event to be avoided by careful forward planning and by the design of an individual relapse prevention programme. Patients themselves are active partners in identifying high-risk situations thought to be associated with a potential for relapse. Intrapersonal factors such as negative and positive emotional states, interpersonal conflict and social pressure can all be determinants of relapse. The patient then has to learn more effective coping mechanisms, including cognitive strategies or personally planned substitute activities and rewarding the use of leisure. Strategies will thus involve both learning how to avoid unnecessary risks and how to deal positively and confidently with inevitable risks. Relapse prevention essentially addresses itself not just to changing a self-destructive habit but beyond that to the maintenance of change, and to the development of self-efficacy and coping skills. The approach is applicable both to abstinence and the normal drinking goal.

Marlatt and Gordon (1985) also addressed lifestyle imbalance in their relapse prevention model. The individual experiencing feelings of self-deprivation may be particularly likely to relapse in high-risk situations. Cognitive factors such as rationalization or denial come into play when individuals are craving alcohol, and they are used to legitimize the drinking behaviour and to reduce feelings of guilt and anxiety. Covert planning of relapse through a series of seemingly irrelevant decisions is also described in this model. Beyond Marlatt and Gordon's pioneering formulation, several other authors have contributed to elaboration of the relapse prevention model (Annis, Herie & Watkin-Merek, 1996; Wanigaratne et al., 1990). Treatment outcome studies of relapse prevention have shown mixed results (Carroll, 1996; Irwin et al., 1999). Successful components include teaching individuals to recover quickly from lapses (Weingardt & Marlatt, 1998) and interventions to improve aftercare participation. Relapse prevention seems to be most effective when applied to alcohol dependent individuals at the more severe end of the spectrum and to patients with polydrug use (see Chapter 7). It can improve psychosocial functioning and may be more effective when combined with pharma-cological treatments (Irwin et al., 1999; Raistrick, Heather & Godfrey, 2006).

Cognitive behavioural 'packages'

Anyone working with people who have drinking problems will recognize that they are a very heterogeneous population, and that different approaches are needed for different patients. It is best to carry out an individual assessment, and on the basis of this assessment to identify the type of treatment best suited to that person. Thus, a treatment 'package' may usefully incorp-orate several cognitive behavioural techniques tailored to the individual's need. These could include broader spectrum cognitive approaches as well as the alcohol-focused approaches considered above. Broader spectrum approaches are included below for completeness.

Broader spectrum cognitive behavioural approaches

The cognitive behavioural approach can be useful in helping problem drinkers to address skills that they are lacking. Drinkers who use alcohol to cope with anxiety or anger, or as a result of negative cognitions associated with low self-esteem and depression, may benefit from techniques such as relaxation training, anger management and cognitive restructuring. These approaches are not specific to alcohol problems, but find their application as treatments aimed at dealing with postulated psychological causes of excessive drinking.

Family interventions

Many different types and intensities of family approach have been employed in the treat-ment of drinking problems, varying from informal chats with husband and wife to sophis-ticated therapeutic interventions based on a specific theory. The needs of female partners of heavy-drinking men have largely been ignored. In situations where it proves difficult to engage problem-drinking men in treatment, stress management sessions may help to ease the stresses and burden experienced by their female partners (Halford et al., 2001). Other family members besides the husband and wife may be involved in therapeutic sessions. Over recent years there have been many advances in family therapy techniques and in the application of these techniques to the alcohol field. There is now a strong evidence base for family work (Copello, Velleman & Templeton, 2005). It is therefore important that anyone working with drinking problems should have some familiarity with family work.

Family work can be used to facilitate engagement of the problem drinker into treatment, can incorporate families into the treatment programme or involve significant others in stand-alone treatment. The community reinforcement and family training (CRAFT) approach teaches behaviour change strategies and is an effective modality for engaging resistant drink-ers into treatment (Meyers et al., 2002). Families and friends benefit from being involved in treatment, and the evidence for cognitive behavioural couple and family therapy is strong (Berglund, Thelander & Jonsson, 2003; Shand et al., 2003) Behavioural marital therapy has been particularly well evaluated (O'Farrell, Choquette & Cutter, 1998). Social behaviour and network therapy usually involves the wider network of family and friends but can be used with families alone (Copello et al., 2002).

Other psychosocial treatment modalities

Insight-oriented psychotherapy and group psychotherapy are included here for completeness. Although neither approach is now thought to be an effective treatment for alcohol problems, an understanding of the general principles underlying both modalities is extremely useful for the clinician working in the addiction field. At the very least, this can help when the 'therapeutic going gets tough' and may offer insights when working with patients who have co-morbid personality problems and post-traumatic stress disorder (PTSD).

Psychodynamic psychotherapy (insight-oriented psychotherapy)

Insight-oriented psychotherapy has not been shown to be an effective treatment for drinking problems in controlled trials. Early in treatment, one ounce of change in drinking behaviour is worth more than ten tonnes of insight. Yet, once abstinence has been achieved, psychotherapy has something to offer the carefully selected patient, and it may, on occasion, be essential to that improvement in the quality of sobriety which is such an important adjunct to recovery. The therapist who with modesty, open-mindedness and guidance, engages in such work is also personally going to benefit and will round out their understanding of the extraordinarily complex human processes which often lie behind a drinking story.

  This is the way in which an experienced nurse therapist described her use of psychotherapeutic insights:

> Most of the time I am not 'doing psychotherapy', at least overtly. I doubt whether most of my patients would regard themselves as 'being in psychotherapy'. I'm in fact making use of psychotherapeutic principles in every interview – I'm working through and with a relationship, and dealing with defence mechanisms. But all this work goes on in a setting which emphasizes the need to keep one's feet on the ground, deal with drinking, pay the bills, get the children to school.

Such deployment of dynamic skills in the everyday clinical setting merges with more formal and intensive psychotherapeutic strategies. We do not favour the routine and intensive deployment of formal psychotherapy as a treatment for drinking problems. Such a perspective must not be misinterpreted as antipathetic to psychotherapy. On the contrary, an understanding of dynamic principles must underpin basic work in this area, and formal psychotherapy can on occasion have an important part to play, particularly after alcohol consumption has been brought under control. However, its deployment requires timing and discrimination.

  Different therapists will have their own views as to whether suitability for psychotherapy is determined restrictively or more freely. What should particularly be cautioned against is the danger of forgetting that suitability for psychotherapy does indeed have to be determined by careful assessment. The enthusiasm of those not specially trained in general psychotherapeutic work may lead to the prescription of psychotherapy for a patient whom no experienced psychotherapist would regard as a suitable patient for such engagement. Many psychotherapists will make the offer of psychotherapy actually conditional on the patient achieving a stable period of sobriety or other life changes.

Group therapy

Group therapy has been widely employed in the treatment of drinking problems, even to the extent of sometimes being viewed as the treatment of choice. Unstructured group chat and psychoeducation have no evidence of benefit, but well-defined therapies with good research behind them (cognitive behavioural treatment and relapse prevention) can be delivered in structured, well-managed therapeutic groups (Najavits, Weiss & Liese, 1996).

  Group work often has a place within the therapeutic structure of a treatment centre. Such groups tend to have an open rather than a closed membership as patients are admitted and discharged. At the other extreme, one may find practitioners who will work with closed groups of, say, 8–10 patients selected for their homogeneity (all women, for instance, or all of the same social background) and who will run these groups in terms of orthodox group-therapy principles.

One can identify variations on some general themes as to the type of the work likely to be accomplished in groups. In *educational* groups patients may learn about the nature of dependence. A second important and general theme is *problem solving*: this may relate to such reality issues, such as how to find a job or deal with debts, or may focus on interpersonal and dynamic issues. Rehearsal of *relapse prevention strategies* is often a useful part of group work as patients share ideas with each other on how sobriety is to be consolidated and relapse avoided. Cohesion of group sentiment can assist in the *definition of goals*, in overcoming *resistance* and in the *strengthening of motivation*. Lastly, the fellowship of the group and the opportunity to share problems may very generally contribute to support and help to overcome feelings of isolation.

The therapist should be willing to take responsibility for excluding any patient who comes to a group when intoxicated. Having anyone who has been drinking participate in a group usually causes such anxiety and anger as to rule out the possibility of constructive work.

Therapies for related problems

A range of life problems may exacerbate or result from excessive drinking, and these are too often overlooked and insufficient help given. Common examples include bereavement and loss, depression and anxiety, PTSD, marital conflict, sexual dysfunction and pathological gambling. Specialized techniques exist for assisting with such difficulties. Although it is unlikely that the therapist who was working on drinking problems will be able to become fully trained in the application of, for instance, sex therapies, he or she should be conversant with what such approaches have to offer and should be able to make appropriate referrals.

What did we learn from Project MATCH and the United Kingdom Alcohol Treatment Trial?

Project MATCH

Project MATCH, a multi-site study carried out in 9 centres in the USA, involved a total of 1726 individuals with a diagnosis of alcohol dependence/abuse who were randomly assigned to one of three distinct, individually delivered treatments: (1) TSF therapy designed to enable engagement in Alcoholics Anonymous (12 sessions); (2) CBT designed to teach coping skills to prevent relapse to drinking (12 sessions); and (3) MET designed to increase motivation for and commitment to change (four sessions) (Project MATCH Research Group, 1997a, 1997b, 1998a, 1998b). There was no untreated control group and treatment was for 12 weeks. Clients were followed up over a 1-year period and a proportion at 3 years after completion of treatment. Two groups were recruited to the study, an aftercare group and an out-patient group. The more severely dependent aftercare sample ($n = 774$; 80% male) was recruited immediately following a period of in-patient or intensive day-hospital treatment. The out-patient sample ($n = 952$; 72% male) had not received any prior treatment.

The three treatments were all associated with positive and comparable outcomes, highlighting commonalities across treatments. Client traits did not prove to be prognostic factors as was originally hypothesized.

The TSF treated out-patients did better at 1-year and 3-year follow-up than the other two groups (Project MATCH Research Group, 1998a). Analysis of the treatment effect in the out-patient group over time showed that the MET group initially did less well in terms of abstinence than the other two groups but had 'caught up' by the time of the 3-year follow-up.

Therapist effects on drinking outcome were minimal (Project MATCH Research Group, 1998c), probably reflecting the fact that they were carefully selected and trained, used manual-guided treatment and were closely supervised (Carroll, 2001). The study design therefore reduced variability among therapists and excluded the possibility of examining their impact on treatment.

It might be argued that the four-session MET was more 'value for money' than the other treatments. Closer scrutiny of the data on treatment intensity suggests that TSF and CBT groups did not get three times as much treatment as the MET clients, particularly when these sessions were combined with the extensive assessment and research contacts.

Project MATCH has been complemented by a naturalistic long-term treatment outcome study, carried out in 15 substance misuse programmes attached to Veterans' Affairs (VA) hospitals in the USA (Ouimette, Finney & Moos, 1997). This study was carried out in a 'real-world' setting in the sense that it was an evaluation of treatment programmes already running at these centres. The effectiveness of 12-step, cognitive behavioural (CB) and an eclectic mix of both treatments was compared in a treatment sample of 3698 male clients who had been in residential substance abuse programmes for an average of 25 days.

Overall, subjects showed substantial declines in substance use at 1-year follow-up, with clients treated in 12-step programmes doing better (more likely to be abstinent) than those in CB or eclectic programmes (Moos et al., 1999). The 12-step group was also more likely to be free of substance abuse problems and employed at 1-year follow-up. This 'real-world' study also failed to find consistent patient-treatment matching effects for 12-step and CB treatments.

The United Kingdom Alcohol Treatment Trial

The United Kingdom Alcohol Treatment Trial (UKATT) was a pragmatic, randomized controlled trial comparing the effectiveness and cost-effectiveness of two treatment modalities: SBNT and MET (UKATT Research Team, 2005a, 2005b). SBNT involved eight 50-minute treatment sessions over 8 weeks, and MET three 50-minute sessions over 8 weeks. Both treatments were associated with statistically significant improvements in alcohol consumption, alcohol dependence and alcohol-related problems at 3-month and 1-year follow-up. MET was significantly cheaper to deliver, but in a full economic evaluation there were no statistically significant differences in cost-effectiveness between the two treatments. The trial analyzed a number of process measures to determine whether the treatments were distinct, and this was found to be the case. At the same time, there was considerable overlap between the two treatment groups in terms of non-specific factors. Orford (2008a) argues that a contextual model of treatment effectiveness emphasizes factors such as client commitment, therapist allegiance and the client–therapist alliance, and views personal change as being embedded within a complex multi-component treatment system.

Pharmacotherapy for relapse prevention

Recent years have seen the introduction of newer pharmacotherapies for the treatment of alcohol dependence, in particular drugs with anti-craving properties. Pharmacotherapy should not be used in isolation but in conjunction with psychosocial treatments. This section will summarize current knowledge on the older (disulfiram) and newer (naltrexone, acamprosate) drugs in the field. The treatment of alcohol withdrawal has been discussed in Chapter 12.

Disulfiram

Since its introduction in the late 1940s, disulfiram (Antabuse®) has been used very widely in the treatment of alcohol problems. Disulfiram blocks the breakdown of alcohol at the acetaldehyde stage by inhibiting the hepatic enzyme aldehyde dehydrogenase or ALDH (see Chapter 2). This leads to an accumulation of acetaldehyde in the body and to the disulfiram–ethanol reaction (DER), characterized by flushing of the face and upper trunk, throbbing headache, palpitations, an increased heart rate, nausea, vomiting and general distress. Ethanol levels as low as 5–10 mg/100 ml (5–10 mg%) can cause a reaction, and so patients taking disulfiram should be advised to avoid medicines with an ethanol concentration of greater than 5 mg%; for instance, cough mixture, mouthwash and other similar over-the-counter preparations. If a large amount of alcohol is consumed with disulfiram, there is a risk of cardiac arrhythmia, hypotension and collapse. The reaction usually starts within 10–30 minutes of drinking and can last for several hours, the peak effect occurring within 8–12 hours. Reactions have been reported up to 2 weeks after stopping disulfiram. The severity of the DER varies greatly: it may be so slight that the patient 'drinks through it' or so severe as to be life-threatening. Some individuals appear to be more sensitive to disulfiram than others, and this may be related, in part, to individual differences in the absorption and metabolism of the drug. The severity of the reaction has been reported to be proportional both to the amount of alcohol consumed and to the dose of the drug.

A mild reaction can be treated with an oral dose of ascorbic acid (1 g), which takes between 30–45 minutes to work (Baxter, 2008). Moderately severe cases can be treated with 1 g of intravenous ascorbic acid, which takes effect within 2–5 minutes. In the event of a severe reaction and cardiovascular collapse, the patient should lie down and the foot of the bed should be elevated. A vasopressor (blood-pressure raising drug) may be needed, together with intravenous vitamin C or an antihistamine. Patients prescribed disulfiram should carry a medical card with emergency instructions. The practice of exposing patients to a challenge dose of alcohol as a therapeutic test is not justified.

The rationale of treatment with disulfiram is that a patient cannot drink while under the protective cover of the drug, and they will therefore only have to make a daily decision to take the medication rather than have to resist the sudden temptation to drink at any moment. Disulfiram is thus not primarily a conditioning treatment, though a variety of secondary learning processes may be involved. While disulfiram is used for its deterrent action, it also has effects on the central nervous system, inhibiting dopamine β-hydroxylase and increasing concentrations of dopamine in the mesolimbic system. Patients taking disulfiram have reported a reduction in desire for alcohol. Disulfiram may also be useful in the treatment of individuals with co-occurring alcohol and cocaine use (Carroll et al., 2004) (see Chapter 7). Caution is needed here, as disulfiram has been reported to increase plasma levels and reduce the clearance of both intranasal and intravenous cocaine (Baker, Jatlow & McCance-Katz, 2007).

Patients with cardiac failure, coronary artery disease, hypertension and stroke, hepatic or renal impairment, respiratory disease, diabetes or epilepsy should not be given disulfiram. Other contraindications include psychosis, severe personality disorder, suicide risk, pregnancy and breast-feeding.

Disulfiram is usually given in a daily dose of 100–250 mg. It is absorbed slowly, and therefore must be taken for a few days so as to build up a satisfactory blood level. Possible side-effects include initial lethargy and fatigue, vomiting, an unpleasant taste in the mouth and halitosis, impotence and unexplained breathlessness. Other less common side-effects include psychosis (usually accompanied by delirium), allergic dermatitis, optic and peripheral neuropathy and hepatic cell damage. Disulfiram interacts with other drugs, enhancing the effect of warfarin and inhibiting the metabolism of tricyclic antidepressants, phenytoin and benzodiazepines, such as diazepam and chlordiazepoxide. The antimicrobial drug metronidazole produces a disulfiram-like reaction with alcohol.

Disulfiram should be used with discretion and its dangers should not be underestimated. Doctors instituting treatment should advise patients of the side-effects and set up arrangements for physical health reviews to include liver function tests and regular ophthalmic reviews. Supervised oral disulfiram appears to be an effective treatment for alcohol dependence when incorporated into a comprehensive treatment programme, used in association with a contingency management plan, CRA (Azrin et al., 1982) or counselling (Chick et al., 1982). Court-mandated disulfiram also has a role in treatment (Martin et al., 2003).

The disadvantages of disulfiram include the potential dangers of the drug–ethanol reaction, its potentially serious side-effects and a covert message that more basic therapeutic work is not needed. However, there are patients who find disulfiram helpful, especially in the early stages of abstinence. Some prefer to take a low maintenance dose over many years while others use it intermittently to cover high-risk periods. Disulfiram is also available in a long-acting implant form, but studies are methodologically weak and suggest that the implant does not give patients a pharmacologically active concentration of disulfiram (Garbutt et al., 1999).

In the light of present evidence, disulfiram has a minor role in the treatment of alcohol problems (Fuller & Gordis, 2004; Hughes & Cook, 1997). The best results are likely to be seen when one or both of the following conditions are fulfilled. Firstly, the use of the drug should be explained to and negotiated with the patient, so that the taking of these tablets becomes not only acceptable but wanted; the patient is not being muzzled or surrendering autonomy but making a free decision to engage in this type of treatment. Secondly, an acceptable degree of supervision should be set up – for instance, the tablet taken in the doctor's office, or in the medical room at work or under the eyes of the wife or partner – or a contingency management plan or therapeutic contract established.

Drugs that attenuate drinking behaviour

Naltrexone and acamprosate are anti-craving medications used as adjuvant pharmacotherapies for alcohol dependence in adults. They have been subject to many trials in which small-to-medium effect sizes have been reported.

Naltrexone

Naltrexone is an opioid receptor antagonist, which is thought to produce its effect by blocking endogenous opioid pathways. First approved for the treatment of alcohol dependence in 1994 by the US Food and Drug Administration, it has been subject to numerous randomized and controlled clinical trials. When used short-term (i.e. for less than 12 weeks) in an oral dose of 50 mg daily, it has been shown to reduce relapse rates in alcohol dependent patients, in combination with out-patient psychosocial treatment (for references see Bouza et al., 2004; Lingford-Hughes, Welch & Nutt, 2004). It has also been shown to reduce the number of drinks consumed by non-treatment-seeking alcohol dependent drinkers, and also to reduce their urges to drink. Naltrexone may reduce the euphoria associated with alcohol intake, and an action on craving has been suggested.

Two large multi-centre trials (one carried out in the USA and one carried out in the UK) failed to replicate the relapse reduction effect in treatment-seeking alcohol dependent patients. The US trial was a long-term study of veterans with chronic, severe alcohol dependence, almost all of whom were men (Krystal et al., 2001). The UK study found that total consumption, liver enzymes and alcohol craving were significantly reduced in compliant patients treated with oral naltrexone as compared to placebo (Chick et al., 2000). It also demonstrated that oral naltrexone was effective when used in association with a range of psychosocial treatments which were less intensive than those applied in the US studies.

Naltrexone has also recently become available in a long-term injected formulation. Due to the once a month dosing, this approach may improve treatment compliance, thus helping the patient whose motivation to stop drinking waxes and wanes frequently. An early trial was positive and was also associated with improvements in quality of life, but a large amount of clinical experience with real-world patients has not yet accumulated (Garbutt et al., 2005; Pettinati et al., 2009).

Naltrexone is a fairly safe medication. Side-effects include nausea, vomiting and abdominal pain, headache, reduced energy, joint and muscle pain and sleeping difficulty. Loss of appetite, diarrhoea, constipation, increased thirst, chest pain, increased sweating, increased energy, irritability, chills, delayed ejaculation and decreased potency are less frequent side-effects. Liver function abnormalities and reversible thrombocytopaenia (reduction in platelet count) have been reported but are rare. Hepatic toxicity is very unlikely with a 50 mg per day dose. Despite these side-effects naltrexone is reasonably well tolerated.

Most people tolerate the daily 50 mg dose, though in some instances it may be sensible to take a lower dose (25 mg) for the first 3–4 days of treatment to minimize side-effects. Individuals who are troubled with persistent craving may need a dose of 100 mg daily (this was the dose taken in the COMBINE study: see below). Treatment is usually for 3–6 months in the first instance. However, the effect may fall off after 6 months and some patients may need longer-term prescribing for up to 1 year (O'Malley et al., 1996). Naltrexone appears to be safe when used with antidepressants, but more studies are needed to evaluate its role in depression and alcohol dependence.

Naltrexone is indicated for use in alcohol dependent patients, particularly in those aiming for a controlled drinking outcome. Some studies suggest a benefit in non-dependent drinkers. Patients do not have to be abstinent before they commence the medication. Indeed, drinking on naltrexone might actually be beneficial as they experience extinction. Naltrexone may also help to prevent a drinking session from developing into a binge session. Patients in receipt of naltrexone should also be engaged in a psychosocial treatment programme and should be motivated to take the drug. Liver toxicity tests should be carried out before starting treatment and at regular intervals while patients remain on the drug. The use of opiates and opioid-containing medications is contraindicated, and patients should be careful about using other drugs with potential liver toxicity, e.g. paracetamol (acetaminophen) and disulfiram. In special instances, naltrexone can be used alongside disulfiram as long as great care is taken to ensure that liver toxicity tests are taken at regular intervals.

In individuals taking naltrexone, pain should be treated with aspirin, paracetamol (acetaminophen) or ibuprofen. When opioid analgesia is needed, naltrexone should be discontinued for 2–3 days. People taking naltrexone should carry a medical card providing information that they are on this drug and some information regarding emergency analgesia. Naltrexone is licensed for use in alcohol dependence in the USA and a number of European countries. It is not licensed for use in alcohol dependence in the UK, but it is available at specialist clinics where its use is authorized on a named-patient basis.

How does naltrexone work? Alcohol is thought to be reinforcing because it stimulates brain opioid activity (see Chapter 2). Opioid antagonists, such as naltrexone, should theoretically block or reduce the effect of alcohol on opioid receptor activity and decrease the pleasure or 'high' experienced by drinkers. This mechanism would explain the lower rates of drinking or relapse in the naltrexone groups in the US studies. Naltrexone may also reduce cravings or urges to drink. Another potential mechanism relates to what happens when someone drinks while taking naltrexone. Here naltrexone is thought to increase the aversive effects of alcohol (e.g. nausea) and/or increase intoxication for a given dose of alcohol.

Acamprosate

Acamprosate (calcium bis-acetyl homotaurinate), a simple derivative of the amino acid taurine, has been used in the treatment of alcohol dependence in France for several years. Clinical trials carried out in a number of European countries suggest that it may help to improve abstinence rates in alcohol dependent patients when used as part of a therapeutic programme (for references see Bouza et al., 2004; Lingford-Hughes, Welch & Nutt, 2004). It has also been associated with an increase in cumulative abstinence duration.

Acamprosate is a safe medication that improves adherence to treatment. It does not interact with alcohol or diazepam, appears to have no addictive potential itself and has been used safely with antidepressants. The recommended treatment dose in Europe is 1998 mg daily for body weight over 60 kg and 1332 mg daily for body weight under 60 kg. In the COMBINE study (see below) the dose was 3 g daily. Acamprosate should not be prescribed to individuals with renal insufficiency or severe hepatic failure, nor to women who are pregnant or breastfeeding. About 10% of patients experience gastrointestinal symptoms including diarrhoea and abdominal discomfort.

The mechanism of action of acamprosate is uncertain (Littleton, 1995). It has been reported to block presynaptic $GABA_B$ receptors and to antagonize glutamatergic NMDA-receptor activation in the hippocampus and nucleus accumbens. It is thought to modulate alcohol withdrawal effects and limit negative reinforcement associated with the cessation of drinking.

The COMBINE study

The COMBINE study was a very large clinical trial of pharmacological and behavioural treatments for alcohol dependence, which was carried out in the USA and involved 1383 subjects. It compared eight treatment groups of recently abstinent alcohol dependent patients who were offered various combinations of medical management (MM) with 16 weeks of oral naltrexone (100 mg daily) or acamprosate (3 g daily), both medications; and/or placebo; and with/without a combined behavioural intervention (CBI) (Anton et al., 2006). A ninth group received CBI only. The CBI integrated CBT, MET and techniques to enhance mutual self-help group participation. All groups showed a substantial reduction in drinking, as measured by the percentage of days abstinent and the time to first drinking day. The trial did not show any evidence of a combining effect. The difference in outcomes between naltrexone and acamprosate was small at the end of 16 weeks and had disappeared at 1-year follow-up. Neither naltrexone nor acamprosate was associated with a better outcome than the non-pharmacological intervention. Although the authors concluded that the results supported the use of naltrexone in primary care settings, scrutiny of the data points to a more complex picture (Bergmark, 2008). Medical management was arguably an excellent treatment in its own right (Orford, 2008b), perhaps unsurprisingly so, as it was more intensive than the sort of treatment routinely provided to alcohol dependent patients in general healthcare settings. Reduction of 'treatment' to a narrow biomedical model cannot adequately explain changes in behaviour occurring in the complex contexts of patients' lives.

Other pharmacotherapies

A number of other drugs have been studied to evaluate their efficacy in maintaining abstinence in alcohol dependent subjects. *Ondansetron*, a specific 5-HT$_3$ antagonist, may have a role in individuals with early-onset, family history positive alcohol dependence. Studies have reported that ondansetron was associated with a reduction in drinking rates in early-onset but not late-onset subjects (Johnson et al., 2000; Kranzler et al., 2003), possibly related to its effect on reducing subjective craving in the former group (Johnson et al., 2002). *Baclofen,* an agonist at the GABA$_B$ receptor historically used as a treatment for spasticity, may also have a role in the treatment of alcohol dependence (Addolorato et al., 2002). *Topiramate,* an antiepileptic drug which has antagonistic action at excitatory glutamate receptors, inhibits dopamine release and enhances GABA function (see Chapter 2), and should theoretically be useful in the treatment of alcohol dependence. Trials have reported its efficacy in reducing drinking behaviour and improving quality of life (Johnson et al., 2007; Olmsted & Kockler, 2008). It should be noted that topiramate is quite a sedative drug and should be avoided in individuals with hepatic impairment. Although the early trials of these drugs have been promising, there is, as yet, insufficient evidence to support their routine use in the treatment of alcohol dependence. Further research is underway to identify and evaluate drugs that may be of benefit in reducing craving, relapse and drinking behaviour in alcohol dependent individuals (Heilig & Egli, 2006).

Drugs used to treat psychiatric co-morbidity

Alcohol dependence is commonly associated with co-morbid psychiatric symptoms in particular mood and anxiety disorders. Judicious treatment of co-morbid mood, anxiety and psychotic disorders should help to ameliorate psychological symptoms and may improve drinking outcomes. The selective serotonin reuptake inhibitors (SSRIs) are effective in improving symptoms of depression and anxiety in alcohol dependent patients (for references see Lingford-Hughes, Welch & Nutt, 2004).

Pregnancy

The use of disulfiram, naltrexone and acamprosate is not recommended in women who are pregnant or breast-feeding. The management of alcohol withdrawal in the pregnant woman is considered in Chapter 12.

The effectiveness of treatments for alcohol use disorders

The Mesa Grande

Over recent years the quality of alcohol treatment trials has improved and there is now a reasonable evidence base. Miller and colleagues have attempted to review and rate controlled outcome studies according to rigorous predefined criteria, thus facilitating a rank ordering of treatment efficacy (Miller & Wilbourne, 2002; Miller, Wilbourne & Hetema, 2003). The most recent review of 381 studies is set out in a large table (Mesa Grande) (Miller, Wilbourne & Hetema, 2003). The psychosocial treatments with the strongest evidence for efficacy were brief interventions, MET, CRA, self-change manual, BSCT, behaviour contracting, social skills training and behavioural marital therapy. Naltrexone and acamprosate also performed well (Table 14.2).

Essentially, behaviour techniques that build on the inner resources of the individual and their social support system, and that facilitate motivation for change and self-efficacy, appear to be effective. As mentioned in Chapter 13, all techniques are more effective when the therapeutic relationship is warm, genuine and empathic (Rogers, 1957).

Treatments at the bottom of the table (not shown) include educational methods, general alcoholism counselling, psychotherapy, confrontational counselling, relaxation training and videotape self-confrontation.

Systematic reviews

Systematic reviews assessing the evidence base on the effectiveness of treatment of alcohol problems have been carried out in Sweden, Australia and Scotland (Berglund, Thelander & Jonsson, 2003; Shand et al., 2003; Slattery et al., 2003). In England, a critical appraisal of the evidence base was published by the National Treatment Agency for Substance Misuse in 2006 (Raistrick, Heather & Godfrey, 2006).

The Scottish Health Technology Assessment concluded that four psychosocial treatment modalities were clinically effective and cost-effective: BSCT; MET; marital and family therapies; and coping and social skills training (Slattery et al., 2003). Acamprosate and supervised oral disulfiram were also recommended for use in combination with psychosocial interventions.

The effective psychosocial interventions highlighted in the Swedish systematic review were broadly similar and included CBT, 12-step treatment and structured interactional therapy strategies involving the family (Berglund, Thelander & Jonsson, 2003). Acamprosate, naltrexone and supervised disulfiram were found to have confirmed effects in long-term treatment.

Implications for real-world treatment

Clinical services need to incorporate evidence-based treatment methods into their repertoire. This is a challenge, because the 'real world' of the community, out-patient or

Table 14.2. The Mesa Grande.

Treatment modality and ranking 1–10
1 Brief intervention
2 Motivational enhancement
3 GABA agonist (acamprosate)
4, 5 Community reinforcement
4, 5 Self-change manual (bibliotherapy)
6 Opiate antagonist (naltrexone)
7 Behavioural self-control training
8 Behaviour contracting
9 Social skills training
10 Behavioural marital therapy

Source: Miller, Wilbourne & Hetema (2003).

in-patient setting can be chaotic, fraught with day-to-day crises, staff shortages and poor morale. There is no 'best' treatment but a number of effective treatments (Raistrick, Heather & Godfrey, 2006). Delivery systems also need to be considered and patients offered more choice in terms of actual treatment, rapid treatment entry and 'meeting them where they are' (Humphreys & Tucker, 2002). Individuals with severe chronic alcohol dependence should have the option to be followed up for lengthy periods, in much the same way that diabetics are followed up in specialized clinics, i.e. treatment needs to be more 'extensive' (Humphreys & Tucker, 2002). Many alcohol dependent individuals live sad, isolated lives, with little in the way of positive features in their social environment. In these situations, the therapeutic intervention must become a positive, enduring feature of their environment. The therapist becomes someone they can rely upon and trust to act as an advocate with rent arrears, to facilitate referral to a physician, someone to whom they can show their holiday photographs or share their grief about the death of a parent, sister or spouse. The therapist may be the only person who remembers their birthday, supports them when they get into trouble with the police (again) or takes the time to ensure that they are admitted to hospital when they are suicidal and then continues to visit.

'Extensive' interventions can take the form of long-term out-patient treatment, peer-managed residential accommodation and extended case-monitoring. These interventions can be combined with pharmacotherapy and other psychosocial treatments. Voluntary and self-help organizations are other 'extensive' resources, many of which engage with individuals indefinitely. A real culture shift, therefore, must take place within services, so that they are more appealing to users. Equally, patients should not be discharged just because they fail to attend three consecutive appointments, particularly if the therapist has failed to find out what has been happening to them. Treatments for alcohol dependence are only effective in the context of the individual strengths and social environment of the patient. Clinicians and therapists lose sight of this at their peril.

There is no one single pathway to recovery, rather a number of different individual paths. Recovery from severe alcohol dependence inevitably involves *personal acceptance of an abstinence goal*. Insight may come from the buffeting of experience, what is heard at an AA meeting or from professional advice. Sometimes a *trigger* or *'Damascus' event* might constitute the turning point (Tuchfield, 1981). Here is an instance as reported in a 10-year follow-up study (Edwards, Oppenheimer & Taylor, 1992).

> A place in Ireland called Knock where the Virgin appeared. . . . I visited the place, atmosphere, and I knew I would never drink again or smoke.

Events as trivial as being teased in the street for a dishevelled appearance, or as serious as drunken carelessness causing the death of a child, illustrate a spectrum of happenings which the drinker may see as responsible for their abrupt and permanent sobriety. Both negative and positive life events may be precursors to achieving sobriety.

Although dramatic events may assist or precipitate change, sobriety is best conceived as something built and *consolidated* over time rather than as a state achieved on a particular day (Moos, Finney & Cronkite, 1990). Important questions attach to the understanding of what in the individual's life may most effectively support sobriety. Research suggests that sobriety is most likely to be sustained in the longer term when the sober state is experienced as rewarding. An example of this kind of positive influence is the reward coming from a loving relationship. Meaningful employment, hobbies, educational activities and holidays are additional examples of activities which can provide substitution for rewards previously found only in drinking.

The present position

In this chapter we have attempted to outline the main psychosocial and pharmacotherapy approaches available for the treatment of drinking problems. We hope that this discussion will stimulate the reader to explore these treatments further and in actuality. The fundamental position taken in this chapter is that choosing the best treatment for the individual patient is a skilled and highly responsible undertaking, which needs to be negotiated and later reviewed with the patient, guided by clinical experience and illuminated by a critical understanding of what an evolving research base can tell.

References

Addolorato G, Caputo F, Caprista E, et al. (2002) Baclofen efficacy in reducing alcohol craving and intake: a preliminary double-blind randomized controlled study. *Alcohol and Alcoholism* **37**, 504–508.

Annis H M, Herie M A, Watkin-Merek L (1996) *Structured Relapse Prevention: An Outpatient Counselling Approach*. Toronto: Addiction Research Foundation of Ontario.

Anton R F, O'Malley S S, Ciraulo D A, et al. (2006) Combined pharmacotherapies and behavioural interventions for alcohol dependence. *Journal of the American Medical Association* **295**, 2003–2017.

Azrin N H (1976) Improvements in the community-reinforcement approach to alcoholism. *Behaviour Research and Therapy* **14**, 339–348.

Azrin N H, Sisson R W, Meyers R, Godley M (1982) Alcoholism treatment by disulfiram and community reinforcement therapy. *Journal of Behaviour Therapy and Experimental Psychiatry* **13**, 105–112.

Baker J R, Jatlow P M, McCance-Katz E F (2007) Disulfiram effects on responses to intravenous cocaine administration. *Drug and Alcohol Dependence* **87**, 202–209.

Baxter K (ed.) (2008) *Stockley's Drug Interactions*[online]. London: Pharmaceutical Press. http://www.medicines complete.com/, accessed 01/01/2009.

Berglund M, Thelander S, Jonsson E (2003) *Treating Alcohol and Drug Abuse: An Evidence-based Review*. Weinheim, Germany: Wiley-VCH.

Bergmark A (2008) On treatment mechanisms – what can we learn from the COMBINE study. *Addiction* **103**, 703–705.

Bouza C, Magro A, Munoz A, Amate J M (2004) Efficacy and safety of naltrexone and acamprosate in the treatment of alcohol dependence: a systematic review. *Addiction* **99**, 811–828.

Bowers T G, Al-Rehda M R (1990) A comparison of outcome with group/marital and standard/individual therapies with alcoholics. *Journal of Studies on Alcohol* **151**, 301–309.

Burke B L, Arkowitz H, Menchola M (2003) The efficacy of motivational interviewing: a meta-analysis of controlled clinical trials. *Journal of Consulting and Clinical Psychology* **71**, 843–861.

Burke B L, Dunn C W, Atkins D, Phelps J S (2004) The emerging evidence base for motivational interviewing: a meta-analytic and qualitative inquiry. *Journal of Cognitive Psychotherapy* **18**, 311–325.

Carroll K M (1996) Relapse prevention as a psychosocial treatment: a review of controlled studies. *Experimental Clinical Psychopharmacology* **41**, 46–54.

Carroll K M (2001) Constrained, confronted and confused: why we really know so little about therapists in treatment outcome research. *Addiction* **96**, 203–206.

Carroll K M, Nich C, Ball S A, et al. (2004) One-year follow-up of disulfiram and psychotherapy for cocaine-alcohol users: sustained effects of treatment. *Addiction* **95**, 1335–1349.

Chick J, Gough K, Falkowski W, et al. (1982) Disufiram treatment of alcoholism. *British Journal of Psychiatry* **61**, 84–89.

Chick J, Anton R, Checinski K, et al. (2000) A multicentre, randomised, double-blind, placebo controlled trial of naltrexone in the treatment of alcohol dependence or misuse. *Alcohol and Alcoholism* **35**, 587–593.

Copello A, Orford J, Hodgson R, Tober G, Barrett C on behalf of the UKATT Research Team (2002) Social behaviour and network therapy: basic principles and early experiences. *Addictive Behaviours* 27, 354–366.

Copello A G, Velleman R D, Templeton L (2005) Family interventions in the treatment of alcohol and drug problems. *Drug and Alcohol Review* 24, 369–385.

Copello A G, Hodgson R, Tober G, Orford J (2009) *Social Behaviour and Network Therapy for Alcohol Problems.* London: Routledge.

Drummond D C, Tiffany S T, Glautier S, Remington B (1995) *Addictive Behaviour: Cue Exposure, Theory and Practice.* Chichester, UK: John Wiley & Sons.

Edwards G, Oppenheimer E, Taylor C (1992) Hearing the noise in the system. Exploration and textual analysis as a method for studying change in drinking behaviour. *British Journal of Addiction* 87, 73–81.

Elkins R L (1980) Covert sensitization and alcoholism: contributions of successful conditioning to subsequent abstinence maintenance. *Addictive Behaviours* 5, 67–89.

Fuller R K, Gordis E (2004) Does disulfiram have a role in alcoholism treatment? *Addiction* 99, 21–24.

Garbutt J C, West S L, Carey T S, Lohr K N, Crews F T (1999) Pharmacological treatment of alcohol dependence: a review of the evidence. *Journal of the American Medical Association* 281, 1318–1325.

Garbutt J C, Kranzler H R, O'Malley S S, et al. (2005) Efficacy and tolerability of long-acting injectable naltrexone for alcohol dependence: a randomized controlled trial. *Journal of the American Medical Association* 293, 1617–1625.

Halford W K, Price J, Kelly A B, Bouma R, Young R McD (2001) Helping the female partners of men abusing alcohol: a comparison of three treatments. *Addiction* 96, 1497–1508.

Heilig M, Egli M (2006) Pharmacological treatment of alcohol dependence: target symptoms and target mechanisms. *Pharmacology and Therapeutics* 111, 855–876.

Hester R K (1995) Behavioural self control training. In *Handbook of Alcoholism Treatment Approaches: Effective Alternatives,* 2nd edn, R K Hester, W R Miller (eds). Needham Heights, MS: Allyn and Bacon, pp. 148–159.

Holder H, Longabaugh R, Miller W R, Rubonis A V (1991) The cost effectiveness of treatment for alcoholism: a first approximation. *Journal of Studies on Alcohol* 52, 517–540.

Hughes J L, Cook C C H (1997) The efficacy of disulfiram: a review of outcome studies. *Addiction* 92, 381–396.

Humphreys K, Tucker J A (2002) Towards more responsive and effective intervention systems for alcohol-related problems. *Addiction* 97, 126–132.

Hunt G M, Azrin N H (1973) A community-reinforcement approach to alcoholism. *Behaviour Research and Therapy* 11, 91–104.

Irwin J, Bowers C, Dunn M, Wang M (1999) Efficacy of relapse prevention: a meta-analytic review. *Journal of Consulting and Clinical Psychology* 67, 563–570.

Jarvis T J, Tebbutt J, Mattick R P, Shand F (2005) *Treatment Approaches for Alcohol and Drug Dependence: An Introductory Guide,* 2nd edn. Chichester, UK: John Wiley & Sons.

Johnson B A, Roache J D, Javors M A, et al. (2000) Ondansetron for reduction of drinking among biologically predisposed alcoholic patients – a randomized controlled trial. *Journal of the American Medical Association* 284, 963–971.

Johnson B A, Roache J D, Ait-Daoud N, Zanca N A, Velazquez M (2002) Ondensetron reduces the craving of biologically predisposed alcoholics. *Psychopharmacology (Berlin)* 160, 408–413.

Johnson B A, Rosenthal N, Capece J A, et al. (2007) Topiramate for alcohol dependence. A randomized controlled trial. *Journal of the American Medical Association* 298, 1641–1651.

Kranzler H R, Pierucci-Lagha A, Feinn R, Hernandez-Avila C (2003) Effects of ondansetron in early- versus late-onset alcoholics: a prospective, open-label study. *Alcoholism: Clinical and Experimental Research* 27, 1150–1155.

Krystal J H, Cramer J A, Krol W F, Kirk G F, Rosenheck R A (2001) Naltrexone in the treatment of alcohol dependence. *New England Journal of Medicine* **345**, 1734–1739.

Lingford-Hughes A, Welch S, Nutt D (2004) Evidence-based guidelines for the pharmacological management of substance misuse, addiction and co-morbidity: recommendations from the British Association for Psychopharmacology. *Journal of Psychopharmacology* **18**, 293–335.

Littleton J (1995) Acamprosate in alcohol dependence: how does it work? *Addiction* **90**, 1179–1188.

Marlatt G A, Gordon J R (1985) *Relapse Prevention*. New York: Guilford Press.

Martin B, Clapp L, Bialkowski D, et al. (2003) Compliance to supervised disulfiram therapy: a comparison of voluntary and court-ordered patients. *American Journal of Addictions* **12**, 137–143.

Meyers R J, Miller W R (2001) *A Community Reinforcement Approach to Addiction Treatment*. International Research Monographs in the Addictions. Cambridge: Cambridge University Press.

Meyers R J, Miller W R, Smith J E, Tonigan J S (2002) A randomised controlled trial of two methods for engaging treatment-refusing drug users through concerned significant others. *Journal of Consulting and Clinical Psychology* **70**, 1182–1185.

Miller W R, Wilbourne P L (2002) Mesa Grande: a methodological analysis of clinical trials of treatments for alcohol use disorders. *Addiction* **97**, 265–277.

Miller W R, Brown J M, Simpson T L, et al. (1995) What works? A methodological analysis of the alcohol treatment outcome literature. In *Handbook of Alcoholism Treatment Approaches: Effective Alternatives*, 2nd edn, R K Hester, W R Miller (eds). Needham Heights, MA: Allyn and Bacon, pp. 12–44.

Miller W R, Andrews N R, Wilbourne P, Bennett M E (1998) A wealth of alternatives: effective treatments for alcohol problems. In *Treating Addictive Behaviours*, 2nd edn, W R Miller, N Heather (eds). New York: Plenum Press, pp. 203–216.

Miller W R, Walters S T, Bennett M E (2001) How effective is alcoholism treatment in the United States. *Journal of Studies on Alcohol* **62**, 211–220.

Miller W R, Wilbourne P D, Hetema J E (2003) What works? A summary of alcohol treatment outcome research. In *Handbook of Alcoholism Treatment Approaches: Effective Alternatives*, 3rd edn, R K Hester, W R Miller (eds). Boston, MA: Allyn and Bacon, pp. 13–63.

Monti P M, Abrams D B, Binkoff J A, et al. (1990) Communication skills training, communication skills training with family and cognitive behavioural mood management training for alcoholics. *Journal of Studies on Alcohol* **51**, 263–270.

Monti P M, Rohsenhow D J, Rubonis A V, et al. (1993) Cue exposure with coping skills treatment for male alcoholics: a preliminary investigation. *Journal of Consulting and Clinical Psychology* **61**, 1011–1019.

Monti P M, Rohsenhow D J, Colby S M, Abrams D B (1995) Coping and social skills training. In *Handbook of Alcoholism Treatment Approaches: Effective Alternatives*, 2nd edn, R K Hester, W R Miller (eds). Needham Heights, MS: Allyn and Bacon, pp. 221–241.

Moos R H, Finney J W, Cronkite E (1990) *Alcoholism Treatment: Context, Process and Outcome*. New York: Oxford University Press.

Moos R H, Finney J W, Ouimette P G, Suchinsky R T (1999) A comparative evaluation of substance abuse treatment orientation, amount of care, and 1-year outcomes. *Alcoholism: Clinical and Experimental Research* **23**, 529–536.

Najavits L M, Weiss R D, Liese B S (1996) Group cognitive behavioural therapy for women with PTSD and substance use disorder. *Journal of Substance Abuse Treatment* **13**, 13–22.

O'Farrell T J, Choquette K A, Cutter H S G, Brown E D, McCourt W F (1993) Behavioural marital therapy with and without additional couples relapse prevention sessions for alcoholics and their wives. *Journal of Studies on Alcohol* **54**, 652–666.

O'Farrell T J, Choquette K A, Cutter H S G (1998) Couples relapse prevention sessions after behavioural marital therapy for male alcoholics: outcomes during the first 3 years after starting treatment. *Journal of Studies on Alcohol* **59**, 357–370.

Olmsted C L, Kockler D R (2008) Topiramate for alcohol dependence. *Annals of Pharmacotherapy* **42**, 1475–1480.

O'Malley S, Jaffe A J, Chang G, et al. (1996) Six-month follow-up of naltrexone and psychotherapy for alcohol dependence. *Archives of General Psychiatry* **53**, 217–224.

Orford J (2008a) Asking the right question in the right way: the need for a shift in research on psychological treatments for addiction. *Addiction* **103**, 875–885.

Orford J (2008b) Joining the queue of dissenters. *Addiction* **103**, 706–707.

Ouimette P C, Finney J W, Moos R H (1997) Twelve-step and cognitive-behavioural treatment for substance abuse: a comparison of treatment effectiveness. *Journal of Consulting and Clinical Psychology* **65**, 230–240.

Pettinati H M, Gastfriend D R, Ding Q, Kranzler H R, O'Malley S S (2009) Effect of extended-release naltrexone (XR-NTX) on quality of life in alcohol dependent patients. *Alcoholism: Clinical and Experimental Research* **33**, 350–356.

Project MATCH Research Group (1997a) Matching alcoholism treatments to client heterogeneity: project MATCH post-treatment drinking outcomes. *Journal of Studies on Alcohol* **58**, 7–29.

Project MATCH Research Group (1997b) Project MATCH secondary a priori hypothesis. *Addiction* **92**, 1671–1698.

Project MATCH Research Group (1998a) Matching alcoholism treatments to client heterogeneity: treatment main effects and matching effects on drinking during treatment. *Journal of Studies on Alcohol* **59**, 631–639.

Project MATCH Research Group (1998b) Matching alcoholism treatments to client heterogeneity: Project MATCH 3-year drinking outcomes. *Alcoholism: Clinical and Experimental Research* **22**, 1300–1311.

Project MATCH Research Group (1998c) Therapist effects in three treatments for alcohol problems. *Psychotherapy Research* **8**, 455–474.

Raistrick D, Heather N, Godfrey C (2006) *Review of the Effectiveness of Treatment for Alcohol Problems*. London: National Treatment Agency for Substance Misuse.

Rogers C R (1957) The necessary and sufficient conditions for therapeutic personality change. *Journal of Consulting Psychology* **21**, 95–103.

Rohsenhow D J, Monti P, Rubonis D, et al. (2001) Cue exposure with coping skills training and communiation skills training for alcohol dependence. *Addiction* **96**, 1161–1174.

Shand F, Gates J, Fawcett J, Mattick R (2003) *The Treatment of Alcohol Problems: A Review of the Evidence*. Canberra, Australia: Commonwealth Department of Health and Ageing.

Slattery J, Chick J, Cochrane M, et al. (2003) *Prevention of Relapse in Alcohol Dependence*. Glasgow: Health Technology Board for Scotland.

Tuchfield B S (1981) Spontaneous remission in alcoholics: empirical observations and theoretical implication. *Quarterly Journal of Studies on Alcohol* **42**, 626–641.

UKATT Research Team (2005a) Effectiveness of treatment for alcohol problems: findings of the randomised UK Alcohol Treatment Trial (UKATT). *British Medical Journal* **331**, 541–544.

UKATT Research Team (2005b) Cost-effectiveness of treatment for alcohol problems: findings of the randomised UK Alcohol Treatment Trial (UKATT). *British Medical Journal* **331**, 544–547.

Wanigaratne S, Wallace W, Pullin J, Keaney F, Farmer R (1990) *Relapse Prevention for Addictive Behaviours. A Manual for Therapists*. Oxford: Blackwell Scientific Publications.

Weingardt K R & Marlatt G A (1998) Sustaining change: helping those who are still using. In *Treating Addictive Behaviours*, 2nd edn, W R Miller, N Heather (eds). New York: Plenum, pp. 337–351.

Further reading

Mitcheson L, Maslin J, Meynen T, et al. (2010) *Applied Cognitive Behavioural Approaches to* the Treatment of Addiction. A Practical Guide. Chichester: Wiley-Blackwell.

Raistrick D, Heather N, Godfrey C (2006) Review of the Effectiveness of Treatment for Alcohol Problems. London: National Treatment Agency for Substance Misuse.

Shand F, Gates J, Fawcett J, Mattick R (2003) The Treatment of Alcohol Problems: A Review of the Evidence. Canberra, Australia: Commonwealth Department of Health and Ageing.

Slattery J, Chick J, Cochrane M, et al. (2003) Prevention of Relapse in Alcohol Dependence. Glasgow: Health Technology Board for Scotland.

15

Treatment: context and content

Alcoholics Anonymous and other mutual-help organizations

> I crawled into Alcoholics Anonymous, physically, mentally and spiritually bankrupt, to find an amazing bunch of men and women who had suffered the same physical and mental agony as myself.
>
> At last there were people who thought like me. Dear God – I was no longer alone. And, slowly, slowly, the fog has started to clear. Today, nearly 4 years later, I have not had a drink and am happy and contented for the first time in nearly 50 years of existing. Now I am really starting to Live with a capital 'L' – and it's just great. I never knew that life could be such fun without booze.

The above quotation is from a member of Alcoholics Anonymous (AA), the largest mutual-help fellowship in the world, and a major asset in the work of the clinician who understands and respects it. It was founded in the USA in 1935 by two alcoholics (Wilson, 1994), and it has grown dramatically to more than 50 000 face-to-face groups and over a million members in its country of origin alone. After its founding in the USA, AA diffused fairly quickly to the rest of North America and then spread to Europe soon after World War II (Eisenbach-Stangl & Rosenqvist, 1998). Today, there are more than 100 000 face-to-face groups in almost 180 countries worldwide. It has also developed a substantial Internet presence, bringing to on-line meetings and chat rooms an unknown number of members who are unwilling or unable to attend face-to-face meetings (or who prefer to supplement face-to-face AA with an on-line component). Alcoholics Anonymous estimates its world membership at over two million; careful survey research suggests that, if anything, that is an understatement (Humphreys, 2004).

Alcoholics Anonymous has helped countless individuals (often when professional intervention has failed), is a repository of astonishing experience and subtle, often humorously conveyed, wisdom, and it has had a profound influence in humanizing social attitudes towards people with drinking problems. It is thus an enormous potential resource, and it is a dereliction of duty if patients go through treatment without AA ever being mentioned or, worse still, if they are deflected from trying AA involvement by some negative statement born of ignorance, misunderstanding or professional precious-ness, e.g. 'I think you would find it all too religious' or 'let's leave your treatment to trained professionals'.

The therapist must be willing to find out how AA operates, what its beliefs and practices are, and how to help patients get the most out of the fellowship. This chapter provides an introduction to these issues, but the best professional education would also include personal visits to several 'open' AA meetings. Open meetings, which are typically labelled as such in AA's meeting directories, welcome all-comers. In contrast, closed meetings are restricted to individuals 'with a sincere desire to stop drinking'.

AA meetings

The AA meeting is of central importance to AA's functioning. It has a unique atmosphere, marked by a seeming informality but with an underlying and purposeful method of working. The number of people at a meeting will vary from group to group, but it is typically around 10–20. Larger meetings tend to sit classroom style, whereas smaller groups typically sit facing each other around a table. Some of those present will have been attending AA for years, whereas the person sitting in the back may have just walked hesitantly through the door for the first time. The chairmanship of each group rotates, and 'elections', such as they are, are usually quick and informal, e.g. 'I lead us for October … Margaret, do you mind leading the group meetings for November?'

The most common sort of meeting is organized around a chosen speaker's story of alcoholism and recovery. Another type of meeting focuses on discussion of the first step, and is geared toward newcomers. In some areas, AA meetings have a tradition of making any meeting where newcomers are present a first-step meeting. Finally, some meetings focus on discussion of a particular topic or topics (e.g. shame, spirituality, criticism, honesty, cravings) suggested on the spot by those present.

The meeting will start with the chairman saying, 'My name is ...' (only first names are used), 'I am an alcoholic'. These words carry immense implications: the speaker is not ashamed of being alcoholic but without reservation acknowledges the condition as an inalienable fact. Note also that the speaker is making a statement about essential identity rather than a disorder per se, i.e. not, 'I have alcoholism' as one might have a cold. The starting point of the evening is thus one individual's reaffirmation, for all present, of what in AA terms must be the starting point of recovery for every individual, namely the admission that he or she is suffering from 'alcoholism'.

The chairman will then greet the assembled attendees, potentially asking any newcomers to raise their hands so that the chairman can specifically welcome them to the meeting. This serves the additional function of cueing experienced members which people at the meeting might appreciate an added greeting, shared cup of coffee or words of encouragement after the meeting ends.

The meeting will then be opened with a reading from one or several AA-related books, most commonly the following preamble.

Alcoholics Anonymous is a fellowship of men and women who share their experience, strength, and hope with each other that they may solve their common problem and help others to recover from alcoholism. The only requirement for membership is a desire to stop drinking. There are no dues or fees for AA membership; we are self-supporting through our own contributions. AA is not allied with any sect, denomination, politics, organization or institution; does not wish to engage in any controversy, neither endorses nor opposes any causes. Our primary purpose is to stay sober and help other alcoholics to achieve sobriety (Alcoholics Anonymous, 2010, preamble).

With these preliminaries out of the way, the substance of the meeting begins. The starter will normally be a speaker who has agreed to relate his or her story of 'What it was like, what happened and what I am like now'. He or she will speak for perhaps 20–30 minutes without interruption, giving an account of their personal background and then going on to describe the development of their drinking problem, the sufferings they endured or inflicted on others, the deceptions and prevarications of their drinking days and then often some turning point or 'rock bottom' experience. They will go on to describe their introduction to AA and their recovery within the programme of that fellowship, and their evolving understanding of the meaning of AA as a way of life. Within this biographical format different speakers each develop their own approach, and the ability of the person who has never given a public speech in any other setting to make a personal statement which is both moving and convincing is no doubt related to the unwritten guidelines, which propose that a personal *story* should be given, rather than an abstract lecture. The story, which is told in unadorned manner by the person with fairly recent experience of recovery, is often better received than the highly polished performance by the person who has told their story many times, but who is by now rather distanced from the acuteness of their experience. And stories that deal with recovery, and which offer practical hints on how to work at recovery, are likely to be better received than drawn-out accounts of drinking days.

These life stories are followed by briefer comments and personal statements from the floor. Very importantly, there is no 'cross talk', meaning interruptions or critiques of someone who is speaking or dialogues between members. Rather, members talk about *their own* 'experience, strength and hope'. Themes raised by prior speakers may, however, be caught up and explored by subsequent speakers, who often stress their identification with the speaker's story – 'That happened to me too...'. No one is forced to speak and it is realized that for weeks the new member may want to do no more than sit and listen. This point is particularly important for therapists to emphasize to patients who have the quite prevalent fear of speaking about personal matters in front of a group.

Reference is often made during the meeting to 'the 12 steps', which enshrine the basic philosophy and programme of action recommended – though not mandated – by AA. These steps are as follows:

1. We admitted we were powerless over alcohol – that our lives had become unmanageable.
2. Came to believe that a Power greater than ourselves could restore us to sanity.
3. Made a decision to turn our will and our lives over to the care of God as we understood Him.
4. Made a searching and fearless moral inventory of ourselves.
5. Admitted to God, to ourselves and to another human being the exact nature of our wrongs.
6. Were entirely ready to have God remove all these defects of character.
7. Humbly asked Him to remove our shortcomings.
8. Made a list of all persons we had harmed, and became willing to make amends to them all.
9. Made direct amends to such people wherever possible, except when to do so would injure them or others.
10. Continued to take personal inventory, and when we were wrong, promptly admitted it.
11. Sought through prayer and meditation to improve our conscious contact with God as we understood Him praying only for knowledge of His will for us and the power to carry that out.
12. Having had a spiritual awakening as the result of these steps we tried to carry this message to alcoholics and to practice these principles in all our affairs (Alcoholics Anonymous, 1977).

A speaker may comment on the meaning that any one of these steps has had for them personally and describe their efforts to achieve this step. For instance, the meaning to be given to

Step 2, with its idea of 'a Power greater than ourselves' (usually referred to as a 'Higher Power') often attracts discussion. The Higher Power is usually interpreted in terms of an open and individually determined concept of God – the 'God *as we understood Him*', of Steps 3 and 11. This seemingly theistic formulation does not in practice debar an atheist from finding help in AA, which indeed is not at all uncommon.

The formal proceedings end with a closing ritual, which might be a reading, a group recitation of a slogan or a prayer. A common one, which embodies some useful advice on coping with life's challenges, is the Serenity Prayer:

God grant me the serenity
To accept the things I cannot change
The courage to change the things I can
And the wisdom to know the difference.

The members then chat and exchange news over tea or coffee, and subtle but positive effort is likely to be made to put the new attender at their ease and draw them into contact. Frequently the new member will after some weeks find a 'sponsor' who will offer personal advice and a special degree of availability – a phone number to contact, an arrangement to meet in the evening to attend an AA meeting and so on. The sponsor is also a role model and a coach in the member's work on the 12 steps.

Besides the meetings themselves, much else is potentially on offer. Members may start to visit each other at home, go out to meals together or share other social activities. In some localities, AA also arranges sober dances, hikes and other outings. Old drinking friends are dropped and new friends found who think and talk AA. In some localities, routine meetings will be supplemented by study groups and AA literature shared and passed around. Weekend retreats, regional and national AA conventions may be attended, and the more experienced member may give time to 'twelfth-stepping' (acting as a sponsor and working with new members), may help with prison or hospital groups, or offer availability as a speaker at meetings of community organizations.

Change processes

What are the essential processes through which AA operates? There have been many attempts to answer this question, and in summary the following dimensions can probably be identified.

Coherent, flexible ideas

In *Persuasion and Healing*, a classic text of psychiatry and anthropology, Jerome Frank (1973) noted that, across cultures, healers offer a philosophy or narrative that explains why the sufferer is ill and how the pain can be relieved. Alcoholics Anonymous fits this characterization, providing a coherent yet flexible philosophy which makes members feel understood and gives meaning to their experience of alcoholism. They are suffering from 'the disease of alcoholism', which is pictured as metaphorically akin to an 'allergy to alcohol'. Their constitution is such that they will react to this drug differently from other people. They can never be 'cured' but the disease will be 'arrested' if they never drink again.

Yet AA's definition of disease is broader than that of traditional medicine, comprising emotional and spiritual elements as well as physical ones. This broad conception allows members more 'latch-on points' with the AA programme than would a purely biological view, in that most alcoholics have problems in addition to drinking to which AA's philosophy can speak.

The flexible nature of AA philosophy is evident in its 'spiritual rather than religious' posture (Kurtz, 1991). The 12 steps unambiguously talk about God as a Higher Power essential to recovery, and yet there are geographic areas (e.g. Sweden) where most AA members are atheist or agnostic (Mäkelä et al., 1996). Relatedly, though the founders of AA were Protestants, it claims among its members countless Catholics, as well as Jews, Muslims and Buddhists (Humphreys, 2004). We will give extensive attention to spiritual issues in Chapter 16. Here, suffice it to say that AA's conception is broad enough to cover almost any conception of a Higher Power that a member wishes to employ.

Action programme

Alcoholics Anonymous offers an action programme, which is outlined in 'the 12 steps'. The 'alcoholic' must join AA and stay close to AA. They will be advised to take things 'one day at a time' and to work for short-term goals. The stories and discussions they listen to at AA meetings and the guidance from their sponsor will provide them with many hints on coping and problem solving. Their first priority is to deal with their drinking, but the programme will also require them to examine psychological problems – their self-centeredness, resentment and tendency to blame others. The 'personal inventory', in which one catalogues honestly one's shortcomings, is a key part of this process of self-examination and may relieve years of accumulated shame and guilt.

It is easy, but wrong-headed, for educated professionals to poke fun at AA's many slogans and seemingly simplistic advice. Most of the practical advice offered by AA members directly parallels that which a scientifically informed cognitive behavioural therapist would offer, albeit in different words. Two of many possible examples make the point. 'Avoid slippery people, places and things' contains the same wisdom as, 'Let's examine what stimuli lead you to drink and then make a plan to avoid those relapse triggers'. 'Watch your stinking thinking' is but a more pithy way of emphasizing the role of automatic cognitive distortions in addiction.

Alcoholics Anonymous is 'a selfish programme' and each individual is working for sobriety for their own sake and not to please anyone else, and they thus give no hostages to fortune. If they relapse they are not rejected but may return any number of times to try again. The programme will finally include 'twelfth-stepping', but by then members should have learnt that in the process of helping other people they will help themselves and confirm their own strength; it is not, however, their job to proselytize, 'pull people down lamp posts' or put their own sobriety at risk.

Rewards of sobriety

The creators of AA appreciated that few people can sustain the motivation to make a difficult change without some rewards along the way. Alcoholics Anonymous carries the message that sobriety offers many benefits, and it helps the individual to discover who they are. It gives them new friends, introduces them to a social network that does not centre on drinking, relieves their loneliness, helps them to structure and employ their time, removes a stigma and confers on them a sense of personal worth. Though the greatest rewards in AA are promised to those who make a long-term commitment to sobriety as a way of life, honours are conferred on the smaller, more readily attainable steps along the way. A classic question of sponsors to sponsees who bemoan how many problems they have yet to solve is, 'Did you drink today?'

If the sponsee says, 'No', the sponsor will say something encouraging like, 'That was the most important thing to do today, and you accomplished it'.

Possibility of recovery

Before change must come hope. The group's philosophy and network of experienced, sober members makes recovery seem possible to even the most disillusioned drinker. This last heading bears on each of the previous headings. It does not 'work' through an abstract set of ideas but through those ideas being found persuasive by the individual. The most apt theoretical definition of the disorder and the pathways to recovery would remain useless if AA did not have the ability to persuade the new member that AA is about him or her as an individual, it can meet their problems and show them personally the way ahead. Alcoholics Anonymous can carry this conviction because its members so evidently know what they are talking about; they too have been through it all and know every stratagem of deceit and denial, while at the same time bearing tangible witness to the possibility of success.

Who will affiliate with AA?

Like other approaches to treatment, AA is not a panacea. Its membership is primarily composed of people who have suffered from moderate or severe alcohol dependence, and group cohesion is therefore built around total acceptance of the abstinence goal. The person who is not dependent and who does not wish to aim for abstinence is unlikely to find AA compatible.

The drinker who goes to a meeting where everyone is of another social background is also unlikely to feel at home, although this problem can be met by the individual shopping around until he or she finds a group of people with whom they can identify. Different AA meetings vary in composition; some operate with a wide mix of social backgrounds, while others seem tacitly to have recruited their membership with a bias toward a particular socio-economic stratum. Some chapters have standing rules of serving a particular subpopulation; for example, men, women, gays and lesbians, non-smokers or physicians. Also, some groups will emphasize the spiritual aspect of AA much more than others. It may therefore take some time and perseverance for the new member to find the group which most suits their needs. Some groups may have a particular reputation for being helpful to the newcomer, who may be guided in their direction.

It is always difficult to predict who will and who will not find AA helpful and patients should be advised to go along to meetings and see for themselves whether AA offers an answer. Therapists should emphasize the diversity of AA meetings when raising the issue, so that the patient knows that if the first group visited seems a poor fit, there are others of quite different character that would warrant investigation before a judgement can be made about whether AA will be of any value to the patient.

How therapists can maximize patients' benefits from AA

As was stated earlier, the therapist should, whenever appropriate, signpost the way to AA. This not only implies being able to provide the appropriate phone number (which is available in the local telephone directory), and perhaps being able to effect a direct introduction to an AA sponsor with whom the patient is likely to identify, but also means having the knowledge and sympathy which will enable them to convey to the patient that attending some AA meetings is likely to be eminently worthwhile. Therapists who, on occasion, attend open AA meetings will enhance their credibility as informants and build up valuable contacts with local groups.

The therapist will know that only a minority of their patients (perhaps no more than 5–10%) will enter into a full and prolonged relationship with AA, but even a lesser exposure can be beneficial. The attitude about trying AA conveyed to the patient should be optimistic, but not dogmatic. Most patients understandably dislike having AA 'rammed down their throat' and, for an oppositional subset, they may resist AA not because it wouldn't help for them but because they want to show the therapist who is the captain of their ship. If a sincere effort at AA affiliation is not productive, the therapist should not scold the patient; rather the task becomes finding other sources of support for sustaining change in drinking behaviour.

Therapists can increase the likelihood that AA will 'stick' by helping the patient talk through important decisions about a 'home group' and a sponsor. This is particularly important for patients who have a history of poor interpersonal relationships. It can be useful for the therapist to enquire, for example, whom the patient is considering asking to be a sponsor, what about the person makes them worthy of such trust and how the patient might explore with the potential sponsor whether the match would be a mutually productive one.

For patients on medication, the therapist can be helpful by providing reassurance that AA does not officially oppose medication prescribed by professionals, even though the occasional errant AA member may make this assertion. The therapist can provide patients concerned about this issue AA's statement on medications, which enjoins members from 'playing doctor' (free of charge on the Internet at http://www.alcoholics-anonymous.org/en_pdfs/p-11_aamembers.pdf).

Finally, because many people – alcoholic or not – are uncomfortable speaking in front of groups, the therapist should offer reassurance that speaking in meetings is not a requirement of membership. In the case of a patient whose discomfort about these matters approaches a phobia, the therapist could suggest exploration of on-line AA meetings.

Co-operation is, of course, a two-way business, and AA needs to understand the workings of the local services and be able to make a direct referral for professional advice if assistance is thought necessary. Many centres have established a fruitful two-way relationship of this sort, and at the national level AA has set up mechanisms for liaison with hospitals and prisons. A centre which is offering a moderate drinking goal for some of its patients will, however, need to talk through this aspect of its work with AA, if misunderstanding is to be avoided. At the extreme, some AA members may be so convinced that AA offers the only true pathway to recovery for all problem drinkers as to make co-operation with other agencies difficult. But such difficulties are rare, and with open communication and mutual respect, problems can usually be sorted out.

Research on AA

For many years, the evidence of AA's efficacy was therefore largely suggestive, being based upon popularity, personal testimony and perceived benefit rather than scientific proof (Edwards, 1995). But recent, rigorous longitudinal research has vindicated the faith of AA members in the healing power of their fellowship.

Timko and colleagues conducted a randomized trial with 345 out-patients being treated for alcohol and/or illegal drug dependence (Timko, DeBenedetti & Billow, 2006). Half received a standard referral to AA and other 12-step organizations (i.e. a list of meetings and encouragement to attend) whereas the other half received a more intensive referral, including being linked to an experienced AA member known to the treatment programme. The intensive referral produced higher rates of 12-step group attendance and greater improvement in alcohol and drug problems at 6-month follow-up.

Timko and colleagues' study was conducted in a sample composed mainly of male, racial minorities. It is worth mentioning therefore that longitudinal, multiple-condition research with a predominantly Caucasian sample evenly divided between women and men also found that AA reduced alcohol consumption and related problems, as well as reducing healthcare costs over time (Humphreys & Moos, 1996).

A detailed analysis of research on AA is beyond the scope of this book, but the interested reader should consult the review by Humphreys (2004).

Other 12-step fellowships

Since AA's founding, countless other organizations have applied the 12 steps to problems as diverse as chronic indebtedness, gambling, smoking and schizophrenia. We adumbrate here the subset of these organizations that are most likely to be of interest to patients with drinking problems and their families.

Al-Anon is an organization which is independent of, but allied with, AA (Al-Anon Family Groups UK and Eire, 1980). It is a self-help organization which caters for the families of 'alcoholics' – for 'anyone who loves an alcoholic'. Most Al-Anon members are spouses or other romantic partners, but designated chapters are available for offspring who are teenagers (Al-Ateen), as well as those who have grown to adulthood (Adult Children of Alcoholics). Al-Anon has its own '12 steps', which mirror AA thinking. Quite often, an AA meeting will be going on in one room and an Al-Anon meeting in the next room, with everyone getting together afterwards over the tea and biscuits.

The functioning of Al-Anon will not be discussed here in detail because its principles and methods of working have much in common with AA. That Al-Anon can fulfil an extremely important function does, however, need to be emphasized, and the therapist should again be able knowledgeably to point the way. Al-Anon may give immediate relief to the husband or wife who has been struggling by every stratagem to stop a spouse from drinking, and who has in the process been experiencing stress and frustration. Al-Anon will teach 'loving detachment' to help such individuals stop trying the impossible task of controlling their mate's behaviour. Instead, the member will be encouraged to examine his or her own behaviour, both in terms of restraining destructive habits and increasing (often long-neglected) self-care. The small but solid research base available on Al-Anon indicates that participation tends to reduce members' resentment, anxiety, depression and anger (Humphreys, 2004).

Twelve-step organizations focused on illegal drugs (e.g. Marijuana Anonymous, Cocaine Anonymous) may be useful to those alcohol dependent patients who also have a drug problem. The largest is Narcotics Anonymous, which contrary to its name welcomes individuals with problems with any drug, narcotic or otherwise. Narcotics Anonymous is widely available in many countries, including Australia, Canada, the UK and the USA, and in most respects is similar to AA in its philosophy and meeting process.

Alternative alcohol mutual-help organizations

Other organizations have deliberately set out to take a different approach to AA. For example, Secular Organization for Sobriety (SOS) and LifeRing Secular Recovery offer a network of groups and a philosophy that contains no inherent spiritual component (Connors & Dermen, 1996; Humphreys, 2004). SMART Recovery also includes no spiritual content and draws its change directly from scientifically supported cognitive behavioural principles. SMART has the added advantage of having established a foothold outside the USA, including in Scotland and Australia.

Two other US-based organizations merit comment. Women for Sobriety (WFS) is a feminist alternative to AA, which has a small but devoted membership (Kaskutas, 1996). Moderation Management® provides group support for moderation of drinking rather than total abstinence (Klaw, Luft & Humphreys, 2003).

No other mutual-help organization for people with drinking problems has become as international or as readily accessible as AA. The main challenge to helping patients take advantage of alternatives to AA is, therefore, difficulty in locating nearby groups to attend. This problem can be ameliorated by accessing the Internet-based groups and chat rooms of these organizations. But, in the long term, expansion of face-to-face groups is likely essential to increasing the range of persons who recover with the aid of a mutual-help organization. Therapists and professional agencies who make efforts to establish new chapters of alternative organizations may see gratifying benefits among some of their alcohol dependent patients who simply do not mesh well with AA.

References

Al-Anon Family Groups UK and Eire (1980) Help for families of problem drinkers. *Health Trends* **12**, 8.

Alcoholics Anonymous (1977) *Twelve Steps and Twelve Traditions*. New York: Alcoholics Anonymous World Services.

Alcoholics Anonymous (2010) Preamble. http://www.alcoholicsanonymous.ie/opencontent/default.asp, accessed March 2010.

Connors G J, Dermen K H (1996) Characteristics of participants in Secular Organizations for Sobriety (SOS). *American Journal of Drug and Alcohol Abuse* **22**, 281–295.

Edwards G (1995) Alcoholics Anonymous as mirror held up to nature. In *Psychotherapy, Psychological Treatments, and the Addictions*, G Edwards, C Dare (eds). Cambridge: Cambridge University Press, pp. 220–239.

Eisenbach-Stangl I, Rosenqvist P (1998) *Diversity in Unity: Studies of Alcoholics Anonymous in Eight Societies*. Helsinki, Finland: Nordic Council for Alcohol and Drug Research.

Frank J D (1973) *Persuasion and Healing: A Comparative Study of Psychotherapy*. Baltimore, MD: Johns Hopkins University Press.

Humphreys K (2004) *Circles of Recovery: Self-help Organisations for Addictions*. Cambridge: Cambridge University Press.

Humphreys K, Moos R (1996) Reduced substance abuse-related health care costs among voluntary participants in Alcoholics Anonymous. *Psychiatric Services* **47**, 709–713.

Kaskutas L A (1996) A road less traveled: choosing the Women for Sobriety Program. *Journal of Drug Issues* **26**, 77–94.

Klaw E, Luft S, Humphreys K (2003) Characteristics and motives of problem drinkers seeking help from Moderation Management self-help groups. *Cognitive and Behavioral Practice* **10**, 385–390.

Kurtz E (1991) *Not-God: A History of Alcoholics Anonymous*. Center City, MN: Hazelden.

Mäkelä K, Arminen I, Bloomfield K, et al. (1996) *Alcoholics Anonymous as a Mutual-Help Movement: A Study in Eight Societies*. Madison, WI: University of Wisconsin Press.

Timko C, DeBenedetti A, Billow R (2006) Intensive referral to 12-step self-help groups and 6-month substance use disorder outcomes. *Addiction* **101**, 678–688.

Wilson W (1994) The society of Alcoholics Anonymous. *American Journal of Psychiatry* **151**, 259–262.

Spiritual and religious issues in treatment

Spiritual and religious issues are now important in all areas of healthcare. This is because of a growing research literature concerned with their influence upon health, their importance as factors to be considered in treatment, and also their influence upon outcome in a wide range of areas of mental and physical health (Koenig, 1998). It is also because of their importance in understanding the whole person, the meaning and purpose that they find in life, their values and relationships, and thus relevance also to ethical considerations. However, if this is true in most (if not all) areas of healthcare, it is especially true in working with people with so called 'addictive' disorders, not least those with drinking problems.

This particular relevance of spiritual and religious issues in the treatment of drinking problems arises for a number of reasons, which will be considered here in turn. These are concerned with history, religion and the nature of drinking problems. We can then turn to a consideration of how spiritual and religious issues might be addressed in treatment, and what influence we should expect that they might have on outcomes. However, before we can consider any of these matters, we must first consider more carefully exactly what spirituality and religion are.

Definitions

Spirituality is a word with a relatively short history (Cook, 2004). Whilst it has its origins in the Christian tradition, it has come to be applied not only to all faith traditions, but also to an aspect of human nature which is generally considered to be universal. Those who are atheist or agnostic, according to this understanding, also experience a spiritual dimension to their lives just as much as those from the world's various faith traditions. Just as there are biological, psychological and social dimensions to being human, so there is a spiritual dimension. In this sense, spirituality is a part of holistic care, of recognizing the totality of what it is to be human.

Beyond this, however, spirituality is a controversial term. For some it is simply not scientific and therefore outside the purview of the medical and social sciences. However, the major controversy is not so much that it is *ultra vires*, as that it is capable of diverse and varied definition, even to the point of self-contradiction. This has led to suggestions that the term either be abandoned completely or else that it should be redefined, using alternative terminology, on a multidimensional basis.

Before we adopt this nihilistic perspective, however, it must also be asserted that whatever some may think, this term is still widely used, not least in the field of addictive disorders. It may also be argued that the diverse definitions are not entirely unrelated, and that some underlying coherence of the term is still affirmed by many clinicians and researchers, not to mention members of mutual-help groups such as Alcoholics Anonymous and members of faith communities. In practice, it is therefore a de facto subject of conversation in this field, which simply does not go away.

What are the various definitions of spirituality? Whilst they are indeed varied, it would seem that (at least within the field of substance misuse) they comprise some combination of the following 13 conceptual components (Cook, 2004):

- relatedness
- transcendence
- humanity
- core/force/soul
- meaning/purpose
- authenticity/truth
- values
- non-materiality
- (non-) religiousness
- wholeness
- self-knowledge
- creativity
- consciousness.

Of these, *relatedness* and *transcendence* are much the most frequently encountered in relation to substance misuse. Thus, for example, a common working definition is of spirituality as relationship with self, others and the wider universe (where the wider universe might variously be understood as 'truth', 'God' or some other 'Higher Power'). The greatest polarization is associated with *(non-) religiousness*, where some writers argue that spirituality and religion are almost diametrically opposed, whereas others cannot conceive of spirituality as divorced from their religious beliefs. The approach adopted here is that all human beings are spiritual, whereas not all are religious. It is therefore possible to be 'spiritual but not religious', but not 'religious but not spiritual'.

It will by now be apparent that a simple, universally acceptable, definition of spirituality is (at least for present purposes) elusive. However, the following definition has been proposed following a study of a large number of papers in this field, and has been adopted as the basis for other work on spirituality and mental health.

> Spirituality is a distinctive, potentially creative and universal dimension of human experience arising both within the inner subjective awareness of individuals and within communities, social groups and traditions. It may be experienced as relationship with that which is intimately 'inner', immanent and personal, within the self and others, and/or as relationship with that which is wholly 'other', transcendent and beyond the self. It is experienced as being of fundamental or ultimate importance and is thus concerned with matters of meaning and purpose in life, truth and values (Cook, 2004, pp. 548–549).

In contrast to all of this, the word *religion* has a very long history, and calls to abandon this term altogether are relatively infrequent. However, it is no less elusive of a clear and universally agreed definition (Bowker, 1999, pp. xv–xxiv). Generally, definitions of the term are concerned with social structures, ritual, tradition, belief and practice. It might therefore be easy to contrast spirituality as individual and subjective with religion as socially defined. Whilst this has some merit, it undoubtedly fails to recognize the social concerns of spirituality (as relatedness, for example) and the psychology of (individual) religious experiences.

Religious belief is a matter of tradition – the handing down from one generation to the next of practices and beliefs. An understanding of those practices and beliefs, according to the world's major faith traditions, is therefore not unimportant in clinical practice. However, in reality, many individuals and local communities adopt elements of various faith traditions and popular beliefs do not always marry exactly with the orthodoxy of the tradition at large. It is always important, therefore, in clinical work to understand what each individual believes and not to make assumptions on the basis of religious or denominational 'labels'.

History

Up until the late eighteenth century, drinking problems (then known as 'chronic inebriety') were largely understood within Europe and North America as being a matter of morality. This was not necessarily the popularly understood moral model that is now so often denounced (i.e. that such people are morally bad in a category apart from other people). It rather reflected a Judeo-Christian understanding of drunkenness as being amongst a range of sins, to which all human beings were more or less subject, all of which were primarily spiritual/religious concerns rather than medical ones. All of this changed in the nineteenth century, under a progressive medicalization of the concept of inebriety.

The nineteenth-century temperance movement understood inebriety as a 'disease of the will', a disease caused by alcohol. However, in the twentieth century, with the repeal of Prohibition in the USA, and the waning of the temperance movement in Europe and North America, a new disease model arose. Associated particularly with the work of Alcoholics Anonymous (AA), this disease model identified certain individuals, 'alcoholics', as suffering from a disease which made them unable to control their drinking. Other people could drink safely and in moderation. Alcoholics could not do this – but this was due to an as yet incompletely understood disease, not any moral failing. This disease model has attracted critics, and it stands alongside hugely influential, and often competing, psychological and scientific models of addiction. But the generally acknowledged effectiveness of AA continues to affirm its credibility, especially in the eyes of those many people who have been helped by it.

The philosophy and experience of AA has subsequently been greatly influential in regard to the treatment of drinking problems around the world (see Chapter 15). It is explicitly not aligned with any particular religious tradition, and is open to atheists and agnostics as well as to members of all the world's major faith traditions. However, AA drew in its early days on the spirituality that its founders identified in the work of Carl Jung and William James and, most especially, the spirituality of the Oxford Group. The Oxford Group, a Christian movement founded by an American Lutheran minister, Frank Buchman, was at the peak of its success in the 1930s. It emphasized confession and repentance of sins, and a life of dependence upon God.

The spirituality of AA, now effectively a 'secular'[iii] spirituality, is at the heart of the help that AA offers to people who struggle with their drinking. It is defined, most importantly, by the philosophy of the '12 steps' of AA – the steps taken by the founders in their own recovery from alcoholism. The nature of this spirituality will be considered further, below.

[iii] Alcoholics Anonymous has been described as a secular spirituality, alongside other secular forms of spirituality, such as sport, aestheticism and psychotherapy (Kurtz, 1996). However, this is not to neglect the important observation that many of its members continue to understand their own spirituality within the framework of traditional religious practice. It might therefore be thought of as a pluralist spirituality, as much as (if not more than) a secular one.

However, what must be noted here is that it has been so very widely influential. It is AA, more than anything else, which has placed spirituality firmly on the contemporary addictions treatment map.

Religion

In Europe and North America, the Temperance movement did more than simply change attitudes to drinking and drunkenness. It spawned a variety of projects aimed at reclaiming the drunkard or, as we would now say, offering treatment for drinking problems. Many of these projects found inspiration and motivation in the Christian tradition. Perhaps most famously, the Salvation Army devoted itself (amongst other concerns) to helping those whose lives had been destroyed by alcohol, but it was not alone. Alongside the secular spirituality that emerged from AA, various Christian groups in Europe and North America continued to concern themselves with rescuing those whose lives were ruined by alcohol, and they did so in explicitly Christian ways. Today, there continue to be numerous projects around the world that offer rehabilitation from addiction within a Christian framework.

For Christianity, concern for those whose lives have been shackled by bonds of addiction has been a part of a broader tradition of concern with social and spiritual bonds from which people need to be set free. Elsewhere in the world, and increasingly also in the West, treatment programmes are integrated with, inspired by and motivated by other faith traditions, including Islam, Buddhism and Native American religion (Abdel-Mawgoud, Fateem & Al-Sharif, 1995; Barrett, 1997; Garrett & Carroll, 2000). These traditions each find their own distinctive point of contact with problems related to alcohol and other drugs.

Buddhism recognizes that all human beings have a tendency to attachment to things, which causes suffering. What might otherwise be identified as 'addiction' is but one manifestation of this, but it is a problem which afflicts us all. Treatments founded on basic tenets of Buddhism, and which are not dissimilar to forms of cognitive behavioural therapy, thus lend themselves readily to the treatment of alcohol dependence (Marlatt & Kristeller, 1999).

In Islam, alcohol use is forbidden on the basis of texts in the Quran, which point out that its use has an adverse impact on relationship with God. The response of this tradition to drinking problems has thus been much more akin to that of the Temperance movement, and prevention (in the form of injunction to total abstinence) is emphasized rather than treatment. However, treatment programmes for other forms of addiction, which incorporate Islamic spiritual practices, have been reported in the scientific and medical literature (Abdel-Mawgoud, Fateem & Al-Sharif, 1995) .

Native American religion is important because of the extremely high rates of alcohol-related problems that Native American peoples have experienced since beverage alcohol was first introduced by European settlers. Whilst this might still leave its importance limited to North America, it also provides an example of the way in which spirituality and religious practices of a faith tradition may be woven into the fabric of treatment programmes based upon the 12 steps of AA or other models. Native American religion understands spiritual reality as more 'real' than the visible order of the world, but addiction represents a closing down of connection with this reality. Treatment is therefore about reconnecting to this reality, and various treatment programmes now integrate traditional Native American practices such as talking circles, sweat lodges, tribal music, pow wows and peyote meetings in support of recovery from alcohol dependence.

Treatment programmes based explicitly upon other faith traditions are relatively unusual in Western countries. However, there is evidence to suggest that similar principles apply in working with individual members of other faith communities. Thus, for example, Morjaria and Orford found that South Asian men in the UK undergoing counselling for drinking problems experienced a reaffirmation of existing beliefs (Hindu or Sikh) during recovery. This contrasted with members of AA who underwent a 'conversion' experience (Morjaria & Orford, 2002). However, both groups found a deeper sense of connectedness with God, and it is this spiritual dynamic of recovery, understood within the particular spiritual or religious tradition of the individual concerned, which seems to be of general importance in the treatment of drinking problems (and other forms of substance misuse).

The nature of drinking problems

As we have seen in the earlier chapters of this book, drinking problems can take many forms. They may be expressed as drinking which is potentially harmful, but has not yet caused actual harm, or else as actual harm of various kinds: biological, psychological and social. To this we might now add spiritual harm – the harm that inappropriate or excessive drinking may cause to faith, morality, values, self-worth and relationships with self, others and a transcendent order, in a variety of ways. It is not so much this spiritual harm, however, that defines drinking problems as an especially spiritual concern. Rather, it is the nature of the problem itself.

The problem itself, we have seen, is also concerned with biological, psychological and social factors. It is not well understood either from a purely individual perspective or from a purely population perspective. It is, rather, about the whole experience of individuals living in community. This whole experience concerns the pressures that come to bear upon people to drink more or to drink less. The individual thus becomes a focal point for decisions which balance harm against good, suffering against pleasure, the present moment against the longer term or self against others.

Many of these decisions are made unconsciously or rapidly and without much thought. No one deliberately chooses to become dependent upon alcohol. Thus, the adolescent who succumbs to peer pressure and drinks to the point of reckless irresponsibility does not set out to cause harm. However, through a series of decisions over a period of time they develop a relationship with alcohol which profoundly affects their relationships with others. Perhaps, at some point, an experience of the reality of this dynamic will provoke a change of course. We know that many young people do 'mature out' of a period of irresponsible or excessive consumption and go on to become moderate drinkers as adults. However, others do not.

At some point, some drinkers find that they are dependent. Alcohol dependence, as we have also seen earlier in this book, is a bio-psycho-social syndrome characterized, amongst other things, by a subjective compulsion to continue (or to reinstate) alcohol consumption. This compulsion characteristically takes the form of a division within the self, or a division of the will, which leads to an internal experience of struggle or conflict (Cook, 2006, pp. 127–170). Thus, those who provide treatment for people with drinking problems have frequently encountered stories of repeatedly failed resolutions to stop drinking. At one level the alcohol dependent person knows that they need to stop. At another level, the desire (or craving) to continue seems to be stronger still.

This inner division of the self has important points of resonance with the world's major faith traditions. We considered briefly, earlier in this chapter, the way in which Christianity, Buddhism, Islam and Native American religion understand this kind of problem. However, it is a fundamentally spiritual problem, concerned with relationships with self, others and a transcendent order of things. It is a disorder of relationship that leads to denial of those things which are most deeply valued, and which provide meaning and purpose in life. It is this inner division of the self that leads to the tragedy of the alcohol dependent person who loses the job that they loved, the lover that they cherished or the integrity that they took pride in. The choices that the dependence syndrome presents, and the disorders of relationships that it establishes, are a fundamentally spiritual problem.

Spirituality and religion in the treatment of drinking problems

There is much clinical wisdom in the published literature on spirituality in the treatment of drinking problems, but there is also much which is vague, confusing or unhelpful. Unfortunately, the research literature on spirituality in treatment is only just beginning to develop the evidence base, and so much of what must be done will still rely upon conjecture, tradition or intuition. Leaving aside conjecture and intuition for a moment, what does tradition tell us?

The best-established tradition, in terms of an explicit relationship of spirituality and drinking problems, is to be found in the philosophy and practice of AA. Different commentators each offer their own analysis of the 12 steps (see Chapter 15). However, given here our working definition of spirituality, and our understanding of the spiritual nature of addiction, a few comments may be made concerning their perspective upon the spirituality of relationship: with alcohol, with a Higher Power, with self and with others.

The steps clearly begin with a recognition of powerlessness (Step 1). Powerlessness (specifically over alcohol, but with the result that whole lives become unmanageable) leads on to identification of the need for belief in a 'Higher Power' (Step 2). In Steps 3, 5, 6 and 11, this Higher Power is unambiguously identified as 'God', but the emphasis is on the individual member defining their Higher Power in the way that best works for them. For example, it is suggested that the Higher Power could be AA itself. What matters is the recognition that there is a higher power than self and that it is in this power that help can be found.

Steps 4–9 outline a process of change which impacts profoundly upon relationships with self, God and others. The process begins with the self – and specifically with a self-reflective moral account. This account needs neither to be excessively self-punitive (as though the individual were worse than others) or self-righteous (as though the individual were better than others). It is rather about regaining moral perspective and this requires honesty with one's self about one's self. The process continues with sharing this account with God (or the Higher Power) and then working it out in relationship with others, with God's help. Most members of AA will require a sponsor, or other person, to help them with this process. It is both a 'one-off' process of putting right the wrongs that have arisen as a result of alcohol dependence and also an ongoing process of living in reordered relationship with self, God and others. Steps 10–12 are concerned with the ongoing process.

The word 'spirituality' does not appear in the 12 steps at all. Only Step 12 refers to a 'spiritual awakening', and only Step 11 refers to what might normally be expected as spiritual matters – prayer and meditation. The spirituality of the 12 steps is practical, relational and (largely) implicit. For most members of AA, the help of another person (usually a 'sponsor') in working through the steps is essential. For some, the embedding of the work of the early stages of the programme within a residential community, often with medical and counselling support, is also helpful. The 12-step programme is, by definition, not something that can be done alone. It involves a very practical approach to relationship with God and other human beings, as well as a radical revision of relationship with self.

The world's major faith traditions have not left texts that are as explicitly applied to the spiritual process of recovery from alcohol dependence as have the founders of AA. However, as we noted above, there are various examples of how recovery from drinking problems may be pursued within programmes structured according to the beliefs and practices of different faith traditions. Within some of these traditions there is much latitude for interpretation. Thus, for example, within Christianity differences of approach may be identified between more liberal and more conservative traditions. Typically, the latter are likely to define a sharper boundary with secular practice (although this is not always or necessarily the case). For example, Teen Challenge provides an example of an approach within which the concept of addiction is understood as more or less coterminous with the theological concept of sin. In this paradigm, recovery from addiction is more or less identical with the process of conversion and Christian growth which is expected in this tradition of all Christians. Less conservative Christians, in contrast, might be expected to rely on medical and other secular treatments, or else on a programme such as that of AA which is not explicitly linked to any particular faith or denomination.

Harold Koenig, writing about the relationship between religious organizations and the delivery of mental health services, identifies five categories of faith-based organizations (Koenig, 2005):

A   Local churches, synagogues, mosques, etc., that provide services
B   Networking and advocacy organizations
C   Groups that provide largely secular services for religious reasons
D   Trained counsellors that utilize a mixture of secular and religious methods
E   Groups and counsellors that provide largely faith-based therapies.

Examples of each of these categories could probably be identified in respect of projects and individuals working with people with drinking problems, but the nature and range of provision varies from country to country. For example, in the UK, the Salvation Army might be identified as working under each of these headings – although probably more under A and C than the others. Christian charities with an evangelical tradition providing residential rehabilitation might most frequently be found under E.

For some Christians, the choice between secular and religious approaches is a difficult one. Anxieties about compromising Christian belief have been expressed in movements that have sought to re-express the 12 steps in more explicitly Christian terms (e.g. Overcomers Outreach). On the other hand, other Christians have written firsthand accounts of how AA does not require any compromise of faith and in fact can be helpful both to the process of recovery and to growth in faith (K, 2002) .

It is also possible to integrate spiritual approaches within completely secular treatment programmes, such as those provided by the National Health Service in the UK (Jackson & Cook, 2005). This is not simply a question of the provision of chaplaincy services, which are a part of all healthcare provision within the UK, but rather a matter of recognizing the spiritual needs of all health service users, and recognizing spirituality as a component of all truly comprehensive assessments and treatment programmes.

Working with the individual

What does all of this mean when working with an individual person with drinking problems?

The first, and most important, lesson is that spirituality and faith are matters which can be discussed in the counselling room or clinic. It takes only a few seconds to ask one or two simple questions about whether someone has any spiritual or religious beliefs that are important to them. After making it clear in this way that such things can be discussed, it usually becomes clear whether the conversation needs to be taken further and, if so, in which direction.

The second conclusion to this chapter is that the context of a faith community, and a spiritual or religious belief system, can be important in planning treatment. This might be at a very explicit level of referral to a faith-based organization offering services for people with drinking problems, or it might be a matter of allaying fears that AA is either 'too religious' or else not a suitable place for a Christian, Muslim or Jew, etc. Or, it might be at a much more implicit level of acknowledging that there are spiritual aspects to all treatment programmes and to most (if not all) kinds of drinking problems.

Thirdly, it is clearly important for health professionals to do their homework. We cannot all be experts on comparative religion, and those who come to us for help do not expect this. They are, after all, the experts on what they believe – which may in any case not be exactly according to what the orthodoxy of their tradition would expect. However, when working in a given locality it is important to know what is available. Where are the nearest AA groups, or residential programmes using a 12-step approach? Are there any faith-based organizations locally working in this field? Where might someone with a strong sense of belonging to a particular faith tradition most feel at home? How might questions about the compatibility of (say) the Christian faith and AA be handled?

Finally, there is a need for professional and spiritual integrity. Sometimes it will be easier working with someone from a different faith tradition or spiritual perspective than one's own – sometimes it will be more difficult. However, the relationship between helping professional and client should never be misused as a place for proselytizing, whether to a particular tradition or to a position of agnosticism or unbelief. Only in exceptional circumstances (for example, when working with those who have survived involvement with cults) is it appropriate to engage someone in questioning the validity of the tradition to which they have belonged. Even then, it may be very important (where appropriate) to involve family or members of a healthy faith community in the process of recovery.

Integrity also involves recognition that all human beings are spiritual beings. Exploration of a client's spirituality implies that one has explored one's own spirituality and is not afraid to grapple with the same kinds of questions that they are grappling with. In fact, spirituality is a great antidote for the so called 'moral model'. Spirituality reminds us that we are all spiritual beings, struggling within ourselves over various desires and motives that draw us in different directions. People afflicted with drinking problems are not morally weak – they are simply human. Those of us who work with them will best be able to help them when we have recognized this common humanity within ourselves as well.

References

Abdel-Mawgoud M, Fateem L, Al-Sharif A I (1995) Development of a comprehensive treatment program for chemical dependency at Al Amal Hospital, Damman. *Journal of Substance Abuse Treatment* 12, 369–376.

Barrett M E (1997) Wat Thamkrabok: A Buddhist drug rehabilitation program in Thailand. *Substance Use and Misuse* 32, 435–459.

Bowker J (1999) *The Oxford Dictionary of World Religions*. Oxford: Oxford University Press.

Cook C C H (2004) Addiction and spirituality. *Addiction* 99, 539–551.

Cook C C H (2006) *Alcohol, Addiction and Christian Ethics*. Cambridge: Cambridge University Press.

Garrett M T, Carroll J J (2000) Mending the broken circle: treatment of substance dependence among Native Americans.

Journal of Counseling and Development **78**, 379–388.

Jackson P, Cook C C H (2005) Introduction of a spirituality group in a community service for people with drinking problems. *Journal of Substance Use* **10**, 375–383.

K D (2002) *Twelve Steps with Jesus*. Luton, UK: New Life.

Koenig H G (1998) *Handbook of Religion and Mental Health*. San Diego, CA: Academic Press.

Koenig H G (2005) *Faith and Mental Health*. Philadelphia, PA: Templeton Foundation Press.

Kurtz E (1996) Twelve step programs. In *Spirituality and the Secular Quest*, P H Van Ness (ed.). London: SCM Press, pp. 277–304.

Marlatt G A, Kristeller J L (1999) Mindfulness and meditation. In *Integrating Spirituality into Treatment: Resources for Practitioners*, W R Miller (ed.). Washington DC: American Psychological Association, pp. 67–84.

Morjaria A, Orford J (2002) The role of religion and spirituality in recovery from drink problems: a qualitative study of Alcoholics Anonymous members and South Asian men. *Addiction Research & Theory* **10**, 225–256.

17

Working towards normal drinking

It is sensible to remember the varied nature of the population coming for help with drinking problems. Not everyone who turns for help because of their drinking is suffering from alcohol dependence. To propose one exclusive goal for everyone, should it be normal drinking or abstinence, is therefore not sensible (Heather & Robertson, 1981). We need, as always, to plan treatment in terms of flexible responses to multiple needs. To claim that no one who has experienced trouble with drinking will ever be able to drink in a trouble-free way is mistaken (Sobell & Sobell, 1987). On the other hand, it is unhelpful to make 'normal drinking' into a slogan or heedlessly to attack the AA position. The probability of successful long-term controlled drinking among the kind of patients who usually present to specialized centres is not high (Davies, 1962; Edwards, 1985, 1994; Helzer et al., 1985). A sense of balance is needed when considering these questions (Heather, 1995).

There are many patients for whom it is inappropriate to attempt such a goal. For those with a history of fully developed alcohol dependence, abstinence is the only feasible objective (Edwards et al., 1983). Equally, there are instances where no one could doubt that, for at least a trial period, it is sensible to go along with and support the patient's wish to reduce their consumption rather than abstain (Booth et al., 1992; Sanchez-Craig, Wilkinson & Davila, 1995). This would often be true of the patient who has been drinking too heavily only recently and intermittently, and who is not manifesting significant dependence symptoms. The following considerations often contribute to the decision-making and are summarized in Table 17.1.

Degree of dependence

In practical terms, if the patient has never experienced withdrawal symptoms of such severity as to have developed morning-relief drinking then (other things being equal) normal drinking is an option. If the patient has experienced withdrawal symptoms and drunk intermittently in the morning but only for the last 6 months or less, normal drinking is possible but questionable. If for 6 months or longer the patient has not only experienced withdrawal symptoms but has repeatedly engaged in morning-relief drinking, a return to normal drinking is unlikely to be achieved. These guidelines are to be read as ways in which the evidence may be examined, rather than as fixed rules. Some authorities regard a Severity of Alcohol Dependence Questionnaire (SADQ) score of greater than 30 on the 60-point scale as precluding normal drinking, but Heather and colleagues have questioned this assumption (Heather et al., 2000).

Evidence of recent sustained normal drinking

If within the last couple of years the patient has been able to drink in a relaxed and controlled manner continuously for 2–3 months, this may indicate that they retain a capacity for a normal style of drinking, and that this capacity may now with due care be strengthened and

Table 17.1. Factors relevant to the choice of a normal drinking goal.

Factors unfavourable to a controlled drinking goal	Favourable factors in support of a controlled drinking goal
Severe dependence	Mild or absent signs of dependence
Previous failures at controlled drinking	Recent sustained normal drinking
Strong preference of the drinker for abstinence	Strong preference of the drinker for normal drinking
Commitment to the Alcoholics Anonymous ethic	
Poorly developed capacity for self-control in other areas	Mature and determined person with evidence of strong self-control in other areas of life
Diagnosis of mental illness or drug misuse	No evidence of mental illness or drug misuse
Severe alcohol-related organ damage	Mild or no physical complications of alcohol misuse
Heavy drinking family or friends	Abstemious family and friends
Heavy drinking at work	Colleagues drink moderately
Social isolation	Strong social network
Employment jeopardized by drinking problems at work	Drinking has not affected employment or work performance
Violent when drinking	Not violent when drinking

extended. The evidence must, however, be approached warily. Careful questioning may reveal that this previous period of 'sustained normal drinking' was less sustained and less 'normal' than the patient at first suggested, and it may have been only a slide towards reinstatement of dependence.

The patient personally wishes to attempt a normal drinking goal

A patient who wants to return to normal drinking may be deluding themselves, and it is then the therapist's responsibility to try to help them to accept abstinence rather than conniving in the delusion – the golden rule for the therapist when talking through these patient choices is to be open-minded but not gullible. Some patients will frankly declare that drinking other than for intoxication is for them a purposeless use of alcohol. On the other hand, a patient may be right in believing they can control their drinking and be strongly committed to attempting that goal.

Personality

The mature and determined person who is good at exercising self-control is more likely to succeed in drinking normally than the person whose capacity for self-control is, in general, not well developed.

Underlying mental illness

The patient who is suffering from any type of mental illness, and as a result uses alcohol to relieve unpleasant feelings, is not in a good position to attempt normal drinking. Whatever its nature, the underlying disorder first has to be treated, but there is always the danger that a relapse into the illness will precipitate loss of control over drinking, although equally it may overthrow an intention of complete abstinence. Underlying brain damage or learning disability usually suggests that normal drinking will not be possible, and a concurrent drug dependence which has not been dealt with successfully also rules out a return to safe use of alcohol. Pathological gambling may threaten maintenance of control over drinking. The euphoria of the win, the depression of the loss or the tension associated with continuous gambling all rather easily invite a return to the heavy use of alcohol.

Alcohol-related physical illness

The decision in this instance must be made in relation to the actual type and degree of illness, but alcohol-related physical illness usually suggests that the patient would be wise to avoid any further drinking and risk of progressive tissue damage.

Social and family support

The patient who is socially isolated and without a family will probably find it more difficult to sustain moderate drinking than the person whose behaviour is being monitored and influenced by close supports. On the other hand, a certain type of family network may positively encourage excessive drinking. Occupation has similarly to be taken into account. Someone who has no job, much time on their hands and no structure to their day may find it hard to control their drinking, while jobs which involve exposure to heavy drinking may make it difficult to pursue a controlled drinking goal.

The clinical skill thus lies in knowing how to weigh and integrate these and other factors when assessing the feasibility of a normal drinking goal, and in learning how to feed information to the patient so as to help their own decision-making. But, whatever the therapist proposes, it is finally the patient who makes the decision.

An interval of sobriety as first step

For some patients normal drinking emerges directly out of more chaotic drinking. Suddenly or gradually the new pattern supersedes the old. Alternatively, the story may be of a shorter or longer initial period of abstinence, followed by a tentative move towards moderate drinking. When drinking follows a period of sobriety, the therapist has the responsibility of working out with the patient whether this is a sadly familiar story of unguardedness and self-deception foreshadowing major relapse or whether this is indeed the evolution of re-established control.

Whether the patient, who is aiming at controlled drinking, does best to do so directly or by the pathway of initial abstinence is not an easy question to answer. Different strategies suit different people. But if the drinking is chaotic and surrounded with problems, in general the patient is likely to do better if they start out afresh from an abstinent base.

Techniques for establishing and maintaining control

Patients are themselves often very inventive in designing ways to keep their drinking within a limit, and it is always useful therefore to explore and encourage these personal strategies. The paragraphs below describe a variety of methods which may be employed (Alden, 1988; Connors, 1993; Heather et al., 1987; Marlatt & Gordon, 1985; Saunders, 1994).

Full initial discussion with the patient

The first step in setting a treatment programme for the individual patient who is aiming at controlled drinking must be to clarify what is expected of treatment and the precise goal that is to be achieved, the methods of working and the mutual level of commitment.

Limiting the type of beverage

Shifting from one type of alcoholic drink to another is often dismissed as the typical strategy of the drinker who refuses to face up to the fact that their problem lies not in the specific drink but in their relationship with any sort of alcohol – the whisky drinker who believes that 'beer will be safe' is classically warned that alcohol is simply alcohol, whatever the label on the bottle. The therapist has to distinguish between self-delusion and sound strategy, but the patient who is going to effect a successful return to normal drinking may often spontaneously discover that a change of beverage is helpful. They choose what they may term a 'social drink' – beer instead of wine perhaps, or wine instead of beer, but in any case a beverage free of old associations.

Limiting the quantity and frequency of intake

The importance of strictly defining with each patient what is to count as 'normal' has already been mentioned. If the patient is making their definition in terms of 'a single of . . .', or 'a glass of . . .', or other such familiar but often rather vague measures (a 'single' is a very uncertain quantity of alcohol if the patient is pouring their own drink), then properly objective measures have to be agreed.

Speed of drinking

A patient may learn to pace their drinking. This may be in terms either of not drinking faster than a slow-drinking companion or of pacing against the clock.

Motivations for drinking

The patient may discover that it is unwise for them to drink in response to mood, for instance when they are angry, depressed or bored. They do better to drink only when they do not 'need' a drink.

Circumstances and company

Drinking is at first often best limited to situations in which that individual's previous experience has shown that control is more likely to be maintained, while drinking situations which can be identified as leading to loss of control are best avoided. For instance, the patient may decide that they will drink with their spouse on Tuesdays in the pub at the corner, but will 'avoid the Saturday night crowd'. They will never drink at work during the day and will not drink when they are on business trips away from home. When guests come to dinner, control will mean no drink before or after dinner but only with the meal (and within explicit limits).

Identifying 'competing activities'

The client may usefully identify activities which can immediately be engaged in to prevent the risk of uncontrolled drinking. For instance, if a housewife knows that she is likely to start drinking in an uncontrolled fashion when she is alone in the middle of the afternoon, then she has to find and plan activities which can divert her from drinking at this time of the day. She may decide on a simple strategy like doing some shopping in the afternoon or calling on a friend and so on. If the dangerous circumstances which particularly invite uncontrolled drinking can thus be neutralized by a competing activity, practice in normal drinking can then be restricted to occasions when the chances of success are more real.

Individual behavioural analysis

The headings above provide ideas about the kinds of strategies which might be suggested for any patient. Essentially what is being learnt is self-control. It may in addition be useful to carry out an individual and more detailed behavioural analysis of the patient's drinking. The aim is to identify the circumstances in which a particular patient tends to drink excessively, using recent instances and the experiences which evolve during treatment. General statements such as, 'I drink when I am bored' are not to be discounted, but are usually of far less value to the planning of treatment than minute analysis of the immediate antecedents and circumstances of, say, last Friday's drinking binge. The analysis identifies the *cues* which are related to excessive drinking, both in internal (mood) and external (event and situation) terms. It is necessary to form an idea of how such cues interact rather than seeing them only in isolation, and to understand the sort of *pathway* that the individual is apt to move along when they indulge in excessive drinking. Such material is then used in planning the package of strategies which go to make up the individual drinking programme.

Formal cognitive behavioural treatment protocols

Heather and colleagues have compared the efficacy of moderation-oriented cue exposure and behavioural self-control training and their report gives details of these approaches (there were no outcome differences) (Heather et al., 2000). Substantial attention to design of protocols has been given by Sanchez-Craig and her colleagues (e.g. Sanchez-Craig et al., 1984).

How testing should the programme be?

The patient must identify risky situations (Marlatt & Gordon, 1985), although it may then be difficult for them to avoid many of these. They may, for instance, have to go away on business trips knowing that a lonely weekend in a hotel is particularly likely to invite heavy solitary drinking. However, not only may exposure to such a risky situation be unavoidable but, for the real effectiveness of treatment, such exposure to temptation may be highly desirable. The patient should not make impossible demands on their own strength and determination, but the essence of therapy is that they should experience some sense of struggle, of temptation and perhaps of craving to drink excessively, *and that temptation and craving should then be successfully resisted*. It is the repeated exposure to the relevant cues and the repeated resistance to an excessive drinking response which will in the end extinguish the potency of those cues. Without experience of craving there can be no long-term extinction of craving. In terms of a familiar analogy, a child who is afraid of dogs is unlikely to overcome that fear simply by avoiding all dogs. Such a normal fear is dealt with in terms of ordinary family wisdom by introducing a dog to the child, and then by praise and close support persuading the child on this occasion not to run away. The objective behaviour towards dogs changes, and then more slowly the anxiety experienced at the approach of a dog begins to fade out.

In similar fashion, the patient who only avoids risk will probably only achieve an objective recovery. Their drinking will be objectively within acceptable social limits, but it will still be associated with subjective unease. Subjective recovery comes about when there has been repeated exposure to cues and repeated resistance to an excessive drinking response. Treatment will, on the other hand, suffer a reverse if on too many occasions the patient does in fact drink excessively; the potency of the risky cue is confirmed rather than extinguished.

Involving the partner

The partner has an important part to play in supporting the patient's work on their problem. They are often accepted as a direct and useful restraining influence, and as the person within whose company normal drinking may most safely be attempted. If, however, their help is effectively to be enlisted their views should be taken into account. Therapy will be handicapped if any reservations the partner has about the patient's normal drinking goal have not been discussed.

Seeing it through

The patient who is aiming at normal drinking is likely to need close support over some months. Treatment which aims at return to normal drinking is far from being a cheap option in terms of service costs, and if such a treatment is to be given its place within the range of what is offered by a treatment service, it cannot be on a casual, unplanned and understaffed basis which fails to provide the proper follow-through of support and which risks irresponsibility.

Monitoring of progress must firstly involve the patient's own regular objective and subjective report at follow-up treatment sessions, and these sessions should probably be at not less than 2-weekly intervals. Verbal reports may usefully be supplemented by asking the patient to keep a drinking diary, and thus to engage in self-monitoring. Feedback of repeat laboratory test results may be helpful with gamma-glutamyl transferase (GGT) and mean corpuscular volume (MCV) hopefully moving toward normal (see Chapter 10). The partner should also be seen regularly both for them to share in the discussion and planning of treatment and for their contribution to monitoring.

One of two alternative decisions will then at some point have to be made in the light of progress and monitoring:

Termination of successful treatment. A successful outcome may be assumed when over about 12 months the patient has achieved both objective and subjective normality in their drinking. Judgement of 'success' is as ever provisional, but at some point treatment and frequency of visits should be wound down. The patient may be left with an open invitation to return if they encounter further difficulties, or it may be wise to offer widely spaced (say 6-monthly) follow-up appointments and 'booster' discussions over the next year or two.

Termination of unsuccessful treatment. The patient who is failing to make progress should not immediately and without review be told to abandon the normal drinking goal. Lack of progress is to be taken in the first instance as a matter for careful analysis of the causes of the difficulty, and on that basis some planned shift in the strategy may be possible. But if the patient still fails in any way to progress, there comes a moment when there is no profit in encouraging them in a frustrating and perhaps damaging pursuit of normal drinking. They may now be persuaded by experience that it is better to opt instead for an abstinence goal, either as the short- or longer-term solution.

Self-help groups that aim to support return to normal drinking

Alcoholics Anonymous and a number of the other mutual-help organizations are usually not appropriate for the drinker who wants to moderate rather than stop their drinking (see Chapter 15). Moderation Management (Kishline, 1999) provides group support for the moderation of drinking using a nine-step cognitive behavioural programme.

Limits on goal choice that may be set by institutional ways of working

Some institutions, such as 12-step facilities, will restrict their work to helping patients towards abstinence, while other types of facility may take controlled drinking as their universal first choice (Donovan & Heather, 1997). Organizational cohesion may be vested in a rigid commitment to one or other narrow choice. Interests of the wide and varied range of people who experience drinking problems may in part be well served by narrow-range institutions with high levels of confidence in what they are doing, and people can often make their own choice as to which type of facility they attend. Within this market dangers do, however, also exist of patients becoming engaged in a narrow approach which is not optimal for them. The situation may be helped by more informed advice by referral agencies, by greater diversity of treatment facilities within a locality and, generally, by an enhanced degree of open-mindedness.

A final word of caution

The decision to advise a patient to aim for total abstinence may sometimes result in that person alternating sobriety with explosive and damaging relapses, rather than their learning how to control their drinking or attenuate relapse. Choice of the abstinence goal does not by itself guarantee anyone's safety. Treatment of every new case is an experiment which requires the patient's informed consent and professional and ethical decisions on the therapist's behalf, and that is so whatever the drinking goal.

That having been said, there are special problems which can attach to work towards normal drinking. What is to be done if in the therapist's experienced judgement normal drinking is for a particular patient likely to lead only to further postponement of the necessary decision to stop drinking? Depending on the circumstances two different types of response can be envisaged:

1 *Supporting a normal drinking goal on an experimental basis and in the short term.* If there are no pressing dangers, it may be acceptable to work along with the patient and let them determine whether normal drinking is attainable. In the process, one way or another, something useful will have been learnt.

2 *Stating firmly that abstinence is, for carefully explained reasons, probably the only feasible goal.* One is dealing here with probabilities rather than certainties, but the therapist may feel that for this patient and on strong balance of probabilities, normal drinking is likely to be unattainable and dangerous in its pursuit. That then should be said. In the long term it may be better for a patient at least temporarily to break contact, but take with them an unambiguous, honest and accurate message, rather than the therapist being drawn into a course of action which they see as against the patient's best interests. It may be the moment for challenge rather than connivance.

Twenty years ago discussion of how treatment can assist return to normal drinking might have been seen as heterodox. Today, with the growing awareness of the need to provide help for people whose drinking problems are of many different degrees and kinds, a discriminating ability to work with some patients or clients towards a moderate drinking goal is a necessary therapeutic skill.

References

Alden L (1988) Behavioral self-management: controlled drinking strategies in a context of secondary prevention. *Journal of Consulting and Clinical Psychology* **56**, 280–286.

Booth P G, Dale B, Slade P D, Dewey M E (1992) A follow-up study of problem drinkers offered a goal choice option. *Journal of Studies on Alcohol* **53**, 594–600.

Connors G J (1993) Drinking moderation training as a contemporary therapeutic approach. In *Innovations in Alcoholism Treatment: State of the Art Reviews and Their Implications for Clinical Practice*, G J Connors (ed.). New York: Haworth Press, pp. 117–134.

Davies D L (1962) Normal drinking by recovered alcohol addicts. *Quarterly Journal of Studies on Alcohol* **23**, 194–204.

Donovan M, Heather N (1997) Acceptability of the controlled-drinking goal among alcohol treatment agencies in New South Wales, Australia. *Journal of Studies on Alcohol* **58**, 253–256.

Edwards G (1985) A later follow-up of a classic case series: D. L. Davies's 1962 report and its significance for the present. *Journal of Studies on Alcohol* **46**, 181–190.

Edwards G (1994) D. L. Davies and 'normal drinking in recovered alcohol addicts': the genesis of a paper. *Drug and Alcohol Dependence* **35**, 249–259.

Edwards G, Duckett A, Oppenheimer E, Sheehan M, Taylor C (1983) What happens to alcoholics? *Lancet* **2**, 269–271.

Heather N (1995) The great controlled drinking consensus: is it premature? *Addiction* **90**, 1160–1162.

Heather N, Robertson I (1981) *Controlled Drinking*. London: Methuen.

Heather N, Robertson I, Macpherson B, Allsop S, Fulton A (1987) Effectiveness of a controlled drinking self-help manual: 1 year follow-up results. *British Journal of Clinical Psychology* **26**, 279–287.

Heather N, Brodie J, Wale S, et al. (2000) A randomized controlled trial of moderation-oriented cue exposure. *Journal of Studies on Alcohol* **61**, 561–570.

Helzer J E, Robins L N, Taylor J R, et al. (1985) The extent of long-term moderate drinking among alcoholics discharged from medical and psychiatric facilities. *New England Journal of Medicine* **312**, 1678–1682.

Kishline A (1999) *Moderate Drinking: The Moderation Management Guide for People Who Want to Reduce their Drinking*. New York: Three Rivers Press.

Marlatt G, Gordon J (1985) *Relapse Prevention*. New York: Guilford Press.

Sanchez-Craig M, Annis H M, Bornet R, MacDonald K R (1984) Random assignment to abstinence and controlled drinking. Evaluation of a cognitive-behavioural program for problem drinkers. *Journal of Consulting and Clinical Psychology* **52**, 390–403.

Sanchez-Craig M, Wilkinson A, Davila R (1995) Empirically based guidelines for moderate drinking: 1-year results from three studies with problem drinkers. *American Journal of Public Health* **85**, 823–828.

Saunders B (1994) The cognitive-behavioural approach to the management of addictive behaviour. In *Seminars on Alcohol and Drug Misuse*, J Chick, R Cantwell (eds). London: Gaskell, pp. 154–173.

Sobell M G, Sobell L C (eds) (1987) *Moderation as a Goal or Outcome of Treatment for Alcohol Problems: A Dialogue*. New York: Haworth Press.

When things go wrong and putting them right

Every attempt has been made in previous chapters of this book to present a perspective that avoids an idealized view of the therapeutic process as an operation smoothly and inevitably moving forward to success, as each patient responds to our wise and well-planned interventions. This chapter seeks further to correct any such caricature and considers some problematic workaday situations.

Going wrong

The person who wishes to treat alcohol problems must develop an appreciation of the ways in which treatment can go wrong. He or she must train their eyes quickly to recognize these situations, and they must be aware of the familiar patterns of events against which to interpret the latest instance of something going awry. They must learn to examine the extent to which the therapist is at fault, and the extent to which it is the patient, and most particularly to analyze what is amiss in the interaction. They must learn not to be discouraged or defeated by such events, but to turn them so far as possible to good therapeutic advantage and to learn from them. One cannot treat alcohol dependence without things very often going wrong, and the essence of treatment is usually a series of trials and errors rather than a straight-line advance. Such a statement is not to be read as a licence for complacency – true, the best-laid treatment plans can fall apart and we must not be too flustered by that fact, but equally true is the insistence that the situation must be recognized and an effort made to put it right.

This chapter does not attempt a consideration of all possible eventualities. Anyone who has experience of this field will see ways in which the list might be extended, and a personal listing of cases where therapy was unproductive (a list kept, as it were, on mental file) is a valuable working tool.

Losing the balances

Much of therapy is a matter of finding balances (and of readily shifting balances), and things often go wide of the mark because balance has been lost. Let's give this statement meaning by considering balance in terms of a number of different paired factors.

Emphasizing the drinking/emphasizing all else

It is possible for things to go wrong because the treatment has become so exclusively focused on the individual's drinking that the person doing that drinking in a complex personal and social setting is overlooked: the drinking is everything. The complementary imbalance is a sensitive awareness of that individual's total life situation, but with the reality of alcohol as a destructively pervasive aspect of that situation discounted: the drinking is hardly anything. To set the balance right is often difficult, and at a certain stage of learning and experience it is particularly the sensitive, open-minded therapist who is apt to fall into the trap of under-estimating the seriousness of the drinking problem. But the admirable desire to see the whole person and to respect the complexities of that individual's life should not be put in opposition to awareness of the true threat of the drinking.

> A man aged 44 had experienced a deprived and troubled childhood. Despite this he managed to contract a seemingly happy marriage and for 16 years all had appeared to go well. Then his wife had an affair, and his world fell to pieces. All his fearful beliefs as to the inevitability of rejection were proved to be well founded. His feelings towards his wife were unforgiving. He determined that an unhappy episode should be the occasion for catastrophe and he divorced, threw in his job, sold his house, gave up his friends and moved to a new city. A couple of years later he overdosed and consequently came under the care of a psychotherapist who spent a year with him, exploring his problems relating to his mother. He frequently turned up for interviews drunk, and this was duly interpreted. He was then admitted to hospital after a further and more serious suicidal attempt. The psychiatrist who saw him on the medical ward the following morning diagnosed a severe and untreated depressive illness, and started him on an antidepressant. He noted that the patient had 'recently engaged in some secondary relief drinking'. The evening following the first dose of the antidepressant the patient developed an acute confusional state: it was one of the night nurses who made the diagnosis of delirium tremens.

Both the psychotherapist and the psychiatrist had focused on important aspects of this man's condition, but each had over-focused and seen things comfortably in terms of their own predilections. Neither had bothered to take a drinking history. It seems likely that the patient was not so much covering up the seriousness of his drinking, as that those who came in contact with him were almost wilfully turning a deaf ear to what he was telling them. A careful reconstruction of the history later suggested a drinking problem going back to the early days of marriage, a marriage much affected by drinking, and a wife who finally moved out because she could no longer tolerate the drinking and the attendant violence. The next move must not be the substitution of an exclusive alcohol focus and a new imbalance for old, but ensuring that treatment of this man's alcohol dependence is accorded its balanced place within the total strategy of his treatment.

There are many different ways of falling into error through seeing the patient as 'an alcoholic' and believing therefore that all their problems are to be understood and treated within that definition alone. A short extract from another case history should correct any notion that the error is always in one direction.

> A 33-year-old building worker had been admitted to an alcohol treatment unit, where a diagnosis of alcoholic hallucinosis was made. It was noted that he had previously been admitted to another hospital with what was now deemed to be the mistaken diagnosis of schizophrenia; the case notes were not borrowed. He was put into the ward therapeutic group but seemed to spend more time listening to imaginary voices than participating. After 3 weeks he was discharged to a hostel for people with drinking problems, which was run on intensive therapeutic community lines. He was put into a challenging group on the evening of his arrival, and shortly thereafter again developed florid schizophrenic symptoms, and was readmitted to the first hospital rather than to the alcohol unit. Their case notes recorded the onset of a schizophrenic illness at the age of 17 years. He had since done fairly well provided he was not too stressed and could find a supportive environment. But this was certainly a patient who over recent years had compounded his suffering by responding to his symptoms with alcohol misuse.

The staff of the alcohol treatment unit had so specialized a perspective that when a case of schizophrenia presented to them they reacted in terms of a predetermined psychological set, and the consequent diagnosis led to a package of group therapy and confrontation for a man whose needs were quite otherwise.

So much for two rather extreme cases, which illustrate the poles of imbalance that can occur. The errors are usually on a smaller scale and more subtle. Perhaps the mass of general agencies tend to underrate the importance of the drinking while the specialized alcohol agencies overcompensate by being too alcohol-focused.

Too ambitious/too unambitious goals

Sometimes patients (or the therapist) become frustrated in therapy because they have unrealistic expectations of what changes may be achieved and at what pace. This dilemma can occur at any stage of treatment. The mistake may be that too great a therapeutic pace is being set, which can readily force the patient into breaking contact, but equally the problem may be in the direction of inertia.

> A 60-year-old man stopped drinking but continued to treat his wife in a curmudgeonly fashion, was at cross purposes with his grown-up children and had no leisure activities other than watching television and grumbling about the quality of the entertainment provided. At the end of a further year he was still sober and still regarding the world with unrelenting enmity.

What is the community psychiatric nurse (CPN) to do the next time they call round on this family and the man purposely turns up the volume on the television, while otherwise angrily staring ahead and not acknowledging the caller's presence? The wife offers a cup of tea in the kitchen and says: 'He's always been that way and I suppose he won't change – a real old misery I call him'. What is the right balance of treatment ambition?

The reality may indeed be that a man of 60 who has for most of his existence defined the world as antagonistic, and who has built up his self-image largely in terms of afflicted righteousness, is unlikely radically to change his ways. His wife's assessment of the situation may be just about right, and she does not seem too put out by his ill-grace. Her father was much like that anyhow, and her husband's behaviour is in accord with what she expects of men. She is happy enough that he is no longer running her short of money.

Yet it seems sad to leave it at that. There is the lingering feeling that the goal is being set too low, that more happiness for two people should be possible than is seen here. The answer is perhaps for the CPN to try setting a moderately more ambitious goal on a trial basis. The goal had better be expressed concretely, and the starting point must be the identification of something which patient and wife themselves at least half hint at being wanted. In this particular instance the wife let drop, 'and he never takes me on holiday of course'. The 'of course' was an important part of the statement; it was clear that the wife's communication with her husband often carried the implication that she expected his response to be negative. A modestly realistic goal in these circumstances was to see if this couple could go away for a week's holiday together and come home with the feeling that they had enjoyed themselves. Working at first through the wife and suggesting that she might for once expect the answer 'yes' from her husband, the holiday was booked. The couple went for a week to the coast, and although the holiday provided much cause for grumbling, in sum the week provided a real sense of shared reward. Beyond the immediate happening a small shake-up had occurred in negative patterns of interaction, and the basis established for the possibility of further, small changes.

Too indulgent/too hard

There is a balance to be struck regarding the degree to which the relationship offered by the therapist to the patient or client is to be supportive and non-judgemental, as contrasted with one which emphasizes elements of tough-minded expectation and hard confrontation. To put the matter in terms of absolutes and contradictions is an oversimplification, but it may be useful to examine this particular idea in terms of two contrasting examples. Firstly, imbalance in the direction of indulgence.

> A social worker of rather little professional experience became highly committed to helping this family. The 30-year-old man was not alcohol dependent, but seemed to use drink to enhance his passivity and incompetence. He seldom worked. He borrowed, pawned and stole. The wife who was faced with this chronically difficult situation tried to prop up the family as best she could. When the social worker arrived on the scene she soon became no more than a provider of gifts, and she protected the man from the consequence of his having cheated on welfare payments. She found him good second-hand clothes so that he could go for a job interview, and when he sold the clothes and did not go to the interview she treated him as an amusingly naughty child.

The social worker was operating on the hypothesis that this patient was deprived and was testing out her 'goodness'; she believed that she 'must not reject him'. Where she may have gone wrong is in her assumption that the opposite to rejection is indulgence.

As an example of the tough-minded imbalance, the following case is illustrative. It relates to consequences of a stance that is quite commonly taken by service agencies in their attempt to screen out the 'unmotivated' patient.

> A man with a drinking problem was to be discharged from prison and it had been agreed that he should then be admitted to hospital. He was homeless. However, the decision was made 'to test this man's sincerity'. The consultant in charge of the treatment unit decided that the man would not be admitted straight away, but should find himself lodgings, go to Alcoholics Anonymous and then present to the community alcohol team for assessment. Coming out of prison after 4 years the man was anxious, a little bit euphoric, very lost, and he immediately made his way to old friends. He was drinking again within hours, and within days had once more committed his familiar offence of breaking and entering. The consultant was confirmed in his sense of wisdom, and took these events as evidence that the patient was 'insufficiently motivated'.

There are occasions when it is therapeutically useful to be nurturing and others on which it is kind and constructive to openly challenge.

Too directive/too afraid of a position

The alternative to forcing one's opinion on a patient is not necessarily the pretence of having no opinions at all. A therapist may have difficulty in treating drinking problems because they give their patients the impression of lacking confidence at a time when that person badly needs to borrow some certainties. An orthodox therapeutic detachment is, for instance, inappropriate in a situation where someone needs very practically to be helped by the therapist's knowledge of how to deal with a drinking crisis, while a dictatorial attitude will be equally counter-productive. Here is an example which bears on this particular and difficult aspect of balance.

> A 40-year-old woman, who over a 2-year period had begun to move towards severe alcohol dependence in the setting of a depressive illness, was visited on the ward by her husband. The husband made himself unpopular with the staff by his unsympathetic and scolding attitude towards his wife. One of the junior nurses exclaimed to the patient: 'I don't see how living with that man you could ever stay sober – you should go and live with that son of yours who seems so fond of you!'

In the treatment of drinking problems, more than in the treatment of many other conditions, the therapist is faced with the problem of directiveness. It often appears glaringly obvious that the patient is engaging in wrong-headed and self-destructive behaviour, is revealing a chaotic inability to make good decisions and order their life well, and manifestly does not know what is best for their own good. This area of practice seems therefore to pose an especially acute challenge to the orthodox notion of the therapist's need to maintain neutrality. The nurse felt that she knew what was good for the patient, and said what she thought. Discussion of this incident in the staff group would usefully bring into the open wider issues related to the limits of directiveness, but the conclusion in this particular instance could only be that the balance had gone wrong. The nurse knew too little about the marriage to give directive advice and she certainly knew too little about that patient's son.

Defeated by poor coping strategies

That the patient's coping styles have to be identified, their utility for the patient understood and their existence adequately dealt with, are ideas common to the treatment of many conditions other than a drinking problem. The therapist who is going to work with drinking problems will do well to cultivate a lively awareness of how coping styles can manifest themselves, as an inadequate response to poor coping strategies is one of the more common reasons for things going wrong.

Poor coping styles: pure or mixed form

Often the patient's difficulty in facing up to the threat posed by their drinking is a manifestation both of a poor coping style and of prevarication. In practice, it is often difficult to determine the extent to which the two different elements are contributing to a given presentation.

In the popular image, the 'alcoholic' is frequently pictured as someone who insists on drinking themself to death while maintaining that no drop of alcohol ever passes their lips. Such crude and primitive defensiveness is relatively uncommon, but when it reaches extreme proportions it can be baffling and a block to all progress, despite every therapeutic stratagem. Here is a case vignette that shows the kind of problems that can be set by entrenched denial.

> A 50-year-old accountant was brought to a psychiatric clinic by his business partner, who said that unless something was done his colleague would have to be pensioned off. The patient's breath smelled heavily of drink, his liver was mildly enlarged and he had bruises from several recent falls. He charmingly acknowledged his gratitude to the partner for taking this trouble, but said that the poor man was overworked, worried and getting things out of proportion. The patient admitted to having an occasional beer at lunchtime, but that was the limit of his drinking. He was then seen with his wife, who said that he was permanently intoxicated, that he was frequently incontinent, that he had recently fallen down stairs when drunk and that empty bottles were falling out of every cupboard. He said that his wife was a dear woman but a terrible worrier, that of course he was often tired at the end of the day (who wasn't), and as for falling down those steps there had been a loose stair rod.

Given that one does not at this point surrender hope entirely, the best approach might first be to try to get some insight into the reasons that could lead a patient to engage in this stonewalling. Usually there are several reasons rather than one. For instance, some people make lifelong use of certain favoured coping styles (in sickness and in health), and this man may, under stress, be reaching for his personally most available coping mechanism out of a limited repertoire. Another explanation may be that this stance is a passive-aggressive response to what he conceives as an attack on his integrity. He sees his partner and his wife as out to dominate him, and he reacts with angry and childish stubbornness.

With these guesses in mind the therapist might then sit down alone with the patient, with the other actors out of the room. With no implication of attack, the therapist will start a discussion on the basis of an openly stated assumption that both he and the patient know what has been going on: namely that the patient has been drinking and realizes, correctly, that he will be judged for this behaviour. The therapist will furthermore immediately lay down ground rules for the interaction by stating that the interview will not be allowed to degenerate into a useless cross-examination, which could offer no fruitful result but only further entrenchment. It can be put to the patient that a lot of people find difficulty in talking openly about the degree of worry and trouble which their drinking is causing – they may be afraid of attack and afraid of being demeaned – and in such circumstances to try to insist that the worrying facts do not exist can be a natural response. The therapist might try to convey that he or she sees this situation from the patient's point of view and then offer possible alternative solutions. It can be put to the patient that if a man drives his car off the road and someone comes up and asks questions, the driver may well respond defensively if they think that it is a policeman who is questioning them, but it will make no sense to treat the person who is offering first-aid as if they were a policeman and hence bleed to death.

The patient may take the line that the therapist is a nice person whom it is a privilege to meet, but that the clinic's valuable time is being wasted on the basis of a most unfortunate mistake – everyone is getting hold of absolutely the wrong end of the stick. What to do next?

It may be possible as a temporary measure to go on leaving the coping style in place, as it were, but to take no notice of it – to allow the patient to hold to the assumption that he has no drinking problem, while the therapist works on the assumption that there is a serious problem which has to be treated. Such a peculiar agreement to differ is unlikely to continue happily for long; either the patient will slide into accepting the therapist's definition of reality or contact will be unprofitable. Another and rather simple approach, which may sometimes be promising, is to concentrate for the time being on the patient's physical health. He may find it acceptable that he is in need of advice on his physical health (an alcohol-free diet for his liver's sake) without any of the loss of face that he fears will result from fully admitting his dependence on alcohol.

If none of these approaches pays dividends, the only course may be to leave the patient with an unambiguous message as to the need for him to open his eyes, and a factual warning of the dangers which will stem from his continuing refusal to admit his drinking problem, and then not to make any offer to see the patient again for a period of some months, unless he so asks. The wife meanwhile may well need help or support in her own right.

The occasional baffling intractableness of a deeply entrenched failure to acknowledge that there is a problem should not itself be ignored. The temptation is almost literally to raise one's voice in the hope that the patient will actually hear, or to confront him with every sort of proof-positive and hope that he will come to his senses. The temptation is in short to resort to the battering ram. Sadly, the consequences of that attack will probably only be the patient strengthening their entrenched position.

The defence of sickness

Sometimes a patient will claim that they continue to drink because they are indeed 'an alcoholic'. They are suffering from an illness that is the explanation of their behaviour, and the responsibility for curing this illness rests with the therapist. The patient may then continue their drinking with the position nicely established that the therapist is to blame. Things go wrong if this position is accepted, but they go equally wrong if the therapist automatically assumes that this person is playing games or working some kind of intentional trickery. They may be taking up this particular version of the sick role because they truly believe that they are sick, damaged and no longer able to control their own behaviour. They are not then so much displaying a defence as manifesting symptoms of learned helplessness. The two different possible meanings of outwardly similar presentations have therefore to be distinguished. In the wrong circumstances, cutting the drinker down with an aggressively neat analysis of the game they are playing is likely to result in the therapist being rid of a difficult patient but nothing else. It may be more useful to try to move this person towards a realization that they can indeed start to take responsibility for not drinking, that they have more resources than they supposed and that it would be misleading if anyone else were to pretend to be able to take over their responsibilities for them. The job is to work for increased self-efficacy and strengthening of motivation.

Absolution

A patient may be able to defend himself or herself from the pain which would otherwise force them to change their behaviour, if they can find a doctor or counsellor who can be persuaded to offer regular absolution. At the same time they may present a picture of pseudo-insight. Intellectually they know what suffering they are causing to themselves and others, but they are able to divorce this insight from any deep feelings provided they are given regular doses of forgiveness. They are, in fact, seeking the therapist's connivance as actor in a repetitive and unproductive play. Here is a case extract that illustrates one such presentation.

> The patient settled into a chair and said that he knew he was an 'alcoholic', had been going to Alcoholics Anonymous for years, and knew that all he now had to do was to get through one day without drink. His wife was threatening to leave him, and after this last 'slip' and all that she had been through, he entirely saw her point of view and did not blame her in the least. He was most dreadfully sorry and knew that he had behaved to her like a swine. Furthermore, he had let the doctor down again and was thoroughly ashamed of himself. He had said exactly the same thing on many occasions with a similar show of contrition coupled with detachment from real feeling.

Things go wrong if the therapist falls into the position of aiding and abetting this cycle of behaviour. Such a story is not uncommon, and the patient may sometimes be a long-term Alcoholics Anonymous (AA) attendee who has managed to get little out of AA. One may suspect that they have used the AA meetings in much the same way as they would employ the interview with the psychiatrist, and that they are nowhere near grasping the real AA message. For the therapist to continue contact on this non-therapeutic or anti-therapeutic basis is useless. It is more helpful to throw the responsibility back on the patient and refuse to be the confessor. An element of challenge and confrontation may produce new possibilities, but there is always the risk that the patient will instead go off and find another therapist who will at least temporarily provide the absolutions.

The romantic defence

Drinking peculiarly lends itself to a romantic defence, an identification with famous drinking poets and playwrights. The following is an abstract from a referral letter.

> This lady is a successful artist and you will certainly know of her husband who is the novelist. She has led a truly amazing life, and if she gets round to telling you about her years in Paris you will find it fascinating. Everyone in her set drinks, and I think one has to accept that drinking is for her essential to the creative life. Recently she has been hitting the bottle and she was seen by

someone last year who rather annoyed her by calling her an alcoholic. She cannot accept help that is conditional upon her giving up drinking.

In this instance the patient's defence has overwhelmed the judgement of an experienced physician, who had been seduced into accepting drinking as symbolizing 'the creative life'. That the drinking was profoundly affecting this woman's ability to work and threatened to destroy her, was being screened out.

If this position is accepted things will very certainly go wrong, with the patient continuing to drink and the therapist effectively neutralized as an amused and admiring spectator of a fascinating way of life, but with the therapeutic position lost. At the start of the contact the therapist has therefore to hold to the position that drinking must be de-symbolized and seen in its reality. The patient may have an immediate sense of relief if they find that they can discard the act that self-destruction is romantic fun.

Endless argument

The problems set by intellectual defence are familiar in any area of psychotherapy. In work with drinking problems the intellectualization is likely to go off in certain special directions – the patient will divert the discussion away from any real therapeutic content towards making the interview a symposium either on the definition of alcohol dependence, or on the determinants of drinking behaviour, or both. The therapeutic response should be to steer the patient away from consideration of generalities and back to the immediacy of their own position. Otherwise the therapist may find themselves engaged in a lengthy analysis of 'the disease concept' while the patient continues to drink.

The patient who knows someone who drinks much more

A block to treatment, which can be no more than a minor distraction but which may sometimes be employed as a major stratagem to escape the reality of the threat that drink poses, is the claim made by the patient that they knew someone who drank much more than they ever did themselves (often the family doctor), or who drank a great deal and never came to harm.

> All right, I drink my share. But I'll tell you this, my old father died at 86 and he drank much more heavily than I have ever done. Absolutely routine, he'd never go outside the house without putting a bottle of whisky in his pocket, just like picking up his tin of tobacco.

To enter a debate with such a patient as to whether their drinking is more or less than the father's is bound to be defeating. The data on the patient's drinking are probably at that stage uncertain and the data on the father's drinking much falsified, so the patient is in a position to prop up their defence by revising all elements of the comparison at will. If one agrees to enter this debate, one gets involved in a kind of pub conversation, with wildly unlikely but incontrovertible assertions being heaped one on the other: 'Look at Winston Churchill. He had the best part of a bottle of brandy every morning before he got out of bed. Greatest Englishman who ever lived . . .' The best way to avoid entanglement in this unproductive argument is to say that it is not the patient's father or Winston Churchill who has come for the consultation, and that they will be left outside the room.

Medical negligence

Sadly, it is not unknown for a doctor treating a drinking problem to find himself or herself facing an action for negligence. At the extreme, there may be risk of action for medical manslaughter.

This is a difficult area of practice, but that does not excuse practitioners from the inalienable responsibility to delivering a high quality of care. As ever, the practitioner's best defence is to ensure that their treatment is of a kind and quality that would be seen as reasonable good practice by their peers. Scrupulous attention to note keeping and letter writing is important. When a patient poses the danger of self-harm or harm to others, it may be good medico-legal as well as good medical practice to consult with another professional and fully record the consultation on file.

Here is a list of the kind of problems which good practice will in this arena seek most strenuously to avoid. Over-prescribing of benzodiazepines to a drinking patient with consequent instatement of benzodiazepine dependence is a not uncommon cause for legal action. Failure of an Accident and Emergency Department (Emergency Room) doctor to diagnose and immediately treat incipient Wernicke's encephalopathy may lead to tragic brain damage for the patient and enormously expensive damages against the hospital and doctor. Failure of a general hospital ward to deal adequately with withdrawal and to maintain a safe environment (see Chapter 12) may see staff held responsible for a very expensive tragedy. Careless prescribing of disulfiram can lead to repeated confusional episodes.

None of these types of accident should ever be allowed to happen, but unfortunately they still continue to occur, thus witnessing to the fact that, in every medical setting, enhanced alertness and better training on drinking problems are much required.

When everything goes wrong

In Table 18.1 some ideas are set out on ways of unblocking a therapeutic impasse. There are times in treating drinking problems when everything seems to go wrong at once, and this is not just in terms of happenings relating to one particular patient but with several patients getting into serious difficulties over the same few weeks. One's most hopeful patient relapses, another seems bent on destroying themselves with their continued drinking, and a patient for whom the therapist had especially warm feelings dies and there is an element of self-blame. These periods occur, and it is necessary for the therapist who runs into such a patch of trouble to remind themselves (or to be reminded by their colleagues) that this kind of practice will inevitably at times be a fraught and perplexing business. Sometimes the therapist may have been taking on all the more difficult cases himself or herself, and there is the possibility that they have become over-stretched, over-tired or careless. But it is more probable that events have randomly clustered. Their self-confidence needs supporting, and they must not be allowed to blame themselves. Sometimes things go wrong because of forgetfulness and oversight: the need for a physical examination is overlooked, the spouse is not seen, what the patient is trying

Table 18.1. When things go wrong: the positive therapeutic response to case problems.

- Problems should be shared. Talk through the situation with a colleague.
- Problems can be two-way. Try to understand your own behaviour, attitudes and expectations as well as those of the patient.
- Identify blocks – in particular the therapeutic approach losing its balance or the unhelpful defence mechanisms that the patient may be using to negate progress.
- Motivation is essential to change – does further work need to be done on readiness to change?
- Check back on the original assessment and formulation, review the case and get a purposive plan in place, with the patient participating, to recover the therapeutic motivation.
- Remember, no-one is omnipotent and therapists have rightful needs.

to say is not heard. Perhaps more dangerously, things go amiss when the therapist becomes overconfident, fails to entertain doubts and assumes that they know all, and that if the patient fails to respond what is needed is more medicine of the same kind. On occasions, the way in which the treatment system is working may also need to be scrutinized, and it may, for instance, be evident that difficulties stem from staff communication being in poor repair or personal tensions between staff members.

Treating the person with a drinking problem is about moving that individual by every available strategy towards alliance with his or her own recovery. The richest arena for learning is the actuality of contact, the experience of things sometimes going wrong, and the discovery that with patience, flexibility and mutual effort things often very happily come right.

Every individual and team should explore the question of how, within their practice circumstances, they are going to address such problems positively and effectively, so as to help the patient through and ensure that they, themselves, learn in the process. Younger and more experienced therapists equally have needs in this regard, and male and female staff members may at times have different kinds of support need. The sharing of problems rather than a drift to isolation is vital, and the availability for staff support of an experienced therapist from outside the team can be valuable. There should be an open and unashamed willingness to see oneself as needy rather than yielding to the destructive belief that one can endlessly give without being given.

Index